FROM THE
BULLET
TO THE
BALLOT

THE JOHN HOPE FRANKLIN SERIES
IN AFRICAN AMERICAN HISTORY AND CULTURE

Waldo E. Martin Jr. and Patricia Sullivan, editors

JAKOBI WILLIAMS

FROM THE BULLET TO THE BALLOT

The Illinois Chapter of the
Black Panther Party and
Racial Coalition Politics
in Chicago

THE UNIVERSITY OF NORTH CAROLINA PRESS • CHAPEL HILL

*This book was published with the assistance of the
John Hope Franklin Fund of the University of North Carolina Press.*

The University of North Carolina Press has been a member of
the Green Press Initiative since 2003.
Portions of Chapters 2 and 3 appeared previously in somewhat
different form in " 'Don't no woman have to do nothing she don't
want to do': Gender, Activism, and the Illinois Black Panther Party,"
in *Black Women, Gender and Families*, Fall 2012. Copyright 2012 by
the Board of Trustees of the University of Illinois. Used with permission
of the University of Illinois Press.

Library of Congress Cataloging-in-Publication Data

Williams, Jakobi.
From the bullet to the ballot : the Illinois Chapter of the Black Panther Party and racial
coalition politics in Chicago / by Jakobi Williams.
p. cm.—(John Hope Franklin series in African American history and culture)
Includes bibliographical references and index.
ISBN 978-0-8078-3816-7 (cloth : alk. paper)
ISBN 978-1-4696-2210-1 (pbk. : alk. paper)
1. Black Panther Party. Illinois Chapter. 2. Black power—Illinois—Chicago—History—
20th century. 3. African Americans—Illinois—Chicago—Politics and government—
20th century. 4. African Americans—Civil rights—Illinois—Chicago—History—20th
century. 5. Civil rights movements—Illinois—Chicago—History—20th century.
6. Hampton, Fred, 1948–1969. 7. Chicago (Ill.)—Politics and government—1951–
8. Chicago (Ill.)—Race relations. I. Title.
F548.9.N4W55 2013
323.1196'073077311—dc23
2012028588

For my grandmother Louella Smith;
my family Cassandra, Surayya, and Amari;
and Joseph A. Brown, S.J., Ph.D.

CONTENTS

ILLUSTRATIONS

MAPS AND FIGURES

ACKNOWLEDGMENTS

This project would not have been possible without the participation of the many former members of the Illinois chapter of the Black Panther Party and its affiliates and the progressive community of my hometown of Chicago. I dedicate this book to them, as their patience and support, insights and words, have greatly informed this study. The project got off the ground thanks to Kathleen Cleaver, who introduced me to renowned storyteller Michael D. McCarty, who then introduced me to all of the ILBPP comrades. A very humble thank you to Illinois chapter members Michael D. McCarty, Hank Gaddis, Bob Lee, Wanda Ross, Lamar Billy "Che" Brooks, David Lemieux, Billy Dunbar, Lynn French, Congressman Bobby Rush, Joan Gray, Yvonne King, John "Oppressed" Preston, Melvin Lewis, Howard Ann Kendrick, Donna Calvin, Willie Calvin, Joan McCarty, Brenda Harris (Nwaji Nefahito), and countless others not mentioned here. I thank Chester Herring for introducing me to Iberia Hampton and Bill Hampton, who continue to open their home to me and provide invaluable information regarding the life and personality of Fred Hampton. Fred Hampton Jr. also helped to kick-start this project back in 2002. Fred Hampton Jr. and Akua Njeri have not received much support and recognition for their activism—I got your back, brother, and your father's legacy lives on. The book is extensive thanks to José "Cha Cha" Jiménez and Michael James. Cha Cha continues to connect me with folks in the movement, as his influence is all over this project, and Michael James remains a pillar in Chicago's activist community.

Many of the Illinois chapter members do not want to provide interviews because they are working on their own projects. This point helps to explain why there has been a lack of scholarship on the chapter. I have made a concerted effort to honor the positions of the Illinois chapter members who provided oral histories for this book. All parties interviewed were informed as to how their words were used for this book. Where necessary, changes were made to clarify positions of interviewees. Lynn French, for example, insisted that she be allowed to clarify her position based on interview material from the documentary *Comrade Sisters*. Some changes she requested were made and some were not. I want to acknowledge her concerns and emphasize that she did not depart from the Illinois chapter because she feared for her life but, rather, because of the exhaustive demands of the national chapter in Oakland that put a significant strain on the resources of the Illinois chapter. Again, I thank all the Illinois chapter members who sat for interviews for this book, and I hope my honesty and integrity will encourage the interviewees and other members to provide oral histories for my other projects.

There is also a host of other folks who equally made this book possible. The faculty, staff, and students of the Ralph J. Bunche Center of African American Studies at the University of California, Los Angeles, ignited my intellectual abilities. The Bunche Center will always be home for me. My advisor Brenda Stevenson is very dear to me, and she continues to be a driving force in my career not only as a scholar but also as a person. She has made herself available to me both inside and outside the academy, as I am dependent upon her tutelage and advice. Scot Brown and Mark Sawyer also continue to be invaluable mentors, and I greatly appreciate their patience and feedback on the project, as I am a bit of a bug-a-boo. Claudia Mitchell-Kernan will always have my heart. To call her a blessing is an understatement, as her personal guidance and professional leadership were crucial to my completion of this project. A warm thank you to my Bunche Center family: Darnell Hunt, Jan Freeman, Veronica Benson, Alex Tucker, Lisbeth Gant-Britton, and Yolanda Jones.

In the Department of History at UCLA, Jan Reiff and Edward Alpers read the manuscript and provided research, scholarship, and editorial suggestions. Robert Hill and Ellen Dubois also offered advice and recommendations for completing the project and encouraged me to allow my passion to engage my research.

In the Department of African American Studies at the University of Illinois at Urbana–Champaign, Sundiata Cha-Jua and Clarence Lang worked diligently with me on the early stages of the revision of the manuscript. Both aided my grasp of black power and its relationship to the long civil rights movement, which helped me to improve my framework for the book (minus theory although strongly suggested by Sundiata). Similarly, Abdul Alkalimat, Jabari Asim, Chris Benson, Ruby Mendenhall, James Anderson, and Christopher Span all offered constructive critiques of my work during my tenure in DAAS. Thank you all. Special thank you to Jennifer Hamer for providing me with personal and professional guidance. I hope the University of Kansas will treat you and Clarence well.

Numerous individuals, archives, repositories, libraries, fellowships, and private collections were made available to me. Thank you Richard Gutman for helping me to secure access to the court-ordered-sealed Chicago Police Department Red Squad files at the Chicago History Museum. Much of the book's scholarship is a result of this access. I want to thank the staff at the Chicago History Museum for their professionalism and their fast response time, which helped the project to stay on track to completion. Panther archivist Billy Jennings provided material and connections to the project. I want to thank the Dr. Huey P. Newton Foundation and the Green Library at Stanford University, Special Collections in the Young Research Library at UCLA, the Vivian G. Harsh Research Collection of Afro-American History and Literature at the Carter G. Woodson Regional Library in Chicago, the History Makers archive in Chicago, and the Chicago Films Archive. Special thanks to Michael James for extensive use of his personal archive that provided various sorts of materials for this project.

Similarly, a special thank you to Howard Ann Kendrick, William Hampton, Billy Dunbar, Paul Sequeira, and several others who offered materials, photos, and artifacts from their personal collections. Funds made available by the University of Kentucky College of Arts and Sciences and the African American and Africana Studies at the University of Kentucky Mini-Grant also aided the publication. Ruth Homrighaus of ruthlessediting.com and Sian Hunter both provided copy/developmental editing for the project. Thank you both, as the project would not have been published without your expertise.

I also want to thank several colleagues of the academy who either read the manuscript or offered advice for the completion of the project. Thank you Komozi Woodard, who peer-reviewed the book. Thank you Darlene Clark Hine, Robert Harris, James Turner, Robert Self, Peniel Joseph, Yohuru Williams, Amrita Myers, Charles Jones, and Curtis Austin. I extend a very special thank you to John Bracey, who suggested the title of the book, and to V. P. Franklin for his constructive feedback. Thank you both for your patience as I held you both hostage at several ASALH and NCBS meetings. I want to also thank my colleagues in the Department of History and across the campus and the dean of Arts and Sciences, Mark Kornbluh, all at the University of Kentucky.

Finally, I thank all my loved ones for their support and faith in the project. My wife, Cassandra, provided most of the funds needed to complete this project, and thus the book is as much a part of her being as it is a part of my intellectual growth. I love you! My uncle-in-law Burie "Chester" Kitching introduced me to the idea of this project, so thank you. I have been on my own since I was thirteen, and I would not be where I am today without a lot of help along the way. Thank you to all of my high school friends whose families took me in for periods of time, teachers, neighbors, and Gangster Disciples on the block, my lunatic family, student peers, colleagues, aunts and uncles, and the ancestors, especially those recently deceased (Jack Turner, Arralean Brown, and Charles Brown), who all in their own unique ways forced me to reach my potential and prevented my early death or incarceration. As I am the oldest of three, I thank my younger siblings, Ogdennia and Rahfielle, for believing in my work, since my potential big-brother rampage left them with no other choice but to do so. I thank my mother, Gwendolyn, and my father, Ogden, for giving me life and for their life choices which forced me to begin adulthood and to develop responsibility at a very early age. To my deceased grandmothers Louella Smith, Nazimova Williams, and Estelle Roach, you all are my heart and I miss you all dearly! I love you Tyion, Tyshaun, and Tyrone "Booman." Last but not least, I extend a deep loving thank you to my family in the Department of Africana Studies at Southern Illinois University at Carbondale: Pamela Smoot, Leonard Gadzekpo, and Tish Whitlock. A special thank you to Joseph A. Brown! Your guidance and love as a mentor and father figure transformed me as an entire person. I hope that I can one day be half the man that you are, and I will continue to appropriate your intellectual property. I love you and thank you! And thank you Eva Baham at Southern University A&M College for your inspiration and continuous support.

ABBREVIATIONS AND ACRONYMS

BPP	Black Panther Party
BSR	Black Stone Rangers
CFM	Chicago Freedom Movement
COINTELPRO	Counter Intelligence Program
CORE	Congress of Racial Equality
FBI	Federal Bureau of Investigation
FHA	Federal Housing Authority
GIU	Gang Intelligence Unit
HUAC	House Un-American Activities Committee
ILBPP	Illinois chapter of the Black Panther Party
JOIN	Jobs Or Income Now
NAACP	National Association for the Advancement of Colored People
RUA	Rising Up Angry
SCLC	Southern Christian Leadership Conference
SDS	Students for a Democratic Society
SNCC	Student Nonviolent Coordinating Committee
UCLA	University of California at Los Angeles
UIC	University of Illinois at Chicago Circle
U OF I	University of Illinois at Urbana–Champaign
YLO	Young Lords Organization
YPO	Young Patriots Organization

I PLEDGE A GRIEVANCE
TO THE FLAG
OF THE IGNITED STATES
OF AMERICA
AND TO THE SICK PUBLIC
FOR WHICH IT STANDS
ONE NATION
INCONCEIVABLE
WITH MOCKERY
AND PREJUDICE FOR ALL
—Rex Amos, *Black Panther
in Fat City, 1965*

INTRODUCTION

The Illinois Chapter of the
Black Panther Party Speaks for Itself

The Black Panther Party for Self Defense originated, to borrow a phrase
from Miriam Ma'at-Ka-Re Monges, "among the black downtrodden."[1] Black
Panthers lived among impoverished African Americans, and the Party's offices were in low-income, urban African American communities. Immersed
in such settings, where the ideology of self-defense is commonplace, the
Party popularized radicalism and armed resistance. The Illinois chapter of
the Black Panther Party (ILBPP) stands not only as an example in the long
African American tradition of radicalism and resistance but also as a paradigm of Black Power as a creative outgrowth of earlier civil rights efforts in
Chicago.

This volume closely examines the Illinois chapter, located in Chicago, and
its leader, Fred Hampton, with an emphasis on these linkages. Hampton was
the young, idealistic, charismatic leader of a multiethnic political movement
in Chicago who was brutally murdered by police officers while he slept.[2] His

vision and activism helped to create and unite pockets of resistance found throughout local communities regardless of color and ethnicity. Fred Hampton's own transition from the National Association for the Advancement of Colored People (NAACP) to the Black Panther Party (BPP) illustrates how armed resistance and revolutionary ideology could be both a response to *and* a continuation of various tenets of the civil rights struggle. Framing this narrative as a social and political history and utilizing the court-ordered-sealed secret police files in Chicago, this volume will fill an enormous gap in the scholarship on the civil rights–Black Power era, the BPP, and racial coalition politics in Chicago. Furthermore, it shows how President Barack Obama's 2008 campaign was a movement that began with Fred Hampton and the original Rainbow Coalition.

Historians who study the black liberation movement, or what Peniel Joseph has dubbed "Black Power Studies," can be divided into roughly three categories, based on their use of biography.[3] One group examines various elements of the black freedom struggle at the national level by focusing on icons such as Rev. Dr. Martin Luther King Jr., Malcolm X, or Amiri Baraka.[4] Another set provides studies of the lives of grassroots activists such as Fannie Lou Hamer, Gloria Richardson, and Ella Baker to explore the local and grassroots histories of the black liberation movement.[5] My work is in concert with the third circle of scholarship, established by historians such as William Chafe, John Dittmer, and Charles Payne, which analyzes the black liberation struggle from the ground up, thereby connecting organizing at the local and regional levels to the national arena.[6]

This volume could be considered the northern complement to Charles Payne's study of organizing traditions in Mississippi and further adds to appreciations of a northern idiom of the civil rights–Black Power era—a tradition that has been identified in the discourse on the black freedom struggle by the various volumes edited by Komozi Woodard, Jeanne Theoharis, and others.[7] In the Chicago context of the black freedom movement, black students are a neglected group who played a pivotal role in the struggle. The black student movement in Chicago operated alongside the Chicago Freedom Movement (CFM) led by Dr. King and the Southern Christian Leadership Conference (SCLC). Youth community groups, social clubs, and gangs were also active in the black student movement. The ILBPP provided a model for politics, methodology, organizing, and community service programs that ushered in a process of self-transformation, which inspired many Chicago area youth to work toward solving their own critical issues. This study parallels Donna Murch's *Living for the City*, on the Bay

Area, and Matthew Countryman's *Up South*, on Philadelphia, while echoing the foundational southern scholarship of John Dittmer and others.[8]

One of the most highly debated topics in black freedom movement studies is the relationship between civil rights and Black Power. The traditional paradigm is the civil rights (nonviolence/reform) vs. Black Power (armed resistance/revolution) framework. Most recent scholarship demonstrates that the best way to frame the relationship is the "Civil Rights and Black Power" or the "long Civil Rights" model.[9] This volume illustrates that several of the tenets in the city's civil rights movement, such as the fight to desegregate schools and recreation and the resistance to the Daley political machine, were continued by the ILBPP in the Black Power movement. Fred Hampton participated and led many of the civil rights campaigns as president of the NAACP Youth Council, and he continued this work as a leader of the ILBPP. This point corresponds to Donna Murch's research that documents NAACP youth leaders who evolved into key leaders of the Black Power movement in the Bay Area in the mid-1960s. Matthew Countryman exhibits similar findings in his work on Philadelphia. My work posits that the activism of Chicago high school students was central to the black freedom movement in Chicago and that many of these students continued as activists and college leaders on local community campuses. This argument, examined alongside other evidence in this volume, contradicts the line of reasoning fueled by the cultural poverty paradigm put forth by scholars such as Gerald Horne and Jeffrey O. G. Ogbar, which suggests that the Black Power movement was propelled by pathological street gangs.[10]

In the Chicago context, the Black Power movement was thrust forward by students and community organizers who developed into successful intellectual, political, and institutional leaders of the struggle. More importantly, the borders between the civil rights and Black Power movements in Chicago were so permeable that only a careful analysis of the local movement would discern the thousands of threads that bound the two together. This major facet of my premise is influenced by recent works produced by Hasan Jeffries, Donna Murch, Peniel Joseph, Judson Jeffries, Yohuru Williams, and Jama Lazerow.[11] In concert with the aforementioned scholarship, my position is that the ILBPP grew out of youth activism in the CFM—particularly the black student movement in the high schools and local colleges. I show how Chicago Panthers attempted to reach the goals of the CFM with campaigns and community service programs to desegregate schools and recreational facilities, improve housing conditions, address high unemployment and poverty, expand school curricula at both the high school and college levels, feed hungry and malnourished children, provide health care for the poor, and eliminate political corruption and police brutality.

This volume will consider the racial, social, and political conditions that existed in Chicago during the late 1960s to demonstrate how the ILBPP's community organizing methods and revolutionary self-defense ideology significantly influenced Chicago's machine politics, grassroots organizing, racial coalitions, and police behavior. Central to this history is ILBPP chairman Fred Hampton, who gained leadership, mobilization, and grassroots organizing skills while a member of the NAACP. Later, as a member of the BPP, he enhanced these skills and developed oratory tools that attracted other organizations and ethnic groups. His speeches, coupled with the Illinois chapter's revolutionary platform, resulted in alliances between the chapter and various local activists and organizations that would eventually evolve into the original Rainbow Coalition in 1968. As a result, there is a direct link involving racial coalition politics in Chicago that stretches from Fred Hampton to U.S. President Barack Obama. This link is one of appropriation rather than mere genealogy (with the exception of Harold Washington), as this book will highlight the disconnect between what the Panthers hoped to accomplish and what their political strategy was later used for by Jesse Jackson, David Axelrod, and Barack Obama.

Beginning in 1968, the ILBPP's original Rainbow Coalition worked to protect the voting rights of the poor, eradicate political corruption, and eliminate police brutality. Scholars such as Bridgette Baldwin and Devin Fergus have argued that these issues were targets of the Party during its latter years—the Panthers' reformist period beginning in 1971.[12] There were more than forty BPP chapters in the United States, each unique and responsive to the urgent concerns of its own location. The ILBPP was not really ahead of its time in its efforts to address such social problems; these conditions afflicted many poor Chicago residents, and the issues were already among those at the forefront of the civil rights agenda. The ideology, discourse, and long-range objectives applied to these problems by the ILBPP's Black Power model, however, were those of revolution rather than reform, as they addressed pressing concerns that needed to be resolved before the hoped-for revolution.[13]

The Black Panther Party for Self Defense

Having acquired permission from Stokely Carmichael and the Lowndes County Freedom Organization in Alabama to use their panther title and symbol, Huey Newton and Bobby Seale established the Black Panther Party for

Self Defense in 1966 in Oakland, California.[14] Like thousands of others, the two men had migrated from the South to escape racism and segregation only to find similar conditions in Oakland—conditions such as unequal access to labor, education, and housing as well as corruption in electoral politics and high rates of incarceration and police brutality. In their attempt to remedy the plight of working-class and oppressed African Americans in their area, Newton and Seale created a new self-empowerment organization in the region's burgeoning environment of radicalism and Black Power ideology.[15]

In advocating self-defense, the Panthers placed themselves in a long tradition of African American activism extending from the nineteenth century to the 1960s.[16] Martin Delany and Maria W. Stewart were advocates of black armed resistance to oppression, and David Walker's *Appeal* is one of the earliest publications advocating such a doctrine.[17] In the 1920s, Cyril Briggs and the African Blood Brotherhood, along with Marcus Garvey's Universal African Legion (the militia unit of the Universal Negro Improvement Association), also advocated armed resistance.[18] Post–World War II proponents of armed self-defense include Robert Williams, the Deacons for Defense and Justice, Paul Robeson, the Revolutionary Action Movement, the Student Nonviolent Coordinating Committee (SNCC), and Malcolm X, to name a few. Robert Williams, head of the NAACP branch in Monroe, North Carolina, established a rifle club made up mostly of black World War II veterans to protect black communities from white violence.[19] The Deacons for Defense and Justice was a black, working-class, armed self-defense organization based in Louisiana and structured to protect civil rights activists and community organizers from white vigilantes, the Ku Klux Klan, and police violence.[20] World-renowned entertainer Paul Robeson had publicly objected to black oppression long before World War II; his objections became far more militant as he established himself as an advocate for armed self-defense after 1945, which caused him to become a target of McCarthyism.[21] The Revolutionary Action Movement, founded by Maxwell Stanford in 1962, was the first organization to promote urban guerrilla warfare as a method of achieving self-determination for African American people and was supported by both Robert Williams and Malcolm X.[22] Originally, SNCC was formed in 1960 as a student-led, nonviolent civil rights group. But it evolved into a radical armed resistance organization by 1965, and several of its key leaders would eventually merge with the BPP.[23] Malcolm X advocated armed resistance as a human right and necessity for African Americans during and after his membership in the Nation of Islam.[24] Founding Panther Bobby Seale dubbed the Party the continuation of Nat Turner, whom he called "the force that pushed forward with speed for freedom and the turning point in the historical cross-road towards liberation."[25]

Recent scholarship by Christopher Strain, Akinyele Umoja, Emilye Crosby, and many others who tackle the history of African American armed self-defense provides numerous examples that these and other ancestors were models influencing the development of the BPP.[26] Scholars have understood the BPP's ideology as an extension of this tradition and acknowledge the Party's difficulty adapting its radical ideology to the turbulent period in which it operated. They have failed to come to a consensus, however, regarding exactly how to fit the Party's complex theoretical approach into the spectrum of African American radicalism and armed resistance. Floyd Hayes and Francis Kiene, for instance, contend that Panther ideology was a version of W. E. B. Du Bois's political thought that attempted to see the black struggle in terms of race and class. African American radical thinkers have struggled with these relationships, they explain, in trying to explain the "changing characters of their society."[27] The BPP's merger of race and class was hampered by both internal and external pressures. Hayes and Kiene argue that the Party's political perspectives were a "dialectical interaction between Black nationalism" and "revolutionary intercommunalism resulting from changing social conditions."[28]

Nikhil Pal Singh, on the other hand, asserts that Panther ideology was a continuation of C. L. R. James's "The Revolutionary Answer to the Negro Question in the United States." In contrast to James, however, the Party believed racism prevented blacks and whites from uniting "in class struggle toward a socialist revolution."[29] Singh's analysis demonstrates that Panthers defined "Black political subjectivity and a revolutionary sense of Black peoplehood" in the failure of the middle-class civil rights movement and working-class struggles for integration, which were opposed to "Black nationalist schemes of separation."[30] The BPP established a dual approach that blurred these two opposing approaches to black liberation. The Party emphasized "separation and Black difference" by means of localized "demands for communal autonomy" and simultaneously advocated "integration and equality" through a commitment to "solidarity with all victims of Americanization at home and around the world."[31] Thus, Party members' adaptation of the black radical tradition of armed resistance was complex.

Clearly, however, the Party's political and social struggle was defiant and highly publicized. Huey Newton and Bobby Seale learned and taught California law to Party members with the purpose of protecting their communities and policing the police. Scholar Chris Booker outlines six key events that "enhanced the organization's prestige, publicized its existence and objectives, and sharpened the hostility of the American establishment against it."[32] First, the BPP provided security for Betty Shabazz during her visit to the Bay Area to be interviewed by *Ramparts* magazine. Twenty armed Panthers marched Shabazz into the magazine's office, which horrified the staff and eventually led to an armed confrontation with police outside the building. Shabazz was escorted to safety by several Panthers, while Newton and other members taunted and intimidated the police, causing the officers to back down. The media coverage of the incident brought widespread attention to the BPP.[33]

The police killing of Denzil Dowell was a second catalyst. George Dowell contacted the Party to investigate his brother's death, and the Panthers concluded that the murder was not an isolated event. The Party held two rallies, attended by more than 150 people, to inform residents of the necessity of armed self-defense.[34] These events not only helped to increase membership and interest in the group but also demonstrated the community's support of and confidence in the organization.

Next, Eldridge Cleaver, Stokely Carmichael (later known as Kwame Ture), H. Rap Brown, and James Farmer became Panthers. Then came the announcement of SNCC's short-lived, tumultuous "merger" with the Party, which significantly increased the group's membership, and the Detroit-based League of Revolutionary Black Workers participated in joint activities with the Panthers. The addition of these young, influential leaders and established organizations "lent the impression of a Panther monopoly on the Black revolutionary leadership of the period . . . [and] cemented the impression that the African American revolutionary left was uniting under the banner of the Black Panther Party."[35]

A fourth spurt in membership followed the sensationalized May 2, 1967, international media coverage of an armed delegation of BPP lobbyists who stormed the California state assembly and interrupted the proceedings to protest a bill aimed at preventing Panthers (and other citizens) from carrying loaded, unconcealed weapons in public places.[36] Before leaving, Bobby Seale read a "Panther Mandate" to reporters that stated that it was the black community's constitutional right, as well as a survival necessity, to arm itself. The incident aired on networks throughout the world. This display of boldness and courage on the part of young black men inspired those of similar identity and instilled fear and anger in those who interpreted the Panthers' defiance as an assault against the established racial hierarchy and social order.

More exposure arose after the October 28, 1967, shoot-out between Huey Newton and two police officers. Newton and Officer Herbert Heanes were seriously injured during the shoot-out, and Officer John Frey was killed. Newton's incarceration following the incident led the BPP to ally with the white leftist Peace and Freedom Party, and together they held domestic and international "Free Huey" rallies that resulted in another increase in membership. The "Free Huey" campaign helped the Party to become a national organization.[37]

Finally, the shoot-out between Panthers and police two days after Martin Luther King's assassination resulted in the first highly publicized Panther death and served as the sixth incident to cause a surge in Party membership and exposure. After being forced to surrender, seventeen-year-old Bobby Hutton was unarmed when he was shot and killed by police. Publicity of his death helped to increase the Panthers' prestige and national support.[38]

The Party's public image was also crucial to increases in membership at the same time that it brought the organization publicity and drew governmental hostility. Jane Rhodes documents how young African American men wearing black leather jackets, black berets, and blue shirts; carrying rifles; marching in an organized fashion; and disparaging the various forms of the American power structure drew many African American youth and Vietnam veterans to the Party. Their dress, Afros, raised black fists, and Black Power rhetoric were also culturally attractive to African American students and other young adults who supported a more radical approach to achieving equality in America. The Panthers' physical and cultural attractiveness, coupled with the media's frequently sensationalized representations of the group, helped to lead many new members toward the Party.[39]

The Illinois Chapter of the Black Panther Party

The history of the BPP in Oakland has captivated students, scholars, and popular culture since 1966, but the account of the Chicago Panthers has been seriously overlooked. Although local issues catalyzed the founding of the ILBPP in 1968, its formation was also influenced by the historical and contemporary convergences that spawned the national BPP headquarters in Oakland. Illinois chairman Fred Hampton was one of the most popular Panther icons, yet there is practically no scholarship available on Hampton or the ILBPP. It has been long rumored that in 1969, Fred Hampton and the ILBPP offered the best possible hope for stability as the national BPP attempted to overcome its crisis. The fact that Fred Hampton may have been chosen to lead the national Party

Bobby Seale (*far left*), Masai Hewitt (*second from right*), and Don Cox (*center*), members of the national BPP Central Committee, at a secret meeting with ILBPP leaders Fred Hampton (*second from left*) and Bobby Rush (*far right*) in the office of attorney Kermit Coleman at the American Civil Liberties Union in Chicago to discuss the possibility of temporarily moving the BPP national headquarters to Chicago, 1969 (Private archive of Howard Ann Kendrick [Campbell])

during its crisis and that Chicago was chosen in secrecy by members of the national BPP Central Committee as the possible temporary national headquarters in 1969 warrants scholarly examination.[40]

The discussion of the ILBPP by scholars and journalists has predominately focused on the assassination of Fred Hampton.[41] Curtis Austin's work is regarded as one of the most detailed of these accounts.[42] In November 2009, Jeff Haas published his memoirs as a movement lawyer centered on the assassination of Fred Hampton and the numerous trials that followed his death.[43] Several studies of black politics in Chicago provide limited accounts of the Party's role in the city prior to Hampton's death.[44]

Jon Rice's article "The World of the Illinois Panthers" is the most current and relevant work on the Illinois chapter. A condensed version of his unpublished dissertation, the piece ably examines the ILBPP, race relations, rifts between Chicago's African American West and South Sides, and class issues.[45] However, Rice fails to provide a critical examination of the Illinois chapter and its day-to-day activities, Daley's Democratic machine, or the origin of the Rainbow Coalition and its functions. These points are in no way critiques of his investigations but, rather, stress important areas for study that can be examined by using his text as a guide. This volume not only explores these overlooked areas and illustrates their significance in Chicago's political landscape but also demonstrates the power of the Illinois chapter's grassroots organizational abilities. With Fred Hampton as their leader and principal organizer, the Illinois Panthers challenged what was arguably the most powerful political entity in the Midwest—Mayor Richard J. Daley's Democratic machine—in a city with a long and violent history of racial tension. More importantly, the ILBPP promoted interethnic coalitions, and its ideologies and activities in the 1960s were markedly different from popular perceptions of the Party both then and now.[46]

Scope and Limitations

This study begins in 1966 for a number of reasons. The BPP was founded in 1966, the same year that Fred Hampton began his political activism in Chicago as a seventeen-year-old youth organizer for the NAACP. Drawing on activist and organizing experience acquired during his tenure in the NAACP, Hampton transformed the political landscape of Chicago before he was assassinated at age twenty-one. He was a very young man with little education and even fewer resources, yet Hampton was able to unify the diverse working-class population of one of the most racially segregated and politically corrupt cities in the United States. As chairman of the ILBPP, Hampton established the Rainbow Coalition in 1968 as "a political coalition that respected ethnic communities of all kinds led by poor, black youth."[47] This racial coalition movement included both nontraditional and customary political alliances and, more importantly, valued these organizations as essential contributors to the movement for political and social change. Although the ILBPP was disbanded in 1974, the legacy of the Party's racial and class coalition building and its survival programs extend well beyond the chapter's demise. Several of the chapter's survival programs thrived well into the mid-1980s, and the free breakfast for children program was adopted by the Chicago public school system and is still heavily relied upon today.

Thus, this study takes as its endpoint three significant political developments of the 1980s and beyond: First, it considers the election of Chicago's first African American mayor, Harold Washington, in 1983. His successful campaign was a result of the political and racial coalition building that Fred Hampton and the Rainbow Coalition began in the 1960s, which proved effective in bringing independent elected officials to office and undermining Mayor Daley's Democratic machine. Next, it also examines Jesse Jackson's presidential bids in 1984 and 1988 and Barack Obama's presidential election in 2008, demonstrating the linkages between the ILBPP's Rainbow Coalition and these campaigns. Influenced by Harold Washington's election, Chicago resident Jesse Jackson appropriated the Panthers' "rainbow coalition" strategy in both of his presidential campaigns before officially appropriating the title of the Chicago Panthers' political creation as his own. Ironically, in 1969, the ILBPP's Rainbow Coalition opposed Jackson's Operation Breadbasket, an SCLC affiliate, due to the coalition's anticapitalist platform. Jesse Jackson appropriated the group's name and its effective, class-conscious grassroots organizing principles to transfer the ILBPP's accomplishments in a racially strained city to a national arena, even though he was not a supporter of such politics prior to Harold Washington's election.[48]

Forty years after the establishment of the ILBPP's Rainbow Coalition, Barack Obama was elected as the first African American president of the United States. Under the counsel of David Axelrod, who himself had commoditized Rainbow Coalition politics for his media consultant company, Obama adapted the group's methods, message, and philosophy for his own political gains after his U.S. congressional defeat in 2000. That race, billed as the "Black Panther against the Professor," saw original Rainbow Coalition and ILBPP founder Bobby Rush mobilize his Rainbow Coalition base to defeat Barack Obama with 61 percent vs. 30 percent of the vote.[49] This volume demonstrates that Chicago was a vibrant city of black activism where the vanguard ILBPP used political agitation and consciousness to build racial coalitions that challenged local and governmental political affairs, and that would eventually lead to the election of the city's first African American mayor and the nation's first African American president.

In addition to its chronological boundaries, this study also limits its consideration of the Illinois chapter largely to the West, South, and North Sides of Chicago. During the period under study, Chicago was (as it remains today) the most racially residentially segregated city in America. More than 90 percent of the city's African American residents live on the West and South Sides. Moreover, the ILBPP was located in the heart of the West Side's African American community before the office moved to the South Side. While an investigation of the Rainbow Coalition necessitates that we look at the North Side and other areas of the city and the surrounding suburbs, the West and South Sides are the central focus of this study.

There are two aspects to completing this study that warrant discussion. First, the Chicago History Museum, formerly the Chicago Historical Society, houses the records of the Chicago Police Department's Intelligence Section and Surveillance Unit, or Red Squad, which contain police reports on all organizations, clubs, and gangs that challenged machine politics in the 1960s and 1970s.[50] Due to the repressive acts of the Red Squad and the numerous lawsuits by Chicago residents that followed, the Red Squad files were sealed by a court order in 1983. I was permitted unlimited access to the sealed records, and a great deal of that primary source material is utilized for and informs this project. Next, one major reason why scholars have yet to fully engage the Illinois chapter is the fact that many of its former members refuse to be interviewed and/or are engaged in producing their own projects. For instance, the Illinois chapter has recently established a nonprofit organization titled the Illinois Black Panther Party History Project. The group is in the process of archiving primary source material from their personal collections and digitizing oral history interviews of members. The project's slogan is "The Illinois Chapter speaks for itself," and the organization intends to publish a book that focuses on the Illinois chapter as they remember it. Fortunately, members within and outside the Illinois Black Panther Party History Project sat for interviews and provided material from their personal collections for this project. To respect the goals of these former members, this project does not claim to be a complete history of the Illinois Panthers. These points are mentioned to exhibit an important challenge to researchers studying the BPP, and the Illinois chapter in particular.

Chapter Layout

This book consists of six chapters. The first chapter provides a context for the BPP's appeal to African American residents of Chicago in 1968 by considering historical patterns of segregation, economic and political exploitation, and violence against them. The chapter ends with a portrait of black Chicago under the Daley machine and an examination of how the failure of the CFM created a search for new leadership among those interested in pursuing social justice. Chapter 2 examines the overlooked story of young people, battling for civil rights and the desegregation of education and recreation, who formed the base of the ILBPP. The important players in this evolution were the "tough ghetto youth" and students who, while members of the Party, reoriented the civil rights agenda toward community-based activism and self-defense. The youth who joined the ILBPP saw it as the vanguard of the social justice movement. In addition, this chapter begins the biography of Fred Hampton, which is threaded throughout the remainder of the book.

The comparison of the ILBPP to the BPP headquartered in Oakland is the subject of Chapter 3. This chapter provides an overview of the organizations' daily activities and suggests how the Illinois chapter differed due to the 1968

Democratic National Convention, its relationship to the mainstream civil rights movement, and its treatment of gender issues. Chapter 3 shows that just because members joined the ILBPP did not mean that they abandoned the civil rights grassroots campaigns they were involved in prior to joining the Party. More importantly, these civil rights ventures were equally important to the ILBPP, as they addressed immediate issues that needed to be resolved before the hoped-for revolution. Chapter 4 recounts the history of the original Rainbow Coalition, which was created as a response to the Daley Democratic machine, to show how the ILBPP created an antiracist, anticlass coalition to fight urban renewal, political corruption, and police brutality in Chicago via grassroots organizing in communities. This kind of grassroots organizing was significant because it occurred in a city with a long history of racial hatred and at a time when racial conflict in the city had reached new heights. The Rainbow Coalition crossed both racial and class lines and even included marginalized groups and gangs that had little or no political consciousness. The success influenced models used nationwide.

Chapter 5 documents law enforcement repression of the Panthers and how it was an integral part of the Panther story in Chicago. The Chicago Police Department has a reputation for overt racism that dates back far before the 1960s. This chapter considers how African American police officers responded to racism in the department and to the racist repression of the Panthers. More important, it examines the atypical law enforcement relationship between the Federal Bureau of Investigation (FBI), the Illinois state attorney's office, and the corrupt Chicago Police Department, which resulted in the murder of Fred Hampton and Mark Clark. The chapter also considers how the connection of local media outlets to the Chicago Police Department's Red Squad and the FBI's Counter Intelligence Program (COINTELPRO) aided in the demise of the Illinois Panthers. A significant amount of analysis is devoted to the Red Squad because, due to its sealed records, it has not borne appropriate responsibility for its repressive acts.

The concluding chapter offers a brief exploration of the Panthers' legacy nationally and in Chicago, with special emphasis on the Panthers' survival programs, as well as on the Rainbow Coalition. The chapter maps the direct link and appropriation of racial coalition politics in Chicago that stretches from Fred Hampton in 1968 to Harold Washington and Jesse Jackson in the 1980s to Barack Obama in 2008. The ILBPP's Rainbow Coalition utilized ethnic and racial coalition building as a strategy to challenge corruption and to provide power to the powerless in Chicago. The Rainbow Coalition was a significant factor in the election of Chicago's first African American mayor,

Harold Washington (who as mayor established what he called his Rainbow Council), and it provided a model of politics that Jesse Jackson, David Axelrod, and Barack Obama were able to exploit as a means to a political end rather than as the foundations for revolutionary reform that the Panthers and their allies sought. I do not "attack" Jackson but point out the history of an organization whose title he later appropriated. The political dimensions regarding Barack Obama also point out the similarities and continuance of the ILBPP's political racial coalition. The purpose of this section is to highlight the direct connection to demonstrate the legacy of the ILBPP. The chapter is not a critical examination of the full body of work of Jackson, Axelrod, or Obama. Finally, this chapter considers the controversy and debate surrounding efforts to name a street after Fred Hampton in Chicago in 2006. This controversy exposed the persistence of the deep animosity of the local establishment toward the city's African American and progressive communities.

This volume contends with major questions of contestation in the field of civil rights–Black Power studies. Where does civil rights end and Black Power begin? What was the role of student movements in the Black Power movement, and what students were involved—high school or college? The history of Fred Hampton and the ILBPP answers these critical questions under debate. The text brings together both the civil rights and the Black Power movements, giving generous consideration to the political dynamics of both streams of the freedom struggle.

This volume argues that the Illinois Panthers' armed resistance was not a complete break with the traditional civil rights movement and that the Panthers drew energy and leadership from the mainstream movement. But then what do we learn when we investigate and take seriously the ILBPP's work? This volume, while a case study of the ILBPP, is also a case study of the diffusion of the energies of the civil rights movement in Chicago via (1) the failure of the CFM, (2) the eclipse of Panther-style radical activism and traditional nonviolent civil rights in Chicago, and (3) the deliberate dismantling of the Panthers by city and federal law enforcement authorities. We find an ILBPP legacy in attitudes toward organizing and in social programs; we find a legacy in the demise of the Daley Democratic machine and of city and federal spying and First Amendment rights violations of the sort perpetuated by the Chicago Police Department's Red Squad and the FBI's COINTELPRO; and we also find a movement that, as an unintended consequence, resulted not only in a win for Barack Obama of a U.S. Senate seat but also in his election as the United States' first African American president.

I look around me, I feel like this is a foreign country. I
don't belong. . . . My brothers been pushed around too
long. Well, I get zapped walking down the street, I'm
not going to cop out. I'd go right out there and shoot.
—African American Chicago resident, in Royko,
  Boss, 161–62

ONE

The Political and Social Climate of Black Chicago, 1900–1970

When the ILBPP was founded in November 1968, black Chicago could fairly
be characterized as poor, angry, and underserved. This chapter highlights
how these local conditions came to be and how they prepared the ground for
the Black Panther Party's appeal to African Americans in Chicago. The first
sections of the chapter describe the historical foundations of black unrest
in migration and patterns of segregation, economic and political exploitation, and violence in Chicago's black neighborhoods. The central sections of
the chapter investigate black Chicago under Mayor Richard J. Daley's Democratic machine, considering how the Daley government's political corruption, urban renewal program, and police intimidation, as well as its failure
to take meaningful steps to improve slums or prevent housing discrimination
and fraud, affected the lives of black Chicagoans. Racial discrimination in
Chicago drew Dr. Martin Luther King Jr. to target the city when the focus of
the nonviolent civil rights movement shifted to the North. The final section

of the chapter reviews the history of the CFM and the reasons for its failure, which left many of those who wished to struggle for civil rights in Chicago searching for a new vision and new leadership.

The Making of Black Chicago

In the early 1900s, just under 32,000 African Americans lived in Chicago, comprising less than 2 percent of the city's population. During World War I, however, an influx of black migrants crowded into the city, looking for economic opportunities denied to them in the South under legally sanctioned racial discrimination. The war halted European immigration, thereby indirectly forcing Chicago industries to hire black migrants as employees—in several cases as strikebreakers—especially in the white ethnic–dominated meatpacking plants. Newspapers like the *Chicago Defender* advertised these opportunities and helped usher more black migrants into the city.[1] By 1930, Chicago housed almost 247,000 African American residents, and continuous migration, largely from the South, almost tripled these figures by 1960, bringing Chicago's total black population to almost 1 million.[2]

These northwardly mobile African Americans became the foundation of Chicago's black industrial working class.[3] Most of Chicago's white residents, however, saw African American population growth as a threat to their power and livelihood. Throughout most of the twentieth century, Chicago's black and white residents would violently jockey for residential space, political power, and job opportunities.

Racial tensions in Chicago became combustible in 1919. Black migrants seeking housing shifted and expanded the border of the South Side's "Black Belt," and African American soldiers returning from World War I challenged the city's established ethnic groups—civilians and veterans alike—for jobs and housing. The segregated Black Belt is the area on the southeast side of the city made up of three communities—Douglas, Bronzeville, and Washington Park—where African Americans lived as a result of racially restrictive covenants and the real threat that violence would accompany any attempts to reside outside these locations.[4]

On Sunday, July 27, 1919, the murder of an African American youth, Eugene Williams, by a white mob at Lake Michigan Beach on Twenty-Ninth Street led to a four-day race riot that remains one of America's deadliest. Williams, a recent grammar school graduate, was floating on a raft that accidentally drifted across the imaginary line that divided the beach between black and white patrons. Enraged by the unintended violation, white adult beachgoers stoned Williams

South Side Black Belt

until he fell unconscious into the lake, where he drowned. A group of black men attempted to get a white police officer to arrest the mob to no avail, so the men took matters into their own hands, attacking the white men who had caused Williams's death. Other whites came to the aid of the men being attacked, causing black bystanders to join the black men who were fighting.[5]

The battle spread west from the beach as far as the vicinity of Thirty-Fifth and State Streets. Some African Americans who were at work during the riot were trapped inside their employment facilities by white mobs waiting outside to kill them. Former alderman Oscar DePriest donned a policeman's uniform and repeatedly drove a patrol wagon into the stockyards to safely bring out every African American trapped inside. No other policeman attempted the deed or assisted DePriest, who risked his own life for those he rescued.[6] Mayor William Hale Thompson did not request that Governor Frank O. Lowden send out the National Guard until 10:30 P.M. on the fourth day. By this time, a thunderstorm and heavy rain had squelched much of the violence. Thirty-eight men and boys, 23 of them black, were killed, and 537 people, 342 of them black, were injured.[7]

During the riot, the Hamburgs, an Irish athletic club (of which future Chicago mayor Richard J. Daley was a member), were in the center of the mayhem, since most of the violence took place in the Black Belt bordering their community of Bridgeport.[8] Other athletic clubs were also involved, among them Ragen's Colts, Aylwards, Our Flag, and Standard. Young men aged fifteen to twenty-two made up the greater part of the "gangs . . . of white youths" who "formed definite nuclei for the crowd and mob formations."[9] The social discomfort caused by the massive migration of African Americans had led to these white attacks. The resentment toward African Americans who served as strikebreakers during World War I and the increasing presence of black workers in industrial facilities that threatened the rigid geographic boundaries to which white ethnic Chicagoans were accustomed were also important factors.[10]

The explosion of violent racial tensions in 1919 set the tone for Chicago race relations for the next five decades. The 1919 riot also marked a change in how African Americans would respond to white violent oppression. Until this time, white ethnics were able to use violence as a tool of control in their relationships with black Chicagoans without fear of repercussion. The "red summer of 1919," however, transformed black Chicago residents from victims into a people who relied on their agency to defend themselves and their community from white violence. Although the threat of white violence would continue to hold sway over black residents for the next fifty years, the city's power structure understood that if and when these black communities decided to "fight fire with fire," more than a thunderstorm would be required to calm their reaction.

During the 1920s, the northward migration of blacks expanded the black community on the South Side, forcing the newly arrived to seek housing in bordering white neighborhoods. White residents responded by bombing the homes of African Americans in both white and black areas—as frequently as once every twenty days over a four-year period between 1917 and 1921.[11] Nonviolent means were also employed to control the racial geography of the area: realtors profited from the South Side's changing demographics by manipulating the racial fears of whites and by exploiting blacks financially.[12] The white realty firm of Frederick H. Bartlett and the Chicago Real Estate Board utilized racial covenants to swindle both black and white residents during community demographic transitions.[13] White residents were manipulated to sell their homes at bargain prices from fear that black families would soon move to their community, which would drive down their property's value. Then these same homes would be resold to both white and black residents at double (sometimes triple) the purchase price. White homebuyers were led to believe that their cultural privilege would protect them from the integration of their neighborhoods, as realtors purposely lied to prospective white buyers that racial covenants were in place to protect the land they purchased from sale to black families. The same realtors would then sell property in the same communities to black families with mortgages that required balloon payments due at the end of five years.

During the 1930s, inadequate housing and unemployment plagued African Americans residing on the South Side of Chicago, where the suffering of the Great Depression was exacerbated by the continued influx of black migrants from the South. Rents for black residents were almost double those for their white counterparts—who could live as close as one block away—as a result of racial covenants. Black families were building shacks in vacant lots, and single men set up hundreds of tents in Washington Park. The population density of black communities was 70,000 people per square mile, compared with 30,000 in the crowded white districts.[14] If the population density of black communities had been reapportioned to the entire city, one history of the city notes, Chicago "would have had a population of thirty-two million rather than just more than three million."[15] Black unemployment had climbed above 50 percent by 1930, and lack of financial stability led to high eviction rates.[16] According to the Unemployment Relief Census of 1933, African American Chicagoans made up only 8 percent of the city's available workers, but they represented 32 percent of unemployed Chicagoans and 34 percent of Chicagoans on public relief.[17]

Before racial covenants were eliminated in 1948, when the U.S. Supreme Court decision *Shelley v. Kraemer* deemed them unconstitutional, Chicago's African American wards made up a city within the city. They were so congested that there was a saying in black Chicago, according to sociologists St. Clair Drake and Horace Cayton, "If you're trying to find a certain Negro in Chicago, stand on the corner of 47th and South Park long enough and you're bound to see him."[18] By the 1950s, African Americans had increased their attempts to integrate white communities, and white residents just as strongly intensified their violent response to maintain and protect segregation.

Black Politics in Early-Twentieth-Century Chicago

For most of the twentieth century, white ethnic politicians controlled the wards in which African Americans made up the majority of residents. African

Americans of influence (most of whom were men) who resided or conducted business within such wards were often pawns of these politicians—for the benefit of each party and at the expense of the overall community. At times, these men were able to wrest power from aldermen and occasionally were able to have aldermen replaced. Nevertheless, aldermen were usually white ethnics who made sure that the ward votes of their "darkies" were under their control, that businesses and organizations were exploited for profit, and that political gains were minimal to nonexistent.

In 1896, there were two black elected officials in the city: Edward "the Iron Master" Wright, who served as Cook County commissioner, and Major John C. Buckner, a member of the Illinois House of Representatives. Both were advocates for black empowerment and attacked those who demeaned their race. They demanded and often received both political and personal respect. Although the black community overwhelmingly supported Republicans until the 1930s, however, neither politician held enough political clout to compete with (Democratic-affiliated) Irish aldermen and ward bosses.[19]

The lack of real black political power resulted in an unusual alliance between black churches and saloons to get black voters to create change. The first documented account of such an alliance dates to 1896, when Rev. Reverdy C. Ransom, pastor of Bethel African Methodist Episcopal Church, and Robert Motts, saloon owner and one of Chicago's first black gambling czars, joined together in an effort to get the 2600–3100 blocks of Dearborn Avenue paved for the benefit of their community and their patrons. Ransom expressed this wish to the ward alderman, Addison Ballard. Unsympathetic to the pastor's request, Ballard informed his constituents that he had no interest in paving the streets. Angered by the alderman's insolent tone, Ransom vowed to put him "out of office if it is the last thing that I do."[20] The pastor rallied his congregation around the problem. Bob Motts agreed to help finance the campaign, donating $1,000. Their joint effort was central to the unseating of Ballard and the election of Alderman Charles "Candyman" Gunther (1896–1900). Gunther thanked his black constituency by paving the Dearborn blocks.[21]

Coalition politics during this period usually combined patronage with bribery, and until the late 1950s, most politicians had relationships with the underworld.[22] This was true of Anglo-Americans, other white ethnic groups, and African Americans. Bob Motts and his predecessor in the saloon business, John "Mushmouth" Johnson, for example, both helped organize black voters in the Second Ward (the first major black urban center in the United

States, extending south from Roosevelt Road to Forty-Third Street and west from Lake Michigan to Wentworth Avenue) and made cash donations to support white aldermen. In return, aldermen would warn them of potential police raids on their establishments.

Unlike Johnson and Motts, Henry "Teenan" Jones, who was also a saloon and gambling proprietor, solidified his influence on the black vote with a direct wire to the desk of all Chicago mayors from 1895 through 1915. His relationship with the mayor's office enabled his business ventures to be free of police raids. Jones's relationship with Mayor Carter Henry Harrison II was so solid that in 1911, when the mayor put all gambling establishments out of business except those run by black proprietors, Teenan Jones's clubs became the hotbed of nightlife in the city. The mayor rationalized that segregation already restricted the number of activities available to African Americans; thus, it would be "therapeutic to permit Negroes to shoot craps within the confines of the Black Belt" of Chicago. White ethnic politicians' habit of using saloon owners as go-betweens to gain the support of black voters finally changed after the Eighteenth Amendment to the U.S. Constitution instituted Prohibition.[23]

Oscar DePriest was elected Chicago's first African American alderman on April 6, 1915. He ran in support of mayoral candidate William Hale "Big Bill" Thompson, who made several preelection promises to black voters during his campaign. DePriest, along with Edward H. Wright, Louis B. Anderson, and Rev. Archibald J. Carey, campaigned in Chicago's African American communities in support of Thompson. In a very close race, the black vote was the deciding factor in Thompson's election as mayor of Chicago. In the majority-Republican and African American Second and Third Wards, Thompson won by a margin of more than two to one. Once Thompson was elected, he made good on many of his preelection promises. His first act as mayor, for example, was to sponsor a resolution declaring August 23, 1915, a holiday in celebration of the fiftieth anniversary of the emancipation of the slaves. The observance of the holiday brought out 22,000 African Americans, who, with exuberant cheers and applause, once again demonstrated their endorsement of the mayor.[24]

Thompson, who served as mayor from 1915 through 1923 and 1927 through 1931, seemed to understand and sympathize with the plight of African Americans in the city. He personally rewarded three of the black men who helped to get him elected. He appointed Wright and Anderson as assistant corporation counsels and Carey as investigator, all positions in the Law Department with a salary of $5,000 a year. White politicians and the white press challenged these appointments, but Thompson defended them. During the celebration of the African American emancipation holiday he helped to establish, he noted, "Too much publicity is given the shortcomings and frailties of the colored man, and too little publicity is given his genius and skill. . . . It is considered presumptuous for an individual of your race to aspire to any employment other than menial tasks, and there have been recent instances where even your right to be considered among the laborers in this city has been challenged." Thompson appointed blacks to white-collar positions in the Water Department and the Department of Health, garnering further criticism from white Chicagoans and the white press. More resentment followed his decision to ban the showing in Chicago of the racist film *Birth of a Nation*.[25]

On the other hand, Thompson also made certain that particular crimes, such as prostitution and gambling in the black wards, went unchecked. It was business as usual—except an African American alderman, Oscar DePriest, was pulling the strings. By the summer of 1916, widely held notions of DePriest's political corruption swirled within the community. Often seen in the gambling clubs owned by Teenan Jones, DePriest was accused of taking bribes. He was indicted on January 18, 1917, along with chief of police Stephen K. Healey, three police lieutenants, and several brothel and saloon/gambling club owners. Teenan Jones turned state's evidence against the alderman and testified that he was DePriest's "bagman." Over a four-month period, he said, he paid DePriest $2,500, and he also paid Police Chief Healey—a claim the officer supported. DePriest's defense lawyers argued that the money collected was campaign contributions, not bribes. The strategy won the alderman an acquittal.[26]

Whether DePriest was guilty of the charges is irrelevant: the trial exposed him as politically corrupt, much like other Chicago aldermen before, during, and after his term. White ethnic alderman "bosses" controlled the black wards to the detriment of their residents, and once DePriest became the first black alderman "boss" of the largest black ward, the Second Ward, he continued the politically corrupt trend of his white ethnic predecessors. He remains a legend in many circles of the black community, since he was able to exploit the underworld culture of the saloons, brothels, and gambling houses, and because he was a black man who boasted a pro-black posture and ruled over the ward's white politicians, exemplifying what power in the ward meant to many black residents. He escaped another indictment on similar charges in 1929 before being elected as the first African American U.S. congressman from the North. DePriest served three terms (1928–1934) as a representative, mainly because he was known to put his race before his party.[27]

In 1920, Second Ward residents elected Ed Wright committeeman, making him the first African American committeeman in the country. He is best known for his ability to leverage political power during his thirty years in Chicago politics. For example, Congressman Martin B. Madden promised Wright that, once elected, Madden would promote an African American to a supervisory position at the post office, but the congressman reneged on his promise. Having learned that African American postal clerks with college degrees were actually working as laborers loading mail trucks on the docks, Wright phoned Congressman Madden in his Washington office. The congressman was summoned from the House floor to take Wright's call, and the committeeman demanded that Madden keep his promise: "I have a committee from the Chicago Post Office sitting at my desk. I have talked to you about the condition in that place. I also told you that there were black men down there that were college-trained and with years of service but being relegated to the lot of common laborers. I am damned tired of you making me an embarrassment to my people. We are delivering something like a 25,000 majority to the damn Republican Party in my ward. I want a black supervisor in the Chicago Postal System before the damn sun goes down this day. Do you hear me?" At 3:30 that afternoon, Dan Hawley became the first black supervisor for the Chicago Postal System.[28]

Wright also famously leveraged the political power of the city's black wards in a confrontation with city coroner Bernard W. Snow. Before Snow was elected coroner (in the early 1920s), he solicited support from Wright's Second Ward Republican organization and promised to deliver an African American deputy coroner. E. M. Cleaves was chosen by Wright for the position, but once elected, Snow refused to appoint Cleaves. Wright escorted Cleaves to Snow's office and demanded to see the coroner right away. Snow's secretary informed the committeeman that he would have to wait five minutes. Wright then kicked down the gate that separated the waiting room from the secretarial area, marched into Snow's office, and shouted, "This is the man you are going to make deputy coroner now while I am standing here. I am damn tired of your promises."[29] Thus, Cleaves became the first African American deputy coroner in Cook County.

Wright's temperament earned him the nickname "Bulldog," along with great respect from Second Ward residents and from politicians whose power stretched from the municipal level to the upper echelons of both state and federal government. In 1923, Illinois governor Len Small appointed Wright as the first African American Illinois commerce commissioner, a position that supervised all public utilities in the state. Wright used his relationship with the governor to put other African Americans in positions of power for the first time, despite segregation laws that forced blacks to live as second-class citizens. In 1923, Governor Small appointed three African American men to powerful state positions: Rev. H. W. Jameson, inspector in the Department of Registration and Education; Dr. S. A. Ware, inspector in the state Department of Health; and Captain Horace G. Burke, parole agent in the state Department of Public Welfare.[30]

Scholar Harold Gosnell contends that machine politics consist of "self-made men who had shown themselves more ruthless than their rivals." Black politicians in Chicago understood this model very well, as most were "tough, talented and ruthless men on the political make" until the city's Democratic machine established hegemony. The political careers of Oscar DePriest and Ed Wright demonstrate the participation and agency of African Americans in Chicago politics, but more important, they highlight the complex and varying political agendas of historical black politics in the city.[31]

Unlike DePriest and Wright, who reaped the protection of the South Side's Black Belt, African American West Side politicians have historically been subjected to more physical violence than their South Side counterparts. During the 1920s, for instance, in one West Side district nicknamed the "bloody" Twentieth Ward for the many political actors killed there, four black men who were involved in varying political affairs were murdered. The best-known story of these slain men is that of Octavius Granady, because his murder set the political tone for West Side black politicians for the next fifty years. Granady was an attorney running for the ward's committeeman position when he was shot more than fifty times in front of several eyewitnesses in broad daylight on Election Day. Newspaper reports indicate that the gunmen were five uniformed police officers and a car full of Italian gangsters. According to the witnesses, the investigation into the murder of Granady was conducted by the same policemen who had killed him. One of these eyewitnesses was eventually murdered. Jurors were repeatedly threatened, the prosecutor's office was burglarized, and the judge's hostility forced the special assistant district attorney to abandon the prosecution of the accused. The case was dismissed.[32] Granady's murder exemplifies the dangers black politicians on the West Side were forced to deal with once they became participants in a political terrain mired in corruption, mafia ties, and assassinations. The deaths of the four West Side black political actors, moreover, demonstrate the extreme methods employed to protect a corroded political system and to maintain control over the few African Americans in the wards of the West Side.

The Establishment of the Democratic Machine

Democrat Anton Cermak was elected mayor in April 1931, marking the end of black political power and achievements in Chicago under the Republican Party of the 1920s. Cermak had done more than any previous Democratic candidate to get the black vote, and he received very little support from the predominately Republican African American Second, Third, and Fourth Wards. Nonetheless, he managed to win forty-five of Chicago's fifty wards. Cermak's election marked the beginning of Democratic machine politics in Chicago, which would dominate the city's political climate for the next fifty years. His first act was to fire more than 3,000 workers, most of them African American. Then he went after the black vice and policy (illegal gambling/lottery) enterprises, which had heavily subsidized the Republican Party during its previous sixteen years of power. He set up a special vice and gambling police detail to work under his direct orders. The organization used violence and harassment to destroy black illegal enterprises, resulting in over 200 arrests of black men and women daily. According to police arrest records, 87 percent of raids on private homes in 1931 took place in the Black Belt.[33] These police invasions not only weakened black-owned illegal operations but also reminded the black community of the consequences of challenging the power structure.

Cermak harassed African Americans because they were Republicans; since Cermak already had the support of most whites and white ethnics in the city, he particularly targeted African Americans. He boldly stated that "if blacks [would] switch their allegiance to the Democratic Party, the action by his police department would be stopped." Cermak was killed in 1933 while accompanying Franklin D. Roosevelt in Florida. According to the standard account, an assassin attempted to kill Roosevelt and mistakenly shot Cermak. Many believe, however, that the mayor's death was a deliberate hit contracted by a Chicago mafia group.[34]

African American voters remained loyal to the Republican Party until 1936. At this time, under liberal mayor Edward J. Kelly, they began converting to the Democratic Party in pursuit of the economic benefits that came from supporting the party in power. Mayor Kelly's platform and his African American political appointees sought to lift the black community and resulted in his gaining its political support. The shift in allegiance among Chicago's African American residents helped to create a Democratic majority.

Most black residents were poor and knew very little about politics. The Democratic machine exploited this factor. Many black Chicago residents, among them newly arrived black migrants, learned quickly that Chicago politics amounted to some form of patronage or bribery.[35] Political relationships between the black community and Democratic machine politicians developed as the twentieth century progressed. Many African Americans willingly supported the machine for racial, cultural, union, institutional, or ideological reasons. As a result of economic necessity, black Chicagoans were concerned with what machine politicians could do for them, so the relationship was founded on reciprocal exploitation—although the politicians overwhelmingly benefited from the deals.[36]

White ethnic Democrats gained power over the black wards by using their influence to neutralize the black community's political control, which had been obtained under their Republican predecessors. During the 1930s, for example, Joseph Tittinger held the Second Ward's Democratic committeeman seat, even though the ward was 95 percent African American. He showed little respect for his constituency: indeed, when black residents needed to meet with the committeeman at his headquarters in the heart of the black community, they had to wait in segregated quarters and until all white persons were seen first. He forced black precinct captains to pay him dues for holding their positions, and he put several white men who lived outside the ward and who were not precinct captains on the city's payroll.[37]

In 1939, African American Republican William Dawson switched parties to replace Tittinger as the Second Ward committeeman. He would become the model for the black political "submachine" of Chicago Democratic machine politics. Dawson repudiated anyone "who wanted to be independent, buck the machine, or refuse to vote a straight Democratic ticket." With his ability to get city jobs for black people, helping to expand the black middle class, he built a political empire out of the black wards on the South Side. He was the black "boss" of the city until he helped to get Richard J. Daley elected in 1955. Dawson fought for patronage jobs but not for civil rights. In 1967, Dawson scolded Dr. Martin Luther King Jr. and the CFM to demonstrate his loyalty to the Democratic machine. Though Daley was able to diminish Dawson's political power by taking control of black economics in the city, Dawson remained one of Daley's useful allies because he always generated the votes Democratic candidates needed to remain in power.[38]

Like most politicians before him, Dawson financially founded his political, civic, and church work in the policy rackets (the illegal lottery/gambling system). Dempsey Travis explains:

> The power of the policy racket in the political and civic life of black Chicago from the 1920s through the 40s is illustrated by the fact that 15,000 people made a living off policy annually. There were 4,200 policy stations on the Southside alone. It has been estimated that nearly 100,000 persons played policy each day, and according to the files in the offices of former Attorney General Homer S. Cummings, one policy operator alone had an annual take of $2,016,000.00, of which thirty percent was profit for the wheel [Democratic machine]. . . . The policy kings were very intertwined with the political, social, civic and religious life on the South and West sides of Chicago; hence, it was difficult to tell the direct source of the money that supported the legitimate businesses, charitable institutions, and churches. . . . Congressman William L. Dawson . . . was known to be friendly and cordial with *all* the policy men.[39]

The Communist Party advocated on behalf of Chicago's African American community.[40] Escalating its efforts during the 1930s, the party drew about 500 new members to its ranks, many of them former Garveyites. The Communists' commitment to the plight of African Americans forced the Democratic Party and the NAACP to increase their involvement in issues of housing and employment. Harry Haywood, a black Communist during this era, contended that the police began to kill party members to squelch the party's successful campaigns.[41] This method had little effect on the Communists or on the black residents who supported them. Internal issues among black Chicagoans weakened this political solidarity, however, thus making it easier for the Democratic machine to gain a majority base in the black wards.

Class-based rifts between poor and more affluent residents forced to live together in segregated districts often hampered racial cohesion. In the 1930s, many recent migrants from southern states were poor and illiterate. More financially stable migrants (those who arrived during 1910–20) were often able to acquire a decent education, and a number of them studied at traditionally white universities.[42] These "old" migrants were known to be condescending toward the uneducated migrants, who reminded them of their past. In addition, many African American Chicagoans who supported the Communist Party developed a political rivalry with fellow black residents who opposed Communism, which was increasingly stigmatized in the late

1930s. This factor helps to explain the disruption of black South Side unity as black anti-Communist sentiment intensified after World War II.[43]

The Communist Party's successful organizing among black Chicagoans was also hampered by anti-Communist persecution in the early 1950s, when Chicago black Communist leaders Claude Lightfoot and William Patterson were both imprisoned under the Smith Act. This act prohibited affiliation with any group that advocated the overthrow of the U.S. government and was the basis for the prosecution of members of the Communist and Socialist Workers Parties. McCarthy-era pundits would frequently dub anyone advocating for the civil rights of African Americans a "communist," resulting in the political silencing of many Chicago black social activists. Police and mafia violence also helped to curtail black radicalism during this time.[44]

Black Chicago's shift to the Democratic Party was by no means total, however. By late 1940, only slightly more than half of Chicago's African Americans voted Democratic, a result of the failure of the New Deal to address their concerns. In a campaign speech in Chicago in 1944, Roosevelt denounced racial discrimination, and the black vote began to swing heavily Democratic on the national level. Locally, the Democratic machine failed to tackle substantive issues of race, resulting in stagnant support among blacks and creating what scholar William J. Grimshaw calls a Democratic contradiction. He contends that the "machine's material favors were offset by its racist public policies . . . restrictive housing covenants, 'double-shift' public schools, segregated and second-class health care, [and] severe employment discrimination," while at the same time the national party had passed desegregation legislation.[45]

By the late 1940s and early 1950s, the financial base for most black politicians—underworld illegal activities, primarily policy wheels—had been appropriated by the mafia via kidnapping, murder, and political collusion. Black politicians, especially Democrats, became heavily financially dependent upon their party affiliation, which essentially eroded their already limited political independence. For this reason, Republican alderman Archibald Carey of the Third Ward (1940–54) greatly respected policy (gambling house) owner Theodore Rowe, who shot it out with the mafia rather than have his enterprise taken from him.[46]

The Daley Machine

The three mayors who held office from 1930 through 1955 were from the same Irish Catholic working-class district of Bridgeport, located on the city's

South Side. Their base was the Irish community and the wards that housed Chicago's poor Eastern and Southern European Catholic immigrants. Most of the mayors' opposition was from middle-class and Protestant wards, demonstrating the persistent cultural and religious differences of the city's political divide. The three black wards did not yield the same level of Democratic support locally as was overwhelmingly given by African Americans to the party on a national scale.[47] These wards held factions of Republicans and Communists who were more attuned to the issues of race that concerned African American voters. Nevertheless, the Democratic machine was able to consistently generate a bare majority of support in local elections.

Richard J. Daley, elected in 1955, was without question Chicago's most powerful machine mayor and the last of the city's big "bosses." He is also regarded as politically the most powerful person in the Midwest during his long tenure. Daley ushered in the most repressive machine for African Americans thus far in Chicago, whereby the tactics of mafia violence and police brutality were understood by his administration as par for the course. He began his rise to power as a youth gang member of the Hamburgs, located in the South Side Irish community of Bridgeport. Unlike that of his two Irish predecessors, Daley's power escalated when much of the white middle class and Protestant opposition moved to neighboring suburbs after World War II. In 1948, when the Supreme Court decision *Shelley v. Kraemer* declared racially restrictive housing covenants unconstitutional, more affluent African Americans sought better housing outside the three black wards that made up the South Side's Black Belt, taking resources and alternative leadership with them. The three black wards—now overwhelmingly poor— fell to the Democratic machine, and when Daley was elected, these wards replaced poor immigrant wards as the machine's electoral stronghold. Ultimately, these two "migrations" of white and black Chicagoans "transformed Chicago into a one-party city."[48]

The African American slums were ripe for exploitation on all levels, especially the political and economic. Almost all the businesses were owned by whites living outside the area who sold egregiously overpriced products. The black vote on the West Side was controlled by the machine's precinct captains, all of whom had a reputation for punishing those who challenged the machine. From 1955 to the late 1960s, machine precinct captains escorted black residents into the voting booth to make sure they voted for Democratic machine candidates. According to a Daley biographer, "Negroes were warned that they would lose their welfare check, their public housing apartment, their menial job, if they didn't vote Democratic." Failure to vote

Democratic could also cost residents a "rejection of a needed license [application or] intense inspection by city building inspectors."[49]

A Panther poll-watcher remembers firsthand how Daley coerced poor black voters on Election Day:

> I remember an incident on the North Side. There was a brother runnin' for Alderman named Don in the ward that housed Cabrini Green. This [was in] '69. We were at St. Dominic's Church. [Don] asked us to be poll watchers because the ward incorporated the Gold Coast and Cabrini was sittin' right there and he felt that they [Daley machine cronies] were gonna steal the election. Now it's the first time that I had ever been a poll watcher, I haven't seen anything that overt [in elections] again. . . . I saw limousines pull up, big, white, ruddy, Irish guys got out, they came into the poll thing, they went right behind the curtain. . . . All you saw was these long black Cadillacs, with these ruddy-faced Irishmen telling folks, "This is how you're gonna vote." They were giving money, they had lists. "You're on public aid, we know, we could have an issue if you don't vote for machine men"—this is 1969. . . . We stood up and said, this is illegal, you're not supposed to do this. In two minutes the police were there takin' us out. We got put out of so many poll places there and got arrested. Fred [Hampton] was at St. Dominic's, and my understandin' is that there were pistols pulled. He was shot at there. I'm surprised that we survived that day. . . . This was politics in Chicago. This was Mayor Daley's way.[50]

William Dawson made sure his fellow African Americans on the South Side followed the Daley machine's protocols. On the West Side, where most African American migrants settled after 1950, white ethnic ward bosses remained in power despite the changing complexion of their constituents.[51]

West Side precinct captains supported the Democratic political machine in the early 1960s by controlling the West Side wards. These wards were sarcastically dubbed "plantation wards" because they mirrored antebellum-era population demographics and racial hierarchy.[52] The majority of the area's residents were African American, but whites controlled all aspects of these districts. White aldermen on the West Side were known as the West Side bloc, and racism was central to controlling the wards. "Of some sixty-three precincts in the all-black 24th ward in 1960," Jon Rice notes, "fifty-nine had white precinct captains."[53] White politicians and gangsters controlled the Twenty-Fourth, Twenty-Fifth, Twenty-Seventh, Twenty-Eighth, and Twenty-Ninth Wards. The populations of these wards were significantly African

American. The Twenty-Fourth Ward's black alderman worked under white ward bosses Carmen Fratto (Italian) and Irwin Horowitz (Jewish); the latter was a big money-raiser for the machine. The Twenty-Fifth Ward's boss was Vito Marzullo (Italian), and the Twenty-Sixth Ward's boss was Matthew Bieszczat (Central European). The Twenty-Seventh Ward's boss was Ed Quigley (Irish), who made about $28,000 a year overseeing the city's sewer system. His alderman was also white. Tony Girolami was the boss of the Twenty-Eighth Ward, and he was assisted by Alderman Joe Jambrone (both Italian). The Twenty-Ninth Ward consisted of mostly slums, and the black alderman took orders from white ward boss and mafia front man Bernie Neistein (Jewish). Numerous majority-black legislative districts were represented in Springfield by John D'Arco, Larry DiPrima, Louie Capuzi, John Touhy, Pete Granata, Vic Arrigo, Matt Ropa, Larry Bartels, Bernie McDevitt, Bob McPartlin, Frank Wolfe, Sam Romano, and Zygmunt Sokolnicki, all of whom were white ethnics.[54]

The economic incentives offered by the machine were desirable for many African Americans, while the members of other ethnic groups tended to be in a better economic position and therefore were less in need of these incentives.[55] For the Daley machine, it was politically and economically fruitful to keep poor African Americans confined in segregated communities, because doing so allowed their votes to be easily controlled. If this group of voters were dispersed throughout other areas of the city, the political machine would lose its docile black voting bloc and collapse.[56]

As mayor, party chairman, and keeper of the budget, Daley eliminated rivals both outside and within the machine—which afforded him an unprecedented base of power from which to control the growing metropolis. He made sure those loyal to him were elevated to positions of power in his administration. Most of Chicago's and Cook County's top political and government positions were held by male Irish cronies of Mayor Daley.[57] When Daley became mayor, Hamburg members from his youth, as well as their sons, were appointed to some of Chicago's top administrative positions.[58] Under Daley's machine, aldermen and city councilmen were not allowed to introduce any significant legislation in the city council or to be credited with policy proposals that could cause them to be held in high regard. Daley controlled a strict hierarchical system to make sure that only legislation that he explicitly approved was brought before the city council, and he buried any other proposals in bureaucracy. Should a buried proposal be discovered to have merit, moreover, "it would be revived, reintroduced in modified form, and passed as the mayor's proposal."[59]

Virtually every element of Chicago, legal and illegal, was under the mayor's control. Daley demanded, "There can be no organizations within the Organization," meaning that all elected officials of his machine were to advance only the machine's interests, not the concerns of the communities they were elected to represent. Though there were few elected officials who dared to challenge Daley's machine, some risked their office in defense of their dignity, race, and constituency. One black alderman of the Daley machine, Robert H. Miller, attempted to advocate for the interest of his constituents, who wanted a person elected to the school board who would support their push for control of their neighborhood schools. Daley subsequently tossed Miller out of the aldermanic position. The man who replaced him, Sammy Rayner Jr., explained his election as follows:

> I really won by default; Richard J. Daley was angry with Alderman
> Robert H. Miller. Miller had voted, in the committee, against
> Mrs. Wendell Green who was Daley's selection for the Chicago
> Public School Board. Although Miller changed his committee vote on
> the council floor in favor of Mrs. Green, Daley wouldn't forgive him
> for going against his wishes. When election time rolled around, Mayor
> Daley simply pulled all of the workers out from under Miller and
> barred them from giving any assistance at all. It was a negative elec-
> tion. They voted against Bob Miller and for me because there
> was nobody to protect Bob at the polls.[60]

Daley's Democratic machine held a firm and decisive grip on the city's black vote. Bernetta Howell, an independent who ran for Congress in 1964, recalls that the threat of punishment and violence that usually forced black voters to do as instructed was so effective that she lost the congressional race by a landslide to Irish Democrat Thomas J. O'Brien, who had died two weeks before the election.[61]

The fear that Howell mentions would eventually transform into an anger that would provide the black oppressed with agency and courage to confront the machine. By the mid-1960s, Chicago's African American community had heavily aligned with fellow creators of change around the country in the struggle for civil and human rights, using the methods of nonviolence as well as armed resistance. The poor black wards attempted to challenge the Daley machine, and some wards elected antimachine aldermen. Chicago's tradition of political corruption had taught its black residents, as a Black Panther publication put it, that having a "black man in office doesn't neces-sarily mean that [blacks are] going to get justice."[62]

People like Gus Savage, an independent congressman of the Third Congressional District, routinely provided his black constituents with information to challenge the machine. He told residents in his district that their voting population was 60 percent black Democrats and 40 percent whites, most of whom were Republican. More importantly, securing two-thirds of all black votes would allow any black candidate to win an election without a single white vote. Earl B. Dickerson had been the last independent candidate to win against machine politics in Chicago in 1938. Savage argued, "Black people lost their concept of nationhood through psychological damage more so than through capture or enslavement. . . . This government will always challenge over 20 million blacks—until we begin to really learn the concepts of power and politics."[63] This kind of bold defiance did not sit well with Daley or his machine politicians, who were threatened by the idea of independent black political power.

As a result, Daley also shifted with the national political swing to the right of those liberal Democratic New Dealers who fell victim to racial fears and ultimately became supporters of conservative and racist policies and practices. Daley responded by transforming his administration to resemble "the character of a Democratic party of the old Deep South."[64] Michael Madigan, known as one of the machine's most sly committeemen, stated in an interview that the smartest political move he witnessed was "Mayor Daley's move from left to the right as the country moved from left to right." He explained: "When Daley was first elected he was a liberal. He enjoyed strong support from the black wards. As late as 1963, were it not for the black wards, he would have lost to Benjamin Adamowski for mayor. But in the mid-sixties there was a shift in public sentiment from the left to the right. He moved very adroitly to reflect that."[65]

Like his southern Democrat counterparts, Daley and his Democratic machine intensified the use of violence to prevent independent African American politicians from challenging the machine in the 1960s. These tactics were so effective that no independent politician had a successful career. Political activist Richard Barnett recalled how he routinely had to purchase tires months before an election because his car's tires were slashed and windows broken every Election Day. Alderman Danny Davis stated he always had to carry his gun due to the frequency of the fights with bottles, bricks, and bats he would have with Twenty-Seventh Ward boss Ed Quigley's goons.[66]

Local Democrats also controlled key positions in the police departments. West Siders argued that white Democrats ruled the West Side, utilizing the police as their enforcers.[67] This fact is best exemplified by the tragic death of Alderman Ben Lewis in 1963. In the early 1960s, black residents became overtly resistant in the Twenty-Fourth Ward, so ward boss Bernie Neistein picked Ben Lewis as the West Side's first African American alderman. Lewis's job was not to represent his constituents but to continue Daley's policy toward the ward's black residents, which only served the interest of the Democratic machine. Yet, according to Richard Barnett, Lewis used this "Uncle Tom" role to get things done for his community. He "prevented high-rise housing projects in the ward, insisted on garbage collections twice a week and fought the idea of double-shifted schools."[68] Danny Davis declared that Lewis set up an insurance company to challenge the Elrod insurance business, which had a monopoly on liquor licenses in the ward. (Essential to Chicago political corruption was the ability to use conflicts of interest to make profits via legitimate businesses. Ward bosses controlled the distribution of liquor licenses in their respective wards, and the ward's liquor store owners were forced to purchase insurance from the bosses' enterprises to secure liquor licenses.) Rumors at the time speculated that Lewis even considered opening a bank to compete with the ward's banking monopoly.[69]

On February 27, 1963, Ben Lewis was shot to death, execution style. He was found handcuffed, with three bullets in the back of his head. Republican alderman of the Chicago city council John Hoellen identified the Chicago police and certain West Side machine operatives as suspects. Not one black alderman—and at the time there were six on the South Side—supported Hoellen's investigation. The police investigator was eventually removed from the case when clues indicated police involvement in Lewis's murder. Unlike in the murder of Granady some thirty-five years earlier, this time "the media and black politicians looked like accomplices" for failing to investigate or support the investigation of Lewis's death.[70] It is evident to many that Alderman Ben Lewis was assassinated for his bold business actions and his commitment to his constituents, which defied the policies of Daley's Democratic machine.

Mayor Daley and his Democratic machine continued to subjugate Chicago's poor black residents until the early 1970s, when the administration began to lose power. As we will see, a contributing factor in this loss of power was the organizing efforts of the ILBPP's Rainbow Coalition and the controversy surrounding the political assassination of Party chairman Fred Hampton. The final political blow that toppled the machine, however, occurred in 1972 via the case *Shakman v. Democratic Organization of Cook County et al.* This court ruling prohibited the firing of local government employees for political reasons. Thus the Daley machine's electoral advantage was diminished because machine candidates were forced to compete on a level playing field. Throughout his tenure as mayor, Daley had been able to manufacture a minimum of 10,000 votes each from nearly all fifty of Chicago's wards. After the *Shakman* ruling, more than twenty-five wards failed to produce Daley's usual number of votes. By 1977, two-thirds of the wards were generating fewer than 10,000 votes for machine candidates.[71] It was apparent that machine politics could not function in a legitimate electoral arena. Ailing in the 1970s, the Democratic power machine in Chicago met its demise in the early 1980s with the election of African American Harold Washington, who utilized the platform of racial coalition politics that was popularized by the ILBPP's Rainbow Coalition.

Black Chicago under Daley's Machine

Chicago, the nation's second-largest city, was one-fourth African American and severely divided by race during Daley's tenure. Denied open housing opportunities, African Americans were forced to live in two ghettos, the older one on the South Side and another recently established as a result of gentrification and urban renewal on the near West Side. The black population on the West Side of Chicago rapidly increased in the 1960s. Urban renewal forced thousands of African American South Siders to relocate to the West Side to the areas of North Lawndale, Near West Side, and both East and West Garfield. As they moved into these areas, they were joined by black migrants from Mississippi, Arkansas, and Louisiana looking for opportunities denied them in the South.

Between 1950 and 1960, at least 75,000 black migrants from the South helped to shift the population of North Lawndale from 13 percent to more than 91 percent African American.[72] In a ten-year span beginning in the 1960s, West Garfield (which was a little over 83 percent white) effectively became entirely African American. East Garfield already had an African American population of 61 percent by 1960, but it too would become an effectively all-black district by 1970. Racial change in the 53-percent-black Near West Side began in 1940.[73]

North Lawndale was the poor black community hardest hit by the policies of Daley's Democratic machine in the 1960s. It contained the city's worst housing, the highest percentage of residents on welfare (31 percent), and the largest average family size, all of which contributed to the city's highest crime rate. Former police superintendents Leroy Martin and Richard Brzeczek corroborated that it was the department's unofficial policy to assign police to

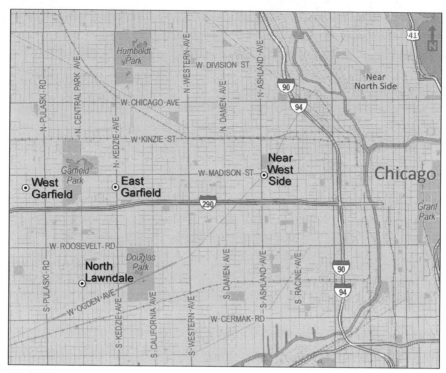

West Side Communities with Changing Racial Demographics, 1950–1970

this district as punishment for misconduct elsewhere. Harold Saffold of the Afro-American Patrolmen's League dubbed the community's youth "West-side Willies" due to their aggressive nature.[74]

During these years of demographic transition, racial tensions between black and white residents were heightened. One African American who moved into a predominately Jewish South Side community when he was a child recalls how he and other black families were greeted: "My family moved in the neighborhood in September of 1964—87th and Kenwood. So we moved into the neighborhood, and we didn't have no resistance, except . . . uh . . . there was a cross burned on our front lawn the first Halloween we were there. They were doin' that to all the black people that were movin' in."[75]

Not all white residents responded to incoming African American families with hate or violence. Some were receptive, and a few were willing to remain residents of these changing areas. A female black resident remembers that her first encounter with her new neighbors was odd and uncomfortable for both parties: "I remember the day we were moving in—we must have been the second or third black family on the block. An older white gentleman from across the street came over and started telling us that his job moved out to some suburb, and he was sayin', 'This commute is getting hard. I'll probably have to move close to my job.' It was like he was saying, 'I'm gonna be movin', but it's not because you're movin' in here,' you know (*laughs*)."[76] Another black female resident details what could have happened to those who tried to move into the white areas of Bridgeport and Cicero, which had a reputation for extreme racial hatred: "We knew we couldn't *go* out to those places (*laughs*). They would, if you just *walked* out there, they would get violent and run you back home."[77]

As part of Daley's urban renewal projects, expressways were built through poor Italian and African American communities in order to expand automobile usage in the 1960s, displacing community residents. Expressways and housing projects displaced 160,000 poor African Americans and about 40,000 whites between 1941 and 1965. Only 3,100 of these people were provided with public housing. The expressways were barriers designed to serve as unofficial borders, reminding poor African Americans where they could and could not reside. The South Side's Dan Ryan Expressway, which runs from Ninety-Fifth Street to Twenty-Second Street (now Cermak), "was shifted several blocks during the planning stage to make one of the ghetto walls," according to Daley's biographer.[78]

Most of Chicago's urban renewal programs were funded with federal dollars.[79] One community resident explains how expressways helped to build two opposing worlds, the affluent white suburbs and the poor, disadvantaged black ghettos in the city: "Powerful forces like real estate interests and the government were puttin' money into buildin' up the suburbs after World War II—expressways were bein' built, and businesses were movin' out that way. I know they say expressways were built for defense, but people were also bein' encouraged to move out to those areas."[80]

Segregation forced the displaced to live virtually on top of one another, especially in the areas packed with high-rise public housing projects. A visitor from California's Bay Area described the housing units as laboratories of inhumanity. Congested confines and the city's neglect of garbage removal from these areas led to an infestation of rats that outnumbered human residents.[81] Chicago's two ghettos—on the South and West Sides—were among the worst slums in the nation because inadequate housing was big business for white real estate agents, inspectors, and property owners. Landlords charged high rents for small, virtually uninhabitable apartments, and the building department, whose purpose was to report and fine such property owners, was easily bought off. Slumlords were a diverse group of investors, as one historian notes: "Universities owned [slum dwellings], and so did churches, fraternal organizations, and prominent establishment types. They avoided public embarrassment because Illinois is one of the few states in which the hidden land trust, concealing the real owners of property, is legal."[82]

Daley attempted to thwart the efforts of those who exposed the conditions of African American slums by arguing that his urban renewal projects were designed to eliminate slums and replace them with superior public housing. A Daley biographer explains:

> Urban renewal was the greatest deceit. True, slum property was being cleared. But it wasn't being replaced by housing for those who were dispossessed. The poor were moved into other marginal neighborhoods, and highly profitable upper middle class developments replaced the slums. The most glaring example was the Sandburg Village high-rise development, about twelve blocks north of the Loop. It was supposed to have been moderate-income housing. It became one of the most popular places for young, well-off moderns to live, if they could afford the $200-plus rents. On the Westside, where conditions were the worst, nothing was being built, although large tracts of land were available. Daley . . . was maintaining black dependency—always a tenant, never an owner, not quite a citizen.[83]

Some of those affected by urban renewal attempted to fight their displacement by attending city council meetings and visiting their community's representatives. Despite their efforts, protest groups lost the war against Daley's urban renewal program. Old and often unusable housing was demolished to make way for potentially lucrative real estate developments, leaving almost 30,000 families, most of whom were poor and African American, without housing. These communities were theoretically able to exercise the franchise to elect city government representatives who would protect their interests, but "City Hall . . . loaded up the Community Conservation Board with its puppets," making effective protest impossible.[84] According to one urban renewal official, unlike the protest groups, most residents were unaware of the goals of urban renewal policies, which he said was "fortunate," for if they knew the true purpose of the policies, "we'd all have to run for cover."[85]

In the 1960s, Daley routinely argued that there was no segregation in the city and that African Americans could live anywhere in Chicago. Even more striking was his claim to the NAACP that "there are no ghettos in Chicago."[86] In 1961, the Federal Civil Rights Commission classified Chicago as "the most segregated city of more than 500,000 in the country," due in part to the city's black population increasing at a rate of 25,000 to 50,000 a year. Only 15 percent of Chicago's new housing units built after 1950 were available to African American residents. Moreover, one in three of Chicago's black residents lived in substandard housing during this period.[87]

Decades of psychological conditioning by means of the threat of violence prevented many African Americans from migrating into mostly white neighborhoods. A white resident recounts her first encounter with her new neighbors, the first black family on the block: "On the day they were moving in, I made a pot of coffee and went over to introduce myself, and I could actually see the fear on this young woman's face as she opened the door. I have never forgotten that. It made me realize how frightening it must be to face a white group. But we became friends."[88] John Walsh, a high school English teacher and known pacifist, bought a three-unit apartment building in Bridgeport at 3309 S. Lowe about a block and a half from Daley's home. In an attempt to integrate the mayor's community, he intended to rent one of the apartments to African Americans. Walsh explains why finding an African American tenant was a difficult task: "Our biggest problem was finding somebody willing to move in. Bridgeport's reputation was well known among Negroes. It was the kind of neighborhood they wouldn't walk through at night, and during the day it wasn't a good idea either. We finally found a young couple and they got as far as the front door. Then the key jammed and they panicked. They turned right around and left. We found two other couples and each time they backed out at the last minute."[89]

Two male college students were brave enough to try the "integrating Daley's neighborhood experiment." Shortly thereafter, a riot broke out. There were at least "four hundred people from the neighborhood fighting with the police, trying to storm the building, a dozen getting arrested, and four policemen being injured."[90] Daley, who lived less than 350 feet from the incident, ignored the mayhem. When this act did not convince the mayor to get rid of the two undesirables, residents took matters into their own hands and evicted the two students while they were away at school. The police assisted them by taking the students' belongings to the police station while residents destroyed the apartment and "smeared excrement on the walls."[91]

The experiment proved that Daley had lied about racial residential segregation in Chicago. John Walsh criticized Daley for his decision not to prevent the rioting or the removal of the black students from the neighborhood: "Daley was guilty of passive hypocrisy. . . . He could have prevented all the trouble. He could have controlled his own people. And he knew what we were doing. Weeks before we moved anybody in, I told the city's Human

Relations Commission about my plan. I promised them that we would rent only one apartment to Negroes and that all the income from the property would be used for improving it. Instead, they let it happen, they let the people in the neighborhood drive us out. And Daley didn't lift a finger."[92]

In 1965, activist/entertainer Dick Gregory led a contingent of both black and white protest marchers to Daley's Bridgeport home to force the mayor to acknowledge their grievances.[93] Daley, as usual, ignored the picketers, but his Bridgeport neighbors did not. A mob of almost 1,000 attacked the picketers with eggs, tomatoes, firecrackers, and rocks, and several women turned their garden hoses on the marchers, while the mob chanted, "Two-four-six-eight, we don't want to integrate" and "Oh, I wish I was an Alabama trooper, that is what I'd really like to be-ee-ee. Cuz if I was an Alabama trooper, I could kill the niggers legally."[94] Daley had the protesters arrested and charged with disorderly conduct, ignoring the assaults of the white mob. Later, in a televised press conference, Daley scolded the civil rights protesters for disturbing his neighborhood of "fine people, hard working people" who had "no feelings one way or another about all of this."[95] His expression of rank indifference toward African Americans pushed the picketers to return to his home every day for the next few weeks.

As these episodes suggest, many white ethnics in Chicago were just as racist as those in the U.S. South. Even though the *Brown v. Board of Education* decision helped to prohibit segregation in public places, in Chicago, there was de facto segregation in most restaurants and hotels, and African Americans knew not to enter the Loop. White racism was particularly virulent on the South Side, "because the blacks were closer."[96]

Realtors convinced white homeowners to cling to their racial fears. They informed targeted homeowners that the changing racial makeup of their area would drive down the value of their homes, thus creating white flight. One female Chicagoan provides a vivid account of the methods realtors used to play off the racial fears of white homeowners and the changing racial demographics of the city's South and West Sides: "For a while some people were resisting leaving. I remember signs in front of some houses that said, 'This house is *not* for sale.' But blockbusters were not only calling you, they'd knock on our door, and if you said your house wasn't for sale, they'd tell you why it should be."[97] As a result, many white homeowners sold their homes cheaply. In turn, these houses were sold to black families at grossly inflated prices. Realtors often raked in profits above 70 percent. During this particular wave of real estate exploitation, banks refused to provide loans in racially changing areas. This forced black families to buy housing via contract, inevitably eliminating accumulated equity, and prevented home improvements in African American communities, which severely hindered the growth of property value in these areas. Federal policies also "encouraged white flight and discouraged community preservation": the Federal Housing Authority (FHA) refused to fund rehabilitation in racially changing communities—neighborhoods transforming into majority–African American districts. Whites fleeing Chicago to the suburbs easily qualified for FHA loans, however, thus creating contrasting all-white areas.[98]

As a result of the overt denial of open housing exemplified by real estate practices and urban renewal policies, coupled with the refusal of banks and the FHA to fund improvements in black communities, slums became common in majority-black areas, and residential segregation in the city was exacerbated.[99] The defeat of the Open Housing Bill in Washington also helped to ghettoize black Chicago.[100]

Daley used the police to control black areas of the city, guaranteeing that the black community and the police would be in constant conflict. Most officers who policed black areas were white and often racist, and they abused their authority. Common complaints were of "abusive language, arbitrary arrests, and searches without provocation, torturing of arrestees, refusal to assist people in distress, and laxness in arresting certain criminals."[101] Daley's Democratic machine controlled key positions in the police department, and these loyalists carried out the orders of the mayor's office—which included controlling black wards. The situation was ripe for rebellion, mirroring the conditions that caused the infamous 1965 Watts uprisings. Early in 1965, Daley turned down an invitation to take part in a secret federal program to prevent riots in major cities. He was the only mayor of the seven invited to reject the invitation from Washington. Daley was so confident of his total control of Chicago's black population and its vote that he believed a riot could not happen in his city.[102]

African American Chicagoans would put Daley's confidence to the test. After weeks of civil rights groups picketing a firehouse on Chicago's West Side, demanding that a black fireman be added to the all-white unit, a hook-and-ladder truck from the firehouse sped out of control and knocked down a light pole, which fell on a black woman and killed her. This incident ignited four days of rioting by African American West Siders.[103] Daley ordered his old Hamburg Club friend, Fire Commissioner Robert J. Quinn, to assign an all-black unit to the firehouse. Quinn did so, but he put a white officer in charge of the firemen. A leader of one of the groups that advocated on behalf of poor black schools stated, "For ten years we've been trying to get them to hire more blacks for the Fire Department, and to integrate that firehouse, and we got nowhere. But when somebody gets killed, they manage to find black firemen in one day."[104] One former African American fireman declared, "At that time black firemen were segregated in two firehouses—all-black firehouses. The riots caused Mayor Daley to move some of these firemen to the Westside so the black residents could see black firemen in the neighborhood, with the hope that maybe then the people wouldn't start up again throwin' rocks and burnin' the firehouses."[105]

No one was killed during the rebellion; about eighty people were injured, and property damage was limited to broken glass and overturned vehicles. The four-day riot occurred about the same time as the Watts riots, a few months after Daley rejected the federal government's efforts to prepare mayors for such an occurrence, and days after he ignored civil rights groups that wanted the school superintendent replaced.[106] Daley clearly underestimated the anger and resilience of the city's African American residents.

Martin Luther King Jr. and the Chicago Freedom Movement

Realizing the real constraints and oppression that African Americans in Chicago were subjected to as a result of the Daley machine's policies, Dr. Martin Luther King Jr. and the SCLC shifted the focus of their civil rights activism to the North in the mid-1960s. According to David Garrow, King and the SCLC chose Chicago as their northern target because the city's black residents experienced overt inequality in housing, employment, and the school system.[107] Rev. Arthur Brazier, leader of the South Side Woodlawn Organization, stated, "King decided to come to Chicago because he thought Chicago was unique in that there was one man, one source of power, who you had to deal with. He knew this wasn't the case in New York or any other city. He thought if Daley could be persuaded of the rightness of open housing and integrated schools that things would be done."[108] King told local activists, "If we can break the system in Chicago, it can be broken anywhere in this country."[109] Edwin Berry of the Urban League agreed: "King thought Daley was a despot and that he ruled with an iron hand, regarding black neighborhoods as plantations to which he anointed his people as overseers. But King also thought that Daley could be effective if he was convinced of the rightness of King's goals."[110] Andrew Young, a member of the SCLC, declared that the group went to Chicago to see "what elements of nonviolence would work."[111] He explained that the SCLC wondered about the potential effectiveness of "voter registration, marches and direct action," asking, "could we end slums and create good housing, could we create jobs and educational opportunities?"[112]

King and his staff were unaware that Daley had already gone "into a wild rage about King," calling him "a dirty son of a bitch, a bastard, a prick . . . a rabble-rouser, [and] a trouble-maker."[113] Although many civil rights leaders in the city welcomed and appreciated King's assistance, Daley's African American municipal cronies, several of whom blatantly disagreed with King that race issues were a problem in Chicago, echoed the mayor's disdain. Jesse Jackson, who was a member of the SCLC at the time, stated, "Daley had blacks on his staff and black officials and some black ministers who marched with Dr. King in the South, went to school with him at Morehouse, but on Daley's plantation, they had press conferences and urged Dr. King to leave Chicago, saying, 'There is no place for you here.' It really broke his heart to see some of his classmates turn on him in Chicago."[114] The South Side's black congressman William Dawson called King an "outside agitator" and stated that "desegregation isn't needed here."[115] Even the Chicago NAACP supported Dawson and called King "intemperate."[116] Black Baptist minister Joseph H. Jackson was not a supporter of civil rights activism, which he proclaimed as action "not far removed from open crime," and he declared that Mayor Daley was a friend of black Chicagoans.[117] These sentiments echoed those of racist leaders and politicians in the South. Nevertheless, the SCLC allied with local civil rights leaders to organize the CFM in 1966.

Via protest marches, King tried to neutralize Daley and demonstrate Chicago's tendency toward violent racial repression. What he and the other southern civil rights leaders who came to Chicago did not understand was that their reliance on the nonviolent strategies of marches, sit-ins, and picketing would not have the same effect in Chicago as they did in the South. In the beginning stages of the CFM, Daley was clever enough to keep his contempt for black grievances hidden from the public. Chicago police officers would calmly place protesters into paddy wagons to be arrested, especially when the news cameras were recording, rather than employ the violent methods of southern officers.[118] This did not deter the protesters, who continued their efforts for the next six months.

In July 1966, the supporters of the CFM marched to City Hall, where King posted fifty demands on the front door, blaming real estate brokers, banks, the FHA, the Democratic Party, the Chicago Board of Education, and local trade unions for conditions in the black ghetto. As historian Jon Rice explains, the document indicated that "profits from the dual housing market, bolstered by policies of banks, the FHA, the local political machine, and the manipulations of the prejudices of white homeowners worked together to produce the conditions of the ghetto and a segregated, unequal school system." Rice continues: "The factors that tied these interests together were economic profit and political control of the poor. The consequences were an unhealthy living environment for the poor and an immense waste of lives and money for society as a whole."[119] The CFM's intentions were to force the city to remedy the situation. In a press conference the following day, the CFM and Daley addressed the issues. After the meeting, however, King stated that the mayor had made no specific commitments regarding any of the movement's complaints, including the pressing concern of creating a civilian police review board to curb police brutality.[120]

A day later, another mass black rebellion, now known as the "hydrant riot," took place on the West Side. On July 12, 1966—a 100-degree day—Fire Chief Quinn ordered that all fire hydrants that had been opened in the black communities be immediately shut down by his firemen to avoid losing water pressure on the West Side. The problem underlying this order lay in black residents' inability to frequent the four swimming pools in the area, all of which were located in all-white, violence-prone neighborhoods. Shutting off the hydrants eliminated African American residents' standard method of finding comfort from the scorching, humid Chicago heat. As a result, fighting broke out between residents and police at a number of hydrant locations. Soon, a riot stretched over several square miles. Looting of stores followed, primarily aimed at those that were white owned and known to sell overpriced items. This time, snipers on rooftops and at windows targeted policemen. The National Guard was deployed to end the mayhem. When it was over, two African Americans had been killed, and several dozen people had been injured, including five policemen. Once the situation was calm, the police returned to the area and shot up several homes in retaliation for the officers injured during the rebellion. This particular uprising was one of forty-three in the United States in 1966—a significant increase from fifteen in 1964.[121]

In a televised press conference, Daley blamed the rebellion on King's protest: "I think you can't charge it directly to Dr. Martin Luther King, but surely some of the people who came in here and have been talking for the last year of violence—they are on his staff. They are responsible in great measure for the instruction that has been given, for the training of these youngsters."[122] King responded: "There is no point in the power structure and anybody else saying because we are peacefully going around trying to change conditions that we are the cause of the riots. That's dishonest, it is untrue, it is unfair to say it to the public."[123] He warned that "those who would make this peaceful revolution impossible will make a violent revolution inevitable."[124] Ironically, the violence had scored a victory for King. Daley was forced to allow the fire hydrants to be used in black residential areas, to provide black residents safe passage to—and protection at—white swimming pools, and to truck portable swimming pools into black communities to prevent another rebellion.[125]

Nonetheless, the nonviolent civil disobedience methods used by King and others in the South were largely ineffective in Chicago. Daley, determined not to let King expose any serious racial issues in Chicago, circumvented the Nobel Peace Prize–winner's efforts with a quick response to all grievances. To combat complaints about segregation in Chicago public schools, School Superintendent Bill Willis was replaced by a progressive educator with experience in racially focused public relations.[126] King moved into a slum to dramatize poor housing conditions, and Daley made sure his inspectors, who usually took bribes from property owners, instead began fining slumlords; the mayor also had the housing units thoroughly cleaned by the city.[127] This left King with only one card to play in the game of Chicago politics: he had to expose the racist practices of real estate agents and the rampant segregation in the city's residential housing.

King decided to march into Chicago's all-white communities to highlight the extent to which the city's housing was not open. Gage Park on the southwest side was the first target. As participants in white flight, many of Gage Park's Lithuanian, Polish, and Italian residents had recently fled the districts of Englewood and Woodlawn, which slowly became African American. The new residents of Gage Park were staunchly segregationist, and they answered the mostly African American march with violence. Several protesters were assaulted, including King, who was hit in the head with a rock.[128] Jesse Jackson, who participated in the demonstration, contends, "It was said that you could not expose segregation in the north because it was subtle. The fact is, it was everything except subtle, it was dynamic, it was real, blatant, ugly, [and] violent."[129]

Fortunately for King and the marchers, the Black Stone Rangers, or "Stones"—a politically conscious Chicago street gang—served as parade marshals. The Stones wanted to play a role in the civil rights movement in Chicago and to win recognition from civil rights organizations as a respectable institution. The Stones demanded inclusion in the march to Gage Park and were invited by CFM leadership to act as marshals on the condition that they swear to adhere to principles of nonviolence. When the marchers were met with violence, nuns and priests were among those who endured the brunt of it. The police assigned to protect the demonstrators fled, and the Black Stone Rangers became the protesters' sole defense. Using baseball gloves to catch the rocks and bottles being thrown by white residents, the Stones protected the marchers on the journey back to their starting point in Englewood.[130]

Undeterred by the violence that occurred during their first protest, the marchers headed into other white communities on August 5, 1966. There were about 1,200 police officers this time, and the white mob swelled to approximately 5,000. Andrew Young remembers the march: "Now in the south we faced mobs but in the south it would be a couple hundred or even fifty or seventy-five. The violence in the south always came from a rabble element. But these were women and children, husbands and wives coming out of their homes becoming a mob. And in some ways it was far more frightening. There were just a rain of rocks and cherry bombs. So you didn't know what it was."[131] Next, the marchers headed into the Catholic Polish and Italian community of Cragin on the northwest side. King did not participate in this protest, but there was a large contingent of clergy, including many white priests and nuns. Again, residents attacked the protesters with bottles and bricks.[132]

Acting on his own, Jesse Jackson announced a march into the predominately Italian suburb of Cicero. African American Chicagoans understood Cicero to be arguably the most racist district in Chicagoland. This was the same area where Jerome Huey was beaten to death by white teens in August 1966 for job hunting in a white neighborhood.[133] Even though about 15,000 African Americans worked in the suburb, not one black person or family was allowed to live there. Community activist Clory Bryant explained black Chicagoans' fear of Cicero: "You don't go under the viaduct honey, because if you do you may not get back. Cicero was on the other side of the viaduct. And you didn't walk through Cicero alone. You didn't let your car break down in Cicero and get out to change your tire."[134]

Parties representing both black and white Chicagoans wanted to halt the march out of fear of a violent racial explosion.[135] King had failed to receive support from allies, such as the federal government and white northern liberals. The SCLC realized that Chicago was too big to deploy the methods used in the South and sustain an aggressive movement that might remedy the city's racial problems. Thus, the SCLC wanted to get the city to redress at least one of the movement's concerns and then end the CFM campaign, because the group believed that it had achieved all that could be accomplished.[136] So King and other members of the CFM used Jackson's threat of a

Chicago Freedom Movement Open Housing Targets, 1966

march into Cicero to force Daley to compromise on what the CFM believed to be the most pressing plight of African American Chicagoans. Scholar Taylor Branch documents that King and his colleagues believed housing was the most important issue in Chicago, as "segregation without signs" was controlled by "human forces that locked [African American] people into slums." For example, the Illinois Association of Real Estate Boards stated, "All we are asking is that the brokers and salesmen have the same right to discriminate as the owners who engage their services."[137]

On August 26, 1966, Daley's office and the CFM drafted and signed a ten-point consensus on open housing, dubbed the "Summit Agreement," which was supported by banks and realtors. Two of the most important points of the agreement stated that the Chicago Housing Authority would build public housing with limited height requirements and that the Mortgage Bankers Association would eliminate race as a criteria for deciding to whom to give mortgages. But there was a loophole in the agreement: it did not include a timetable for implementation, and there were no real enforcement procedures established to penalize violators. As part of the compromise, King agreed to end all marches, especially the march to Cicero.[138]

Both Daley and King reported to the media the benefits of the Summit Agreement. King said, "It is the first step in a thousand-mile journey, but an important step . . . one of the most significant programs ever conceived to make open housing a reality. . . . Never before have such far-reaching and creative concepts been made." Daley announced, "I'm satisfied that the people of Chicago and the suburbs and the whole metropolitan area will accept this program in the light of the people who endorsed it. This program was worked out by the people of the Chicago Freedom Movement, labor unions, business groups and civic groups."[139]

King's announcement immediately split the CFM into two factions. The faction that separated from King was made up primarily of Chicago community activists. Daley had made a number of promises to this group in order to silence them, but his promises were never fulfilled (which is why King and the SCLC were in Chicago in the first place). Clory Bryant summed up the disdain these residents felt for the Summit Agreement: "We don't care about summits taking place without us. We don't care about covenants. We want contracts in black and white. With some hard answers for us, with some signatures, and some people we can hold responsible to and some time frames. But none of this was there."[140] The splinter faction of the CFM consisted of groups such as the Westside Organization, the Congress of Racial Equality (CORE), and others more attuned to self-defense than to nonviolence.[141] These groups had allied with the CFM to achieve their civil rights, but they ultimately decided to march into Cicero without Jackson or King. Chester Robinson, a member of the Westside Organization, explained their reasoning: "We are not marching into Cicero to appeal to the white conscience. But to demonstrate to everybody that rank and file people now are a new breed, a new kind of cat without fear. We do not come hat in hand, scratching our head, shuffling our feet to beg for a few concessions. In this march we are serving notice beginning today, every Negro conceives, acts, and lives out the assumption that he can walk anywhere. That he is a human like anybody and is to be treated like anybody else."[142] To this faction of the CFM, the march into Cicero symbolized the urgent need for common black residents of Chicago to continue the struggle for equality in their city.

Bob Lucas of CORE led about 250 marchers, under the protection of approximately 3,000 police officers, into Cicero. When the white mob threw bricks and bottles, the protesters attempted to catch them and throw the items back. There were also several brief fistfights between members of the groups.[143] Although no one was seriously injured, the police again failed to adequately protect the protesters. In contrast, when the Nazi Party marched through the predominately black South Side, the police capably safeguarded the hate group by positioning officers on rooftops and elevated platforms.[144]

Three months after the Cicero campaign, Alderman Thomas Keane announced at a City Hall meeting that "there is no Summit Agreement" and that open housing was "a goal to be reached."[145] What the splinter faction of the CFM believed would happen had come to pass: nonviolent civil disobedience had failed in the North, and politically mobilized black Chicago residents, many of whom had already rejected the strategy, allied with self-defense groups to attempt to achieve their civil rights agenda. According to scholar Taylor Branch, the Chicago settlement for open housing "and all its shortcomings remained an eyesore" for King and the SCLC.[146]

On April 4, 1968, Dr. Martin Luther King Jr. was assassinated in Memphis, Tennessee. Riots erupted in almost every major city in America.[147] Before rebellions exploded in Chicago, groups like the Woodlawn Organization, independent black aldermen, and even well-organized street gangs attempted to calm residents and discourage rioting on the South Side, to no avail. The rebellion began on the West Side before spilling over to other parts of the city.[148] In response, Daley announced his infamous "shoot to kill" order to stop the black rebellion:

> I have conferred with the superintendent of police this morning and I gave him the following instructions: I said to him very emphatically and very definitely that an order be issued by him immediately and under his signature to shoot to kill any arsonist or anyone with a molotov cocktail in his hand because they're potential murderers, and to issue a police order to shoot to maim or cripple anyone looting any stores in our city. Above all the crime of arson is to me the most hideous and worst crime of any and should be dealt with in this fashion. I was most disappointed to know that every policeman out on his beat was supposed to use his own discretion and this decision was his. In my opinion, policemen should have had instructions to shoot arsonists and looters—arsonists to kill and looters to maim and detain.[149]

Unfortunately, Chicago's black residents had to rely on the subjective ability of police officers—many of whom were staunch racists or were unsympathetic to King and issues of civil rights—to distinguish between riot participants and common black residents in the city's streets. Daley's order suggested that the protection of property was more important to him than black lives.

Several black Chicagoans stated that their vilification of Daley dated from this order to shoot to kill, maim, or cripple all looters during protests and riots. One resident contended that Daley was power-mad and that he was worse than Hitler. Another argued that Daley believed in good government—which to him was equated with repression of leftist dissent.[150] Black police officers, lawyers, civic and religious leaders, and celebrities such as Sammy Davis Jr. vehemently attacked Daley for the order.[151] Yet Daley's stance on black rebellion met with approval in other areas of the country. A bulletin informed residents of San Leandro, California, of their police department's adoption of a "shoot to kill" policy. Even though the suburb had "little to no black population," the leadership of the small town outside Oakland announced that it would follow "the lead of Chicago's Mayor Daley" to have police shoot first to kill rioters and looters.[152] Even more sinister, Cook County sheriff Joseph I. Woods recruited more than 3,000 civilian volunteers for his riot-control unit to control potential outbreaks in the black community, thus sending a clear message to Chicago's black residents. Most of these volunteers were white and were to be trained to handle arms by local government.[153]

Conclusion

Chicago's Democratic machine governed the city's political scene beginning in the New Deal era of the 1930s and ending in the 1980s.[154] The machine affected Chicago's black populace in various ways during this time. As a group, African Americans, whether elite or poor, in support of or in opposition to machine politics, suffered as a result. As scholar William Grimshaw put it, "Chicago's black communities have been treated as though they are islands: separate, unequal, and apart from the rest of the city."[155]

The failures of the CFM and its protests against urban renewal policies and police brutality, along with the realities of Chicago's racial residential segregation and white political, economic, and social supremacy, all figured in the anger of African American residents. One father of four described his despair from the balcony of the high-rise project slum where his family was forced to live:

> I look around me, I feel like this is a foreign country. I don't belong.
> My boss is a Jew, he lives in the suburbs. My foreman is a Pole. They

think colored people don't know much. I take home ninety-one dollars a week, and I'm never gonna be the foreman. No brother ever gonna be the foreman where I work. See down there? See that pool, that little bathtub? They put that there after the riots. How many kids could get in that pool? Fifty maybe? Well we got five hundred kids, maybe more than that, all playing out on these balconies. See this balcony, these outside hallways? That's my kids' playground. And when that wire fence tears through those little babies fall through and die. Man this is real isolation. Even the police are afraid to come in here. . . . Last year there was all that trouble, the police were clearing everybody off the streets, and these little boys, they were playing, they didn't know any better, and the police took those little boys and threw them down into a pile on the sidewalk. . . . Then they started loading them into a wagon. I came down and I said, "You got my little brother in there." They said, "Get out, nigger, or you'll be in there, too." I came back up here and I got my gun and I started shooting. I don't know if I hit any-body, but I was trying. I feel like this—if I got killed up here, I wouldn't be in the wrong. Cat can be walking down the street minding his own business and a cop grabs him, shakes him, throws him in the car. Twelve of my friends got arrested last week just that way. My brothers been pushed around too long. Well, I get zapped walking down the street, I'm not going to cop out. I'd go right out there and shoot."[156]

Similar sentiments led many black Chicago residents to adopt the Black Panther program of self-defense and self-determination to attempt to achieve the goals of their civil rights agenda.

See, bein' black is like havin' somethin' on your face that no one ever tells you is there. People look at you different all the time. It's like there is something always wrong with you. That's one feeling. The other feeling is that whatever happens black around the city, people think you know about it—you're somehow responsible for it. You're constantly being judged for something, and it's never positive.

—Keith Roberts (pseud.), interview by Lawrence, in Rosen, *South Side*, 114

As an African American, sometimes you feel that you're no more than a black box sitting over in the corner—(*pause*) without identity—or any importance for how you fit in, or are needed by the larger society. Just maybe tolerated, or depending on the mood of society, maybe even wiped out.

—William Galloway (pseud.), interview by Lawrence, in Rosen, *South Side*, 114

TWO

The Illinois Chapter of the Black Panther Party

African American novelist William Gardner Smith, writing in 1970, declared that the 1967 race revolts in Chicago marked the entry of black "tough ghetto youth into the race battle . . . [formerly] led by intellectuals or the middle class." Because the older leaders "could not cope" with the new activists, the "Panthers had to be born."[1] Smith's perspective reflects the "brothers off the block" misinterpretation that usually characterizes the Panthers; in the case of the Panthers, however, the "toughs" were also intellectuals who had some college, activist, or military experience. Nevertheless, Smith's analysis suggests the extent to which the founding of the ILBPP was an outgrowth of shifts in the "race battle" specific to Chicago. These shifts included growing disillusionment with the CFM following its failures of 1966, as many "tough ghetto youth" participated in the campaign, and a loss of faith in the ability of the mainstream nonviolent civil rights movement to defeat Chicago's Daley Democratic machine. Several "ghetto" youth became the leaders of the Chicago movement and subsequently merged aspects of the civil rights agenda with community-based activism and self-defense. This hybrid strategy was not an aberration, as recent scholarship points out that the civil rights and Black Power movements were parallel. Many Chicagoans who were members of civil rights organizations were also practitioners of Black Power ideology. This chapter investigates the origins of the BPP in the Chicago context, looking first at the ways in which the founding of the Chicago chapter grew out of earlier civil rights activism and armed resistance in the city and then at how the passionate energy of Chicago's black student movement—a movement led by "organic intellectuals" such as Fred Hampton, who became chairman of the ILBPP—was channeled into the Panthers' Chicago organization via intensive recruitment efforts.

Fred Hampton and the NAACP

The Hamptons were one of many African American families who migrated from the South to Chicago in search of economic and social opportunity. In the 1940s, the Hamptons left Haynesville, Louisiana, and moved to Argo, Illinois. The family stayed in Argo only for a short time, because the children continuously fought with white classmates, before moving to Blue Island, Illinois, for seven years.[2] In 1958, Maywood, Illinois, would be the family's last stop.[3] Frederick Allen Hampton was born on August 30, 1948, in Chicago, Illinois, at Cook County Hospital, the youngest of three children born to Francis and Iberia Hampton. According to his mother and older brother, William, Fred Hampton was a sensitive and observant child who was protective of both his brother and his sister, Delores (Dee Dee), and who demanded and got respect from his peers and elders. As a child, he was athletic and loved baseball. His aspiration in life was to become a lawyer, not because he wanted to become rich but because he wanted to help African Americans and society at large by means of the law.[4] Francis Hampton remembers his young son telling him, "Daddy, I've got to help the people uplift themselves."[5]

According to two of Fred Hampton's childhood friends who grew up with him in Maywood, Hampton demonstrated his intelligence in diverse ways and was a natural leader even while young. At Irving Elementary School in Maywood, he was captain of the patrol boys, whose responsibility was to control traffic as they assisted fellow students to safely cross city streets. He also conducted morning homework sessions, which often included both black and white students, at his home before school.[6]

Fred Hampton in T-Shirt at
ILBPP headquarters, 1969
(Private archive of Howard
Ann Kendrick [Campbell])

Later, Hampton attended Proviso East High School—it had 2,400 students, about one-fourth of whom were African American—where he improved upon his activist spirit and community organizing skills.[7] Iberia Hampton recalls that Fred was involved in various campaigns that usually resulted in some form of school punishment, and she had to get him readmitted to class several times.[8] In 1965, for example, one of Fred Hampton's peers, Eugene Moore, was unjustly arrested, and Hampton convinced a number of schoolmates to follow him to the Maywood police station, where they held a protest rally until the young man was released.[9] Later, Hampton was elected to the high school's Interracial Cross Section Committee, where he opposed racism and other injustices in the school.[10] As a member of this committee, he helped white students to acknowledge and reform their personal racist outlooks.[11] He was also elected president of the Junior Achievement program. He organized the class picnic and led campaigns against racist conditions at the school, as well as the unfair treatment of black students and athletes.[12] When his efforts did not generate any tangible changes by the school's administration, Hampton convinced students to take the drastic step of boycotting the senior prom.[13]

One of Hampton's schoolmates declares that Hampton's leadership, knowledge, and charisma helped other students to become agents of change, despite the efforts of a few white teachers to discredit the young activist.[14] Educator and community activist Jim Ivory recalls that one of Hampton's chief concerns while a high school student was to improve the quality of education for his Maywood peers:

> I used to enjoy talking with [Fred] about his vision for students at Proviso East. . . . Fred always felt that the students at Proviso East were being treated unfairly. He felt that they were getting poor training and that they were not prepared for a high tech world. He felt also that there was a lack of motivation on the part of some of the teachers. The kids were being flunked out and counseled out rather than having programs geared toward remedial programs. Our mutual interest was around the area of trying to get quality education for the young people in Maywood.[15]

According to Charles Anderson, the African American dean of attendance at Proviso East High School in the late 1960s, Hampton's activism is the only reason that Anderson was hired for the position. Anderson contends that he had applied for the dean's job for six years and had never been given an interview until Hampton intervened with a contingent of students who demanded more African American staff.[16] Don Williams, president of the West Suburban Division of the NAACP, contends that Hampton's activism was instrumental in increasing the number of African American teachers on the high school staff from five to sixteen.[17]

Upon graduation in 1968, Hampton took classes at Crane Junior College (now Malcolm X College) and the University of Illinois at Chicago Circle (UIC) to pursue a law degree. He continued to think critically and analyze issues pertinent to poor African Americans.[18] William Taylor, who worked with Hampton in the summer of 1967, remembers that Hampton was adamant about the need to create an economic policy to help the underrepresented segments of society.[19] Organizing around the issues of welfare, health, education, and employment in the black community, he worked with Rev. Claude Porter and other local ministers to develop civil rights enterprises, such as "uplift" programs, and to improve black voter registration in the community.[20]

Hampton's activism as a youth was best exemplified by his years as a member of the NAACP. Donald Williams recruited Hampton during his first year of college in 1966. The group wanted to add a youth branch to its division to address concerns surrounding recreation and education. Williams recalls, "What we needed was a young person who had rapport with the youth—someone intelligent, committed, responsible, and who accepted the NAACP's ideals."[21] Fred Hampton embodied all of Williams's desired qualities. The two met when Williams was a practicing pharmacist at a drugstore on Thirteenth and Randolph, which Proviso East High School's star basketball player, Al Newness, frequently patronized. Williams attempted to recruit Newness, since he was popular and potentially could convince other youth to join the branch. Newness declined, however, and suggested that Fred Hampton would be a more suitable candidate. During the summer of 1966, Hampton and Williams met, and the two discovered they had similar interests. Hampton agreed to join and recruit youth members but insisted that Proviso East High School would be the location of his first campaign.[22]

Hampton was concerned with a number of negative conditions at the high school, notably the discipline policy toward African Americans and the lunch program, which he claimed was unsatisfactory. He received the support of the NAACP's board to meet with the school's administration and with Superintendent Norman Green to address the list of problems.[23] Jim Ivory, who was involved in the NAACP with Hampton, spoke to approximately 200 to 300 Proviso East students about their concerns, and the next day they marched to the Maywood board meeting to discuss the issues. Not all the students could fit into the meeting room. The police were called, and tear gas was used, causing many of the students to respond by breaking shop windows on Fifth Avenue. Hampton and Ivory were arrested and accused of inciting mob action.[24] After several more meetings and a few more school and community disturbances, the administration was forced to directly respond to the list of concerns.[25]

In 1967, Fred Hampton was elected president of the Maywood Youth Branch of the NAACP. He intensified organizing around civil rights issues, such as support for civil rights workers in the South, the development of local recreational facilities, education, employment, and open housing.[26] The youth branch usually assisted the adult branch on various civil rights campaigns. Hampton was responsible for sending food and clothing to Mississippi to aid organizers. He helped to establish and run a cultural center on Madison Street in Maywood that contained books relating to the black experience, and he distributed apparel to youth who identified with the black freedom movement.[27] During another black student operation, Hampton was arrested while attempting to get a black candidate on the ballot for homecoming queen at Proviso East. When he was unsuccessful, he urged students to boycott the homecoming football game. He gained credibility with students by sponsoring parties for children at Irving Elementary School every Friday night and because he bought NAACP T-shirts for the kids.[28] Hampton had worked out an arrangement with elementary school district 89 to use the gym at Washington school for dances as well, which helped to increase the NAACP Youth Council's membership from 125 associates to well over 700 members in one year.[29] His influence increased to the point where he was able to calm both black and white Proviso East students after a race riot erupted at the school in 1968.[30]

Hampton used his organizing skills to gain support from adults in the community as well. He petitioned Maywood's administration about human relations and problems with the police department.[31] Hampton held a rally in Maywood in early 1967 for employment and open housing, and he insisted that community members become operatives and participants in the struggle for civil rights. That same day, he challenged Republican U.S. senator Charles Percy to address the Chicago African American community's needs concerning education, health, and recreation facilities, and he encouraged residents to challenge the senator as well.[32] He also assisted Jesse Jackson and Dick Gregory with various organizing campaigns and boycotts.[33] He even invited members of SNCC, among them Stokely Carmichael, to Maywood to speak to the NAACP Youth Branch and to advise him on ongoing organizing operations.[34] On a number of occasions, Hampton was a guest on the television show *Russ Meeks Up in Here*, and he appeared on a show produced by Warner Saunders, where he introduced the city to the youth activism taking place on the West Side. His appearances served as another recruiting tool.[35]

Fred Hampton is perhaps best remembered for his oratorical skills. He was popularly known as a "charismatic," "dynamic," and "powerful speaker."[36] Paul Wade recalls how Hampton studied the speeches of Dr. King and Malcolm X.[37] According to community activist Bob Wiggins, Hampton was like all great speakers before him, as he understood his audience and knew when to be intellectual and when to provide a common message.[38] U.S. Congressman Danny Davis, who attended many meetings with Fred Hampton, contends that it was odd to him for Hampton, who was so young, to be so "profound," especially since he could "excite audiences with the passion he displayed."[39] Entertainer Tyrone Davis recalls an incident that took place at Mr. Ricky's, a lounge on Fifty-Fifth Street where Fred Hampton utilized his oratorical superiority to command the attention of an entire nightclub:

He had everybody stop the music and I thought to myself, this is a stick-up or this man is crazy. Finally he started talking strongly and loud and I was amazed how he got those Black folks to stop partying and to listen to him. I never even saw Dr. Martin Luther King do that. I mean he got their full attention and he made sense. He made sense and even got me to full attention and I got fired up . . . and after he got through speaking and went and started dancing and partying for awhile. It was amazing. . . . I asked him about the worth of politics and he said to me . . . I'll never forget it . . . "Brother Tyrone, we all can contribute in our own way; as long as you're living you're involved in politics." I remembered that statement and I tried to put it into practice.[40]

Hampton was so impressive as a spokesperson that in 1967 he was chosen to be one of the main speakers at an NAACP function. The event included better-known presenters, such as Richard G. Hatcher, the mayor of Gary, Indiana, and one of the first two African American mayors elected in a major American city.[41] According to James Montgomery, who defended Hampton and Jim Ivory when they were arrested for inciting mob action during an NAACP-led student protest operation, when Hampton took the stand during the trial, his "frank, honest, [and] confrontational rhetoric" resulted in the two men being acquitted of the charges.[42]

Before Fred Hampton joined the NAACP, he had organized different groups in an attempt to compel the city of Maywood to build a swimming pool in the suburb. African Americans in Maywood were not allowed to swim in the nearest pool—located in Melrose Park—because it was reserved only for white people. His mother remembered that Hampton, who "never swam," escorted groups of black children to swim at a pool in nearby Brookfield, since Maywood refused to allow the children access. "Sometimes he would make two trips. He would ride the bus with one group and then come back and take another load. They [black children] could only swim at certain times. Fred made arrangements for the kids to be able to swim because Maywood said they couldn't build a pool. . . . Fred would march to Maywood village hall on meeting nights to ask for this pool," she recalled.[43]

Hampton continued to fight for the swimming pool as a member of both the NAACP and the BPP. In 1966, Hampton led 500 angry young people on a nonviolent march in Maywood to protest the segregation of the swimming pool on the grounds that public resources were being denied to the black community.[44] Hampton and his young cohort approached Maywood's trustees and business leaders for assistance. They helped him to organize a meeting around the issue, but they also insisted that they could do no more. Many Maywood residents attended the meeting, including dozens of white community members. Mr. Portes from Portes Drugs in Melrose Park offered around $25,000 to build the pool.

The pool was eventually completed in 1970, after Hampton's assassination.[45] After a long, drawn-out fight, the pool was also named after Fred Hampton. As Ted Elbert declared at the contentious village meeting: "All who followed the progress of the swimming pool must agree that without Fred Hampton there would be no swimming pool. . . . If there is hesitancy about naming the pool after someone who's been in jail, then consider there would be no churches named 'St. Paul' and no schools named after Thoreau, and the city of Chicago would not have named a junior college after 'Malcolm X.' If we send our Maywood children to a school named after Washington, a slave owner, we can surely name our pool after Fred Hampton. Anything less would be a cop-out!"[46]

The marches for a swimming pool in Maywood transformed the political consciousness of many black youth. Their political awareness resonated throughout the West Side for many years and also resulted in black student activism.[47] During these marches, Hampton exhorted youth activists that by demonstrating, they were helping themselves, and to always remember that fact.[48] Fred Hampton seemed to have an effect on all who came into contact with him. In spite of his young age, he was an "effective grassroots organizer" and a "gifted and charismatic orator," and he was "dedicated to the struggle" for African American liberation.[49] Rev. Harry McNelty remembers Hampton in this way: "He never gave up what he believed in. . . . He was responsible for the swimming pool, Black teachers and coaches at Proviso East and West High Schools and Triton, village jobs and open housing. Many people are in positions today because of Fred Hampton. . . . He was a wonderful person, full of energy and joy. Those who had the pleasure of meeting him developed a love for him."[50]

In Jesse Jackson's opinion, Hampton sacrificed his middle-class privilege because he was sensitive to the plight of African Americans, especially the disadvantaged.[51] Yvonne King, a former leader in the ILBPP, characterized Hampton as a "phenomenal young man who was fearless, arrogant, and selfless. He provided a role model for those who were dedicated to the struggle; who were maybe not as creative or as skillful as he was, but they certainly became so because of him and others."[52] Beginning in 1968, Hampton would put these skills to work on behalf of the ILBPP.

The Founding of the Illinois Chapter of the Black Panther Party

The Black Panther Party for Self Defense was founded in Oakland, California, by Bobby Seale and Huey P. Newton in 1966. The organization began as a small group of young black men who conducted police patrols to eliminate police brutality in African American communities. The Panthers reasoned that police power exercised against black sections of American cities operated in the same manner as colonial powers did in policing colonized subjects: "By staging confrontations with police," one historian of the Panthers notes, "Newton and Seale sought to dramatize how a form of colonial power was actually deployed against black people in the urban areas of the U.S. under the auspices of policing."[53] Encounters with police catapulted the Panthers into national prominence. Their storming of the California state legislature in May 1967 was reported in almost every major media outlet in America. Huey Newton's October 28 shoot-out with two officers, which resulted in the death of one officer and the wounding of Newton, led to his arrest and a domestically and internationally influential "Free Huey" campaign.

By 1968, the BPP was popular not only as a result of its defiance toward law enforcement but also because its socialist ideology resonated with African American youth. The Party echoed a statement by writer, poet, and activist James Baldwin: "To be black and conscious in America is to be in a constant state of rage."[54] Panthers believed the statement to be "very true of black people in general in this country" due to racism and the unequal distribution of wealth.[55] The group's spokespersons often referred to America as a "fascist nation." They defined fascism as capitalism plus racism practiced by an open dictatorship of finance capitalism. To Panthers, "finance capital" meant not only banks, trusts, and monopolies but also people such as businessmen, demagogues, politicians, and police whom they identified as terrorists reaping vengeance against the working class.[56] The *Black Panther* newspaper and members' speaking tours communicated the Party's message and purpose to African American communities and helped the Party establish branches in numerous cities.

Fred Hampton was directly introduced to Panther ideology during a member's tour stop in Chicago. Lennie Eggleston, a Panther from the Los Angeles chapter, was conducting a speaking tour for the Party and, as recalled by Joan Elbert, president of the Lutheran Human Relations Association, won Hampton over to the Party's ideology. Elbert had been asked by Karl Lutze, the director of the Lutheran association, to house Eggleston, and Hampton was her neighbor. Elbert remembers,

> [Eggleston] was a volatile person and interesting, but a little intimidating. Not knowing what to do with this guy all day, I called Fred and asked if he could come over and talk to him. Fred did. They not only talked, they argued, shouted, and debated philosophy and politics until three in the morning. The next evening several ministers sponsoring the evening's program came to our house for dinner. Fred came too. At one point, Brother Lenny turned to one of the black pastors who happened to be wearing a clerical collar and asked him why he was wearing the "white man's collar." (Brother Lenny was a Muslim.) Before the pastor could respond, Fred put his hand on Brother Lenny's shoulder and said quietly, "Don't put down a brother in front of the man." I thought it was very perceptive and fearless of Fred to speak up to this angry man who must have been twice his age.[57]

Hampton, who was still a member of the NAACP, considered himself a black nationalist and regarded racial unity as fundamental and poor whites as adversaries. Eggleston introduced Hampton to the importance of class solidarity, an approach that would transcend race and unite the poor in order to create a viable revolution against the U.S. power structure.[58] Hampton agreed that a movement encompassing all the poor, regardless of race, would be revolutionary and would be effective in addressing concerns he held, and the idea strongly resonated with his Maywood experiences. Other poor communities in Chicago were alienated, he knew, just as the city's poor African American slums were. Hampton believed that this ideological concept could potentially unify underprivileged black areas and revolutionize all of American society.[59]

Shortly after his encounter with Eggleston, Hampton contemplated joining the BPP, but the group had yet to establish a chapter in Chicago. Chapters were officially recognized only upon receipt of a valid charter from the national headquarters in Oakland. Unbeknownst to Hampton at the time, however, young men on both the West and South Sides had organized unofficial and separate entities of the Party.

In 1968, the South Side BPP faction led by former SNCC members Bobby Rush and Bob Brown, who had been heavily involved in the CFM, reached out to Alderman Sam Rayner, who helped them open a BPP office on 2350 West Madison Street (the South Side faction opened its office on the West Side) and to acquire a phone line. Hampton met the South Side faction at a leadership conference organized by former CFM leader Phil Cohran at the Afro-Arts Theater on Thirty-Ninth and Drexel. Hampton was one of the presenters, and his speech fired up the crowd of young radicals.[60] Bobby Rush and Bob Brown needed a speaker for their newly formed South Side BPP unit. Hampton, a speaker looking to join the BPP, was a natural choice.[61] When Hampton left the NAACP to join the South Side faction of the ILBPP, several members joined him in the newly established Panther chapter. Joann Lombard stated that she left with Hampton because "he knew about problems facing the community and the world," and Hampton believed the Party could be a solution to the issues that plagued poor African American communities.[62]

On the West Side, Drew Ferguson and Jewel Cook also formed a BPP chapter in the East Garfield area made up of former members of Deacons for Defense and Justice, local young adults, and some Vice Lords. In August 1968, they held a rally at the Senate Theater and met twenty former SNCC members turned Black Panthers led by Rush and Brown (the South Side faction). The two groups quarreled about who was the real Chicago BPP chapter, to no avail.[63]

In September 1968, a small delegation of the South Side faction led by Rush went to Oakland to gain approval to start a Panther chapter in Chicago, but they were denied. The Rush-led contingent was told that another group, the West Side faction, had already been recognized, even though they had not received an official charter from the BPP national headquarters. Dejected, Rush's group returned to Chicago. A short time later, they received a call from Oakland. Two Oakland Panthers who were on a flight from New York to California had gotten into an argument about whether the flight's distance from New York to California was the same as the flight distance from California to Cuba. One of the men decided to ask the stewardess for her input to settle the debate. During this period, highjacking a plane was not an unlikely occurrence. Thus, the stewardess rationalized that the two Panthers wanted to highjack the plane to Cuba. She contacted the flight's captain, who made an emergency landing in Chicago, where the two men were arrested. The only Chicago BPP group with a phone was the Rush-led contingent, so Oakland called the South Side faction, who secured the release from jail of the two Panthers. For this reason, the South Side contingent was awarded an official charter and thus became the Illinois chapter of the BPP in 1968.[64]

When the West Side faction heard the news, the two contingents decided to merge, and on November 1, 1968, the group officially opened its headquarters at 2350 West Madison Street.[65] The founding members included Fred Hampton, Bobby Rush, Bob Brown, Bob Clay, Rufus "Chaka" Walls, Jewel Cook, Drew Ferguson, and Henry English, among others. They all agreed to appoint Hampton as the main spokesperson, not only because of his oratorical prowess but because, according to Henry English, Hampton's "brain was like a sponge": he was able to quickly read books and disseminate the knowledge he gained.[66] Chicago Panthers targeted three "levels of oppression": (1) the "greedy, exploiting, rich, avaricious businessman" who took advantage of the black community; (2) the "misleading, lying, tricky, demagogic politician" who played upon the community's woes; and (3) the "atrocious, murdering, brutalizing, intimidating, fascist, pig cops."[67] Their immediate target was Daley's Democratic machine, which controlled all three entities of oppression. The ILBPP then began reaching out to other groups that were also engaged in campaigns against the Daley Democratic machine. (See Fig. 1.)

The chapter's unofficial existence was reported in both progressive and mainstream newspapers. Lu Palmer, a journalist at the *Chicago Daily News*, claims to have written the first story on the Illinois Black Panthers.[68] The *Militant* reported the formation of the group and noted that one of its first activities was to organize a "Free Huey" benefit event.[69] The *Chicago Tribune* documented that the first evidence of the group's presence in Chicago came from an undercover police officer. The policeman provided the reporter with information from his surveillance report, indicating that thirty members of the Panthers were at a "Free Huey" meeting at the Senate Theater on 3158 W. Madison Street. The article stated that the group members marched into the facility in military formation wearing black berets and black leather jackets.[70] Bobby Seale was supposed to speak at the event to announce the official opening of a Panther chapter in Chicago, but he was unable to attend. He did fly into Chicago the next day, however, to support the establishment of the chapter. The street gangs—the Black Stone Rangers (BSR), Egyptian Cobras, and Vice Lords—were described by one speaker at the rally as the "warriors that are needed" in the struggle.[71] The reporter sensationalized the fact that the Panthers were recruiting throughout the Midwest among known street gangs.[72]

The Illinois chapter was set up to mirror the leadership and organization of its Oakland headquarters. There was no single leader. A Central Committee comprised the leadership of the national organization, and likewise, the Illinois chapter had a Central Staff made up of six (later seven) members. The Central Committee consisted of minister positions, whereas the Illinois chapter's Central Staff positions were called deputy ministers. There was a deputy minister of information (Rufus Walls); education (Lamar Billy "Che" Brooks); communication (Iris Shinn and, later, Ann Campbell); defense (Bobby Rush); culture (Christina "Chuckles" May); labor (Dianne Dunn and, later, Yvonne King); and finance (Drew Ferguson). There was also a chairman (Fred Hampton), who served as the group's spokesperson.[73] The chapter also had at least three field lieutenants—Jewel Cook, Bob Lee, and Joan Gray—whose main responsibility was grassroots organizing. Each member was assigned to a cadre headed by a deputy minister. The deputy ministers' responsibilities included overseeing their cadre and assuring that comrades under their command carried out their assigned daily duties.[74]

It is important to note that the Illinois chapter was successful not only because of the dynamic leadership of Fred Hampton but also because of the perseverance and dedication of the rank and file. These non-officer members were continuously on call, doing what needed to be done and becoming leaders in their own right. This was the real threat of the BPP: the Party was not just an organization but a structured group of young leaders.

The Panthers believed in reaching out to the *Lumpenproletariat*— America's underclass society, which included common criminals and gang members whose actions demonstrated their rejection of America's political and economic structures. The Illinois chapter wanted to organize gangs and end black-on-black violence and thus attempted to form an alliance with the larger black gangs.[75] A conservative estimate of the Chicago branch membership at the time of its founding in the late fall of 1968 was about fifty members.[76] Despite this emphasis on outreach to disaffected groups, however, most of the Panther recruits came from neighboring colleges and universities, not from gangs—in large part as a result of strong recruitment drives targeting Illinois students. Hampton was a student at Crane Junior College, which had a highly politically active student population. Bobby Rush was associated with UIC. Many of the ILBPP's initial members came from UIC and other city colleges, as well as from the streets of Chicago.[77]

The Black Student Movement in Chicago

Traditionally, the student movement in the 1960s is understood as a protest movement for civil rights or as an antiwar movement. Organizations such as SNCC, Students for a Democratic Society (SDS), CORE, and some leftist groups take center stage in analysis of the subject. Some analysts investigate black students' battles on college campuses for the establishment of black studies programs, but Chicago figures in this discourse primarily in the context of the 1968 Democratic National Convention.[78] Black students, however, were at the forefront of civil rights struggles in Chicago during the late 1960s, and it was as activists in this student-led movement that many of the Chicago Panthers, including chairman Fred Hampton, first developed their grassroots organizing and leadership skills—and it was in the context of their interactions with school officials and Chicago police that they first formed their opinions of the social, political, and economic situation of Chicago's black population.[79]

Overcrowding in neighborhood schools was a major concern for African American Chicagoans in 1963. Hirsh High School on the city's South Side, for example, was built to hold 1,800 students, but more than 2,300 students attended. Activists such as Robert Lucas of CORE and Al Raby of the Coordinating Council of Community Organizations led campaigns against the Chicago school board to address this problem. Superintendent Bill Willis instituted a plan that set up trailers in the parking lots of overcrowded black high schools to remedy the situation, because he was against building additions to dilapidated black schools and he opposed integrating the city's white schools. Protesters who objected to the method called the trailers "Willis wagons" and proceeded to lobby the school board for a better solution.

On October 17, Larry Landry, leader of the High School Friends of SNCC, led 225,000 students on a one-day boycott of Chicago schools. Mayor Richard J. Daley immediately unleashed Alderman Kenneth Campbell, Alderman Claude Holman, and Congressman William Dawson—black officials elected through Daley's Democratic machine—to make the situation disappear.[80] The two aldermen and the congressman formed an organization called the Assembly to End Prejudice, Injustice, and Poverty to mislead the protesters and convince them that serious efforts would be made to eliminate overcrowding. About 400 local African Methodist Episcopal and Baptist church pastors also announced their support for Daley and urged protesters to abandon their campaign. In February 1964, 172,350 students staged another one-day boycott. The school board did not change its decision to use trailers; as a result, the campaign for school reform in black communities continued for another two years.[81]

In 1965, Daley accused the agitators of being influenced and led by Communists. This was a common Cold War strategy used by racists and segregationists who wanted to thwart all moves toward real equality in the hopes that labeling or blacklisting civil rights advocates as "reds" would force these marked people to abandon their crusade. Undeterred by the accusations, however, black school reform activists challenged Daley to prove their Communist ties or provide tangible solutions to their grievances.[82] The mayor was unresponsive on both issues. The school reform campaign grew, encompassing both open housing and integration of white schools. Shortly thereafter, Dr. King and the SCLC joined the activists, leading to the birth of the CFM.[83]

Both college and high school students stressed the need for pupils to align community struggles with the education system. The students' chief concern was that the black community had to control its schools in order to improve the quality of education at what community members believed were grossly inadequate institutions. At the college level, curriculum was the most pressing issue, but black college students also assisted their high school peers in their struggle to break down the racial divide. In 1968, Chicago's African American college students established the Congress of Black College Students and held their first meeting at the Umoja Student Center at 251 East Thirty-Ninth Street. Students representing all of Chicago's Black Student Associations were in attendance.[84] The group's formation signaled the development of a new dimension of black student involvement in academic and community concerns. The congress coordinated and unified the city's various student organizations and emphatically supported the black community's civil rights struggle.[85]

Black college students from Roosevelt University championed the idea of merit as a criterion for hiring schoolteachers in the black community. They confronted the Chicago school board with the theme of "Black control of Black schools in Black communities." The organization hoped this approach would give the community the means to install black administrators in positions of power, thereby ensuring that the results of programs were "meaningful, responsive, and pertinent to the needs of Black people." The students argued that the school system was a model of "colonial educational policy" and believed that community control was but one major tool to direct their destiny.[86]

Challenges to the Chicago school board's power by black college students were not narrowly focused on community control: they also addressed the status of integrated schools in the city by demanding more courses that were relevant and responsive to the needs of their diverse student populations. The students insisted that white teachers were welcome in the community schools—but explicitly as contributors, not as leaders. Merit, defined in terms of the teacher's ability to respond to and get responses from the students, would be a deciding factor in a teacher's tenure process with community schools. This process was expected to remedy the high dropout rates of black students and better prepare them for higher education.[87]

From January 6 through January 9, 1969, black students at Roosevelt University organized Afro-American Culture Week and invited speakers to campus to voice their opinions on the issue of community control of schools. The speakers included Roy Woods, a director at radio station WVON, who spoke about black culture and history; Professor James Turner of Northwestern University, who advocated black unity, criticized materialism, and conceded that violence might be used as an alternative of last resort; and Ann Kolhien, the principal of Hyde Park High School, who spoke about the deplorable conditions of many black Chicago schools, the city's minimal efforts to improve them, and the importance of a good education.[88]

That same week, Illinois Black Panther leaders Fred Hampton, Bobby Rush, and Ruth Iris Shinn appeared on *Chicago*, a program hosted by Ronnie Barrett, a white male Chicago television personality. Their message was in sync with the project of the Roosevelt students: When asked about the school system in Chicago, for example, they argued that students in high schools and colleges had to control their schools. The Chicago Panthers informed viewers that local black high school students had made a list of demands, and if their demands were not met, Chicago could expect the same problems as California. Students in California, particularly those led by the Brown

Berets, had staged walkouts and other protest campaigns to dramatize the racial divide and subpar facilities of their educational system.[89]

The type of agitation that the Panthers alluded to had already taken place in some Chicago schools and would inevitably unfold in several others. Black students at Harper High School, for example, formed various organizations—among them the Black Students for Defense and Black Unity, the Afro-American History Club, and Black Students for Advancement—to challenge the school's administration to develop more inclusive curricula, to invest in black students' academic progression, and to protect themselves from violence in the racially changing community.[90] Black students staged walkouts at numerous schools around the city to protest the lack of adequate curriculum, and some of these episodes erupted into violence.

The protest events at Bowen High School on the southeast side and Gage Park High School on the southwest side both warrant examination for the level of violence that occurred in these communities, where racial demographics were changing. Bowen High School was located in Calumet Heights, a once predominately Jewish community rapidly being integrated by African American families. One of these new arrivals, William Galloway, secured a teaching position at Bowen in the fall of 1967. He was one of few black teachers at the school, and he contends that during a faculty meeting, the principal, an Irish American woman, apologized to the white faculty for having to hire black teachers—setting the racial tone for the next few years. The school administrators separated students by race in some classes and pitted groups and individuals against one another.[91] An African American student at Bowen in the late 1960s who was the first president of the school's Afro Club explains that the administration's actions led to the radicalization of black students at the high school:

> So the problem for us at Bowen was never the student body. . . .
> There was never no fist fights between blacks and whites, or Jewish
> and black, or even Irish and black. Our problem was the administra-
> tion. And it was these things that led to the black power movement
> startin' at Bowen High School. . . . So you got an administration that
> is anti-black, and you got a small minority group like us dropped in
> an all-white, primarily Jewish environment—and with all the black
> power stuff goin' on at that time, naturally you gonna have a little
> resistance.[92]

Black students at Bowen in April 1968 advocated for a black history curriculum but were turned down. Their next big fight with school administrators was over a memorial service for Dr. King, which the administrators refused to hold. The black students' frustration with school officials eventually resulted in a full-scale riot, which frightened the administrators into asking the mayor to send the National Guard—already in Chicago to deal with the West Side riots following King's assassination—to their area. Guard troops responded and loaded numerous students onto buses, though just as many students were able to elude the guardsmen. These students reorganized at Stony Island Park with black students from Chicago Vocational High School and South Shore High School who had also held walkouts that day. The groups converged, making their way to Eighty-Seventh Street.[93] The students wreaked havoc on white-owned businesses on the southeast side. According to one witness, "They tore up everything in their path on their way home."[94]

The agitation at Gage Park High School, however, was far more violent and lasted much longer. Between 1966 and 1977, there were numerous racial clashes at the school. Gage Park, a predominately white area that housed members of the American Nazi Party, was undergoing a change in its racial demographic. At the high school, the objections of established residents to the demographic change and the insistence of African American newcomers that their civil rights be respected played out violently among the area's youth.

The first incident took place in February 1966 on the school's steps, when black students defended themselves from attacks instituted by their white classmates. The melee ended with one white person stabbed and four black students and one white student arrested.[95] Tensions failed to subside over the next couple of years, and in May 1968 Gage Park's black students staged a school boycott after a black youth was hospitalized for injuries sustained in an attack by a white student who had dropped out of school. Students felt that the administration had failed to protect the school's 240 African American pupils not only from the 2,160 matriculated white students but also from the school's white dropouts, who frequently badgered black students on their way home after school. Black students did not want to engage in a race war, as evidenced by the picket signs of the boycotters, which read "We Want Peace." Nevertheless, they were angry with white school officials for what they believed was an indirectly racist approach to dealing with the dilemma. An unidentified female African American student explained that the administration had "done nothing to prevent white drop-outs, kick-outs, and thugs from hanging around the school and harassing the black students." She continued: "We realize, on the other hand, that if Negro drop-outs were found near the school they would be subjected to arrest. . . . We are anxious to keep the peace, as are many of the white students here. But when police are called to the school . . . we have no doubt that they are here to protect the white students who are in the majority. They are not here to protect us."[96] This scenario played out several more times during the month of May and later in 1968.

During the week of May 13, 1969, interracial violence between black and white Gage Park High School students took place over a consecutive three-day period. Initially, a disturbance involving over 400 students erupted in front of the school. A few days later, it was reported that more than 40 African American youths attacked 2 female white students on the third floor of the school. Three black males were arrested.[97]

Racial strife continued for the next two academic years, but further violent confrontations did not erupt until October 1969. By this time, the black student population had increased from 1.5 percent to 11.2 percent of the student body. On a Tuesday in 1969, white students stoned black students as they boarded buses to return home, and a rock-throwing battle ensued. No one was seriously injured, but nineteen students were arrested by Chicago police. The next day, black students responded with clashes in the restrooms. As a result, police were forced to escort small groups of black students throughout the school day.[98]

Over the next several years, racial clashes between black and white Gage Park High School students increased dramatically. Over time, the incidents also included skirmishes between black students and police and, eventually, violent confrontations between black and white parents, all of which escalated racial issues at the school. In 1970, more than 500 African American high school students held a protest march to highlight the indifference of the school's white administration to the problems of black students. The associate superintendent, Julien Drayton, responded to the students' complaints by proposing to change the boundaries of the school district to increase the population of white students and decrease the number of black pupils. According to this rationale, racial issues would not have been a concern if Gage Park High School had not been integrated. White parents and students, along with the school administration, supported the measure. Nazi hate groups and the National Socialist Party of America advocated the need to maintain segregation to protect Gage Park's all-white community. White Gage Park residents subsequently held protests to keep their high school all white. At one point, 100 African American male members of Operation PUSH (People United to Save Humanity) had to position themselves around the school to protect black students from the area's white residents. The men could not prevent another violent racial fracas from taking place.[99]

On November 15, 1972, one-third of the white students who had boycotted the school since September returned to classes. Their return increased their numbers, which meant that white students outnumbered blacks three to one. A male black student came to the aid of a female black student who was being attacked by two white male students, igniting a riot between whites and blacks that once again included students, parents, and teachers. Thirty people were injured, and Chicago police arrested 26 participants, 22 of them white. Participants included 15 white and 3 black students, as well as 7 white adults and 1 black adult. The Chicago Transit Authority supplied the police with buses to make sure the black students got home safely. The next day, over 100 police officers were stationed around the school, but rioting broke out again. The police seemed to be either ineffectual in or uncommitted to protecting black students from the more than 4,500 white youths in and around the school.[100]

Other schools with black students became sites of protest as well. About 400 black Harper High School students staged a walkout in an effort to present solidarity with their Gage Park classmates after the incidents.[101] In a more telling accord, three years later, the Chicago Park District agreed to allow the American Nazi Party to hold a rally in the Gage Park field house auditorium to protest the influx of black students at Gage Park High School and black residents in the area. This same group had been implicated in fostering racial violence at the high school by passing out hate literature and recruiting white students.[102] African American residents' fight against the boundary change proposal and the school's racist administration continued for several years.[103]

The students of Bowen, Gage Park, and other Chicago area high schools carried the struggle to college campuses. These students demanded that black student unions on college campuses participate in educational and organizational programs in black communities.[104] Moreover, they learned from examples at other institutions around the country. African American students at San Francisco State University were beaten on numerous occasions, for example, during their struggle to force the school to provide a black studies curriculum.[105]

Black college students at Northwestern University and Woodrow Wilson Junior College (now Kennedy–King College) insisted on a more nuanced and aggressive approach to the political position of black students on college campuses and their relation to the black community at large. At Northwestern, black students called for a revolution by black people in response to what the students identified as a system of oppression and exploitation. They insisted that the role of black students had to be to understand the needs of the black community, to analyze ideological problems, to work with community activists, and to gain the necessary skills to establish self-determination for the race. These particular students linked their situations to those of colonized people abroad, thus underscoring the necessity for organized resistance to gain liberation: "Black students must find new and more meaningful testing grounds for theory and action. We must organize ourselves and then submit our skills and ability to the will of the Brothers and Sisters in the colony."[106]

At Wilson Junior College, the dean reported to authorities that there were three incidents at the institution involving black student protest and unrest over curriculum. Two teachers were under constant pressure from black students to teach African American history. One incident involved hundreds of black students entering one instructor's classroom and "taking over the class, attempting to teach Afro-American History themselves."[107] The college's black students generally congregated at a place close to the facility called "the Hole," where according to undercover police officers, a large amount of radical literature was on the book racks, including a section on Black Power. At the Hole, students discussed their plans for a black boycott at Parker High School, adjacent to Chicago State College at Sixty-Ninth Street and Stewart Avenue. A number of Black Stone Rangers were seen talking to students who had walked out—probably in an effort to assist the students' campaign.[108] Students at Wilson Junior College refused in February 1969 to honor the school's closure for Lincoln's birthday when Wilson refused to schedule an official holiday in observance of Malcolm X's birthday.[109]

SNCC played an important role in Chicago's black student movement. The organization was heavily involved on several of the city's college campuses. Many of SNCC's members had participated in the civil rights struggle in the South. Stokely Carmichael's coining of the term "Black Power" resonated with several Chicago SNCC members, as well as with many of the black students. The ideal of achieving black power, coupled with the establishment and popularization of Oakland's Black Panther Party, strongly influenced many of Chicago's black students. SNCC members such as Bobby Rush and Bob Brown would ultimately organize a Black Panther group.[110]

All of the aforementioned episodes initiated by black students at Chicago's high schools, colleges, and universities demonstrate a heightened political awareness of the predicament of African Americans in the city. Although the black student movement took place outside the control of the city's traditional African American political organizing (aside from that of groups like SNCC), student groups were front and center in the struggle against the racist power structure in Chicago. Many of the student activists would go on to join the ILBPP, and several were founding members, most notably the eventual chairman of the organization, Fred Hampton. His involvement in the undervalued activism of Chicago's black student movement stretched from his grammar school to his college days.

The Illinois Chapter's Recruitment Strategies

Branches of the BPP were established throughout Illinois in 1969. The first branch outside Chicago was in Fred Hampton's Maywood community. Others followed in Argo, Rockford, Joliet, Peoria, and, later, East St. Louis.

The ILBPP attempted to increase its ranks by sponsoring speaking engagements at high schools and college campuses throughout Chicago and the state.[111] Chicago Panthers recruited heavily at local high schools—so much so that fears were heightened among Chicago police, who were already monitoring the activity of black high school students, because of several race riots sparked by the mobilizing of the city's black student movement when many of these students joined the Party. At Hyde Park High School, whose principal had recently spoken at an event at Roosevelt University with Panther presenters, the Party amplified its recruitment efforts to circumvent countermobilization campaigns of the BSR. The Rangers at this time viewed the Party as a rival street gang trespassing on Ranger territory in the Woodlawn area, trying to recruit the gang's current and potential members. According to an interview report, the leader of the BSR informed police that he told the Panthers to stay out of his neighborhood. His objection to the group was partly due to the Party's limited success in recruiting members of the Rangers' rivals, the Disciples.[112] Tension between the Rangers and the Panthers over recruitment was so high that rumors circulated that there would be a war between the groups.[113] Most other recruitment efforts were less constrained. At Parker High School on Sixty-Ninth Street, for example, students took the initiative to seek out and organize their own branch of the Chicago Panthers. Students handed out BPP applications for membership and flyers inviting interested students to attend a meeting. The flyer read, "To all students interested in the organization of a Black Panther Party at Parker High School . . . Meet today . . . 10th period . . . Community Room."[114]

The Illinois Panthers' recruitment operations on college campuses received greater attention as the group attempted to solidify branches in other parts of the state. In January 1969, organizers in the group traveled down-state to the University of Illinois at Urbana–Champaign (U of I), where they held a meeting in the Natural History Building and a gathering at the Douglass Center to recruit members.[115] The event was sponsored by U of I's Black Student Association and SDS.[116] Hampton, Rush, and Dianne Dunn met with David Addison, president of the Black Student Association at U of I, over coffee before the Party's event, perhaps to get an idea of what, if any, problems existed for African Americans on the campus.[117] At the student event, Dunn, who was married to another Panther (William Dunn) and was six months pregnant, declared that she could "whip any three honkies in the room."[118] She used such rhetoric in an attempt to persuade more women to either join the party or get involved in the African American liberation struggle. Rush outlined the Panthers' ten-point program to the large audience of students. When Hampton spoke, he criticized "universities, whites, police, and 'black students who are acting like the enemy.'"[119] Aware that their presence on campus would bring undercover officers to their presentation, Chicago Panthers refused to allow U of I audience members to photograph them. Unfortunately, William O'Neal had to forcefully remove a photographer from the room, and Dianne Dunn forced a young woman to put her camera away. Both incidents frightened some of the white students who attended the speaking engagement.[120] At the end of their presentation, Panthers took donations, and John Lee Johnson, a U of I student and Panther, told fellow students interested in joining the Party to contact him. He also posed the question "How many would join?," and many hands were raised.[121] Fred Hampton responded, "Y'know, we've been getting that response everywhere we go."[122] Hampton then asked all white people to leave the room so the campus's black students could conduct a strategy session.[123]

The Chicago Panthers returned the next month to follow up on promises made during the strategy session. On this trip, campus police began to harass the group in an attempt to curtail their organizing. Without provocation, Lamar Billy "Che" Brooks and William Dunn were arrested for disorderly conduct. Witnesses stated the officers approached Brooks and called him a "bad ass."[124] Brooks responded in like verbal accord, so the officers arrested him. Dunn was detained when he approached the officers to ask why Brooks was being arrested. The Black Student Association and SDS collected bond money for the two Panthers.[125] More important, the Party's trip to the campus was spied upon by Chicago and Urbana–Champaign police. According to surveillance reports, the group arrived on February 2 and got a room at Chief Illini Motel, which served as their base of operation. Rush was

Fred Hampton, accompanied by members of the Young Lords, speaking to college
students, UIC, 1969 (Private archive of Howard Ann Kendrick [Campbell])

accompanied by at least one armed guard at all times. Then on February 5,
the Panthers switched their base of operation to the Courtesy Motel due
to police surveillance. The Panthers believed that their room was searched
while they were out. To impede the organization's progress in the college
town, thirteen Panthers—Fred Hampton, Bobby Rush, Nathaniel Junior,
Billy "Che" Brooks, Ted Boston, Dianne Dunn, Jeldean Eldridge, Ronald
"Doc" Satchel, Christina May, Donna Washington, Phyllis Clarke, Robert
Bruce, and William Dunn—were arrested on the trumped-up charge of de-
frauding an innkeeper. According to police, four members rented rooms,
but fifteen people occupied the rooms. Upon their release, the group continued their recruitment work.[126] One U of I student, Brenda Harris (also commonly known by members as China Doll), dropped out of school to join the
ILBPP as a result of the Panthers' visits to campus. Later, Harris would be one
of several victims in the December 4, 1969, police raid on Fred Hampton's
apartment that resulted in his death.[127]

Campus visits enabled the Party to establish branches at several Illinois
colleges and universities. (See Fig. 2.) Invited by the Black Student Association to give a speech at Roosevelt University for an informal meeting

FIGURE TWO

**COLLEGES AND UNIVERSITIES THAT HOUSED
ILBPP REPRESENTATIVES**

Chicago State University

Crane Junior College (now Malcolm X College)

Illinois Institute of Technology

Northeastern Illinois University

Northwestern University

Roosevelt University

Southern Illinois University, Carbondale

University of Illinois at Chicago Circle

University of Illinois at Urbana–Champaign

Wilber Wright Junior College

Woodrow Wilson Junior College (now Kennedy–King College)

Compiled from Chicago Police Department Red Squad files and interviews with various Illinois Panthers

in December 1968 and for the black students' revival week that following January, Fred Hampton gladly accepted, as the chairman seized every opportunity to recruit members and inform the masses. During his December speech, Hampton explained to the audience that to join the Party, one had to endure a six-week process of mastering certain political ideological literature (the *Autobiography of Malcolm X, Quotations of Chairman Mao Tse-Tung* [known as the *Red Book*], and *Guerrilla Warfare* by Che Guevara were listed as examples) and completing physical self-defense training. Hampton insisted that the Party was a self-defense-oriented political organization that aimed to protect the black community against racist police, and he emphasized that the group was the only police force the black community had ever had. Although white people could not join the Party, he stated that they could work in coalition with the Panthers, as had members of other white groups such as SDS, the Peace and Freedom Party, and the Young Socialist Alliance (the youth arm of the Socialist Workers Party).[128]

In response to an audience member's characterization of the BPP as a violent organization, Hampton countered that the group was not about violence but about self-defense, information, religion, and culture, and that the group had ministers for these categories. He elaborated: "If all we were talking about was violence, we would just have my job—Minister of Defense. If 'the man' wants to talk about the Bible, he can meet Reverend Hampton. If he wants to talk about education, he can meet Fred Hampton, Ph.D. But if he is going to talk about brutalizing black people, then he's going to meet Fred Hampton . . . revolutionary, and liberator."[129]

Hampton attacked the idea of black capitalism, a concept advocated by CORE (and others, such as Jesse Jackson), as a redefined form of oppression: "Capitalism is oppression," he said, and thus black capitalism is oppression dictated by black people.[130] He urged white students to become involved by forging coalitions, sending donations, and becoming "a 1968 counterpart to John Brown."[131] Finally, he clearly explained that the Party rejected hatred of white people and did not "define the enemy by his color but by his deed."[132] He concluded that the Panthers did believe in the teachings of Martin Luther King Jr. but did not believe in "preaching nonviolence to the Ku Klux Klan."[133]

The next month, members held another meeting at the campus during revival week. Rufus Walls was one of the key speakers, and he reiterated the points raised during the group's previous visit: that the BPP was against capitalism and racism and that the group served as police for black people. He spoke explicitly against white police officers who volunteered to work in the ghetto, which he argued was a way for them to gain an opportunity to abuse black people. And he urged black citizens to arm themselves with guns against oppression. Hampton called for new members and explained that new members would have to commit themselves to staffing community programs.[134]

Wilson Junior College, then located on Seventy-First Street and Stewart Avenue, was also a hotbed of Panther activity. It was reported that over a several-day period in October 1968, about a dozen members of the Young Socialist Alliance and the BPP recruited around the school.[135] Billy "Che" Brooks, deputy minister of education, was a student at the institution and was identified as the leader of the Panthers there. A Chicago police report reveals that black students organized around the Panthers, and student members of the Party recruited heavily, passing out leaflets and information. An anonymous staff member informed the officer that "white enrollment in the school has dropped to less than 1 percent because of fear of the activities of Negro students in the school . . . [and because] the Black Panthers of The Student Government groups have literally taken over the school."[136] An FBI investigation, prompted by fears that the situation, "left unchecked," would produce "drastic results," produced evidence of Panther organization at the college that disturbed the investigating officers, who desperately wanted to intervene to restore the school to white administrative control.[137] Student Party members placed signs all over the school describing their revolutionary philosophy: "Black Power comes from the barrel of a gun."[138] The school's president decided to allow the signs to remain on display, and there were no incidents of violence.[139]

There was also considerable activity at colleges that other Central Staff members attended. At Crane Junior College, Fred Hampton's former school, recruitment was intense. Fred Hampton, Bobby Rush, and Rufus Wall were among several Panthers who visited Crane to recruit new members and to support student protesters who were advocating for African American studies courses. They were invited by the student Afro-American Club, which had been approached by the Party with the intention of building a coalition.[140]

At Bobby Rush's former institution of higher learning, UIC, the Party held a "Free Huey" rally attended by 65 white and 177 black students. The rally was sponsored by the Young Socialist Alliance, and Fred Hampton was among several speakers who talked about the incarceration of Huey Newton. All those present at the event stressed the necessity of supporting both the Panthers and the black community in Chicago. Moreover, those in attendance advocated that the Party must lead the charge for change in Chicago. Such a change could reverberate throughout the Midwest, since Chicago during this period was the political and economic center of the nation, a hub for its airlines, gasoline production, railroads, and so forth.[141] A few months later, Chicago Panthers held another meeting at UIC led by Robert L. Carter, associate director of the Education Assistance Program at the campus. Carter was able to answer all questions directed toward the Party's speaker. For this reason, the reporting investigator assumed that Carter was a Chicago Panther, although his affiliation remains unclear. Carter was, however, a known activist who had had several confrontations with UIC police and avidly supported other militant organizations on campus. Two female Panthers, Christina May (minister of culture) and Clidra, gave speeches as well. Cynthia Conley and Nee McDearnon, leaders of a female group called Black Liberators, from Saint Louis, Missouri, were there to meet Chicago Panthers because they wanted to establish a chapter in their hometown.[142]

The Panthers were invited to UIC on numerous occasions; one such instance was to participate in a memorial service on Dr. King's birthday.[143] The Chicago Panthers also visited the Illinois Institute of Technology, Northeastern Illinois University, and Wright Junior College. Panthers' efforts on college campuses increased the power and influence of the Chicago branch of the Party. Chicago Panthers' successful recruitment campaigns led Chicago police officers to attempt to infiltrate their mobilization movement, with little success.[144]

While students comprised a large target group for recruitment, the Panthers also attempted to convince high school dropouts, gang members, and other members of the African American community to join their cause. Panthers recruited in pool halls and other popular youth hangouts.[145] Leroy Danzy, a manager at Burger King at 7125 S. Ashland, reported to Chicago police that Panther youth were recruiting in the area.[146] One police report indicates that the Chicago Police Department's Red Squad also had youth officers who supplied them with information. One of these youth officers reported that the Chicago Panthers and Deacons for Defense and Justice also recruited in Ada Park on 112th Place and Throop among youth aged sixteen and older.[147]

Chicago Panthers also held numerous meetings in the community. Most of these meetings took place in the Louis Theater, located at 110 East Thirty-Fifth Street. At these meetings, various members presented speeches that informed residents of the Party's progress, of BPP community service programs, of how to organize to address the community's ills, and of how to protect themselves legally and physically from police brutality. Members at such meetings often criticized the media (black radio stations and newspapers included) and the police.[148]

Political Activism and Armed Resistance in Chicago in the 1960s

Before the CFM tackled the political, economic, and social oppression of African American Chicagoans, many local groups were already engaged in battle with the Daley Democratic machine. After Alderman Ben Lewis was murdered in 1963, Edward "Fats" Crawford and many other West Side activists formed an armed group, the Friends of Ben Lewis, to protect black independent politicians from the political–police–mob triumvirate responsible for the death and violence visited upon many black West Siders engaged in political affairs. In 1965, the group met Earnest Thomas, an organizer for the Deacons for Defense and Justice, a black self-defense group based in Louisiana. After this encounter, the Friends of Ben Lewis reconstituted their political organization as a Chicago chapter of the Deacons for Defense and Justice. In May 1966, the group officially opened its office at 1230 Pulaski Road on Chicago's West Side. This armed group provided protection for the black community from racist whites and police brutality. It established a charter with the National Rifle Association and armed itself with m-1 assault rifles. Group members used these arms to monitor the police, to attempt to eliminate discrimination against black residents by local store owners, and to keep surveillance at a Nazi rally in all-white Gage Park.[149]

By the fall of 1966, Thomas had returned to Louisiana, and Fats Crawford assumed the leadership position of the organization. Under Crawford's command, according to Deacons historian Lance Hill, the Chicago Deacons became allied with a number of other local Black Power groups to found the Community Coalition for Black Power, which in addition to the Deacons included segments of radical CORE and SNCC members, the W. E. B. Du Bois Club, and members of the BSR and Vice Lords, two youth gangs.[150] The Deacons for Defense and Justice supplied financial and material support to civil rights activists in the South and attempted to curb black-on-black violence among young black male West Siders. In retaliation for the Deacons' armed political defiance, police officers from the Fillmore District station shot up the group's office on October 2, 1966.[151]

Frederick "Doug" Andrews, founder of the local community group Garfield Organization, was also involved in political activism on the West Side. According to Judge Eugene Pincham, Richard Barnett, Bernetta Barrett, and Danny Davis, Andrews was so popular among the West Side's African American populace that he could have been elected mayor of the West Side if such an office had existed. In 1968, he led a "boycott the polls" campaign that cost the Democratic Party about 30,000 votes. President Richard Nixon rewarded Andrews's political effort by providing financial support to the Garfield Organization, and it was rumored that Andrews was also compensated with control over several Burger King franchises on the West Side. Russell Meeks, a well-known local activist, also worked to topple Democratic machine politics in Chicago; Meeks founded Search for Truth, a community-based watchdog group, and promoted gangs like the Vice Lords and the Egyptian Cobras. Hundreds of friends and followers of these leaders and groups would later join the ILBPP.[152]

In 1965, a collective of grassroots West Side organizations came together to challenge injustices in their districts. The community leaders of these organizations held a number of meetings, called the West Side Summit, with Mayor Daley and his representatives. West Siders' demands included (1) resignation of precinct captains who did not live in the community, (2) a civilian review board on police brutality, (3) a local voice in federally funded programs, (4) equal job opportunity in the city, (5) city influence over bank loan policies, and (6) community influence in community schools. The summit failed to produce any substantial measures that addressed these demands, but the requests would become the central platform of both the nonviolent CFM and local grassroots Black Power groups, including the ILBPP. Among the followers of the West Side community leaders were Jewel Cook and Lamar Billy "Che" Brooks, both of whom would later become founding members of the ILBPP.[153]

The CFM's nonviolent, direct-action approach failed to eliminate racial discrimination in the Daley administration's policies. The disappointment forced local organizations to reestablish their earlier defiant and aggressive approach toward meeting their goals, which had been put on hold to allow King to lead the Chicago Freedom campaign. These methods highlighted deep-rooted differences between South Side and West Side African American residents. Class diversity on the South Side stifled community-wide activism, as middle-class blacks kept a distance between themselves and their poorer counterparts. The South Side's all-black wards were a more established part of town due to decades of segregation, which had enabled a minority of African American families to attain economic wealth. Urban renewal and gentrification forced many poor South Siders to move to the West Side, but a number of middle-class families took advantage of their ability to integrate certain majority-white areas on the South Side, such as the Chatham neighborhood. Here, these black middle-class residents were able to achieve financial success and some political power as teachers, barbers, morticians, and postal workers. Understandably, many of these middle-class residents viewed the militant actions of underprivileged African Americans as a threat to their advancement and therefore attempted to distance themselves from such groups. The Contract Buyers League, for example, a group of community activists that operated in African American areas on both the South and West Sides, split into two opposing camps because South Siders perceived West Siders as too radical.[154]

Successful South Side middle-class blacks were members of civil rights organizations and received better services and police protection than the majority of black Chicagoans, who were financially disadvantaged. Many of these poverty-stricken folks were members of Black Power groups and lived in slums or housing projects such as the Robert Taylor Homes, the Henry Horner Homes, and the Cabrini-Green complex.[155] These residents were usually members of groups such as the Friends of Ben Lewis, led by Fats Crawford; Deacons for Defense and Justice, also led by Fats Crawford; Garfield Organization, led by Frederick "Doug" Andrews; the Contract Buyers

League, led by Ruth Wells; the West Englewood Citizens Committee, led by Rev. John Clinkscale and Bob Lucas; and the Black Concerned Society. Moreover, poverty-stricken residents were the targets of police control and brutality, and they often responded violently to such treatment, especially on the West Side, where all of Chicago's major race riots of the 1960s began.

West Side black inhabitants, however, did not monopolize black militancy in Chicago. Although civil rights and Black Power organizations may have disagreed on certain strategies and methodological approaches, almost all groups placed police brutality at or near the top of their list of challenges. In August 1968, the SCLC's South Side–based civil rights group, Operation Breadbasket, under the leadership of Rev. Jesse Jackson, held a meeting with more than 2,000 in attendance. The organization was engaged in a multicity boycott campaign against A&P stores in Chicago, Memphis, New York, New Jersey, Philadelphia, and Atlanta. Attendees held a strategy session to figure out how to empower black police officers, who the organization believed should control the black community.[156] Later that year, the South Side's West Englewood Citizens Committee went to the Seventh District police station to present Police Commander Miles with a list of demands. The main requirements on their list were an end to police brutality and the establishment of a line of communication between the police and the black community. Commander Miles agreed to either attend or send a representative to the committee's next meeting, but he did not make any concessions.[157]

In 1968, a benefit program for incarcerated national Panther chairman Huey Newton was held on Chicago's West Side at the Senate Theater, located at 3128 W. Madison. The event was sponsored by the Black Concerned Society (a collective of Civil Rights and Black Power grassroots organizations), and about 350 people attended—all African American except for about 4 European Americans who were members of the Young Socialist Alliance. Other Black Power groups represented there included the Garfield Organization and the Westside Organization. Gangs such as the Vice Lords (a West Side street gang), the Egyptian Cobras (a South Side street gang), and the BSR (a South Side street gang) were also in attendance. There were also about 30 members of the BPP, which had not yet announced its official opening of a branch in the city, but the event nonetheless fueled rumors that Bobby Seale was in town to formally inaugurate the Party in Chicago.

The program consisted of several speakers, all of whom addressed what they believed to be critical issues in the black community.[158] Russell Meeks stated that Chicago's stop-and-frisk law was designed to harass black people in ghetto areas and that the black community must challenge the law on an "individual basis." He declared, "Then police would stop-and-frisk at their own risk." Meeks also insisted that gun registration was also a measure designed for black people, because whites in suburbs like Cicero were not required to register their firearms. He opposed "white domination," especially in black areas, and planned to testify before the U.S. Senate about this concern and black America's response to King's assassination. Meeks gave his support to Newton and demanded that black Chicagoans must control their schools.[159]

Fats Crawford thanked the people of the West Side for donating money to bail him out of jail. He stated that he was arrested on a trumped-up charge because Daley wanted him off the streets. Crawford demanded that black people unite to oppose Alderman Holmon, who wanted to put youth who participated in civil disturbances in detention camps. Crawford's arrest caused him to realize that West Side leadership must not be placed in the hands of one or two people, but that each leader should have a team of twelve people ready to replace him if he was arrested or killed. He argued that 96 percent of the inmates in Cook County jails were African American because whites were allowed to take advantage of recognizance bonds but black citizens were not.[160]

Fox Williams, president of the Egyptian Cobras, introduced his spokesman, Lamont Pearce, who informed the crowd that gangs on the West Side no longer battled one another. His group and the Vice Lords, he said, had united to help West Side black brothers and sisters by offering protection from police violence and by becoming entrepreneurs. The Vice Lords already owned legitimate businesses and were attempting to open a gas station and car wash; they also planned to only hire black workers who were enrolled in some type of school, even high school, because they believed that education was fundamental to gaining freedom.

James Turner, a professor at Northwestern University, stated that the pressing issue among black Chicagoans was that everyone wanted to be the leader; thus he indicated that only a few activists could occupy the role. He believed that black residents should have multiple leading organizations and should organize and fight the white power structure with a planned battle and not with futile unplanned riots.[161]

The critical issues addressed during the event were police brutality and harassment, community control of schools, identifying community leaders, racism in the court system, and education and entrepreneurship. The speakers demonstrated consensus that it was necessary to take a militant or radical approach to ending oppression in their communities. Meeks opposed racial profiling and advocated community-controlled schools. Fats Crawford wanted to curb unlawful arrest and detainment of black males and to re-evaluate leadership roles on the West Side. The Egyptian Cobras promoted education, entrepreneurship, and an end to black-on-black violence. James Turner believed black riots were a distraction from developing tangible plans to deconstruct white supremacy. While each man suggested different approaches to dealing with the social and political predicaments of black Chicagoans, the passion they all demonstrated suggests the intensification of political militancy and radicalism in black Chicago at this time. For exam-ple, in February 1969, the Black Liberation Alliance favored co-ops and food-buying clubs because they believed the process would benefit poor black families.[162] Chicago's civil rights movement was no longer completely led by establishment icons; rather, grassroots intellectuals, all of whom worked to remedy the plight of poor African American residents, had seized the reins.

Chicago was in tune with much of black America. After seventeen-year-old Bobby Hutton was gunned down in Oakland, becoming the first Oakland Panther killed, Betty Shabazz sent a telegram of condolence to the Hutton family via Kathleen Cleaver.[163] The telegram read, "If the generation before him had not been afraid, he perhaps would be alive today." Asserting that it was time for black Americans to defend themselves, Shabazz implied that her generation should have practiced armed self-defense so the offspring of her generation would not have to put their lives on the line for racial equal-ity in America.[164] Chicago's African American residents already understood self-defense ideology, which had been in practice for decades before the BPP established a chapter in Illinois. It would be the young activists of Chicago's black student movement who would take up the self-defense challenge ar-ticulated by Shabazz.

Who Joined and Why: Rank-and-File Chicago Panthers

The rank and file were the pulse of the BPP, and they are the most overlooked and undervalued members of the organization. While the martyrs and icons of the popular and controversial Party have consistently overshadowed the efforts of the rank and file, the non-officers were the movers and shakers of the Party. These young men and women carried out the necessary but daunting day-to-day tasks of the organization with dedication, showcas-ing an impressive work ethic, and without complaint. Whereas most young people are concerned with dating, partying, school, employment, and keep-ing pace with contemporary popular culture trends, the young adults and teenagers who became Panthers usually had a difficult time maintaining intimate relationships, were too tired for revelry, generally dropped out of school, and in many cases were financially unstable. They were loyal to the Panthers, the social justice movement, and the potential revolution.

Although these members shared similar activist attributes in their youth, their journeys to the ILBPP were quite different. Michael McCarty and Hank "Poison" Gaddis, for instance, were two young men who were heavily involved in the black student movement in Chicago, the CFM, and the NAACP Youth Council. The lack of police response to a violent experience led McCarty to become active in political affairs: "In 1966, I got jumped on by a gang. Me and a buddy of mine. And at some point we got split up, and I saw a police car, and my buddy was still back in this building, possibly being beaten, possibly being killed. So I staggered over to the police car and told them what happened. [The officer] looked at me, 'So?'" Frustrated by the officer's lack of interest and frightened by the gang's continued pursuit, McCarty asked to be taken to the police station. There, he did not find the help he sought: "So I'm thinking this is an aberration, this is one cop. So I go in the police station. At this point, I'm bleeding. Everything's starting to swell up. My face and head are all starting to swell up, and all the cops were white. They just started laughing at me. And they basically ignored me until my father showed up. Yeah. So that is when I had my first personal experience with the fact that the police were not there to serve and protect me." For McCarty, the experience was his "awakening" to the civil rights movement, which he realized was not "just something that was happening someplace else" but, indeed, "was happening here." "That's when I started reading," he said. "I started reading about what was going on. I started reading about Black History and I discovered all of this stuff." His discoveries led him to join the youth wing of the NAACP.[165]

McCarty decided to become a Panther after watching a news program that showed armed Panthers storming the California state legislature on May 2, 1967. He first encountered information about the Party in *Ramparts*, where he read about the Panthers' ten-point program. He watched the Sacramento incident on the news: "Here were these brothers armed with guns and law books policing the police," he said. "They's some badass brothers. Woo. So right away I'm intrigued by this." After reading more articles and a book about Black Power, he became interested in "these badass brothers standing up to the cops": "Now for a brother from Chicago, the idea of somebody who's gonna stand up to a cop has to be like, 'Damn.' You gotta be bad. So I was intrigued by the organization. And in some way, shape, or form I got wind that there was a chapter here in Chicago on Western and Madison, not too far. I be around there, man. So I went down there."[166]

Hank Gaddis's father put his son on the front lines of racial and political protest when Hank was just eight years old. Gaddis's early exposure to civil rights activism explains his consistent involvement in grassroots movements throughout his teenage and young adult years: "Prior to joining the Party, I was already involved in the movement. . . . And the reason I was involved at eight years old was because my father was very movement oriented, but I was the youngest of eight children. And since he had so many mouths to feed as a manual laborer, he couldn't afford to be directly involved in demonstrations, 'cause we were getting arrested. And he couldn't afford to have to pay bail money, so what he did was kind of be involved in the movement vicariously through me, and so when I would get arrested all he had to do was go down to the police station and sign his name and I was released." Gaddis began participating in the movement when King came to Chicago; later, he was part of the movement to desegregate the Chicago Board of Education and remove its superintendent, whom many regarded as racist, and he participated in the Coordinating Council of Community Organizations before joining the NAACP Youth Council.[167]

Like McCarty and other black youth nationwide, Gaddis also first became aware of the Panthers as a result of the California legislature episode. He became a Panther after Fred Hampton and others left the NAACP Youth Council to join the Party. Hampton's ideological influence convinced Gaddis that the BPP at the time was more keenly aware of the needs of African Americans than the NAACP was:

In 1968, we had an Illinois NAACP Youth Council state meeting, and Fred Hampton was the Chairman. We had a preliminary session of the Youth Council at which Fred was the keynote speaker, and I had never heard him speak before then, and his oratorical skills just blew me away. What he was talking about, I was like, "Wait a minute. NAACP is talking like this?" 'Cause he was a brother who had the oratorical style and abilities like Martin Luther King, but the ideology that he professed was more in line with Malcolm X. And then to top it off he was like eighteen or nineteen years old—and he always looked much more mature than his age.

After the speech we went back to the motel room, and everybody was talking, and Fred asked a question: "Have any of ya'll heard of Huey Newton and the Black Panther Party?" And nobody had really.

I spoke up and said, "Yeah. Them some crazy motherfuckers out there in California that took guns into the state legislature." And he said, "Yeah, brother." He said, "Well, I've been in touch with Huey Newton and Bobby Seale, and they've authorized me to form a Black Panther Party here." And I said, "Oh, okay. That sounds good to me." And so some weeks later, once I found out where they were opening up the office at 2350 West Madison on the West Side of Chicago, I went over and joined the Party.[168]

Wanda Ross was a young UIC student eager to become active in the movement. Ross was indirectly recruited by the ILBPP. She was not involved in a political organization before she joined the Party, but she was attracted to the dedication and activism exemplified by Panthers who were students at her institution: "At Circle, we had a lot of different people comin' from different organizations, the Young Patriots, a guy from the Communist Party, the Black Panther Party. Then I met—I don't even think I'd been there for more than two or three months—Chuckles, Christina May, she was the minister of culture of the Chicago Panthers. She was the first one that I ever knew that was in the Party. She was an artist, and she was pushin' to get us involved. Fred [Hampton] had come to talk. He impressed me. He didn't impress me that much—Chuckles impressed me more."

Ross was a member of a dance group that performed African dance at an independent black theater called the Apple Arts Theater. She and her group "started goin' over to the Panther office," and Hampton invited them to perform at Panther recruitment events: "[The party] had speakin' engagements, but they wanted to make it a cultural show, so actually, that's really what pulled me in. We were goin' to political education classes, cause we wanted to know what's happenin', and one by one, the girls in the dance group kinda fell off, but I was kinda stickin' with it. I don't remember doin' many shows, but that was one of the hooks beside the P.E. [political education] classes that got me really interested in joining the party."[169]

Unlike Wanda Ross, McCarty and Gaddis were not recruited by the Party. Both, who at the time were members of the NAACP Youth Council, joined the Panthers for different reasons. Nevertheless, these former members present firsthand accounts of how they grew from common youth to political intellectuals in underprivileged Chicago's struggle against the Daley machine. McCarty, Gaddis, and Ross represent the majority of the Illinois chapter's membership and offer examples of rank-and-file Panthers who played significant roles in the day-to-day functioning of the Party. Michael McCarty was a member of the education cadre headed by Deputy Minister of Education Billy "Che" Brooks, for which he taught political education classes. Hank Gaddis, on the other hand, was one of the Party's important grassroots organizers, assisting Deputy Field Lieutenant Bob Lee with politicizing various groups and organizations—one of which, the Young Patriots, became affiliated with the Illinois chapter's Rainbow Coalition. Wanda Ross became the chief organizer of the Illinois Panthers' first successful community service initiative: the Party's Free Breakfast for Children Program. These brief accounts demonstrate the complexities of youth activism in Chicago and emphasize the linkages and overlaps of political action during this period.

Conclusion

Long before there was a Black Panther Party for Self Defense in Oakland, the Chicago black student movement was concerned with day-to-day issues of self-defense in school and after school. White students outnumbered black students, and school fights triggered race riots. In addition to concerns about the lack of school discipline and police protection against white mobs and the problems of self-defense, black students were concerned with the lack of diversity in the curriculum. Those issues galvanized black students in both high school and college as they began to agitate for more black history, black teachers, and black studies courses.

Most of the ILBPP's members were high school or college students or were affiliated with grassroots community and national political organizations. Many Illinois Panthers were also activists before they joined the Party, which contradicts popular perceptions of the group as made up of thugs and criminals. While the *Lumpenproletariat* was present, at least in the Illinois chapter this element was minimal. Thus, Chicago youth who became members decided to continue the work they were already involved in via an organization they believed to be the vanguard of the overall social justice movement. It is ironic that popular perceptions of the Party as a violent and confrontational entity drew the youth to the organization, even though these characteristics were generalized misrepresentations of the armed self-defense movement.

THREE

Chicago and Oakland

A Comparative Analysis of the Illinois Chapter of the Black Panther Party and National Headquarters

"There is no single BPP," Mumia Abu-Jamal has written. Rather, "there are many, unified in one national organization, to be sure, but separated by the various regional and cultural influences that form and inform consciousness." Between 1966 and 1982, there were more than forty BPP chapters across America and abroad. These chapters differed from one another, as well as from the national headquarters in Oakland, in their methodology, ideology, and activities. For example, many New York Panthers were Muslims because of the influence of Malcolm X, but others identified themselves as Yoruba, Santeria, and Puerto Rican—which differed greatly not only from popular perceptions of the Party but also from the exclusively African American founding branch in Oakland. Thus, when analyzing the BPP, we must understand that the "macrocosm cannot truly be found in the microcosm."[1]

This chapter investigates the ways in which the ILBPP hewed to the Party line, as well as how it differed from the national organization as a whole.

Many aspects of the Illinois Party reflected the ideology, programs, and direction of Oakland. The group worked to combat police brutality and build coalitions, engaged in fund-raising and public relations activities, and ran candidates for office and the Model Cities Board. The ILBPP had these activities in common with many of the forty-plus Black Panther chapters. Nevertheless, the differences are significant. The unique qualities of the Illinois chapter are apparent in three aspects of the group's history in particular: its involvement in the protests of the 1968 Democratic National Convention, its relationship to the mainstream civil rights movement, and its treatment of gender issues.

Following Oakland's Lead

COMBATING POLICE BRUTALITY AND HARASSMENT

All Panther chapters shared a willingness to confront police brutality and harassment. The Party gained national attention via various displays of legal methods of self-defense against police violence waged upon the black community. The Chicago Panthers were no exception: they addressed both police brutality and racial profiling. Chicago police used fear to harass black Chicagoans and, more importantly, to control poor communities. Chicago police would often stop any car in an African American neighborhood that was two years old or older and force all of its occupants to exit it to be searched. If a driver committed a traffic violation, such as turning left and failing to signal, police officers did not necessarily have the authority to search the driver or the car's other occupants. Instead of recognizing the illegality of Chicago police tactics, however, the courts ignored them, indirectly reinforcing their use.[2]

Bobby Rush, the Illinois chapter's deputy minister of defense, responded to such police methods by announcing that the members of the BPP were the "protectors of the black community" and they intended to "deal with" police brutality.[3] Panthers believed that the police only understood the language of the gun. To eliminate the African American community's fear of police, Rush stated, "We plan to arm the total black community so when the pigs come down on us, we will be equal. . . . Black people have been on the defensive for all these years. The trend now is not to wait to be attacked. We advocate offensive violence against the power structure. . . . We are at war, and the Minister of Defense must be in charge."[4] In "peace" time, Chairman Fred Hampton was in charge. Hampton supported Rush's opposition to police brutality by promoting the Party as an organization of "revolutionaries dedicated in the overthrow of the brutal, racist American system." He argued, "The only way to deal with the system is to deal with the enforcers of the system. The pigs are the enforcers. They come into the black community and brutalize and victimize black people. We intend to put a stop to that kind of violence."[5]

SURVIVAL PROGRAMS

Confronting the police for self-defense was only one purpose of the BPP. The Party also implemented a number of "survival programs," or community service programs. Indeed, in 1971 tensions arose between Eldridge Cleaver, who headed the Panthers' International Section, and Huey Newton, the national chairman, over the direction of the Party. Cleaver favored military action against the U.S. government, and Newton wanted to centralize the Party's efforts around the group's community service programs. Newton expelled the entire International Section and the New York chapter, which caused the Party to split into two factions. The Chicago chapter sided with the national office, opting to deemphasize the military dimension of Black Panther activity and to focus primarily on the Party's survival programs, community organizations, coalition building, and electoral politics.[6] In his study of political repression, Robert Justin Goldstein argues that 1971 marked the end of the revolutionary character of the BPP: after that year, the Party focused mostly on its survival programs.[7]

The Panthers' survival programs included free breakfast for children, free medical research health clinics and the sickle-cell anemia campaign, free food, free busing to prisons, free daycare centers, free clothing, free ambulance service, and many other efforts. Illinois Panthers even established an emergency heat program to pressure landlords to ensure that furnaces and boilers were repaired and working properly during winter months.[8]

The Illinois chapter's most popular programs were its free breakfast for children and its free medical research health clinics and sickle-cell anemia campaign. There were five different breakfast programs on the West Side alone.[9] Barbara Sankey was the director of three sites.[10] The first site was established at the Better Boys Foundation on 1512 South Pulaski Road in 1969, and by May of that year there was also one site on the North Side and another on the South Side.[11] All the other sites were in community centers and black churches or white ethnic Catholic churches.[12] Donna Murch points out that in many cities where BPP chapters were established, "Panther community programs would have been impossible without the support of local churches."[13] This fact set the Illinois chapter's free breakfast program on a par with most other BPP chapters, unlike the Los Angeles chapter. For

ILBPP free breakfast program, male members serving children, Chicago, 1969
(Courtesy of Paul Sequeira)

instance, the Los Angeles chapter received support from the African American community for the breakfast program, but some churches in Los Angeles and Watts were reluctant to allow the Party to use their facilities because of police pressure. Los Angeles Panthers suggested that the black community demand that its churches "open their facilities for community use," since the churches were near the Central Avenue Panther office.[14]

Wanda Ross was another chief organizer of the Illinois Panthers' breakfast program. One of her daily duties consisted of soliciting money and food from residents, philanthropists, celebrities, and both local and corporate businesses. She recalls her involvement with the program:

> I joined the Party, and my first real responsibility was the breakfast program. . . . I didn't know the skills I had until I was in the situation to say, "Okay, we need to figure out a plan and we need to go out and solicit money from people who may not have a concept of what the Panthers are about." . . . The mid-level black people in corporations were the ones that we approached for donations to the breakfast program,

it's like, "Okay, you're the community person at A&P, what can you do? We're the community, we need this, we need that." . . . It was truly learning on the fly. . . . We got to the point that we were gettin' at least six hundred dollars a week in donations, which was a lot of money then. . . . Basically, on a daily basis, I was out in the street beggin' for money and food, purchasing food and supplies, and making sure all the breakfast sites had everything they needed.[15]

Panthers such as Wanda Ross represented the backbone of the Illinois chapter. It was little-known members like her whose efficient grassroots community organizing and management skills secured the sustainability and reputation of the chapter's much-utilized programs. As Panther Lynn French put it: "Being a Black Panther in the Black community was a position of respect. People . . . whether they agreed with us or not respected our commitment."[16]

Panther Yvonne King, a member of the Illinois chapter's Central Staff, describes the political purpose of the chapter's survival programs:

When we developed survival programs, service programs, programs to meet some of the basic needs of the black community, it was done not because we believed we could answer, we could meet all of the needs of black people. No. It was done more as an organizing vehicle. Our survival programs heightened the contradiction that existed between the black people and the government. When we were able to feed thousands, literally thousands of children every morning in various cities in the country, parents began to ask, why wasn't the government doing that? The government had all the resources at its disposal.[17]

Fred Hampton echoed King's sentiment: "A lot of people think it's charity what we do. It takes the people from a stage to another stage, to another stage. And any program is revolutionary if it's an advancing program; revolution is change, unending, they just keep on changing. That's what we do. We take the people in there and take them through those changes and before you know it, they are in fact not only knowing what socialism is, they did not know it, they are endorsing it and they are participating in it, they are observing and they are supporting socialism."[18] The ILBPP's free breakfast for children program fed more than 400 children each morning and served as an example to all other Panther chapters.[19]

The Chicago Panthers' Spurgeon "Jake" Winters People's Free Medical Care Center, located in the North Lawndale community on Sixteenth Street between Avers and Springfield, was established in January 1970.[20] One of its goals was to reverse the infant mortality rate in the black community, which was twice that of white Chicago.[21] Sending medical teams from door to door, the clinic served more than 2,000 black Chicagoans in its first two months.[22] Bobby Rush emphasized the chronic need for medical service in poor African American communities:

> In that area, where you have a high infant mortality rate, where you have lead poisoning, where you have inadequate medical service, we saw the basic needs for free medical service and we worked hard and worked over a long period of time to make that a reality. Now up till this day in the black community, you have doctors there who are more concerned with private wealth rather than public health. The concept behind the medical center is that we would take the profit out of the medical profession. Our medical center is a direct result of the basic need in the black community for free medical service.[23]

The ILBPP clinic was named after a fallen comrade, Jake Winters, who was killed on November 13, 1969, during a shootout with two Chicago policemen, who also died. The medical center stood above all other chapter clinics, including Oakland's, as it was able to address both chronic and less serious problems of patients. The staff of the Winters clinic "included obstetricians, gynecologists, pediatricians, and general practitioners."[24] Ronald "Doc" Satchel outlined how the clinic was able to meet the community's health needs and to be a more comprehensive resource for black patients: "We can have patients come through and see a doctor, actually gets through, get a test what have you, then they comes in and see the people's advocate. That's a community person, a person in power that acts like a liaison between the center here itself and the community. He asks them what kind of service they got here in the center, you know, any other criticism of the medical center itself. It's also to deal with problems outside, medical problems, you know. People's advocate also has a resource file. In this file we have teachers, sociologists, speech therapists, social workers."[25] In May 1971, the Winters Clinic became the first BPP medical center to conduct free sickle-cell testing: 600 children were examined in three days.[26] In addition, it held blood drives for Cook County Hospital (Chicago's only free hospital), which was frequented by much of the African American community.[27]

COALITION BUILDING

All BPP chapters engaged in coalition building. The Party made numerous efforts to create coalitions with nonblack groups. For example, the Brown

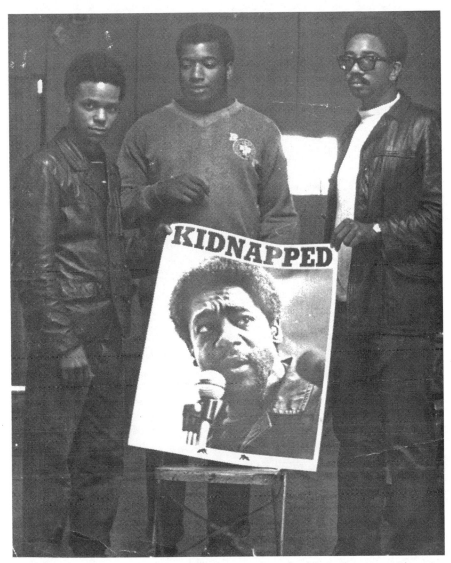

ILBPP members Ronald "Doc" Satchel, Fred Hampton, and Bobby Rush posing with poster indicating the group's opposition to the arrest of Bobby Seale during the Chicago Eight trial, 1969 (Courtesy of Paul Sequeira)

Caucus of the Peace and Freedom Party pledged its support for the BPP's efforts to end racism in America.[28] During a speaking engagement at Roosevelt University, Fred Hampton urged white students to become involved in the Party's political affairs by forging coalitions, sending donations, and becoming "a 1968 counterpart to John Brown."[29] The Illinois chapter's most rewarding coalition endeavor would be the establishment of the Rainbow Coalition.[30]

Each chapter also attempted to build coalitions and relationships with organizations that contrasted ideologically with the Party's platform. The SCLC's Operation Breadbasket in Chicago, headed by Jesse Jackson, was a group whose goals conflicted with Panther principles.[31] The Illinois Party, which was anticapitalist, considered Operation Breadbasket to be an example of the problems of a profit-driven America. When Jackson's group led a campaign to replace non-minority business owners in black neighborhoods with African American business proprietors, the Panthers viewed this process as merely replacing the (usually white) avaricious businessmen who exploited Chicago's black communities for profit with black faces whose goals mimicked those of their white predecessors. Nevertheless, Chicago Panthers understood the political and economic influence that Jesse Jackson had over the city and made attempts to build a coalition with his organization. The two political units worked in solidarity on several campaigns to address issues pertinent to the city's African American community. The most widely reported episode was their boycott of A&P stores and Rothschild's Liquor Company. Operation Breadbasket already had a successful national boycott in place against A&P stores.[32] Illinois Panthers decided to lead the charge in opposition to Rothschild's liquor stores. Drew Ferguson, deputy minister of finance, gave an interview about the strategy behind the Rothschild's boycott in which he accused the business of exploiting the black community for profit and failing to support black people in any way. He stated that the boycott had been 50 percent effective after only two weeks, and he recited five demands, all of which had to be met if the boycott were to end: Rothschild's had to hire a black vice president, whom the Panthers would screen and select; join the Black Westside Businessmen's Association; donate 20 percent of its total West Side income to the East Garfield Organization to be used to provide food for children; deposit the firm's gross income into black banks with a memorandum stating that potential black businessmen could borrow the money to start or expand businesses; and clean up, prevent loitering in, and physically refurbish the immediate neighborhood surrounding its stores.[33]

According to Ferguson, Rothschild's was targeted because liquor stores were the "biggest exploiters of black communities" and were one of the many evils from which black Chicagoans suffered—the worst of these being the police.[34] He stated that the liquor stores controlled the minds of many people in the black community. He asserted, moreover, that the company, which also cashed checks—welfare checks included—did so to prey on the poor, many of whom, he argued, were addicted to the products the company distributed.[35] Panthers were not participants on the picket lines, but they offered their presence at picket sites to protect protesters (assisted by Vice Lords) and to demonstrate solidarity with the community and demonstrators. Rothschild's was just one of many of the varying businesses, from drugstores to funeral homes, on the Panthers' list of enemies of the community.[36]

The Oakland Police Department told one *Chicago Tribune* reporter that the Panthers' recent activity in Chicago fit a pattern of organizing used by the Party throughout the Midwest and in some southern states. Oakland police indicated that Chicago Panthers had been trying to recruit the Black Stone Rangers, which was another method of coalition building. The Party wanted to politicize gangs, encouraging members to eliminate their negative and criminal activity and join the Panthers. This pattern was used, according to a writer for the *Chicago Tribune*, "in every city where [a] Panther chapter was established."[37]

A telling example of the Party's strategy in coalition building occurred when Eldridge Cleaver was hired to teach a course titled "Dehumanization and Regeneration in the American Social Order" at the University of California at Los Angeles (UCLA). Forging coalitions with students and academics was only one goal of Cleaver's course. It was also a conscious attempt to demonstrate that the BPP was not a violent group. The class served as a recruitment tool: it was a means to disseminate Panther propaganda, and it was an alternative way to exhibit the organization's genuine concern about conditions that plagued black America.[38] The Illinois Panthers did not teach classes on college campuses, but they did establish branches on most of the city's high school and college campuses and in the Illinois towns of Maywood, Argo, Rockford, Joliet, Peoria, and East Saint Louis for similar reasons.[39]

FUND-RAISING

Fund-raising was crucial to the BPP's maintenance and stability. Numerous celebrities and wealthy individuals held fund-raisers to financially support the Panthers. Donations were used to pay for community service programs and members' legal expenses. There was even an effort to produce a Panther film to raise money, and actor/political activist Ossie Davis was considered as a possible director. The Party believed Davis to be a perfect fit due to his political support for the group, as well as his artistic experience. He played a key role in raising funds to secure the freedom of arrested Party members.[40]

In Chicago, people of prominence were significant in the ILBPP's fund-raising operations. Radio disc jockeys and television personalities directly aided Chicago Panthers with bail money. According to one police report, when Fred Hampton was arrested in January 1969 outside Marina Towers Channel 32, his bond was set at $7,000. Channel 32 television panelist Howard Miller posted Hampton's bond. This same report indicates that Chicago Panthers had "big white people" behind them.[41] The officer claimed that Hampton let it slip that a downstate industrialist named Altofer, whom the policeman indicated had recently run against then-governor Richard Buell Ogilvie in the Republican primary, would give members of the ILBPP "all the money they needed."[42]

On trips to college campuses and other locations for speaking engagements and during participation in varying programs, Panthers usually asked for financial offerings. A white male college student who wrote an article for the *Champaign–Urbana Courier* stated that during one BPP campus event, the group asked those in attendance to contribute money to their organization. The author declared that he donated out of fear, clearly suggesting that the Panthers were intimidating and that he did not support the group.[43] Police observing an event held at the Church of the Holy Covenant on 925 West Diversey described it as a meeting consisting of a "revolutionary contingent."[44] The police documented that the Panthers used their time at the church as a fund-raiser and collected about $30.[45]

PUBLIC RELATIONS

Like their national counterparts in Oakland—who were constantly criticized by the mainstream media—Chicago Panthers were often scrutinized by the local press and depicted as a gang or a racist organization.[46] Oakland Party members usually responded to misrepresentations of the group with news conferences, appearances on talk radio shows, and commentaries in the group's newspaper, the *Black Panther*, or via their own radio broadcasts. Discussing Stokely Carmichael's visit to Cuba and Eldridge Cleaver's exile there, the Oakland Police Department reported that George Mason Murray, an English professor at San Francisco State College recently named minister of finance by the BPP, had just visited Cuba and made a series of tape recordings broadcast by Havana Radio outlining the Panthers' revolutionary ideology.[47]

The Illinois Party also used newsletters to respond to critics and appeared on popular Chicago television talk shows. In February 1969, the ILBPP released a newsletter to reply to comments made in the *Daily Defender* by a journalist who blamed the militant leadership of Eldridge Cleaver, H. Rap Brown, and Stokely Carmichael for Party members' exile and oppression. The newsletter was also a reaction to the Progressive Labor Party's criticism of Cleaver's statement in opposition to the contemporary political process, in which he suggested that voters should "piss in voting booths."[48]

The newsletter was written by Rufus "Chaka" Walls, deputy minister of information, and it argued that the aforementioned critiques were an insult to what he called the "black colony." Walls was also angry with the journalist for dubbing the BPP "a mere gang." He continued that the Party was a revolutionary organization and the only one with a program that did active work in the black colony toward black liberation. Walls declared that the Party was respected on every continent and was equated with groups like the Mau Mau, the Dirty Dozen, and the National Liberation Front, and none of these groups had been identified as "gangs." He lashed out at what he called attacks on the Panthers waged by "the pigs" and by those ignorant of the Party's survival programs. Walls called into question the *Daily Defender*'s position of scolding Panthers' efforts, lamenting that the newspaper had yet to defend anyone in the black community. According to Walls, exile and oppression were the result of black people not protecting their leaders. He addressed the Progressive Labor Party's comments with a declaration that the BPP "welcomes and combats criticism with truth and active work in the community toward alleviating the appalling conditions due to the effects of genocidal programs."[49]

In early January 1969, Fred Hampton, Rufus Walls, and Ruth Iris Shinn (the deputy minister of communications) appeared on the ABC-Channel 7 television program *For Blacks Only* to explain to viewers the Party's purpose and to attempt to refute previous misrepresentations of the group as a gang or a racist organization. Hampton spoke first, explaining the need to defeat the evils of capitalism and racism and to make drastic changes to the U.S. political system. When asked about his opinion on waging a nonviolent revolution, Hampton stated that he believed that there is no such thing as a nonviolent revolution, and thus the black man's dialogue had to be guns and weapons against the power structure—which he declared to be the only language the U.S. government understood. He asserted that the Party was trained in guerrilla warfare tactics and was ready to fight as needed, particularly in urban settings. Hampton also wanted Chicago residents to know that he was willing to give up his life to help others gain real equality through liberation. He stressed that the Panthers were not a military unit, though they supported revolutionary change; that he had some college education; and that he had adopted his political position after reading a lot.[50]

Rufus Walls weighed in next, defining the Party's intention in terms of its desire to stop the political structure from oppressing black people. When asked about how the group would respond if the majority of black America did not want a revolutionary transformation of the current political and economic systems, Walls simply stated that Mao Tse-Tung did not have majority support during the Chinese Revolution when it began, but today he controls China. Thus, he believed the BPP would control the hypothetical majority of blacks who may not at that time have recognized the benefits of revolutionary change. Ruth Iris Shinn declared that not only would women be active participants in the potential liberation struggle but that Panther women would also be ready to help with medical aid to injured members when needed.[51]

The same month, Hampton, Shinn, and Bobby Rush appeared on the television show *Chicago* (hosted by local white male television personality Ronnie Barrett) to reiterate a message similar to the one outlined above. Barrett almost apologized for having the Panthers on his show, but he wanted people to hear the Party's platform—even if he and his audience disagreed with the group. He was visibly shaken by the Chicago Panthers' dialogue, which led him to break for a commercial, and he attempted to end the segment prematurely before the commercial break. When the program resumed, however, the Panthers were still on the panel. They insisted on providing the public with more information about their platform and community service programs and were allowed to do so without confrontation. The three members proclaimed that the BPP was the "police for the black community" and warned that if representatives of the system continued to "abuse African American residents," Panthers would attempt to "locate such offenders and give them what they deserved."[52]

ELECTORAL POLITICS

The BPP was formed in 1966, one year after the passage of the Voting Rights Act, when there were fewer than 300 black elected officials in the United States.[53] Close to none of these officials were in the South, where more than half the nation's African Americans lived and where blacks made up the majority in many areas.[54] Oakland's political system—a white-dominated power structure—mirrored the South's political configuration, and the Panthers became convinced that they needed to address the issue of black political representation. Panthers concluded that the lack of black elected officials helped maintain a political system that was unresponsive, racist, and opposed to the interests of black people.[55] It took the Party six years to become engaged in electoral politics, with the goal of transforming the U.S. political agenda. In 1972, Huey Newton and Bobby Seale decided to dismantle all chapters and to concentrate the Panthers' resources in Oakland in order to centralize their power in that city's political arena. The Illinois and Winston-Salem chapters were the only exceptions, because of the strength of their community service programs and fund-raising capabilities. In 1972, both Bobby Seale and Elaine Brown ran competitive, though unsuccessful, races for political offices in Oakland. Seale placed second in the mayoral runoff election, while Brown failed to win a city council seat.[56] In Chicago, female Panthers Yvonne King, Lynn French, Ernestine Crossley, Pamela Jones, and Beverlina Powell campaigned for seats on the city's Model Cities Board, a federally funded community program.[57]

The Panthers in Daley's Chicago

DEMOCRATIC NATIONAL CONVENTION

The ILBPP had two central concerns that it emphasized over and above its community service programs. These issues were police brutality and political corruption—both of which the chapter believed were hallmarks of Mayor Richard J. Daley's Democratic machine. Via rallies and various speaking engagements, Chicago Panthers promoted their Party as a real opposing force to Daley's powerful political organization. In addition, the group opposed the war in Vietnam, in solidarity with other organizations. Panthers not only objected to the American conflict in Vietnam but passionately resisted African Americans' involvement in the military on the grounds that the U.S. government had historically taken positions that would lead to the destruction of African Americans. The Chicago Panthers insisted that black citizens should not be forced to serve in the military, which they believed was oppressing other colored people worldwide, and should not be compelled to represent a government that subjugated African Americans domestically.[58]

In 1968, various students, activists, and organizations converged on Chicago for the Democratic National Convention, primarily to protest the Vietnam War. Chicago Panthers anticipated that Mayor Daley would utilize the most efficient tool in what they regarded as an arsenal of political corruption: his command of police power. Daley would not allow civil disobedience—or what he may have considered to be lawlessness—to take place during the convention.

In preparation for the convention, Mayor Daley and the Chicago Police Department had begun to investigate groups outside the city that they considered to be either serious security threats or sources of potential political agitation during the event. The police department's Subversive Unit utilized confidential informants stationed in California to spy on the Panthers. One of these nonpolice agents, the wife of a Chicago Police Department patrolman, happened to live in California. The patrolman was scheduled to resign from the department to join his wife in California.[59] The patrolman's wife became a trusted companion of many Panthers in the Los Angeles area, and she relayed information to her husband that he then transferred to the proper authorities in his department. Her first report indicated that members of the California BPP planned to be in Chicago for the Democratic National Convention. She claimed that Party members had phony passports, intended to blow up undisclosed locations, and were to perform other acts of terror. She also stated that the group wanted to kill California governor Ronald Reagan.[60]

The Chicago patrolman's wife spent most of her time undercover working in Van Nuys, where she routinely spied on Million Donn and Ida Kinny of San Fernando—alleged organizers for the BPP. She provided Chicago police with several accounts that detailed the travel plans of Party members to the convention and information of a detailed discussion among both black and white activists who planned to move to Miami, Florida, to form an affiliate group there.[61] In a follow-up interview, the patrolman's wife declared that some Panthers and white leftists were traveling from California to Chicago for the convention in a car driven by Million Donn, and others would arrive courtesy of a small aircraft. She stated that members of the Revolutionary Action Movement, the BSR, and the Disciples were all affiliated with Panthers in Chicago.[62] She also made a list of strategies that Party members planned to use to undermine the Democratic National Convention. Party members, the informant claimed, would create incidents involving white police officers in black areas of the city to draw police officers away from the convention site, enabling the Yippies to demonstrate more effectively; would "initiate 'phony' police brutality complaints"; would lace delegates' food and drinks with LSD using BPP associates who worked in Chicago area hotels; would introduce LSD to the water system at the amphitheater where the convention was being held; would solicit delegates to pay for sexual services "and then embarrass the delegates with complaints"; and would "tie incendiary devices to bats," which would then "explode" when the bats landed, "creating numerous fires."[63] Her reports helped to heighten the alarm of Chicago police. More important, the information strengthened Mayor Daley's conviction that he needed to prohibit all demonstrations during the convention, which helps to explain his violent response to all protests.

There were several other non-law-enforcement participants who dissemi-nated information to the Chicago Police Department's Subversive Unit. One confidential informant (identified only as a white female) told Chicago in-vestigators that Mike James, a national officer for SDS, was in California to meet with Peggy Terry—who at the time was the vice presidential candi-date for the Peace and Freedom Party—and others to discuss demonstra-tion methods for the Democratic National Convention. This informant also provided investigators with Panther Eldridge Cleaver's entire schedule for his trip to Chicago on a speaking tour, including where he intended to sleep and the college campuses he was to visit.[64] Another confidential informant stated that the Party intended to bring guns into the city and hide them in pool rooms and clubs between Sixty-Third Street and Cottage Grove and be-tween Sixty-Third Street and Stony Island, in preparation for an anticipated riot during the convention.[65]

In early August 1968, the Subversive Unit conducted a series of interviews over a two-day period with a frequent patron of the Baroque Lounge, located on 1510 East Fifty-Third Street in the Hyde Park district of Chicago's South Side. The confidential informant reported that he had overheard a group of Panthers talking about the transport of arms and about training films. One of these films was the movie *Battle of Algiers*. According to the informant, the Panthers stated that the movie should be seen by all who planned to take part in disturbances at the Democratic National Convention and that recent incidents civil unrest in Gary, Indiana, and Cleveland, Ohio, were training sessions for actions to take place in Chicago. The report also claimed that Operation Breadbasket had funded the Party's plan of action, and Panthers used the money to purchase weapons.[66]

As a result of these testimonies, Mayor Daley and the police department took steps to defend the city and the convention from potential acts of vio-lence. Consequently, the 1968 Democratic National Convention in Chicago resulted in one of America's most notorious incidents of police brutality, as authorities responded to the largely peaceful protests of the gathered youth with overwhelming force. When comedian Dick Gregory, already engaged in a campaign against the Daley machine over open housing, attempted to lead a multiracial march for peace on Michigan Avenue from downtown Chicago to his home on Fifty-Fifth Street, for example, the police and National Guard were ordered by Daley not to let the protest march past Eighteenth Street, because the administration feared that if marchers were allowed to enter the heart of the city's Black Belt, the protesters might attract South Side residents to join the demonstration. City officials believed such an act could potentially increase the number of marchers to well over 100,000, and troops would not be able to control the protest rally.[67] The Black Stone Rangers were involved in the march as marshals to protect the participants.[68] Dick Gregory and delegates of the Democratic National Convention who joined the protest were arrested for attempting to walk past Eighteenth Street.[69]

Tensions increased and turned violent when Chicago police refused to allow any activists or groups near the main hotels or the convention hall. As the groups attempted to get closer to the convention site, police blocked their paths and ordered the demonstrators to retreat. Many of the activists and groups had come to Chicago ready for a violent clash with police, and officers, in turn, were prepared to defend the convention site if such a conflict erupted. As expected, confrontations ensued and lasted about four days. Determined to restore order, Daley unleashed his police force, and their brutality against both protesters and the media was captured on camera and broadcast internationally. The city pitted nearly 12,000 police officers, 7,500 army soldiers, 7,500 members of the Illinois National Guard, and 1,000 FBI and Secret Service agents against the demonstrators. When the convention was over, nearly 600 people had been arrested, and more than 119 policemen and 100 protesters had been injured.[70]

The majority of the wounded protesters were white middle-class youth. This phenomenon upset many white Americans, and the media set out to investigate what was widely regarded as an abuse of police power. Many black residents resented the media's concern for the white protesters who were brutalized by the police and National Guard during the convention. One unidentified Panther explained that black citizens were brutalized daily by police without prompting media concern, and only when white people suffered similar offenses did the media want to discuss police brutality and enlist black residents to help them. The Panthers adamantly declared that African Americans would defend themselves from police brutality. A female Illinois Panther and mother explained to one reporter while wielding a rifle that she was ready to die for liberation.[71]

In the aftermath, eight people were tried before a grand jury for conspiracy to provoke a disturbance. Dubbed the "Chicago Eight," they were charged with crossing state lines to incite a riot under the 1968 Civil Rights Act—the first people to be charged under this provision of the act.[72] Bobby Seale was the only African American co-conspirator on trial. He attempted to represent himself and exchanged verbal assaults with the judge. Consequently, he was gagged and chained to his chair on October 29, 1969, and he remained restrained during the trial until November 3. Seale's trial was severed from those of the other seven defendants on November 5. The judge declared a mistrial on the conspiracy charges and sentenced Seale to four years in prison for contempt—the longest sentence ever handed down for a contempt charge at that time—which Seale did not serve.[73]

The protests at the Democratic National Convention in 1968 were a unique national event that in many ways came to symbolize the problems of Daley's Chicago, highlighting the mayor's stranglehold on political protest, the brutality of the city's police force, and (though this did not come to light for many years) the city government's infiltration of protest groups. The Chicago Panthers—more so than their comrades from Oakland—were at the heart of the action. Although the Illinois Panthers' ultimate goal to end capitalism in America was in line with the national Party, their immediate and arguably more important objective was the dismantling of the Daley Democratic machine's control of Chicago residents. The Party's leadership of several protests at the convention demonstrated the credibility and influence that the Illinois Panthers had achieved as a result of their collecting youth activists in Chicago under the rubric of class solidarity to protest Daley's Democratic machine.

CIVIL RIGHTS AND THE BLACK PANTHER PARTY

Both Huey Newton and Stokely Carmichael agreed that neither communism nor socialism was appropriate for African Americans, because the two theories of government only tackled economic issues and did not solve America's race dilemma.[74] Scholar Nikhil Pal Singh points out that the Panthers believed racism kept blacks and whites from uniting in class struggle toward a socialist revolution. As a result, the Party defined "Black political subjectivity and a revolutionary sense of Black peoplehood" in the failure of the middle-class civil rights movement and working-class "Black nationalist schemes of separation."[75] Singh contends that the Panthers established a dual approach that blurred the two opposing spheres: one side emphasized "separation and Black difference" by localized "demands for communal autonomy," and the other side stressed "integration and equality" by a commitment to "solidarity with all victims of Americanization at home and around the world."[76] Singh asserts that the BPP argued that "Black Nationalism and Civil Rights each provided what were essentially 'bourgeois' answers to the properly 'revolutionary' needs of America's black poor."[77]

Though Singh is convincing in his assessment of the Party's ideology as a national organization, one identifying characteristic of the ILBPP was its continuance of the civil rights agenda in Chicago. Though the Chicago

Panthers followed Oakland's lead in promoting revolution as the only real approach to revamping the American establishment, they did not abandon their campaigns and connections to the city's civil rights struggle. As we have seen, many of the Illinois chapter members were highly involved in the Christian-led civil rights organizations before joining the Party, and they continued their involvement as Panthers. More important, civil rights community and religious groups offered their support and the use of their facilities to Panthers. St. Bartholomew's Church on Sixty-Eighth Street and Stewart and the Mennonite Church on Seventy-Third Street and Laflin Avenue, both on Chicago's South Side, were used as meeting places by the Illinois Party.[78] In addition, Rev. John Clinkscale of Lebanon Baptist Church at 1501 West Marquette allowed the Chicago Panthers to use his church for meetings. Cusboard James, a community organizer in the vicinity, reportedly worked with the Party at the church on coordinating demonstrations in the area.[79]

Various black and white Protestant and Catholic churches and civil rights organizations worked diligently with the Illinois chapter. Many of these representatives may have echoed the sentiments of author James Baldwin and Rev. John Eckels, both of whom consistently expressed support for Bobby Seale and the BPP, the black liberation movement, and a black revolution. Eckels stated, "Nat Turner was a preacher, and that's the kind of preacher I am. . . . Religion to me means freeing people's bodies and minds and souls."[80] Illinois Panthers did not hesitate to inform all who would listen that they were students of Rev. Dr. Martin Luther King Jr.'s nonviolent direct action and civil disobedience philosophy. Chicago Panthers' "ultimate goal," in Fred Hampton's view, was "to end racial and class oppression"; as historian Jon Rice points out, King had the same goal.[81] Hampton clearly explained that the BPP did not rely on or advocate hatred of white people and did not "define the enemy by his color but by his deed."[82] He noted that the Party did believe in the teachings of Dr. King but that it did not believe in "preaching nonviolence to the Ku Klux Klan."[83]

A police surveillance report of a speech by Fred Hampton at the Church of the Holy Covenant highlights why Panthers continued to support civil rights groups, and vice versa. Although the methods of the Panthers and civil rights groups often conflicted, both factions agreed on the importance of supporting the local working class and opposing Mayor Daley: "Don't talk of working within the structure, this is no fucking good. Don't talk of changing the white man's attitudes; this could go on for another 400 years," Hampton told his audience. "Black men having jobs is not the answer either," he continued.

"Martin Luther King had a job; he did more for the black man than anyone else when he was killed." Hampton noted, "We were brought to this country and we had jobs, but no freedom. Our fight is for liberation." And he attacked the Daley administration, calling Daley "the worst animal I have ever seen."[84]

Indeed, when the Illinois chapter emerged in November 1968, its members took the lead in Chicago's liberation movement. The Party coordinated with civil rights groups on community control matters. For example, the West Englewood Citizens Committee led by Clinkscale, Robert Lucas of CORE, and the ILBPP held meetings (at Lebanon Baptist Church) with the Seventh District police station's Commander Miles about putting an end to police brutality.[85] The Party was also committed to the black community's battle with the Chicago archdiocese over alleged racism in the Catholic Church—a little-known affiliation. Chicago Panthers played a key role in a dispute at St. Dorothy's Catholic Church and took part in the black holiday observance of the birthday of Martin Luther King Jr. St. Dorothy's case was led by a confederation of about fifteen black groups that confronted John Cardinal Cody over demands that black priests be named pastors of black parishes.[86]

According to members of the Chicago Police Department's Tactical Unit, Panthers participated in solidarity with several civil rights community groups in an act of nonviolent civil disobedience at St. James Church. The Concerned Black Catholics, Whites Concerned about the Black Community, and five members of the ILBPP conducted a black unity mass pray-in and other demonstrations to protest the reassignment of Father Rollins Lambert from St. James to St. Dorothy's parish as pastor. The Panthers stood in the back of the church while members of the other groups—which consisted of about fifty-six black and white women—sang songs and read prayers to disrupt the Sunday morning mass at St. James. One prayer was as follows:

After each invocation say—HEAR US LORD

That we as Black people may never stop striving for Our place in the sun.
That we might recognize Our blackness as a thing of pride and beauty.
That more of Our Black Brothers and Sisters might be brought into the One Black Fold.
That we might always have the courage to carry out OUR THING— whatever it may be.
That the Lord may strengthen Our faith in each other and love for one another.
That Archbishop Cody might soon come to understand OUR BLACK THING.

That Father Rollins Lambert might soon return to St. James as pastor.
That Father George Clements be brought back to St. Dorothy as pastor.
That ALL of Our Black priests might be put in leadership positions in
    Our Church.
That the churches in the Black community might be run by Black
    people.
That we might never have dissension among Our Black People.
That Rev. Dr. Martin Luther King Jr. might be recognized as a saint by
    all Black People.[87]

The officers reported that when some of those in attendance at the mass abruptly left and expressed their disgust at the acts of the demonstrators, the Panthers showed discipline, and there were no incidents or arrests.[88]

In their civil rights activism, then, the Illinois Panthers displayed a willingness to interpret their revolutionary agenda broadly, aiding Chicago's black communities in the struggle against white power structures of all kinds. While the image of leather-clad Panthers fighting on behalf of the parishioners of Catholic churches for their right to worship under the leadership of a favored pastor is one that does not square particularly well with our image of the Panthers as militant, revolutionary socialists, it makes sense in the context of the Illinois chapter, many of whose members cut their teeth as activists in the mainstream, Christian-influenced civil rights movement.

GENDER DYNAMICS AND THE ILLINOIS CHAPTER

When the BPP formed in 1966, women's liberation was considered an aberration by many "progressive" organizations. For African American women, the "double jeopardy" of racial and gender oppression was a problem that the black struggle for civil rights and self-determination did not necessarily address. Like most American men in the era, many male members of the BPP took an old-fashioned view of gender roles, especially during the organization's formative years (1966–69).

In large part due to the autobiographies of female icons such as Elaine Brown and Assata Shakur, who document their roles and experiences as women in the Party, gender inequality in the BPP is a subject of concern among academics who study the group.[89] As Robyn Spencer notes, "Scholarly analysis of the nuances of black women's experiences in Black Power organizations has remained limited. Black women have fallen through the analytical cracks of the frameworks scholars have used to analyze gender and

Black Power."[90] This section adds to other recent efforts to bring more relief to the complex and contradictory gender dynamics within the organization by comparing the Illinois chapter to its national headquarters in Oakland. The comparison is not an attempt to argue that the ILBPP was wholly less sexist than the national headquarters but, rather, posits that the macrocosm cannot truly be found in the microcosm; the local chapter experiences need to be separated from the shadow cast by the national headquarters, which fuels popular perceptions and fosters dominant discourse about the organization. A comparison between the BPP national headquarters in Oakland and the ILBPP reveals how the ILBPP wrestled unevenly, yet creatively, with gender politics in leadership, sex, and parenting roles.

Jeffrey O. G. Ogbar documents that some women Panthers argue that the experiences of female members of the Oakland chapter—who were at times subjected to sexism and subordination—"were not the norm for the country." Ogbar's interview of ILBPP member Akua Njeri (formerly Deborah Johnson), the significant other of slain leader Fred Hampton, indicates that she "did not feel marginalized as a Panther woman in Chicago." She states, "Men did not try to take advantage of sisters in our chapter. We had respect. Men and women both cleaned and cooked for the children. We also trained together. We were all Panthers."[91] Furthermore, Charles Jones posits that another local chapter, the People's Party II in Houston, Texas, was also committed "to the revolutionary principle of gender equality."[92]

While there were many women members of the ILBPP, only eight experiences are used in this examination. One obstacle to writing history about people who were members of iconic groups such as the BPP and are still alive is that many of them prefer to tell their own stories. Thus, to supplement the first-person interviews, primary sources such as lectures/presentations and interviews made available via documentaries are employed along with secondary sources that examine other local BPP chapters. An examination of recent edited works published on the BPP at the local level by scholars such as Judson Jeffries, Peniel Joseph, Yohuru Williams, and Jama Lazerow reveals the limited amount of scholarship that analyzes the Panthers' gender dynamics.[93] The few who explore the subject, a couple from the aforementioned edited works, are used in this study. Robyn Spencer's and Donna Murch's works on Oakland are also valuable sources.

Although Paul Alkebulan's work on women and the BPP is more recent, Tracye Matthews provides perhaps the most balanced and nuanced analysis of gender dynamics and the BPP.[94] Matthews argues that the gender ideology of the Party, both as it was formally stated and as it was exemplified by organizational practices, was played out in most aspects of Party activities and affected its ability to function as an effective political organization.[95] She contends that "black women were critical players in the BPP," but she also argues that women were not defined by Panther leadership as active and productive participants in the black liberation struggle; rather, men were deemed the primary actors and agents of change. Focusing on the most controversial leaders of the BPP's national headquarters, Matthews notes that Huey Newton's and Eldridge Cleaver's historical analyses of black women posited black females as co-conspirators in the castration process and as distant observers waiting for black men to become courageous enough to liberate them and their children; the formulations of both men asserted that black men were not real men unless they enforced patriarchy and male dominance in sexual and familial relationships. Matthews notes that both Newton and Cleaver ignored the historical legacy of black men and women who rejected gender hierarchies.[96] In addition, Matthews documents how the gender politics of both Cleaver and Newton progressively changed over time, as the "ideological development of Party members was an ongoing process."[97]

Matthews describes the Panthers' official policy regarding gender dynamics as complex, however. She notes that the Party provided women opportunities for political activism not typically present in other civil rights and black power groups.[98] Moreover, she argues that the "Party was in fact a very important place for challenging ideas, not just about women's roles but also men's roles . . . in trying to define a new revolutionary black man, a revolutionary black woman."[99] The BPP provided direction for other civil rights and black power organizations on how to make progress toward gender equality. According to Donna Murch, the organization advocated "new legislation to ban police brutality and discrimination based on gender and sexual orientation in jobs and housing, adoption and child custody, taxation, and inheritance laws."[100] It was one of few civil rights and black power groups that included women as equals, and many women joined the group primarily for this reason. As Robyn Spencer notes, the BPP's ideas and practices of gender evolved over the course of the group's early life as female membership increased and such members challenged the Panthers' gendered politics.[101] For instance, the Des Moines, Iowa, chapter and the New Haven, Connecticut, chapter were founded, organized, and led by women, with Mary Rem setting up the Des Moines branch and Ericka Huggins establishing the New Haven chapter. These leaders made aggressive attempts to institute and maintain gender equality and neutrality in their respective units and addressed women's issues in their communities.[102]

Ann Campbell, Communications Secretary, ILBPP, 1969 (Private archive of Howard Ann Kendrick [Campbell])

Research and interviews centered on the Illinois chapter echo Matthews's position and confirm Ogbar's argument that in at least some chapters, women's roles were more complex than a simple reading of Newton and Cleaver would suggest. Some ILBPP members contend that gender diversity was not a divisive issue in the Chicago branch because "women's liberation was not perceived as a problem in the Illinois Party."[103] The Illinois chapter gave women a prominent place as leaders—a place they did not have in Oakland. Women occupied a number of Central Staff positions, headed up committees and programs, and held other positions of responsibility.[104] "It was a place where women rose to leadership," contends Joan Gray. "We learned how to lead organizations, how to build institutions, how to take charge, how to negotiate. . . . We learned those skills there in the Party along with the men."[105] Within the first year after the group's inception, there was a woman section leader, a woman field secretary, and a woman on the security staff. Barbara Sankey was the director of three free breakfast program facilities. Ann Campbell held a seat on the Central Staff as communications secretary. Yvonne King was a member of the Central Staff as deputy minister of labor, and she

Christina "Chuckles" May, Deputy Minister of Culture, ILBPP, 1968 (Private archive of Howard Ann Kendrick [Campbell])

was also a field secretary, owing to her talent as a community organizer.[106] Field secretary was an important position, as these members were sent out to some of the Illinois state branches and were often given directives from national headquarters to go address an issue in another chapter in the Midwest. Several women (among them Joan Gray) filled these assignments.[107]

Yvonne King notes that women worked on the free busing to prisons program and held leadership positions similar to those of their male comrades. She contends that all members in the Illinois chapter seriously enforced the Party's position that women's roles in the organization were the same as men's roles: "We were fortunate that many of the brothers who were in leadership in the central staff, particularly Fred, . . . really encouraged the sisters. Michael [McCarty] mentioned . . . how Fred could make you believe you could walk through a wall and get to the other side. That's how he made us feel, and it helped us to develop not only as women, but as people within the chapter, but he particularly encouraged women to speak, to represent, to take on responsibility, and we were held accountable."[108] Ahmad Rahmad, once a member of the Illinois chapter, mentioned that it was where he "first took orders from a woman who wasn't [his] mother."[109]

The BPP's ten-point platform and survival programs "outlined the Party's plan to make sweeping changes in police brutality, housing, employment, education, and other institutions that had a negative impact on the black community. While the government and media focused their public attention on the Party's initial insistence on the right to bear arms, Party members focused their attention on the ten-point platform and program, and much of that responsibility was taken on by women."[110] Moreover, Donna Murch notes that by 1969, "women made up the majority of the rank and file, and their influence was clearly visible in the Party's survival and political education efforts."[111]

Lynn French, one of the Illinois chapter's more prominent members, emphasizes the extent to which women took on substantive roles in the ILBPP: "There are an awful lot of women who are unsung heroes in the Party, and although the mental image that many people have is of a defiant young black male with a leather jacket and a beret and his fist raised, they should remember that there were a whole lot of sisters out there struggling too. And committing heroic acts every day."[112] Many of the women who joined the Party brought organizing and educational experience to the group, as many women members came from "middle-class families or had attended college" prior to joining the Panthers. "In fact, an internal skills survey conducted in 1973 revealed higher rates of college attendance among female Party members in comparison to their male counterparts."[113] Much of the Illinois chapter's success and sustainability was due to the work and leadership of its female members.[114]

Joan Kelley-Williams served in the Los Angeles, Berkeley, and Oakland chapters for ten years. She joined the Party because it was the only group at the time that made a real attempt to address gender equality:

Probably for me the thing that differentiated the Black Panther Party from any other organization was . . . that women were seen as equals when I first got involved with the Party. There were other organizations, black organizations at the time that for the most part had women walking two steps behind, whether it was in African garb or in traditional garb, it didn't matter. Women really weren't even remotely considered to be peers or policy makers in the organization and that just did not appeal to me, because tomboy at heart that I was, that and thinking I was as smart as any other man, was not going to make any organization appeal to me.[115]

Yvonne King also argues that the Party was revolutionary as it was one of the few male-dominated organizations that addressed women's issues.

This was the 1960s and 1970s, and even in progressive organizations women were . . . [relegated] to stereotypical roles. . . . And here was [the BPP] that not only provided the opportunity [for women as leaders] . . . but it was a policy. . . . Men and women were treated the same and I believed it and asserted myself as such. And many of the women did and we challenged the sexism, maybe not overtly, but through our belief in the Party's policy and its principle. . . . Part of the Party's legacy has to be that it provided that opportunity and women took that opportunity and it showed through our commitment, hard work, and our love for the Party and the people. . . . And we held up the men because they believed in the goals.[116]

Many male Chicago Panthers made a conscious effort to prevent and eradicate sexism and all forms of gender inequality within the organization. Some women members believe that the Chicago chapter did better than other branches at trying to address the gender issue.[117] More important, like some women in other chapters, female ILBPP members did not allow their male comrades to disrespect women or practice gender discrimination. Lynn French, for example, claimed that she was not required to be subordinate to men in the Illinois chapter, nor was there any sexual harassment. "Not in Chicago," she said. "We [women] would not accept it."[118]

As Matthews has documented, despite the organization's efforts to level the gender playing field, there is evidence that the Party was inconsistent in its gender dynamics. For instance, the Party posted ads in the *Black Panther* to acquire assistance with the publication. One advertisement at the bottom of a page reads, "Jive Sisters—Don't read this . . . The Black Panthers need typists!"[119] The ad suggests the presence of gender conflicts over women's roles in the Party. Furthermore, Brenda Harris recounts how male members of the Illinois chapter's rank and file often made comments to female members that were offensive. She recalls that some female members were called "prostitutes" or comments were made about "their big booties";

she was once called a "banana face bitch," and sometimes a woman faced the danger of being "sexually exploited if she didn't have the wherewithal to stand up for herself." Harris continues: "If you were a woman . . . it depended upon your position in the Party how you were treated." She contends that women in leadership positions or "women who were in relationships with the leadership" were not subjected to such treatment. Moreover, the Illinois chapter's leadership "was very enlightened" and made attempts to prevent such occurrences or to punish those who mistreated their comrades, and they even challenged the sexism of the national leadership. Recounting one visit by a BPP minister from national headquarters who spent the night with the Chicago group, Harris remembers that "he was looking for some [female members]" to have sex with him. The Illinois leadership made it clear to him that "we didn't have to go with him" and that the minister would respect the women in the Illinois chapter. Harris recalls, "Since we lived in a sexist society individuals were sexist," and while the Illinois chapter "was not perfect," it advocated a gender policy that was "anti-sexist and progressive."[120]

Even Fred Hampton, who demanded that female members be regarded as equals by their male comrades, struggled to be consistent in his attitude regarding gender. Hampton stated that washing dishes and sweeping floors was "women's work," although men should learn to do this kind of work in case they had to take on these jobs someday. On the other hand, Hampton also stated that women played an important part in the Panther movement, in that they were required to do "the same things" that male members did.[121]

In the face of inquiries about sexism and negative gender politics in their organization, Illinois Panthers have insisted emphatically that the problem was minimal in the Illinois chapter. Yvonne King stated that sexism was present, but as far as she was concerned, it was not a real problem: "Male chauvinism was an issue. . . . But it . . . didn't have center stage. We recognized male chauvinism, but our primary concern, particularly in the Illinois chapter, was the chain of command. It wasn't so much who was giving the order, but whether or not that person had the authority to give the order."[122] Hank Gaddis insisted that women, including King, were treated equally: "Let me say that women of the Party served, and there was no gender distinction as far as [King's] role on the central staff. She ate, drank, bathed, and very seldomly slept. I mean, she did not work any less than Fred or any other functioning member, and as far as [King's] role in a leadership position, there was no gender distinction."[123]

King related similar sentiments with regard to her male comrades:

As comrades, we lived communally. At least . . . during the time that I was a member of the Party from 1969 through 1974, most of our members lived communally. So you know we worked together, we lived together, we loved together, and we struggled together, we suffered together. You know, some of us were underground together, in prisons together. . . . There were difficulties because of levels of consciousness, because of power relationships, some people abused their positions. But overall the comradeship in the Black Panther Party was very special. A sincere one.[124]

Most Chicago Panthers maintain that sexism was not an issue in their chapter because they made every effort to terminate individuals who refused to adhere to their policy of gender equality. Former Illinois chapter member Joan Gray remembers that Fred Hampton conducted a "big meeting" to address sexism and misogyny in the chapter. "Don't no woman have to do nothing she don't want to do," Gray recalls Fred Hampton saying in an angry rant. Hampton stated, "You lazy ass punks, you couldn't get no pussy on your own so you gonna try to force somebody to have sex with you? . . . This is not gonna happen here." According to Gray, Hampton "wasn't tolerating any kind of abuse, period, inside of the Party. He was very clear about that and anybody [who violated this policy] was dealt with by Fred, Rush, and the others."[125] Gray recounts how the leadership in the ILBPP responded after an incident regarding the mistreatment of female members by male members took place. "The energy that was prevalent in some [other chapters] I have to say was not the rule [in the Illinois chapter]. When Fred [Hampton] and Bobby Rush found out [they commanded those men to line up] . . . and [the women] had sticks and we would go down the line and pop 'em upside the head or on the butt. But [gender discrimination/sexism] was acknowledged and dealt with."[126]

The Illinois chapter not only regulated sexism; it also investigated the concern in other chapters in the Midwest. Hank Gaddis recalled an episode when he and other field marshals expelled an entire chapter in Milwaukee for violating Panther principles on gender dynamics:

The Milwaukee Chapter had become blatant with renegade ideas, and so we were sent up there to assess the situation and take the appropriate actions. So we went up: Bob [Lee] and I went up to Milwaukee and we got there and we found that the leadership had declined into a group of male chauvinists that had basically put the sisters there into the role of indentured sex slaves and just rampant male chauvinism. Basically the sisters' duties were to service the male leadership of the Chapter, and so we purged all those motherfuckers—all the males. We called them in . . . and we talked to them and heard what they had to say, and then we told them, "Hey, we've been authorized to purge all of ya'll. You're purged, and then you're gonna have to establish yourself to demonstrate that you're worthy of representing an organization called the Black Panther Party." And then what we did was, we put the sisters in charge, made them the leadership, and so Milwaukee began to reconstitute itself.[127]

While the Illinois Panthers' attempts, recalled in this anecdote and other quotations above, to level the playing field for women and to stamp out sexual harassment and exploitation was laudable, Panthers' reflections underline a degree of hypermasculinity in the Party that the speakers fail to acknowledge as indicative of gender inequality. Female Panthers' explanations for why they departed the Illinois chapter provide significant evidence to illustrate this point.

Most women who left the Illinois chapter declare that they did not sever ties as a result of sexism or gender discrimination but, rather, because of the direction of the organization and its leadership after Hampton's assassination, and to pursue individual goals.[128] However, some women left the chapter because of the way they were treated as mothers. The Party as a national entity represented a real community, as many members both male and female lived communally. Panthers adopted collective parenting and cared for one another's children as they carried out their everyday required tasks. In Oakland, the unit established the opportunity for "women to be mothers and active political organizers." Robyn Spencer documents that a memo addressed to the leadership in Oakland, "dated August 16, 1972, brought up the need for a dialogue on planned parenthood within the party, policies for expectant mothers, [and] the creation of an infirmary" to ensure that female members could be mothers and revolutionaries.[129] Such a policy was later established in the ILBPP by Lynn French and other female members during the latter years of the group, and the directive was influenced by Lynn French and fellow female ILBPP members who later relocated to Oakland.

Since policies recognizing parenthood were not adopted in Chicago until 1972, many women in the ILBPP resented the fact that their membership conflicted with their duty as mothers. Joan McCarty recounts she could not "raise her child and still be a Party member." She continues: "[The Illinois] chapter did not have daycare" or a "mechanism" in place "like a school like Oakland" for mothers in the Party. Moreover, "there was the issue of safety.

I [was willing] to put my life on the line [for the Party] but I [would] not put my child [in harm's way]. . . . There was always a chance of a raid."[130] Akua Njeri left the ILBPP in 1971 because "there was no structure set up to work within the Party" and care for her child while being a full-time member:

> A lot of things that didn't happen or did happen spoke to the people's inability to deal with being a parent in the context of the revolutionary struggle. A number of people left the Party. . . . It was just really difficult for me to survive with a child without abdicating the responsibility of his growth and development to my mother, and I didn't think it was her full responsibility to take care of him while I continued to do Party work. I did, honestly, . . . continue to try to work for the breakfast program, sell 200 newspapers and so on, but I didn't spend the time that needed to be spent with my son.[131]

Lynn French was one of many Panther women who had to care for her child while she was engaged in her duties for the Party. She recounts that her young daughter was just as immersed in the organization as the members themselves were:

> My daughter's first words weren't "Mama" or "Dada," it was "Power Peop." She would raise her arm up and go "Power Peop," because we had a free breakfast program in Berkeley where we were living at the Berkeley branch, and she would like to eat with the children. She was just about seven or eight months old and she would get around in the walker and we'd give her scrambled eggs on the tray to the walker and she would try to feed herself. We looked up one morning and she was at the front door as the children were leaving. They would all go "Power to the People," and she was at the front door going "Power Peop," "Power Peop."[132]

These reflections provide evidence of gender discrimination, even though the former members do not necessarily identify this aspect as such. Nurturing and parenting have traditionally been categorized as "women's work" by society at large, and motherhood did not fit with the hypermasculine conceptions of "revolutionary work" that dominated Panther ideology.

Kathleen Cleaver documents that after Huey Newton's murder charges were dismissed in January 1972, the BPP had transitioned into a "reformist community action group" from the revolutionary vanguard of the people.[133] She states, "Newton announced that the Panthers had been wrong to attack police, that they would return to church, participate in electoral politics, support black capitalist ventures, and work within the system."[134] Shortly thereafter, Oakland demanded that all chapters be disbanded and each affiliate's two most highly regarded members be sent to Oakland to work for the electoral campaigns of Bobby Seale and Elaine Brown. Donna Murch points out that one intention of this "large-scale internal reorganization" was to "divert resources and (wo)manpower to the national headquarters in the East Bay."[135] Lynn French and Yvonne King were two of a number of female Illinois Panthers relocated to Oakland. The move caused several female Panthers to depart from the organization because of what they believed to be the Party's lack of respect for their motherhood. French remembers:

> I guess it was late spring of '71, late spring, early summer when my daughter was an infant. A call came out from the Central Committee that each chapter was to send two loyal Party members out there for a meeting. . . . And I was told that we would be leaving on a Friday evening and returning by Sunday evening and there was no need to take my daughter, Tanya, with me because there was no point in putting her through all of that. So I left her with some very supportive people who lived in public housing behind our office. And I had been there maybe six hours when June Hilliard informed me that I was a permanent resident of the Bay Area and would not be retuning to Chicago. That caught me a little off guard, especially with my child being in Chicago, and it took me probably about six weeks to get her. I got her because Ericka Huggins was going back east to pick up her child and she stopped and as a surprise, she just rang the doorbell one night, and had Tanya in her arms and had brought her back to me.[136]

For French, the separation from her infant daughter as a result of her dedication to the struggle for African American liberation on behalf of the Party was too much to bear. She was not alone in this view. Akua Njeri, Joan McCarty, and other female Illinois Panthers attribute their departure from the Party to the fact that as long as the women were Party members, their children really did not belong to them.

Despite conscientious efforts of both male and female members to eliminate gender discrimination, then, the Illinois chapter, like the BPP as a whole, perpetuated a certain type of discriminatory behavior. This behavior, along with the demands of membership—and the continuous police harassment that caused many Panthers to constantly fear for their lives—drove some women out of the Party. Lynn French stated that some of these concerns are what led to her eventual departure:

> I left the Party through a process; it wasn't just an overnight snap decision. The first link in the chain was way back in 1971 when I was sent to California without my child. And that was something that always stayed in the back of my mind, that we were under the control of someone who wouldn't take a relationship between a mother and a child seriously. Another major factor in that process was that we had accumulated an amazing amount of support, both financial and community-based in Chicago, and it was tapped continuously. Just greater and greater demands of what we were to send to California, and that got to be too frustrating and too much, it was just beyond what I could handle. We also had really been eaten up, I believe, in retrospect, by the fear as a result of Fred being murdered. There was always a paranoia of who you could trust, who you couldn't trust, being followed all the time. When I was pregnant with my child, she was born a month after the due date the doctors had given me, and it had gotten to the point there was an undercover policeman coming up to me on the street saying, "You haven't had that baby yet." It was just a mind game they were playing with us, and the pressure was incredible. My parents gave me a very graceful out, because they had to take a trip and my mother called and asked would I come take care of the kids for a couple of weeks while they went away on business. And I complied, and it made it easier for me to just not come back.[137]

The Illinois Panthers were relatively more consistent than their national counterparts in implementing real gender equality and placing female comrades in positions of power and influence, albeit with the aforementioned limitations. The narratives of ILBPP women, especially those who went from Chicago to Oakland on orders from national headquarters, outline the differences between the two units regarding gender dynamics. Robyn Spencer and Donna Murch provide examples of the influx of women members and their influence on the evolution of the BPP policy and ideology regarding gender issues. However, in Chicago, the experiences of female members exhibit that men who violated the Party's policy on gender equality were swiftly reprimanded, women were agents of change and enforcement of Party policy, and women held key and influential positions in terms of both leadership and the rank and file, as women were the backbone of the chapter. Moreover, female ILBPP members sought to negotiate their roles as both revolutionaries and mothers in direct response to the Party's overall gender dynamics.

The average age of ILBPP members was between eighteen and twenty-four years, as most chapter members were either high school or college students. Records of actual membership to determine the ratio of men to women are nonexistent for a number of reasons. Records were destroyed; there were three raids conducted by Chicago police and the FBI on the chapter's headquarters in 1969, and in one raid the police set fire to the office. Another reason is that the ILBPP did not advertise its membership. Despite these factors, one can draw the conclusion that the ILBPP was not prepared to deal with its members' responsibilities as parents, and these youthful members may not have anticipated child care as part of the revolutionary struggle. After all, the ILBPP women in this study became mothers while members of the chapter. Nevertheless, considering the youth of the chapter's membership, the members realized a fairly high level of gender equality in their Panther chapter.

Conclusion

Each BPP chapter centered its ideology on the Party's political platform and community service programs. Nevertheless, state and city chapters of the Panthers differed significantly from the national headquarters, which used local issues in Oakland to direct its state and city affiliates. None of the forty-plus chapters and branches had representation on the Central Committee to address their interests. For example, the New York chapter emphasized race and worked with cultural nationalists to fight for class issues concerning housing and drugs, while the national BPP focused on free breakfast, clothing, and health care, which were pertinent to Oakland's poor black communities but also had resonance in other urban American centers. The Illinois chapter was concerned chiefly with police brutality, political corruption, and exploitation by the Daley Democratic machine.[138] Despite their similarities with Oakland, the Illinois Panthers differed in key respects: in their experiences with the Democratic National Convention, which was held in Chicago shortly after the Party's inception; in their revolutionary platform, which grew out of their recruitment of civil rights grassroots community organizers and college students; and finally, in their sincere efforts to incorporate and maintain gender equality among their membership by placing women in real positions of power and responsibility.

There was another way in which the Illinois chapter stood out, moreover: it built a number of alliances with other organizations to form the Rainbow Coalition, its most lasting contribution to Chicago and national politics. The next chapter examines this development.

Ever since the pigs found out that we in the Young Patriots of Uptown are a part of the *rainbow coalition* with the Black Panthers and the Young Lords, they been worried as hell. When we wear our gold Young Patriots berets we're continually harassed by the cops in the neighborhood. The cops have threatened people in our neighborhood that if they join us they'll get the shit beat out of them. Plain clothes pigs are always watching our office on Wilson Ave., trying to discourage new guys from coming around and talking with us.... We stick together to protect ourselves, and we stand beside all other political organizations and gangs who stand for the people and are against attacks by the police.

—"Stone Grease Grapevine," *Rising Up Angry,* 1, no. 1 (July 1969)

FOUR

The Original Rainbow Coalition

One year after the violent confrontations at the 1968 Democratic National Convention in Chicago, Fred Hampton and the Illinois Panthers, along with several white leftist groups, held a rally to protest the trial of the Chicago Eight, who were charged with conspiracy after the incident, and to express support for their defense. The gathering took place in Grant Park near Michigan Avenue and consisted of speeches and workshops. In addition to its stated purpose, the rally also represented an effort to demonstrate to the Daley administration that the city's leftist groups maintained strong racial coalition ties. Rennie Davis, one of the Chicago Eight, spoke at the event, informing Daley that "the battle for Chicago continues today."[1] Fred Hampton, who had recently been released from prison after having his sentence reduced to four months (for allegedly robbing a Good Humor ice cream truck and distributing the goodies to children in the community), was introduced by Sylvia Kushner, a middle-aged woman who was the secretary of the Chicago Peace

Council. Her presence alongside Hampton illustrated that Illinois Panthers' coalition building was not limited to the youth.[2]

In 1968, the Illinois Panthers took steps to extend such efforts by creating the Rainbow Coalition, "a political coalition that respected ethnic communities of all kinds" that was "led by poor, black youth." It later became famous when Harold Washington used it as a base for his successful bid for mayor of Chicago in 1983.[3] The key factors that bonded the racial coalition were opposition to the Daley Democratic machine's perceived political corruption, police brutality, urban renewal, and gentrification. In its efforts to restore financial glory to Uptown and Lincoln Park and along the Gold Coast, Mayor Daley's administration exhausted every method to displace the people who called these areas home—people who identified themselves as "pig farmers and Indians off the reservation."[4] The Rainbow Coalition opposed Daley's destructive urban renewal programs and the police brutality that so often plagued Chicago's poor neighborhoods by making efforts to eradicate political divisiveness centered in racism, to teach communities how to empower themselves via grassroots organizing, and to develop a classless society.[5] The organization was autonomous, as the groups consulted and exchanged ideas and information.

The long history of political activism and coalition politics in Chicago notwithstanding, the Rainbow Coalition was the first of its kind, not only because it was established and led by teenagers and young people but also because poor ethnic groups led by (indeed, for the first time *including*) African Americans organized as one entity to fight for political power that was denied to them all and to significantly reduce the rigid racial and ethnic tension between these groups, which had persisted since the nineteenth century. Chicago in the 1960s was one of the most racially, residentially, and politically segregated cities in America. Cross-class unity was nonexistent, and both de jure and de facto racism were common. Racial tensions were at an all-time high in Chicago at the time that the Rainbow Coalition was created. There were at least three major race riots between 1965 and 1968.[6] Chicago's African American student movement to desegregate public schools and Dr. Martin Luther King Jr.'s efforts to desegregate housing in the city also offer vivid examples of violent racial explosions. Despite the racial tensions looming over Chicago residents, the ILBPP and its Rainbow Coalition were able to persuade many of the city's youth to become a united political force regardless of race, class, age, sex, religion, fraternal, political, or any other affiliations. The ILBPP's leadership role in racial coalition building was crucial to the Illinois chapter's success. Furthermore, the coming together of these young people—many of whom had been little more than street gangsters before the Panthers—to advocate as one political entity made the Democratic machine tremble, prompting a police response of greater repression and surveillance, as the quotation that opens this chapter suggests.

The Origins of the Rainbow Coalition

Fred Hampton was the face of the Rainbow Coalition, and Robert E. Lee III—known as Bob Lee—served as the legman of the organization. Hampton gave speeches and sat for interviews on behalf of the Rainbow Coalition, but Bob Lee was the mover and shaker of the group.[7] Lee was out in the street politicizing North Side groups and introducing them to the BPP.[8] Bob Lee had moved from Houston, Texas, to Chicago in 1968 as a VISTA (Volunteers in Service to America) volunteer stationed at the Isham YMCA. He was the recreation leader of the facility during the day and a counselor at night. Lee worked exclusively with gang members in the area, who were African Americans, Puerto Ricans, and southern whites. After the assassination of Rev. Martin Luther King Jr. in 1968, Lee joined the ILBPP for the purpose of conducting community organizing. He acquired effective grassroots organizing skills by observing activists in his mother's nightclub, the activism of his father, and the labor struggles of the Longshoreman's Union that was directly across the street from his home. Lee declares, "I was raised around organizing. Any nightclub in the South during segregation; all the conversations that I listened to in the club were [organizing] work. So I had an instinct by being raised in [an organizing] world. . . . So when I met Fred [Hampton] and told him about my organizing on the North Side, he told me to continue the work and report only to him."[9] Because of Lee's familiarity with and experience as an organizer of white youth on Chicago's North Side, Hampton appointed Lee as field secretary and section leader for the area.[10] The North Side was comprised mostly of segregated, nonblack neighborhoods.

Illinois Panthers Bob Lee, Hank "Poison" Gaddis, Jerry Dunnigan, and Ruby Smith were already organizing in Uptown with the Young Patriots (YPO), unbeknownst to Hampton and other Illinois Panther leadership. After Lee informed Hampton of their activities, the two men met on the roof of the Panthers' headquarters alone to thwart police surveillance. Bob Lee remembers: "[Fred Hampton and I] believed that solidarity in Chicago was stronger than anywhere else. We knew [our organization] would not last long, and we knew that we had to move fast. We didn't fool ourselves. . . . There was a mystique in the Party about my cadre because no one knew what [Poison and I] were doing. I only dialogued with Fred [Hampton]."[11] Like Lee, Hampton also had an extensive background working in coalition with both ideologically similar and different organizations and activists.[12] After Hampton was informed of Lee's successful racial coalition building with white ethnics on Chicago's North Side, he introduced the idea to the public, and the Party set out to establish linkages throughout the city—and later the nation.[13]

It was Hampton who coined the term "Rainbow Coalition." In Chicago, the name became the code word for class struggle.[14] "Fred Hampton introduced class struggle," declares Bob Lee, "[via] rallies and his speeches that set up the ideology in which I was able to apply."[15] The ILBPP met and attempted to build alliances with five youth groups from different racial, ethnic, and class backgrounds. These included the BSR, a South Side gang that developed a social consciousness; SDS, a revolutionary, politically organized group of white college students; the Young Lords, a socially conscious Puerto Rican gang; the YPO, a gang of Appalachian white migrants; and Rising Up Angry (RUA), a club of young greasers from Logan Square.[16]

Even though Illinois Panthers led the Rainbow Coalition, there was no official head of the group. The organization was structured as a partnership in a united front. The leaders and members of the ILBPP, the YPO, the Young Lords, and RUA conducted meetings periodically to maintain lines of communication, to discuss critical issues, and to assist one another's community campaigns as joint political activities.[17] The YPO, the Young Lords, and RUA accepted the leadership of the Panthers; however, the groups were clear that their role was not to organize in the black community but in their own, to heighten the contradictions there, and to educate their own people. This focus made the Rainbow Coalition very effective.[18] The three groups also mirrored the community service programs that the BPP had established. These were surprising achievements for such a young and diverse group of activists. As Gaddis put it, "[Regarding] the Rainbow Coalition and some of the other tremendous things that we were doing . . . the thing that people may lose sight of, is that we were sixteen, seventeen, eighteen, nineteen-year-olds, not steeped in tradition of any organizational structure and discipline, but we had a rudimentary knowledge of that. We were fortunate enough to have charismatic, visionary people at the top."[19]

The members of the BPP brought to the formation of this interracial coalition their experiences organizing a group that was itself an intraracial coalition whose members were from various backgrounds within the black community: the middle class, the poor, college students and graduates, ex-convicts, war veterans, and reformed gang members.[20] Indeed, Fred Hampton and Bob Lee organized the Rainbow Coalition to model "the anti-racist direction in which the organization sought to move."[21] Some of the groups that joined were gangs before they were approached by Chicago Panther field secretaries. The Party believed that gang members made good potential community organizers because the gangs were made up of disaffected youth from poor neighborhoods in transition as a result of urban renewal.[22] What these youth required, Chicago Panthers believed, was guidance toward politicization as a response to the plight of their communities. Thus, Panthers made numerous attempts to politicize Chicago area gangs by appealing to what all of the gangs had in common with the Panthers: opposition to the Daley machine's urban renewal policies, which were destroying the neighborhoods in which the gang members lived, and to the police brutality and mistreatment that was common in these neighborhoods. These efforts were remarkably successful, leading to both formal organizational affiliation through the Rainbow Coalition and unofficial alliances between the Panthers and the Conservative Vice Lords and Disciples.[23]

The Rainbow Coalition came out of the North Side of Chicago. Initially, it was set up via an alliance with the YPO as a result of Bob Lee's interactions with the group.[24] Fred Hampton then enticed José "Cha Cha" Jiménez and the Young Lords to join the organization. Shortly thereafter, RUA came into the fold.[25] The rainbow became the symbol of the group because it epitomized the unity of different colors, which was the message the organization wanted to convey.

JOIN (Jobs Or Income Now) Community Union member Charles Geary, an ex-Pentecostal minister from Horse Branch, Kentucky, designed the buttons worn by affiliates of the group. The Uptown community organization used discarded buttons from the Nixon/Agnew campaign and painted them red for the indigenous folk, brown for those of Latino heritage, black for black people, yellow for people of Asian heritage, and white for working-class hillbillies from Kentucky, West Virginia and other parts of Appalachia.[26] Howard

Original Rainbow Coalition Locations

Alk of the Film Group brought Panthers Fred Hampton and Bob Lee, members of the YPO and Young Lords, and other activists together for an advance screening of the company's documentary, *American Revolution II.* At this screening, Geary passed out the Rainbow Coalition buttons he had created. From that day forward, Fred Hampton referred to the organizations' alliance as the Rainbow Coalition.[27]

The Rainbow Coalition sent representatives to almost every Chicago community. Race was not a deterrent to choosing which neighborhoods to approach. It targeted the Chicano or Mexican community, the Puerto Rican community, the black community, and the poor and working-class white ethnic community. The organization usually focused on working with young people. Members went to the parks and hung out in bars and pool halls to spread the gospel of social change and justice. Many people who were members of street gangs became politically conscious citizens as a result of the Rainbow Coalition's efforts.[28] During the summer of 1969, the Rainbow Coalition held a press conference to demonstrate its unity. Afterward,

The original Rainbow Coalition at a press conference on April 4, 1969, calling for interracial unity one year after the assassination of Martin Luther King Jr. *Standing, left to right*: Andy Keniston, Hi Thurman, William Fesperman, Bobby McGinnis, Mike James, Bud Paulin, Bobby Rush, Elisa McElroy, and Alfredo Matias. *Seated*: Jewnbug Boykin, Nathaniel Junior, and Luis Cuzo. (Courtesy of Michael James Archives)

representatives from the YPO, Young Lords, ILBPP, and RUA gathered for a photograph.[29] These young activists represented a truly diverse association, one that fostered both unsurprising political alliances, such as that between certain factions of SDS and the Panthers, and unusual ones, including the relationship that developed between the white southern Young Patriots and Chicago's Black Panthers.

The Young Patriots

The first group outside the South and West Sides of Chicago that the Party attempted to build alliances with was Uptown's Young Patriots, a group of poor southern white migrants mostly from the Appalachian Mountains of West Virginia, Kentucky, and North Carolina.[30] The YPO formed after the dissolution of JOIN Community Union, an initiative of SDS. The group's intention was to create an interracial movement of the poor that addressed unemployment and a wide number of related issues. According to one of the group's members, it "organized rent strikes, a welfare union, [a] food coop, and [a] community theater" in Uptown.[31] In 1968, one of JOIN's leaders, Peggy Terry, a southern white welfare mother living in Uptown, left the organization to join Panther Eldridge Cleaver as his running mate on the Peace and Freedom Party ticket in his bid for U.S. president. Afterward, numerous JOIN members departed to form their own organizations. One of these groups would evolve into the YPO.[32] The earliest Chicago Police Department Red Squad report of a meeting between Illinois Panthers and Young Patriots dates to early February 1969, but in fact Bob Lee established linkages with the YPO in the fall of 1968.[33]

Uptown, on Chicago's North Side, is situated between Foster Avenue on the north; Lake Michigan on the east; Montrose Avenue (Ravenswood Avenue to Clark Street) and Irving Park Road (Clark Street to Lake Michigan) on the south; and Ravenswood Avenue (Foster Avenue to Montrose Avenue) and Clark Street (Montrose Avenue to Irving Park Road) on the west. Residents of Uptown described the community as a "Southern ghetto."[34] Many of the area's occupants had migrated from the South to the North for better jobs and opportunities. A large number of the residents were on welfare.[35] Uptown was a prime recruiting zone for white supremacists. It was also home to some of Chicago's worst slums, inhabited by poor white people.[36] Todd Gitlin and Nanci Hollander's book *Uptown: Poor Whites in Chicago* provides vivid details about life in the neighborhood, demonstrating that abject white poverty was by no means confined to rural areas in the South. The authors lived in the community from 1965 through 1967 in order to document the everyday lives of Uptown's residents and the horrid conditions in which they lived.[37] Panther field secretary Bob Lee situated himself in Uptown to make connections with residents because urban renewal policies had affected the area.

Bob Lee and the YPO met by accident. Lee was invited by Charlotte Engelmann, a white attorney, to speak at the Church of Three Crosses on the near North Side. The congregation of the church consisted of predominately upper-middle-class whites. Engelmann had also invited the YPO to speak that night. Lee remarks, "In theory, [one] does not put southern whites and the Panthers together. It was a mistake in programming. When I got a phone call and was asked to speak, I was not informed about the Young Patriots attending. My intention was to introduce the [Illinois] Black Panther Party because [the organization] was new to the city of Chicago. . . . The event was my first speaking engagement."[38] Unbeknownst to Lee, he left the event that evening having acquired a political grassroots connection that would lead to the formation of the Rainbow Coalition.

The YPO had been invited to speak about police brutality. Bob Lee was surprised by the intense hostility and class dialogue between the two white groups, and he was unaccustomed to the way that the middle-class group verbally attacked the YPO. "Coming from the South," Lee contends, "it was a culture shock for me. I had never seen that before, because in the South whites were united around race. . . . I had never seen whites attack poor whites before. I had never seen poor whites having to explain themselves to other whites before. . . . When I [was called upon] to speak, I made my speech, and it was an emotional tie-in with the [Young Patriots] because I felt the hostility towards them. And that was the beginning of [our alliance]."[39] After the event, the minister of the church allowed Lee and the YPO to use his office to continue their discussion in private about police brutality, in order to avoid the camera crew that was filming the event for the documentary *American Revolution II*. Two of the leaders of the YPO were Bill "Preacherman" Fesperman, who was originally from North Carolina, and "Jewnbug" Boykin.[40] Lee officially introduced himself to the Young Patriots as Robert E. Lee III. They were amused by the fact that Lee, a southern black man, was named after the Confederate general, but they regarded this as one of several factors they had in common—factors Lee had highlighted earlier that evening.[41]

Bob Lee introduced the youth to the ideology of the BPP and its community service programs, and he encouraged forming a coalition with the group due to its similar gripe with the Daley administration and its interest in fighting police brutality. The two organizations were able to have a meaningful dialogue about their parallel dilemmas. YPO members were receptive to the concept of class solidarity and were easily persuaded to work with the Panthers.[42] Jewnbug Boykin stated that the Panthers were a group he could "respect for their name and what they are trying to do," because, he said, "part of me understands it and I feel it."[43] Lee asserts that the YPO accepted him, but the group was concerned about convincing the poor southern white community to accept working with Panthers, as the Ku Klux Klan and other neo-Nazi hate groups held a heavy influence over the residents of Uptown. Thus, the YPO agreed to help Lee meet with residents of Uptown, laying the groundwork for his arrival.[44]

At the meeting in the fall of 1968, Lee announced that the BPP was in the process of training YPO members in how to set up a free breakfast for children program and other community service projects to assist and organize Uptown occupants.[45] Lee addressed those in attendance with passion and determination:

Panthers are here, for Uptown, for anyone who lives in Uptown. Brown, green, yellow, purple or pink . . . We come here with our hearts open

Field Marshall Bob Lee, ILBPP, organizing Appalachian white migrants during a community meeting in Uptown, 1968 (Courtesy of Paul Sequeira)

and you cats to supervise us, where we can be of help to you. [The Young Patriots] have the same color of skin though. Now we going to have to deal with the concept of poverty, man. We are going to erase the color thang, see. . . . There's welfare up here. . . . There's police brutality up here, there's rats and roaches. There's poverty up here. That's the first thing we can unite on. . . . Once you realize man, that your house is funky with rats and roaches, the same way a black dude's house is . . . Once you realize that your brothers have been brutalized by the cops the same way the Westside and Southside [are]. Once you realize that you are getting an inadequate education in these high schools and junior high schools over here, the same way the Southside and the Westside [are]. Once you realize that you are paying taxes, taxes for the cops to whoop your ass, you're paying them . . . You're paying for them to come in and beat your children, you're paying them to run you off the corner and you're paying them to kill you, deal from there. The same thing is happening on the Southside and the Westside, and if you can realize that concept of poverty . . . a revolution can begin.[46]

Many Uptown residents were apprehensive about the YPO's rationale for agreeing to form an allegiance with Illinois Panthers, but Fesperman and

Boykin set out to convince their poor white neighbors to back their decision to join the Party's Rainbow Coalition. They reasoned that an alliance would help the YPO deal with police brutality, poverty, slumlords, and urban renewal.[47] Bill Fesperman advocated that the YPO should aim to establish "proper housing for the poor people" and "proper jobs for the people that [have] no education to get jobs . . . so that people can live."[48] Jewnbug Boykin assured Uptown residents that the YPO was not a gang but a community organization with a four-point platform: "One thing we're for is better housing for people in the neighborhood, another is stopping police harassment. Another is trying to end urban renewal from kicking people out of the neighborhood and the fourth thing is to have better relations between the people in the neighborhood who [don't] know each other. We out to help the community in the best way we know how."[49]

The YPO opened an office at 2512 N. Lincoln. The group initially was made up of white working-class males from the Appalachian Mountains, and its symbol was the Confederate flag. Young Patriots, according to Fesperman, wore the flag to remind them of their southern heritage and the need for tolerance: "A hundred years ago, this flag that I wear on my cap represents the Confederate States of America, we were beat down, and we beat down people for a hundred years and we know what it's like to beat down people. And we beat down people hard. We are getting ourselves together, we're angry about it cause we are beaten down today. . . . We're just folks who trying to get things straight in our community."[50]

The YPO's introduction by the Panthers to class solidarity that transcended racial divisions also forced the white group to reassess its traditional identification with the Confederate flag.[51] The group continued to use the flag as a symbol of southern heritage, but its adoption of BPP ideology led members to end their reliance on racist representations that were also characteristic of the flag. Shortly after the YPO was politicized by the Panthers, the group incorporated other ethnicities and races into its ranks. Besides white ethnic southerners, there were Spanish, Indian, Italian, Cuban, and African American members. The diversity of the group reflected the symbolism of the Rainbow Coalition.[52]

The YPO quickly became the leading political representative of Uptown and Lincoln Park. Bob Lee organized the YPO utilizing Panther ideology. Together, the two groups helped to form the Uptown Coalition of Poor People.[53] The community coalition attempted to unite residents against owners they regarded as slumlords. Members argued that too many of the buildings in their community were uninhabitable, and tenants were forced to pay

Bill "Preacherman" Fesperman, Fred Hampton, Bobby Rush, and Lamar Billy "Che" Brooks
at Rainbow Coalition rally at band shell in Grant Park, 1969
(Courtesy of Paul Sequeira)

exorbitant rents for inadequate housing.[54] The YPO also set up community
service programs modeled after the BPP's programs. The community coalition also challenged the Model Cities Board and police brutality.[55]

Young Patriots outside their Free Health Clinic, 1969 (Courtesy of Michael James Archives)

Chicago police investigators reported that in February 1969, Bob Lee and two other Panthers, along with a number of YPO members, attended a meeting held by the Model Cities committee. The contingent was there to protest the committee's building project proposal, which the group believed would negatively affect the Uptown community. About 200 Uptown residents stormed the assembly to demand that the money allocated by the federal government to improve their community be used to actually assist the poor occupants of the area. Cuban American Luis Cuzo, field marshal of the Young Lords, also attended the meeting, as his community, Lincoln Park, was under siege by urban developers. The YPO accused the Model Cities council of utilizing the funds to aid Uptown's business owners and not its residents. Members of the YPO took control of the meeting to prevent the Model Cities committee from voting on the measure. One Panther frisked a police investigator before kicking him out of the meeting. The group insisted that another meeting be held on a later date so that community citizens could attend and express their views on the committee's proposal.[56] The Rainbow Coalition "diligently badgered" the Model Cities Board and the Uptown Conservation Community Council "with shouting, foot-stomping, [and] threats of possible violence" from February to September 1969.[57] It is unclear how successful their campaign was, but the

Free Health Clinic, Uptown Chicago, 1969 (Courtesy of Paul Sequeira)

group did not waver in its numerous attempts to influence Model Cities councilmen.[58]

The YPO, along with an unspecified number of Uptown residents, also held several meetings with the Chicago Police Department to address the issues of police brutality and harassment. Many of the police who patrolled Uptown were former members of white gangs who used to clash with the Young Patriots during their high school days. Scores of these officers were

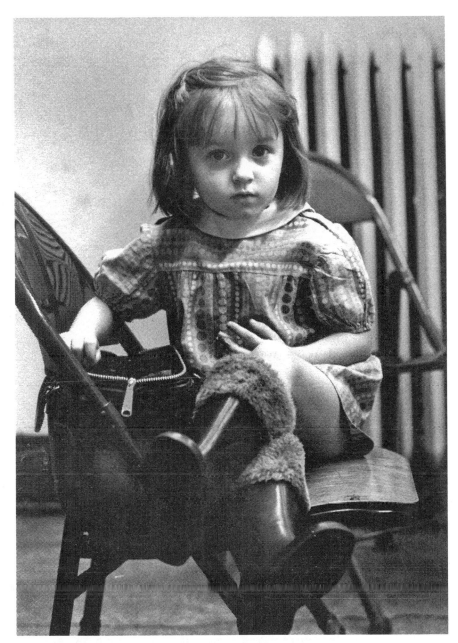

Free Health Clinic, Uptown Chicago, 1969, child with Dr. Valise
(Courtesy of Paul Sequeira)

also southern white migrants who sympathized with white supremacist groups and despised the YPO for working with the Panthers.[59] Chicago police sergeant Cramer and Panther Bob Lee served as the liaisons between

Panther-inspired Young Patriots' free breakfast program in Uptown, 1969
(Courtesy of Paul Sequeira)

the police and the community. The residents selected Lee as chairman of the Uptown Police Brutality Committee. The community hoped to establish a rapport with the area's police, as residents believed this would curb the tension between themselves and law enforcement.[60]

Instead, police officers increased their harassment of the YPO because it had joined the Rainbow Coalition. According to the YPO, the police would threaten to beat people in the neighborhood who expressed an interest in joining the organization. As a result, the group stepped up its efforts to build alliances with other political organizations and with gangs in order to solidify a collective stance against attacks by the police.[61] Bob Lee recounts an incident following a community meeting with residents in Uptown that solidified Uptown's support of the Panthers and the Rainbow Coalition. Lee was accosted by officers as he left the meeting and was placed in the backseat of a police cruiser. Uptown residents surrounded the vehicle and demanded his release. "Those brothers and sisters from the white community ran down there man," Lee recalls; "I'll never forget it because Preacherman [Fesperman] was standing in front of the police car with his wife and two children along with other white families . . . and the cops couldn't move . . . and the cop up front called it in and was told to let me out of the car. And that's when I knew we had the support of Uptown."[62]

During another communitywide effort, the YPO forced Steiner's Furniture Company at 2040 N. Lincoln to end what the residents of Lincoln Park believed to be fraudulent business practices. According to the group, Steiner exploited poor people by having them "sign blank contracts, selling repossessed furniture [as] new, telling them many different prices, misrepresenting how furniture was to be financed, charging people too much, refusing to give duplicates of contracts to customers, and refusing to give customers a statement releasing them from payment once the furniture [was] repossessed." Because of these practices, members of the community broke the windows of the furniture store. This act was repeated numerous times. Consequently, the insurance company threatened to terminate Steiner's contract because his business was deemed to be a high risk. In fact, the insurance agent forced the furniture company to meet the demands of the YPO: Steiner had to make a public statement to the community about how he would serve rather than exploit the community, and Steiner then had to allow people in the community to set up a system to enforce his new fair-business practices. Steiner agreed to the terms. A community negotiating committee supplied the furniture company with a new fair-business practice statement, and the insurance company agreed to continue to insure Steiner's business. The YPO demonstrated that a united community was a powerful entity.[63]

Drawing strength from community support, the YPO allied with the BPP under the umbrella of the Rainbow Coalition to focus attention on the Daley administration. Fesperman, field secretary of the YPO, dubbed Daley a "monster" and advocated for an end to capitalism and racism: "The jaws of the monster in Chicago are grinding up the flesh, and spitting out the blood of the poor and oppressed people, blacks, Southside and Westside, the browns in the North Side, and the reds, and the yellow and yes, the whites. . . . A gun on the side of the pigs means two things: it means racism and it means capitalism. And a gun on the side of a revolutionary, on the side of the people, means solidarity and socialism. . . . Capitalism and racism out shoot the people." Fesperman traveled around Chicago spreading the message of the Rainbow Coalition. He told people that the Young Lords, the YPO, and the ILBPP were united to intensify the struggle against the Daley Democratic machine. More important, Fesperman served as an example to others of how Illinois Panthers helped people end the paralysis that racism imposed on them: "As struggle is, our struggle is beyond comprehension to me. . . . I felt for a long time and other brothers and Uptown felt . . . that certain places we walked and certain organizations that nobody saw us—until we met [the] Illinois

Chapter of the Black Panther Party and they met us. We said let's put that theory into practice about ridding ourselves of that racism."[64]

The Young Lords Organization

The Puerto Rican Young Lords also joined the movement as a result of the influence of the Illinois Panthers. The Puerto Rican community in the 1960s was located in Lincoln Park on the near northwest side of Chicago along Division Street. Lincoln Park is bordered on the north by Diversey Parkway, on the west by Clybourn Avenue, on the south by North Avenue, and on the east by the public park (Lincoln Park) that borders the lakefront of Lake Michigan. Before 1950, Lincoln Park was the home of Poles, Jews, Scandinavians, and a modest number of Puerto Ricans. The Puerto Rican population of the area exploded in the early 1950s as a result of immigration due to unemployment. In 1949, Luis Muñoz Marín, governor of Puerto Rico, established Operation Commonwealth in an attempt to achieve self-rule from the United States. Another objective of Operation Commonwealth promoted Puerto Rican emigration to the United States to alleviate the island's economic woes, as about 60 percent of the country's citizens were unemployed. As a result, from 1950 through 1955, a mass migration from Puerto Rico occurred, and immigrants settled in the Lincoln Park neighborhood of Chicago. From 1955 through 1960, construction of the Carl Sandburg Village replaced the homes of tens of thousands of Lincoln Park's Puerto Rican residents.[65] In 1960, Mayor Daley's urban renewal projects aimed to keep the area predominately white and wealthy; there were already more than 84,000 white ethnic inhabitants.[66]

As was the case in African American communities in the 1960s, Lincoln Park's ward aldermen and precinct captains were white. Moreover, the Puerto Rican community had a severe police brutality and harassment problem. Officers used Lincoln Park to reach their traffic ticket quota, and the police department did not contain many Puerto Ricans because of minimum height requirements. These issues and other tensions eventually led to a rebellion. On one June night in 1966, the Puerto Ricans of Lincoln Park refused to be docile in the face of police brutality, and a riot ensued that lasted several nights and left one youth dead, a few dozen injured, and stores along Division Street looted. Similar to rebellions involving poor African Americans, this particular Puerto Rican uprising was exacerbated by discrimination in employment and housing. Mirroring his southern segregationist counterparts, Daley ignored Puerto Ricans' concerns and blamed the violence on "outsiders."[67]

José "Cha Cha" Jiménez, 1969 (Courtesy of Paul Sequeira)

The Young Lords began as a club in 1959. It was formed by José "Cha Cha" Jiménez, Orlando Dávila, Santos Guzman, Joe Vicente, Benny Perez, Angel Del Rivero, and Fermín Perez in order to protect themselves from white ethnic gangs in the Lincoln Park area. José Jiménez was born on August 8, 1948, in Caguas, Puerto Rico. His parents immigrated to Chicago by way of Massachusetts in 1950, and like other immigrants from the island, they worked in factories and as farmhands. Jiménez was only eleven years old when he helped to establish the Young Lords.[68] The club quickly grew into a large

Puerto Rican gang, forming branches in local high schools and surrounding communities. The parents of the gang members were some of the first Puerto Rican immigrants to Chicago.[69]

In 1964, Jiménez was elected president of the Young Lords, and in 1968 he reorganized the group by transforming it from a Puerto Rican gang into a Lincoln Park community organization. The group was renamed the Young Lords Organization (YLO), and its effectiveness benefited from both the place and time it occupied. Lincoln Park was near some of the protest demonstrations of the Democratic National Convention in 1968, and the youth gang learned from the political dissent that shadowed the convention. The group saw the ILBPP working in the African American community and SDS working with students, and the Puerto Rican youth group decided to organize their community in a similar fashion. At the same time, Lincoln Park was in the middle of a transformation. Puerto Ricans were being displaced by urban renewal.[70] Jiménez recounts the anger and confusion of Puerto Rican residents during this period:

> We were being evicted. We saw our families being thrown out on the street by the sheriff. . . . That was the beginning of urban renewal. So we saw my uncles and aunts being kicked out, and I lived on Bissell Street and Dickens Street and the whole block was bought up by a development company and everyone was told to move out. One month the rent was eighty dollars, then the next month it was four hundred. . . . My family when we came from Puerto Rico, we settled around Clark and Superior. At that time it was called La Clark by all Puerto Ricans who lived between Ohio and North Avenue, La Salle and Clark streets. . . . The neighborhood was completely wiped out when the Carl Sandburg Village development was set up there and slowly we moved West and North to Lincoln Park into Division and Damon, which the area today is known as Humboldt Park. Around that time, Lincoln Park became the center, the primary barrio of the Puerto Rican community.[71]

After the Young Lords became a community organization, the composition of the membership also changed. The YLO expanded from an exclusively Puerto Rican group to include African Americans, whites, and other Latinos.[72] At least one-fifth of the organization was Mexican American or Chicano, as the YLO saw a need to work together with other Latinos to build a unified political base for the Latin community.[73]

The ideology of the YLO shifted to reflect the growth of political awareness in minority and community youth groups citywide. Even before the

YLO joined the Panthers' Rainbow Coalition, it was very politically active. Its community campaigns secured the support of Lincoln Park's residents. Members became the social workers of their community by sponsoring picnics and giving food baskets to needy families. The group held dances and toy drives for Lincoln Park's children. The YLO also took the initiative to build coalitions with other groups. Members met with all Latin organizations and organizers in the city to form a chain of unity. On February 14–16, 1969, the YLO joined with Black Active and Determined, a political organization located in the Cabrini Green housing projects, to organize the Third World Unity Conference in Chicago.[74]

In December 1968, the YLO challenged three realty companies, Bissell, Crown, and Romano, for attempting to force Puerto Ricans to move out of Lincoln Park.[75] According to José "Cha Cha" Jiménez, at least one of these companies, Bissell Realty, "had political connections to the Daley Democratic machine. . . . Lincoln Park, the 43rd Ward had mafia ties dating back to the 1930s. . . . Personally, I knew there were mafia ties because my father used to run numbers when I was younger and he used to turn in his money to the Bissell Realty office."[76] The YLO accused the companies of trying to buy most of the properties in the area to drive up rent, thereby forcing the poor to relocate. Residents responded by breaking the real estate companies' windows and destroying furnaces in buildings owned by those accused of being slumlords. The YLO led this campaign, which won the support of the community. In January 1969, the group confronted the Community Conservation Council over the issue of urban renewal. The contingent forced the council to include Latinos, blacks, and working-class whites from Lincoln Park in the decision-making process. That same month, the YLO led a community meeting to establish the Community School Planning Committee. The committee's role was to represent Lincoln Park at school board meetings in order to pressure the city to improve area schools. In February 1969, the YLO led 300 residents to the Police Community Relations Workshop to protest police brutality and harassment, the police defense of slumlords, and a police shooting that resulted in the death of a fifteen-year-old black youth. The political activity of the YLO demonstrated the resilience and determination of the Lincoln Park organization, which made it an ideal candidate for the Chicago Panthers' Rainbow Coalition.[77]

The actions of the YLO caught the attention of the ILBPP. Chicago Panthers had already organized and incorporated the YPO into the Rainbow Coalition. Fred Hampton personally approached the YLO to encourage them to join the Rainbow Coalition. A day before their encounter, about fifty or sixty

YLO members had made headlines by using nonviolent direct action to take over the Chicago Avenue police station. The group forcefully occupied the facility to protest a police officers' propaganda campaign in Lincoln Park that painted the group as criminals in an effort to destroy community support for the youth organization. The YLO had been in contact with the Black Panthers in Oakland prior to the event and were unaware that there was a chapter of the BPP in Illinois. So Fred Hampton met with the group and offered guidance, as the YLO did not have much support. Hampton told the YLO that the group had to study what was taking place at the international level and relate it to the movement happening in Chicago. Soon after, the YLO joined the Party's Rainbow Coalition.[78]

The YLO adopted Panther ideology and methodology. For instance, to join the group, a potential member had to take political education classes and karate instruction, as well as to conduct community service. The organization offered a free breakfast for children program, set up a Puerto Rican cultural center, and opened a medical center in Lincoln Park.[79] Also, according to Jiménez, the YLO created "the first community daycare center in the city so that women could join us in our movement. We had women in our organization from the very beginning."[80]

The first request of the Rainbow Coalition was that the YLO build alliances with gangs in Lincoln Park with the aim of politicizing the groups. On two occasions, the YLO established citywide truces among the gangs. At this time, there were about seven different gangs in Lincoln Park alone: Hudsons, North Parks, Mohawks, Paragons, Latin Eagles, Black Eagles, and a Puerto Rican biker gang called the Horsemen. The Young Lords had people from all the different gangs within their organization, and these members were dispatched to work within the gangs. The purpose was to organize these gangs to get them involved in the main issue at that time, which was the removal of poor people from the inner city. As a result, the YLO and the gangs "became friends" and perceived "a common enemy" in those who attempted to evict the poor; as Jiménez recalled, "Lincoln Park had a very large concentration of Puerto Ricans" at the time, "but it was also a mixed community . . . a working class community."[81] Thus, it was possible for the YLO to find common cause with other gangs on issues that affected the poor.

In the summer of 1969, the YLO, along with other unspecified organizations, occupied the McCormick Theological Seminary to protest the forced removal of Lincoln Park's poor residents as a result of gentrification and urban renewal.[82] The incident began at a meeting on Lincoln Avenue sponsored by the Concerned Citizens of Lincoln Park. The group wanted to negotiate with the seminary to have it invest money in low-income housing in the area. Mc-Cormick Theological Seminary had purchased a number of properties in Lincoln Park and was viewed by residents as a participant in the forced removal of its poor neighbors. The institution ignored the community's concern, so the YLO seized the seminary's administration and classroom buildings.[83] The next morning, people from the community brought the youth food to demonstrate their support for their effort. "They came in with the kids . . . so they wouldn't shoot at us," Jiménez explained. "So it was a community effort that kept the police away from probably annihilating us at that time."[84] The YLO occupied the facility for nearly a week and eventually forced the clergy of the religious institution to invest over half a million dollars in housing for poor and working-class people in Lincoln Park.[85]

The YLO also attempted to curtail police brutality; these efforts intensified after the death of member Manuel Ramos, who was shot and killed on May 4, 1969, by off-duty policeman James Lamb from the Bridgeport district (Daley's community). When he was shot, Ramos was standing outside a birthday party for Orlando Dávila, president of the YLO. Lamb claimed that he was threatened with a gun, but the weapon was never found.[86] The Young Lords detained Lamb and turned him over to the police. According to Jiménez, this action did not have the desired result: "We went to court and instead of them arresting the police[man], they arrested four Young Lords, we called them the Quatro Lords at that time. We went through trials and again nothing was done about it. . . . During that time there was a lot of police brutality going on. . . . There were no Latinos on the police force at that time and very few African Americans. . . . It was a way to educate the people about police brutality."[87] A coroner's jury decided that Ramos's death was justifiable homicide.

The Rainbow Coalition responded with a series of marches to protest what it classified as state murder. The YLO, the YPO, SDS, and the Panthers, along with 2,000 other Chicagoans, first marched on the Bridgeport police station. Days later, Cook County state's attorney Edward V. Hanrahan announced that he would be at the Eighteenth District police station on Chicago Avenue. The Rainbow Coalition, along with several thousand supporters, marched to the station to confront Hanrahan, but he did not appear. The next day, several thousand people attended Ramos's funeral. The large turnout for the marches and the funeral brought publicity and support to the Rainbow Coalition. Membership in the affiliated organizations spiked as a result.[88]

The marches related to Ramos's death were the first in a series. The Albizu Campos march started on Halstead and Armitage and went to Humboldt Park.[89] It was a march for self-determination and served as a tool to

Young Lords demonstrate in support of Pedro Medina, 1969
(Courtesy of Michael James Archives)

teach the Puerto Rican community about the concept. "We were the first organization in this country to have a massive rally for self, for the independence of Puerto Rico," Jiménez claimed.[90] The march started with only about a thousand people, but by the time participants reached Humboldt Park, there were about 10,000 in the audience. Jiménez said, "We had no one supporting self-determination for Puerto Rico in our area. No one, everyone was afraid to go against old Mayor Daley at that time. And so we were the ones who created and developed that movement, the Young Lords, Rising Up Angry and other groups like ourselves."[91]

On July 26, 1969, the YLO led a march from Western and Sacramento down Division Street to protest the unprovoked beating of a member of the Latin Disciples. The YLO and the Comancheros used the incident to persuade several gangs that were not politically active (Latin Kings, Horsemen, and Stompers) to form a truce and to participate in the event. Even though the YLO opposed the destructive activities of street gangs, the group led the march because it believed police brutality to be a far more important community concern than eliminating gangs.[92]

On June 11, 1969, the YLO seized the Armitage Methodist Church on Armitage and Dayton. The church's congregation was looking to sell or rent the facility but did not want to conduct business with the Young Lords. The YLO mobilized the community to force the church to agree to a settlement by staging a sit-in at the church that ended four days later after the facility's officials accepted the group's demand.[93] The organization then used the church as its headquarters and for a daycare center. The city responded to the YLO's relentless activities against urban renewal policies by refusing to grant a permit for the daycare center.[94] Moreover, city inspectors found eleven expensive code violations that had to be repaired. One infraction resulted in the demand that the church's basement floor be raised three feet. The YLO was ordered to spend more than $10,000 on improvements to acquire a license for the daycare program.[95] To make matters worse, the police raided and vandalized the church while the Young Lords were at an urban renewal meeting protesting against the forced removal of Lincoln Park's Puerto Rican residents.[96]

Rev. Bruce Johnson, one of the pastors of the Armitage Methodist Church, supported the YLO and its programs, and he participated in a number of the organization's protests, marches, and community meetings. Red Squad officers report that Johnson was also an associate of several civil rights organizations.[97] He helped the youth group acquire the facility and collect resources for its programs.[98] On Sunday, September 28, 1969, Johnson and his wife, Eugenia, were murdered. It is not clear if Johnson's staunch support for the YLO led to his death. However, his death added an exclamation point to a string of incidents waged by the city against the YLO.[99] Jiménez explained: "We were clear on who were our friends and who were our enemies. That was made pretty clear to us by Mayor Daley."[100]

On Wednesday, September 10, 1969, the Young Lords and the Chicago Panthers held a memorial service for Larry Roberson and Ho Chi Minh at the Armitage Methodist Church. Chicago Panther Larry Roberson had been killed earlier that month during a shootout with police after he tried to intervene in the arrest of several African American residents on West Madison Street. Ho Chi Minh, president of the Democratic Republic of Vietnam (Communist North), had died on September 2. Fred Hampton was the main speaker at the event, along with several members of the YLO. The memorial service was a further effort to express the Rainbow Coalition's solidarity with and dedication to the struggle of working-class Chicagoans.[101]

In 1969, members of the YLO traveled to other American cities to establish branches of the political group in Puerto Rican communities. Its largest and most successful affiliate was the New York branch, primarily because that city had the highest concentration of Puerto Ricans in the United States. As in Chicago, the Young Lords Party in New York allied with the BPP. The Lords and the Panthers worked together on the Bronx housing coalition to establish the right of tenants to confront their landlords. Together, the organizations addressed police brutality, deplorable housing, poor hospital care, insufficient food, and inadequate education.[102] Denise Oliver-Velez, who at different times was a member of both the BPP and the Young Lords in New York, provides an account of her day-to-day life as a member of both organizations and the dedication required by that choice:

> After you did your community program work, there would usually be forums. We did a lot of political education with older people in the community. We did literacy training for people in the community. We worked with brothers and sisters coming out of prison. We then took people out to Staten Island to a guy named Mike Smith's house, who was a doctor, to detox them from drugs. Cause you couldn't be on drugs in the organization. Then you came back and maybe you got something to eat, and then you went to study hall. Then you were in study hall, if you were good, you were in study hall just 'cause you had to study. If you had committed some infraction in the organization, then you were punished to study hall. So you might be reading Lenin until three o'clock in the morning, and then you had to get up at four again to start your day. We did not go home for Christmas or holidays to see our families. We did not get breaks; we did not go on vacations. You quit your job when you joined the party. You couldn't sort of maintain an existence with one foot in the job. You had to be in the organization twenty-four hours a day, which put a lot of pressure on us to raise money to sustain a cadre of people. We lived collectively, we lived in communes, we ate collectively. Sometimes four of us would go to this restaurant called La Calanya and split a pork chop. And that's how we lived. And that's sort of the day-to-day life in the Young Lords.[103]

Rising Up Angry

The group Rising Up Angry was equally committed to the ILBPP's Rainbow Coalition. Like the YPO, RUA developed as a result of the unraveling of SDS's JOIN Community Union. After JOIN's leader Peggy Terry left the group in 1968 to run as a vice presidential candidate on the Peace and Freedom Party ticket headed by Panther Eldridge Cleaver, one faction of former JOIN members helped to form the YPO in the Chicago community of Uptown. Another group of former JOIN members, led by Mike James, established their own group with the purpose of promoting "revolutionary ideas and [to] help build a progressive organization of poor and working class whites beyond Uptown."[104]

Mike James was born in New York City in 1942 and was raised in Connecticut. He earned a bachelor's degree from Lake Forest College in 1964 and attended graduate school at the University of California at Berkeley. While at Berkeley, James was involved in the free speech movement, discovered SDS, and participated in the Oakland Community Union Project. He moved to Chicago in the spring of 1966 and worked as a community organizer for Uptown's JOIN Community Union.[105] The group of young organizers and former JOIN members who allied with Mike James were inspired by the Puerto Rican YLO in Lincoln Park, which used the slogan "educate to liberate"; by the BPP and its "serve the people" programs; and by Lenin's advocacy for the importance of a newspaper "in a pre-Party situation."[106]

Thus, the young men and women commenced to form an organization and a newspaper, but they lacked a name. In the early spring of 1969, the group met in a farmhouse in Fairborn, Ohio, to discuss extending their organization to reach other working-class white youth. That Saturday night, they went to Yellow Springs, Ohio, to watch the film *Wild in the Streets*, which Mike James describes as portraying a reactionary focus on youth rebellion. One line in the movie's theme song was "There's a new sun, rising up angry in the sky." The phrase "rising up angry" became the name of their organization and the title of the group's newspaper.[107]

Mike James, Steve Tappis, Diane Fager, Patrick Sturgis, Bob Lawson, Norie Davis, and several others cofounded RUA in 1969.[108] RUA was a group of middle-class youth from Logan Square on Chicago's North Side. In the 1960s, Logan Square had over 90,000 residents, of which more than 95 percent were white.[109] The community is bordered by Diversity Avenue on the north, Metra/Milwaukee District North Line Railroad on the west, the Soo Line Railroad on the south, and the North Branch of the Chicago River on the east. Most RUA members were students immersed in the countercultural trends of the time. They were peace advocates who rejected the Vietnam War and opposed the repressive policies of the Daley administration.

The group first gained popularity by publishing its monthly newspaper, *Rising Up Angry*, which disseminated information about North Side youth groups and community organizations. Much like the effect of the *Black*

Panther on the black community, RUA's newspaper provided North Siders with a glimpse into the day-to-day struggles of residents, gangs, and organizations alike. The group distributed the newspaper all over Chicago, especially at high schools and junior colleges and in parks where groups of young people were known to congregate.[110] Mike James often worked North Side corners, selling the paper while yelling, "Sisters and brothers, its time to take the chain from the brain, time to get back in the people's game, time to move it from the lower level to the higher, from the shallower to the deeper, and from the abstract to the concrete!"[111] RUA wanted readers to know that the organization did more than just publish a newspaper. Each edition explained that RUA was a disparate group of individuals who worked together as a collective for the progress of all Chicagoans, regardless of race or class.[112]

Members of RUA believed that the Panthers were about helping all people, regardless of race. The Panthers' slogan, "Power to the People," resonated with RUA. Moreover, the leftist group was in staunch opposition to the Daley administration because of the mayor's attacks on dissent. The Panthers were major targets of Daley's attacks—which led RUA to sympathize with the organization. The Panthers' free breakfast for children program, medical clinics, and other community service ventures were so effective in highlighting the contradictions in Daley's policies that the programs won the respect of Chicago's residents in and outside the black community. The success of the Illinois Panthers' free breakfast for children program caused the mayor to demand that city officials develop their own breakfast program. This was another major reason why RUA joined the Panthers' Rainbow Coalition: RUA was impressed with the Panthers because, despite their advocacy of using weapons to create change, the Party challenged the power structure via education and community service programs.[113] Mike James summed up the common stance of the two groups on the relationships between action and education: "There is nothing like some action to get people involved. . . . After you get some action, then you got to educate to liberate. You got to get people who are kind of turned on by the action, fighting the police, fighting the man, fighting the system. Get into some educational mode to learn about the historical precedents, the historical situation with a picture to the future."[114]

Fred Hampton informed RUA that the Panthers had moved beyond self-defense ideology in order to build a strong racial coalition. Hampton stated, "We're still about that, but that alone can be reactionary. It can be like a street gang just defending its territory, instead of all the gangs—Black and White and Latin—getting together and defending the people from the avaricious greedy businessman, the Mickey Mouse politicians and the pigs. . . .

We serve the people. We help old ladies out of taxis. We fight the pigs. We're about a people thing. Revolutionaries aren't frantic. They're calm. They're the best lovers, because they believe in the people and love the people." Hampton believed that Chicago's poor communities had to unite not only to end racism but also to wage an effective campaign against their real common oppressor, capitalism. All who joined the coalition were required to educate the masses about the ideology of racial coalitions. The Panthers advocated that the fight against oppression must involve all people.[115]

Thus, RUA joined the Rainbow Coalition for a number of reasons. Mike James had a strong belief at the time that "white activists of conscience or white radicals needed to work with white poor and working class youth, overcoming racism, and have them join the Movement, join the struggle along with black and Latinos to overthrow the racist-capitalist-imperialists who were running the show."[116] James contends that he looked to the BPP and the YLO as models and that the successes he had organizing "poor southern whites in JOIN and Uptown could be recreated in primarily white communities and neighborhoods throughout Chicago and beyond."[117]

One of RUA's major goals was to incorporate fellow North Side residents, particularly white ethnics, into the movement led by the Panthers. Thus, the group attempted to influence—and possibly change—the ideology of its constituents with regard to race and class, as an article in its paper explained:

> We used to fight for b.s. reasons. . . . We used to put down blacks and
> Latins, and hippies. . . . OK, we've gone through changes. . . . The
> bullshit gang-bopping, [Puerto Rican], Black or hippie fighting, we
> should try and cool it out. It doesn't mean we're chicken. . . . All of us
> coming from a gang, club, neighborhood, park or school . . . should get
> hip to each other. We can do it through Rising Up Angry. Get together
> among ourselves, learn new things, do new things, and build new ties
> and new friendships. . . . So dig the people; understand them, teach
> them and show them. . . . There's no gimmick to counteract all the
> crap overnight that the younger brothers and sisters, like us, were
> pumped with most of their lives. . . . One of the most important things
> we've got to do is dig the younger brothers and sisters. They're part of
> our future.[118]

RUA also used its newspaper to appeal to the sentiments of white ethnics. For instance, Chicago has long had a large and vibrant Irish community. RUA wrote articles on Ireland's independence campaigns and on people like James Connolly, who in the early 1900s led Ireland's workers against the

British for freedom. Fully aware that older Irish Chicagoans would identify Connolly as a revolutionary people's hero, the group evoked his actions to relate Ireland's struggles to Chicago's racial coalition movement.[119] RUA focused on this approach to appeal to the city's white ethnic communities. Although it is unclear if these efforts influenced older Irish Chicagoans, the method resonated with the younger generation.[120]

RUA members spent a significant amount of time in North Side high schools attempting to politicize white youth. At Senn High School, RUA targeted youth organizations. At Foreman High School, the group aimed its attention at the white ethnic gang the Gaylords. The city's Gang Intelligence Unit (GIU) was present at many schools that had gang activity, and thus officers apprehended RUA organizers along with SDS members (who were equally interested in politically influencing white youth) on several occasions. The persistence of RUA and the repeated arrests of its members won the group great respect among fellow white youth.[121] RUA members also invested countless hours at schools with changing racial demographics. The group set out to curtail and prevent racial tensions among Chicago's youth.[122]

During the fall of 1969, racial tensions mounted at Austin High School as the demographic makeup of its student population shifted dramatically in one year due to real estate block busting. The community transformed from a majority-white to a 65 percent African American district. As a result, black students who had been victims of racial assaults when they were outnumbered at the school soon became the aggressors and attacked white students. A violent racial episode erupted at Tilden High School that same week. RUA took the initiative to attempt to remedy the situation, bringing in the Panthers to help resolve the conflict. The episode demonstrates that some African Americans had to be persuaded not only to work with whites but to recognize the Daley machine as their real oppressor. During meetings with both black and white students, RUA members continuously quoted Panther rhetoric: "We don't hate white people; we hate the oppressor. If he happens to be white, or black, we hate him."[123]

Due to RUA's efforts to politicize gangs, members of the Mohawks, Hudsons, and North Parks (all white ethnic gangs on Chicago's North Side) agreed to end their rivalries and set up an organization called CORP. The purpose of the group was to protect and serve its communities. RUA was also able to work out agreements with gangs that were not interested in political action, such as the Latin Kings, so that people outside these gangs would be able to organize in their territory and feel at home.[124] The Latin Kings did not enter the fold until after the death of Fred Hampton.[125] RUA's influence on the white gangs' coalition resulted in the development of a consensus among the gangs regarding where to aim their rage. The white gangs turned away from violence against one another and other gangs and focused their anger on the Daley administration.[126]

RUA also influenced the Latin Eagles, whose members passed out a leaflet in July 1969 stating that the Eagles were no longer a gang but an organization with an office on 3352 N. Halsted. The Latin Eagles informed their community that they intended to be a support group to improve their neighborhood: "This is to inform the hungry that we are going to feed you, the badly housed we will back you up against the slum lords. This is to inform the police that we are willing to protect ourselves and our community against those of you who have been harassing us, you serve the rich, the people who oppress us. We serve our people and we will protect them."[127]

RUA also exploited the pop culture trends of the time to bring people of various racial, ethnic, and class backgrounds together so the groups could learn about one another's issues/agenda and identify commonalities. RUA established what the group called People's Dances, "mixing rock and roll, blues, and radical politics."[128] The first dance was held in 1969 at the old Wobbly Hall on Lincoln Avenue. Other dances took place at "Alice's Revisited on Wrightwood, in the old Columbia College Theater building on Sheffield, at the People's Church on Lawrence in Uptown, and the MoMing Dance Center at Kenmore and Barry."[129] RUA also sponsored a "People's Celebration" on July 4, 1969, in Caldwell Woods, and the organization created a group titled Cooperative Energy Supply "that put on mega dances with food, poetry, theater, and rock and roll."[130] Cooperative Energy Supply held events at the Midland Hotel (which the group renamed "the Great Hall of the People") that brought in people from neighborhoods throughout Chicago and the suburbs. RUA used these dances and events to create racial and class solidarity among Chicago's youth.[131] RUA also ran an outreach program, Friends of Angry, "that made contact and involved young people throughout the city, bringing them to the People's Dances, anti-war demonstrations . . . the BPP, [and taught] young people about their rights when busted by police."[132]

Following the example of the Illinois Panthers, RUA regularly held political education meetings to consider plans and actions and developed community service programs to address the needs and problems of people in their neighborhood. RUA began with a breakfast for children program held in the Church of the Holy Covenant at Wilton and Diversey. The same church also housed the organization's Fritzi Englestein Free People's Health Clinic. Health clinic participants tested patients, advocated against what they believed to be an

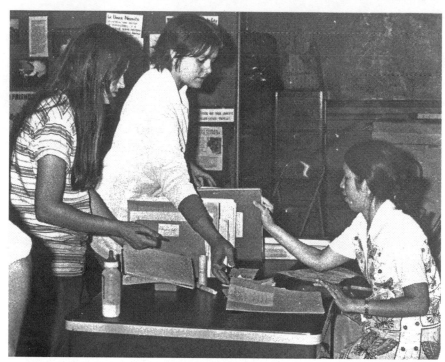

RUA Free Health Clinic, 1969 (Courtesy of Michael James Archives)

inadequate medical system, and helped residents to deal with hospital bureaucracies. The clinic also promoted the concept of "preventative medicine, which included early checking, screening, and preemptive treatment, and also reflected [the group's] early interest in wholesome food, and [their] love of sport."[133] Believing that sports served as part of preventative medicine, RUA created the People's Sports Institute, which was able to retain the services of author and former pro football player David Meggyesy, who toured Chicago colleges to promote the concept.[134]

RUA also created the People's Legal Program, which provided residents with legal advice and served as counsel in court. An adjunct of the RUA legal clinic was the busing-to-prison program, again modeled after a Panther initiative. According to Mike James, the busing program did not last long, as RUA "soon learned that the rate of white incarceration was miniscule to that of blacks and Latinos."[135] The legal clinic also took up the cause of housing and police brutality. With the support of reporters Pam Zekman and Bill Curry, RUA's legal clinic was able to "expose dismal housing conditions in Uptown, Lakeview, and Albany Park."[136] Members of the legal clinic also challenged Chicago police superintendent James Conlisk's public relations

RUA breakfast for kids, 1969 (Courtesy of Michael James Archives)

program by exposing police brutality in the community; this action resulted in members of the legal clinic being "physically attacked by police and Democratic Party hacks."[137]

Antiwar efforts were also an initiative of RUA, as the group attempted to recruit and organize veterans in opposition to the Vietnam War. RUA launched its GI Program to assist returning soldiers with the transition to civilian life and anger management. Returning vets and a network of marines formerly incarcerated at the Glenview Naval Air Station made up the core of the GI Program. The group organized a massive march against the war in Foss Park in North Chicago at the Great Lakes Naval Training Center. The slogan of RUA's GI Program during the demonstration was "SOS—Stop Our Ships, Save Our Sailors."[138]

RUA also established a number of other community service programs. Projects included "employment; draft and abortion counseling; sex education; drug education and emergency phones; legal and medical aid; a daycare center; and sensitivity groups."[139] The organization sought to take a broader approach to its programs and encompass more areas than the Panthers' community service models.

RUA's political activity mirrored that of the other groups involved with the Rainbow Coalition. RUA helped residents who rented apartments in Logan

Square's Sugar Building, owned by the realty firm Draper and Kramer. Tenants conducted a rent strike to protest what they believed to be horrid living conditions. All the tenants signed a petition agreeing not to pay their rent until the company installed lighting in the halls, replaced the carpeting, fixed the plumbing, and exterminated the vermin on the premises. Draper and Kramer responded by issuing eviction notices. According to RUA, the company did not want to make improvements to the building because the property was valuable to urban renewal speculators regardless of its condition. RUA vowed to use arms to protect tenants from forced evictions if necessary.[140]

RUA was crucial to the Rainbow Coalition's labor struggle with Chicago's construction industry. During the fall of 1969, African American workers held numerous demonstrations against several construction companies, demanding more jobs. During this same period, white construction workers opposed potential job cuts in the construction industry and viewed African American demands as a threat to their own job security. RUA set out to inform white workers that their struggle would be more effective if it was aligned with that of the African American protesters. The group argued that the demographics of the construction industry highlighted the contradictions of the Daley administration's neutral stance on the issue. Of the 625 elevator operators in the building and trades industry in Chicago, only 1 was from a minority group. Even more striking was the fact that there were only 16 minority pipe fitters out of more than 7,800. This trend was reflected in all construction industry trades in the city.[141] RUA pointed out that not only was this situation unjust, but white residents also had trouble getting construction jobs unless they had a relative in the union or were able to convince a politician to lobby on their behalf. Moreover, automation was eliminating unskilled labor in all construction trades. RUA wanted white construction workers to understand that what threatened their job security was not black laborers but technology and local government policy. The newspaper made this argument:

> In the last 10 years the number of unskilled jobs dropped from 13 million to 4 million. Usually, black people are the first to lose their jobs. It's gotten so bad that unemployment for black youth is up to about 20%, equal to the Great Depression of the 30's. The rate of unemployment for young whites is twice that of older whites. . . . So we must understand who the real enemy is. Black people who want equality are not the enemy. . . . The enemy is the system that pits us against each other. . . . If white construction workers in Chicago or Pittsburgh were to go on

strike, they wouldn't want the black to cross the picket line. And if black factory workers in Chicago or Pittsburgh were to strike . . . they'd want white workers to go out with them. . . . The more men and women who go out, the better the chance that the workers' demands will be met. . . . That just means that it's much better for us to stick together.[142]

RUA spread this message to white workers in the hope that they would realize that Democratic machine policies protected property and businesses and not workers, regardless of race. As a result, RUA was able to influence a number of white ethnics to adopt the concept of class solidarity and to forge cross-racial coalitions.

In another labor organizing effort, RUA supported César Chávez and the United Farm Workers. In a display of solidarity, RUA "joined with others city-wide in mounting an ongoing boycott of Jewel Supermarkets for their refusal to honor the UFW."[143] About 600 members of the farm workers' union came to Chicago, and RUA helped organize a welcome rally for them. According to Mike James, in addition to supporting labor in the construction industry and farming, RUA advocated on behalf of working people via "strikes and labor actions both in their workplaces and in the streets."[144]

The YPO, YLO, and RUA all spent significant time attempting to transform gangs in their communities into political entities. Illinois Panthers influenced the groups to do so, as the party had made strides in transforming gangs in African American communities on both the West and South Sides of Chicago. The Rainbow Coalition envisioned including nontraditional groups like gangs in Chicago's politically violent and cut-throat arena to strengthen the city's poor communities, which were vulnerable to political exploitation.

Gangs

The Gang Intelligence Unit of the Chicago Police Department was created in 1967. RUA believed that the GIU was formed as a result of the efforts of most of the city gangs to become political entities to fight the Daley Democratic machine. The GIU replaced the Youth Group Intelligence Unit, which was set up to prevent gang violence. According to RUA, the goal of the Youth Group Intelligence Unit was to transform gangs into political units for the Democratic Party. For instance, the Conservative Vice Lords from the city's West Side had entrepreneurial aspirations, and to reach those goals, the group became a political body of the Daley administration under the tutelage of state senator Bernie Neistein.

The mission of the GIU, however, was to destroy rather than reform gangs. Another purpose of the GIU was to keep "track of the activities of alleged gang members and monitor their interactions with social and civil rights activists."[145] By the spring of 1969, the number of GIU officers had increased from 37 to 200, coinciding with the increasing number of youth groups working in coalition with the BPP. Before 1969, the GIU was more tolerant of white ethnic gangs than of those composed of blacks, Latinos, and hippies. Indeed, white ethnic gangs were used to help control the other groups, and many former white gang members became police officers. By the summer of 1969, however, police attacks on white ethnic organizations (such as the YPO and RUA) and several white street gangs were making it clear that the special treatment once afforded such groups was no longer an unofficial policy of the Chicago police.[146]

The GIU classified some groups as gangs that other officials did not consider to be gangs, and most of the groups investigated were of African American and Latino background.[147] As a result, RUA developed a list of fourteen recommendations for organizations seeking to protect themselves where they were most vulnerable to GIU persecution. RUA advised groups to eliminate internal disputes, to beware of police traps in the form of solicitation for guns and money, and to secure community support, as the officers would exhaust every effort to persuade residents to identify activists as violent gang members in order to justify police harassment.[148]

The ILBPP sought to transform Chicago gangs into political units in order to increase Panther membership, to get the former gang members to work in coalition with the Party, and to encourage gangs to cease their negative and criminal activities.[149] Fred Hampton personally worked with the BSR as well as the Conservative Vice Lords. The Black Stone Rangers were located on the South Side primarily, and the Vice Lords were on the West Side.[150] Eugene "Bull" Hairston, one of the "Main 21" (the twenty-one leaders of the BSR), was incarcerated in Menard with Hampton. Hairston was more politically attuned to the movement than Jeff Fort, head of the Rangers. Hairston schooled Hampton on how to deal with the brutality of the correctional officers at Menard. The prison guards used to come to Hampton's cell to beat him. The Ranger told Hampton not to let the guards get into his cell—that he had to meet the guards at the door. This method forced the guards to come in one at a time, so he could prevent them from surrounding him. Before Hampton's imprisonment in Menard, he had also met David Barksdale, leader of the Black Disciples, in Cook County Jail.[151]

Chicago Panthers heavily recruited the warring BSR and Black Disciples, as they were the largest black gangs in the city. More importantly, like the various white ethnic gangs before this period, many black gangs were struggling for empowerment in Chicago's political arena.[152] The Panthers reasoned that uniting the groups would eliminate their rivalry and gang violence.[153] In May 1969, the Chicago Police Department raided Black Disciple headquarters shortly after the Disciples formed an alliance with the Panthers. Chicago Panther leadership responded, "The Black Disciples, the Black Panthers, and all segments of the people are saying to the pigs, 'Its either they stop their repressive acts of barbarism or we're going to start shooting.'"[154] As a result, the Chicago Police Department's GIU targeted the alliance. Nevertheless, the Panthers' Rainbow Coalition was able to influence most of the city's gangs to organize themselves and to end violence. In July 1969, Leonard Sengall of the BSR and Norman Swift of the Black Disciples held a press conference to announce a new truce between the gangs.[155]

The Panthers worked particularly hard to incorporate the Rangers into the Party. As there were about 5,000 Black Stone Rangers, Panthers rationalized that if the group could be incorporated into the party's ranks and transformed via Panther ideology, the merger could solidify the ILBPP as a powerful and formidable political force. Although Jeff Fort and Fred Hampton highly respected each other, the two leaders did not get along. Tensions rose as the Chicago Panthers increased their efforts to persuade the gang to join the movement.[156] More important, disagreements between the Panthers and the Rangers captured the attention of the FBI. One of the FBI's goals was to prevent such an alliance, so it attempted to increase friction between the groups. In December 1968, agents sent an anonymous letter to Fort that stated that Panthers had attacked his reputation; this was an attempt to incite Fort to take violent action against the Party.[157]

According to an informer working for the Chicago Police Department, Panthers and Rangers met a number of times to discuss a merger, and these meetings provide possible evidence that the FBI may have succeeded in exacerbating the rift between the groups. On the morning of December 18, 1968, the two factions met in Jackson Park on Chicago's South Side to display their armed might and firepower after a Panther was shot by a Ranger for selling newspapers in Woodlawn.[158] The two groups later gathered at the Kenwood Oakland Community Organization at 4612 S. Greenwood, where the informant told of Jeff Fort giving Bobby Rush a machine gun. As the members of the groups returned to the West Side, the police stopped one of the Panther cars and arrested the occupants, Henry English, Rufus Walls, and Jerry Dunnigan. At 10:20 that night, five carloads of Panthers (about 25 to 30) attended a meeting with the Rangers (about 100) at the

First Presbyterian Church at 6400 S. Kimbark. Rangers guarded the church with guns and walkie-talkies. According to a police source, Jeff Fort announced, "See the might of the Stones!" and then "treated" the Panthers "to a display of firearms."

Chicago Panthers continued to meet with the Rangers in an attempt to get them to join the Party. Jeff Fort was the main spokesman for the Rangers, and Cephus Inu spoke for the Panthers. Neither group wanted to join the other, but they promised to support one another in time of need. Jeff Fort claimed to be able to get cases of guns when needed and said he would supply the Panthers with weapons. He also gave Bobby Rush a check to "help get the Black Panthers out of jail [who had earlier been] locked up" in his gang's territory. The Main 21, the governing body of the BSR, then agreed to meet at the Panthers' headquarters on Christmas Day.[159]

Instead, the groups met on December 26, 1968, at a South Side bar. Still, the Panthers were unsuccessful in convincing Fort to join the Party. The following day, Fort called Hampton, and the two men threatened each other by proposing that each group had until December 28, 1968, to merge. Fort demanded the Panthers join the Rangers, and Hampton ordered the Rangers to become Panthers. It seems the FBI's ploy had worked. To intensify the tensions between the groups, agents sent Fort another anonymous letter that stated that Panthers had "put out a hit" on him. The letter's possible intention was to provoke Fort to kill Panther members or leaders. Agents did not send a similar letter to the Chicago Panthers, because they believed the organization was not "as violence prone as the Rangers," for whom, the agents argued, "violent type activity—shooting and the like—is second nature."[160]

Despite the divisive action taken by local and federal law enforcement, the ILBPP influenced most Chicago gangs, directly or indirectly, to transform into political entities. For example, the Young Comancheros of the south suburb of Chicago Heights became politically active and adopted Panther community service methodology. Even though the group had not had any contact with the Party, they gathered information from reading newspapers. The Young Comancheros Organization was formed in the summer of 1969 by a group of Chicano youth to combat what they argued were the abuses of the town's police. As demonstrated by other youth organizations in the city, the Young Comancheros realized that a unified community was the only way to achieve their goal. *Rising Up Angry* reported, "The Y.C.O. will unite, for our power is unity. As a minority or as individuals we stand the chance of being wiped off the face of the earth. We are a people with pride. We are a people with dignity. We are a people with a history and culture and we will survive in spite of them and we will win because of them."[161]

Students for a Democratic Society

The ILBPP also influenced the white leftist group Students for a Democratic Society, which supported the Rainbow Coalition. Despite popular perceptions, SDS had no formal coalition or alliance in Chicago with the Panthers, due to the methodological differences between the two groups over using violence as a method of agitation. In 1968, Bobby Rush, Rufus "Chaka" Walls, and a delegation of Illinois chapter members went to the national meeting of SDS held at the old Chicago Coliseum. At this meeting, ideological constraints caused SDS to fracture into two competing groups: the Progressive Labor Party and the Weathermen. Primarily on account of the friction within the student group, SDS never became a direct divisional entity of the Rainbow Coalition.[162] Nevertheless, Panthers and SDS members participated alongside one another in common causes. A representative of Chicago's Rainbow Coalition, "Preacherman" Fesperman of the YPO, participated in the United Front against Fascism Conference in Oakland, California, in July 1969. He joined Jeff Jones of SDS, the Panthers' Elaine Brown and Don Cox, lawyers William Kunstler and Charles Garry, activist Ron Dellums, and others on the panel titled "Political Prisoners and Political Freedom."[163]

In an attempt to quell the tension between SDS and the Panthers, Jeff Jones used his discussion time on the panel to outline the two groups' ideological similarities. He advocated that the student movement on college campuses be intricately linked to the liberation struggle of black and brown people, both domestically and abroad. He insisted that Panthers allow SDS to work in coalition with the party, because SDS wanted the student movement to encompass "the working class movement with support for the right of self-determination." He believed that SDS's involvement had to incorporate "over increased struggle, over increased militancy, over increased alliance, alliances with the working class, with the colonized people, the people oppressed by U.S. imperialism and fascism."[164]

Clearly, SDS and the ILBPP occupied a common stance against oppression. They disagreed intensely, however, about the uses of violence. The Weathermen faction of SDS wanted to use violence to forge a revolution to overthrow the American establishment. The Progressive Labor Party element of the group wanted to maintain traditional organizing that was the hallmark of SDS. The Illinois Panthers advocated self-determination by all poor people, forging racial alliances along class lines, and using armed resistance—not violence—as a tool of self-defense. The Weathermen's action caused the Party to distance itself from the group and SDS to assure the public that the Panthers vehemently opposed violence as an instrument of change.

Conclusion: The Expansion of the Rainbow Coalition

This chapter outlines not only Fred Hampton's proposal for a Rainbow Coalition in Chicago but also documents Bob Lee's genius at organizing that vision into a political reality. It also magnifies the grassroots leadership that orbited around Fred Hampton and the ILBPP. The original Rainbow Coalition reveals how grassroots activists on the fringes of Chicago's political arena spread from group to group and from neighborhood to neighborhood. These youth activists were concerned about the urban renewal programs that threatened their daily lives in neighborhoods facing massive evictions. The BPP offered these youth a perspective that helped them to develop their sense of identity, as grassroots political work gave them a new sense of themselves and the future possibilities of their neighborhoods. Furthermore, this chapter also highlights the nuances in the white working-class communities of Chicago. Rather than lump all poor whites together, this history shows that the struggle brought in young people from at least three different camps: those in desegregated schools who wanted to get along with their new black classmates, those who joined hate groups to attack black students, and those who saw enough commonality in social class and aspirations to join with other racial and ethnic groups in the Rainbow Coalition.

The Rainbow Coalition and its components originated in Chicago. Initially, it was a local phenomenon.[165] The group was able to establish alliances between white ethnics, Puerto Ricans, and the city's various racial and ethnic street gangs. There were also efforts to develop coalitions in Chinatown, and the coalition worked with individual Asians in Uptown, though it did not partner with any particular Asian organization.[166] One of the most significant and underappreciated aspects of the ILBPP's Rainbow Coalition is the fact that "the Black Panther Party extended a hand to suffering white folks." As Bob Lee notes, "That's rare in America; when white folks reach out for the help of [black people]."[167]

The national leadership of the BPP made sure that each established chapter practiced the organization's method of forging class alliances with other groups. The Rainbow Coalition's success in Chicago displayed the Party's aspirations, which had yet to achieve similar results elsewhere. Bob Lee's innate ability as an organizer garnered national attention, and so the national leadership—the Central Committee of the BPP in Oakland, in collaboration with the Illinois chapter's Central Staff—decided to put Bob Lee and Bill Fesperman on the road together, ensuring that the Rainbow Coalition spread to other cities.[168] Beginning in early 1970, the two activists traveled to other cities and organized sections of the Rainbow Coalition.[169] Most of their major stops were in the U.S. South, beginning in Washington, D.C.

The two men used the documentary *American Revolution II* as their recruitment tool; they identified the film as the seed of the Rainbow Coalition. According to Lee, "People were hungry for building political racial alliances and wanted democracy to work," and the film *American Revolution II* "legitimized the Rainbow Coalition concept."[170] Even film critic Roger Ebert recognized the poignancy of the documentary: he gave the movie four stars and stated that "the film comes alive."[171] According to Lee, poor southern whites were receptive to the activists' insistence on building racial coalitions because Fesperman sported a Confederate flag on his beret, and Lee was named after the Confederate general Robert E. Lee. The fact that the organizers are southerners also brought southern whites into the fold.[172]

In addition, Illinois Panther field secretary Yvonne King worked with some of the members of the Rainbow Coalition to set up an affiliate to work in conjunction with the Panther chapter in Detroit. King contends that during this process, she and other Illinois field secretaries dealt with neighboring chapters and "did whatever we were instructed to do."[173] Rainbow Coalition organizers established working alliances with other ethnic groups in various U.S. cities. For instance, Panthers on the West Coast worked with the Brown Berets and the Peace and Freedom Party (a white radical political organization opposed to the two-party system).[174] The Mexican American Brown Berets vowed to assist the Panthers' efforts to combat racism in America.[175] In 1968, Panthers helped the Peace and Freedom Party collect signatures to be placed on that year's election ballot.[176] Later, BPP members ran for political office on Peace and Freedom Party tickets. In 1968, Eldridge Cleaver ran for U.S. president. In 1973, Bobby Seale was a candidate for mayor of Oakland, and Elaine Brown ran for a city council seat.[177]

The Rainbow Coalition concept also took root in Texas. In Houston, the Black Panther Party was originally called the People's Party II and led by Carl Hampton, who was shot and killed by police snipers in 1970.[178] The People's Party II had formed alliances with a white radical group called the John Brown Revolutionary League, led by Bartee Hale. Together, the groups worked with a Chicano group, the Mexican American Youth Organization, and allied with Casa de los Siete in Dallas.[179] Other poor white ethnics in Texas allied with the Party because they identified with the ideology of class struggle against economic oppression and disenfranchisement.[180]

In New York, Rainbow Coalition organizers established links with the Young Lords and the I Wor Kuen, a Chinese organization whose name meant "the harmonious and righteous fist" and referred to the Chinese Boxer Rebellion. Activists also worked with people from the American Indian movement.[181] Alliances were built in San Francisco with the Chinese Red Guard.[182] Panthers even built coalitions with groups outside the United States. Kathleen Cleaver states, "Committees of solidarity with the Black Panthers were formed in Sweden, Denmark, the Netherlands, Belgium, Britain, France, and West Germany. The Scandinavian and the West Germans were the most dynamic and the best organized as they were tied to strong student movements in countries where socialist parties were well-represented in the national government."[183]

The spirit that motivated Chicago's Rainbow Coalition was one that invited people of all stripes—from different races, different classes, different ages, and different parts of the city—to fight injustice and a corrupt city government. Naturally, such an organization drew intense official scrutiny. In 1973, Chicago police ran the license plates of cars parked outside Panther headquarters because the cars had Missouri tags. One vehicle was registered to Susan Rosenblum, a white female student at Washington University in Saint Louis who, it turns out, conducted food drives, advocated for social reform and women's liberation, and supported the antiwar effort. Along with five white associates, she sold the *Black Panther* newspaper and helped to organize the free breakfast for children program located on Tenth and Rutger in Saint Louis.[184] Rosenblum's interest in the ILBPP speaks to its success in coalition building across race and geography, and the police surveillance of Rosenblum suggests the sort of police response the Panthers provoked. The political assassination of Fred Hampton, discussed in the following chapter, displays the extremes that law enforcement under the direction of the Daley Democratic machine relied upon to silence the dissent that the Chicago Panthers encouraged.

Fred Hampton stated that he is scared that he will be killed. He believed that he was "in it too deep to get out without being killed" because there has already been an attempt on his life. Hampton had all his pockets on his pants and jacket sewed shut so no one can say that he reached in his pocket for a weapon if he is killed. He believes the government wants him dead to start guerilla warfare in Chicago so that certain people can say, "I told you so," cause they know if he is killed there will be a complete destruction of the city and this is not his goal.

—"Interview Report: Black Panther Party," February 8, 1969, box 229, folder 3, item 49, Red Squad papers

FIVE

Law Enforcement Repression and the Assassination of Chairman Fred Hampton

From the beginning, law enforcement repression was an integral part of the Panthers' history in Chicago. The ILBPP attracted an impressive amount of attention from both city and federal law enforcement agencies. At one level, this was a consequence of the toxic relationship between Chicago's black community and the racist Chicago Police Department in the 1960s and 1970s, which played out in numerous violent episodes. The ILBPP made attempts at reconciliation, which only exacerbated the division. But the repression of the Panthers by law enforcement agents was far more than the simple product of a local conflict: it also involved the active meddling of the FBI through its COINTELPRO program. The FBI identified the Panthers as a major threat—perhaps *the* major threat—to the nation's internal security and set out to destroy the organization. Both the Chicago Police Department's intelligence arm, the Red Squad, and FBI agents enlisted the local media in efforts to discredit the Panthers. They also shared intelligence, spied on the group's meetings, planted informants, and attempted to sow seeds of internal discord. Most notably, the agencies cooperated in the assassination of Fred Hampton—an act that went a long way toward accomplishing their purpose of destroying the ILBPP. This chapter investigates the law enforcement repression of the Illinois Panthers (which lived up to the Panthers' most inflated rhetoric about the violation of their civil rights by "pigs") and the assassination of Fred Hampton both to emphasize the scale of these efforts and to tie them to the Party's unraveling following Hampton's death.

Black Chicago's Relationship with the Chicago Police Department, 1968–1974

During the period of the Illinois chapter's existence (1968–74), the Chicago Police Department was markedly racist as a result of the city's long history of racial and ethnic segregation and tension. The 1966 Chicago Freedom Movement for open housing exacerbated the tensions between Chicago police and the city's black citizens: many officers were residents of the communities that were targeted by movement activists, putting them on the defensive and increasing their feelings of alienation from the African American neighborhoods they patrolled. Residents of Chicago's predominately black communities consistently complained to their political representatives about the racist nature of many of the police assigned to their areas, to no avail.[1]

In 1969, thirty-nine African American Chicagoans were killed by police officers, and not one of these cases went to court, nor was a single indictment filed against the police.[2] Charles Cox was arrested on May 1, 1969. When he was taken into custody, he was in good health. He was pronounced dead the next day by police officers. The officers insisted that Cox's death was the result of a drug overdose. However, Dr. Earl N. Caldwell, a pathologist at the Veterans' Administration Hospital, concluded that Cox died from severe blows to the head while in police custody.[3] In May 1969 alone, Chicago's black residents made numerous complaints about police brutality and police killings, none of which resulted in the prosecution or punishment of accused white officers.[4] In July 1969, a white rookie policeman shot and killed nineteen-year-old Linda Anderson. The officer had been summoned to Anderson's apartment to respond to a disturbance. Upon being denied entrance, neighbors claimed, the cop used a shotgun to shoot at Anderson's voice coming from the other side of the door. Anderson was struck in the face and killed. The officer was reprimanded with a one-day suspension for violating General Order 67-14, which forbade firing through a closed door. He was never prosecuted for killing Anderson.[5]

The non-prosecution of police violence was a trend practiced across America. In Oakland, two white officers, Richard V. Williams and Robert W. Farrell, were both discharged from the force and arrested for assault with firearms on an occupied building after witnesses saw the two men shooting dozens of shots into the Panther headquarters while intoxicated on duty. Unlike in Chicago, this episode represents the rare occasion of police being held responsible for their acts of violence.[6] More importantly, the Chicago Police Department did not hesitate to prosecute black officers accused of using excessive force on white residents.[7]

One study of the Chicago Police Department's use of force in 1969 and 1970 found that African Americans were six times more likely to be killed by a police officer than were whites. Furthermore, such cases were likely to be marked by police misconduct: "In fifty-eight cases the police said their victim had a weapon, yet in only three of those cases was a weapon found. Twenty-eight of these cases showed clear evidence of police misconduct."[8]

Black residents attributed such results to racism in the police department. Many Chicago police officers were members of the Ku Klux Klan and other hate groups; others simply had no interest in enforcing legislation that protected the civil rights and liberties of African Americans. A report in the *Black Panther* in 1968 noted that one officer who had been on the force for fourteen years "admitted during a police board hearing that he is a Klansman," and several other officers were suspected of membership.[9] Another officer stationed in the black community of North Lawndale "drove to work with KKK spray painted on the trunk of his car."[10] Klan headquarters even bragged about the number of members on the police force.[11]

In response to residents' complaints, one police commander rationalized that officers were more "aggressive" in poor communities in order to root out and destroy Communist influence. Commander Connolly stated, "In the past, the poor neighborhoods have been exploited by persons . . . who have been less than American. There are so many of these anti-American, pink, even red organizations. I said the potential in a poor neighborhood is disproportionate than any other neighborhood for people being exploited by these types of people."[12] The group the officer was indirectly referring to was the Black Panther Party.

In response to rampant racism and discrimination in the Chicago Police Department, Renault Robinson helped to form the Afro-American Patrolman's League in 1969. The group's goals consisted of putting in place a fair process for promotions, ending police brutality in the black community and against black officers, and ending the Irish domination of the police department.[13] The black patrolmen who were its members objected to their fellow white officers' tolerance for Nazis and Klansmen and their rampant hatred of the Panthers.[14] During preparation for one of several raids on the Panthers' headquarters, the black patrolmen listened to white officers expressing their hatred of the BPP and enthusiasm for the raid: "'Boy, I'd love to blow one of those fuckers' heads off. Just one shot from any of them and I'm killing a motherfucker today,' one officer said, and got in reply several 'fuckin' A's'!"[15]

Members of the Afro-American Patrolman's League such as Renault Robinson, Howard Saffold, and Buzz Palmer respected the Panthers. More importantly, the officers acknowledged racism in the ranks of the Chicago Police Department.[16] They violated the policemen's "blue code," an unwritten rule that said that officers would offer one another silence and support, forming a fraternity-style brotherhood. Black patrolmen refused to ignore wanton racial brutality and adamantly advocated against such behavior toward the black community, and particularly against the Chicago Panthers. The predominately Irish police department responded to the Afro-American Patrolman's League with harassment, suspension, and arrest of its members.[17] An extensive collection of Red Squad files on the Afro-American Patrolman's League makes it clear that the Daley administration intended to destroy the league and its leader, Renault Robinson.[18] The administration's responses to members of the Afro-American Patrolman's League who stood against both their colleagues and Mayor Daley were so extreme and so obvious that the organization filed and won a multimillion-dollar racial discrimination lawsuit against the Chicago Police Department.[19]

The Red Squad

According to scholar Frank Donner, for more than 100 years, "urban police have served as the protective arm of the economic and political interest of the capitalist system."[20] Over this time, specialized units like the Chicago Police Department's "Red Squad" have been formed and employed predominately for political repression, to stifle protest and dissent, and to protect the status quo, the power structure, and political culture.[21]

The official name of the Chicago Police unit called the Red Squad varied over time. It was best known as the Subversive Unit, housed in the Intelligence Section of the Bureau of Investigative Services of the Chicago Police Department. The Red Squad evolved with political and social trends. Formed in the 1920s, it focused on persons suspected of having Communist Party ties or being involved in labor union radicalism. Its activities in the 1930s and 1940s are not well documented, although a number of files in the Chicago History Museum's collection from these decades indicate the Red Squad's continuing interest in suspected Communist Party or labor union "radicals." In the 1950s, the Red Squad was strongly influenced by the House Un-American Activities Committee (HUAC), and the two organizations shared information. As a result of Cold War politics, leftists and social protest activists, such as those involved in the civil rights movement, became targets of the police group.[22] Red Squad operatives provided HUAC with information both clandestinely and as witnesses at public hearings. HUAC's literature in the 1940s and 1950s supplied the Red Squad with names of local individuals and organizations suspected of having Communist ties, and the Red Squad took the initiative to investigate these people and groups. Legislation specifically aimed at Communist Party members—the Alien Registration Act and the McCarran Acts—provided the Red Squad with legal protection and justification for its intelligence activities.[23] In Chicago, the Red Squad under Daley was so successful in and notorious for stomping out opposition that the city earned the moniker "The National Capital of Police Repression."[24]

The Chicago Police Department's political surveillance operation served as the example for other cities' police departments to emulate, primarily due to its "size, number, and range of targets or operational scope and diversity."[25] Having grown and adapted to political and social changes for more than seventy-five years, the police department's no-holds-barred approach to anarchism, syndicalism, and Communism more than prepared officers for the city's antiwar activities and inner-city rebellions in the 1960s.[26] Red Squad agents were so sophisticated that officers were able to travel to California to spy on the Panthers. Agents also acquired confidential informants to infiltrate the group in other states, extending all the way to California.[27]

The Chicago Police Department's Red Squad maintained friendly relationships with Chicago's far-right and racist groups. Red Squad sergeant Joseph Grubisic recruited undercover confidential informers at John Birch Society meetings.[28] The Red Squad also had a cordial relationship with the Legion of Justice, a white-only group made up of suburban ethnics who were opposed to Rev. Dr. Martin Luther King Jr. and open housing and who advocated the violent maintenance of racial segregation. The Legion of Justice collaborated with Red Squad officers to burglarize, bug, harass, threaten, and use "terrorist-style raids against left-wing groups."[29] Frank Donner describes the milieu in which the Red Squad flourished: "The power of the unit and its freedom from accountability were nourished by a superpatriotic 'Americanist' tradition, a socially conservative constituency rooted in compact ethnic neighborhoods, a boss-ridden political structure, a right-wing press, racism both within the police department and in the city as a whole, and a corrupt police department. Indiscriminate targeting and autonomy were further assured by the power needs of the Daley administration and its political machine, which used the department's counter subversive resources as a weapon against critics."[30] Donner's analysis underscores the factors that explain how Red Squad officers functioned under the Daley machine's control as a weapon against dissent.

The Chicago Police Department's political surveillance operation was dissolved in 1975 after a group of concerned citizens, through the Alliance to End Repression and the American Civil Liberties Union, filed suit against the city of Chicago to shut down the Red Squad. Climaxing eleven years of litigation, a June 1984 jury verdict and a December 1985 court decision found the Chicago Police Subversive Activities Unit guilty of violating the First Amendment of the U.S. Constitution by spying on and disrupting peaceful political dissent. The court cases revealed that in addition to groups the Red Squad regarded as subversive (like the Panthers), the unit had repressed lawful political, religious, and civic groups that challenged local government power for more than fifty years. The Boy Scouts, the United Methodist Church, the League of Women Voters, the NAACP, the Jewish War Veterans, and the Chicago Peace Council were targets of the machine-controlled Red Squad. It even infiltrated the legal team of the Alliance to End Repression during the lawsuit. Over half a million dollars in damage awards were paid to approximately thirty plaintiffs. As a result, the Chicago Police Department's Red Squad files were sealed by a court order to prevent further lawsuits.[31]

FBI's COINTELPRO, the State's Attorney's Office, and the Red Squad

Chicago's Red Squad found its kindred organization at the federal level in the FBI. Created to protect, and arguably to serve, vested social, political, and economic interests in the nation, the FBI has not always functioned as a democratic institution.[32] The FBI's most famous director, John Edgar Hoover, disliked political leftists, believed in white supremacy, and aligned his position with U.S. elites to maintain blacks in a subordinate economic position. He believed that any activity that disturbed the race and class hierarchy in America was a threat, and the FBI usually targeted individuals and groups carrying out such activities.[33] The FBI's COINTELPRO was launched against the BPP in 1968 in part because of Hoover's belief that the Panthers were the "most influential" revolutionary organization in America.[34] In 1969, Hoover declared the BPP the "greatest threat to internal security" of the United States and set out to destroy the organization.[35] Subsequently, the Panthers became the target of 233 of 295 COINTELPRO initiatives aimed at African American political organizations.[36]

A U.S. Senate report describes the origin and ideology of the program in some detail:

> COINTELPRO is the FBI acronym for a series of covert action programs directed against domestic groups. In these programs, the Bureau went beyond the collection of intelligence to secret action defined to "disrupt" and "neutralize" target groups and individuals. The techniques were adopted wholesale from wartime counterintelligence, and ranged from the trivial (mailing reprints of Reader's Digest articles to college administrators) to the degrading (sending anonymous poison-pen letters intended to break up marriages) and the dangerous (encouraging gang warfare and falsely labeling members of a violent group as police informers). . . . COINTELPRO began in 1956, in part because of frustration with Supreme Court rulings limiting the Government's power to proceed overtly against dissident groups; it ended in 1971 with the threat of public exposure. In the intervening 15 years, the Bureau conducted a sophisticated vigilante operation aimed squarely at preventing the exercise of First Amendment rights of speech and association, on the theory that preventing the growth of dangerous groups and the propagation of dangerous ideas would protect the national security and deter violence. Many of the techniques used would be intolerable in a democratic society even if all of the targets had been involved in violent activity, but COINTELPRO went far beyond that. The unexpressed major premise of the programs was that a law enforcement agency has the duty to do whatever is necessary to combat perceived threats to the existing social and political order.[37]

The FBI's secret war against the Panthers exhausted all of COINTELPRO's methods, including a media offensive, silencing the Panther newspaper, attacking the breakfast for children program, preventing coalitions, neutralizing Panther supporters, exacerbating intergroup/intraparty tensions, infiltrating the organization, sponsoring raids and pretext arrests, encouraging malicious prosecutions, and even assassinating Panthers.[38]

In Chicago, the FBI gave in to pressure from the Daley administration to share information. "To an extent not duplicated in any other city, the Chicago subversive activities unit worked closely with other intelligence agencies, both state and federal."[39] "Chicago represented an advanced level of police–FBI cooperation."[40] Information from bureau files in Chicago on the Panthers was given to Chicago police upon request, and the Chicago Police Department files were open to the bureau. A special agent who acted as a liaison between the FBI's Racial Matters Squad (which was responsible for monitoring Panther activity in Chicago) and the Red Squad from 1967 through July 1969 testified that he visited Chicago police officers between three and five times a week to exchange information. The bureau and Chicago police both maintained paid informants in the BPP and shared informant reports, and the FBI provided information that was used by Chicago police in planning raids against the Chicago Panthers.[41] The FBI provided Cook County state's attorney Edward V. Hanrahan with intelligence on the Party that resulted in four police raids on Chicago Panthers' headquarters in 1969 alone. The fourth raid ended in Hampton's death.[42]

Law enforcement agencies relied on raids and pretext arrests to harass Panthers and to deplete their funds. The idea was to routinely arrest members to force the group to spend financial resources needed for their social programs to bail out their comrades. During the summer of 1969, Chicago Panthers were arrested 111 times, mostly on minor charges, with only a few taken to trial. Several of these arrests were a result of raids on the Party's West Side headquarters. The first raid took place on June 9, as the FBI stormed the Party's office on the phony charge that a fugitive, George Sams, wanted in New Haven, Connecticut, was hiding there.[43] Sams, working as an FBI provocateur in the New York chapter, murdered Panther Alex Rackley after accusing him of being an informant. George Sams had been employed with the FBI since 1967, when he was assigned to infiltrate Stokely Carmichael's faction of SNCC before he joined the BPP.[44] Since Sams worked for the FBI, the agency knew he had been to the Chicago Panthers' headquarters but was not in the Panthers' facility at the time of the raid. Although the fugitive was never found, the FBI used the bogus decree as an opportunity to arrest eleven Panthers and to destroy Party resources.[45] Indeed, Sams's fugitive status was used by law enforcement as a neutralization tool to wage predawn raids on Panther facilities around the country, putting a massive strain on Party resources.[46]

On July 31, 1969, the Chicago Panthers' headquarters was raided again, this time by the Chicago police. During the raid, officers not only destroyed

Aftermath of police raid on the ILBPP headquarters, October 1969
(Courtesy of Paul Sequeira)

the office itself but also seized legal guns, confiscated $3,000, trashed food that had been collected for the Party's free breakfast program, and seized petitions that thousands of people had signed demanding an appeal bond for Fred Hampton.[47] On October 3, 1969, three blue-and-white squad cars approached the headquarters of the ILBPP. Unprovoked, the officers shot up the office. Three Panthers in training inside the facility returned fire, injuring several officers. Eventually, the police gained entrance to the Panther office and arrested the three men. Presumably angered by the incident, the police officers destroyed furniture, newspapers, and food and confiscated money that financed Panther community service programs. The officers also set fire to the Party's headquarters. Clearly, their intent was not only to apprehend Panthers occupying the facility but also to destroy the Party's infrastructure.[48] Bobby Seale called these police actions "naked state terror."[49]

In addition to such direct attacks, the FBI used agents to infiltrate targeted organizations, an old, effective tool of the FBI and local police agencies. When the FBI initiated its COINTELPRO attacks on the Party in 1968, there were about 3,300 "racial ghetto-type informants" on its payroll; that number had increased to more than 7,500 by 1971.[50] In 1969, the FBI paid its 67 informants in the BPP $7.4 million for information gathering.[51] The best-known government spy in the Illinois chapter was William O'Neal. The FBI hired O'Neal to infiltrate the Chicago Panthers after he had been arrested for car theft and impersonating an FBI agent. The charges against O'Neal were dropped, and he received a monthly stipend from 1969 through 1972 that ultimately totaled approximately $30,000. After joining the Party, O'Neal rapidly moved up the Panthers ranks, and he was eventually assigned as chief of security and Fred Hampton's primary bodyguard. O'Neal's undercover work produced a twelve-volume, 4,000-page surveillance file on Fred Hampton, among other intelligence that ultimately contributed to Hampton's death. In 1969 alone, O'Neal furnished so much information that the FBI filled six volumes with memos on the Panthers. He also played a critical role in the sabotage of the Party's alliance with the BSR.[52]

In November 1969, Bobby Seale and other leaders set out to purge spies. As a result of infiltrators occupying key security positions in the Party, a number of legitimate members were ejected as snitches and provocateurs, allowing the moles to become even more entrenched. As repression intensified against the Panthers, these infiltrators advocated for and implemented brutal means of combating spies to enhance the Party's reputation of being a violent group. FBI provocateur O'Neal, for example, was responsible for weeding out infiltrators in the ILBPP. He made an electric chair to intimidate accused members. Fred Hampton prevented him from using such devices.[53] On other occasions, O'Neal attempted to convince members to bomb City Hall, participate in robberies, conduct illegal drug activity, and engage in other criminal behavior, to no avail.[54] At the end of 1969, about 10 percent of the BPP's membership consisted of local and federal law enforcement infiltrators.[55] Paranoia and accusations caused many Panthers to leave the organization. Bobby Seale estimates that 30 to 40 percent of all Panthers had left the group by 1970.[56] The aforementioned aspect of law enforcement repression along with Hampton's political assassination caused many members to depart the Illinois chapter in 1970 and 1971.[57]

The Chicago Police Department was also efficient in infiltrating the ILBPP. The following account of a Chicago undercover police officer's ability to penetrate Panther functions highlights how such occurrences took place. A confidential investigator working undercover in a pool hall on 2334 W. Madison engaged in a conversation with Walter Jordan, who told him that he had recently been approached by a male Panther who wanted to recruit him. A check in the police department's Records and Inquiry Section revealed that Jordan had applied for an appointment as a police cadet but was rejected due to an arrest for a burglary charge. Jordan indicated that he was interested in becoming a Panther and agreed to introduce the investigator to a Party recruiter to inquire about joining the organization. After two attempts, the two men were introduced to an alleged Panther named Zeke by Jackie, a taxi driver who reportedly was also a Panther recruiter.[58]

Eventually, the officer and Jordan attended a meeting at Chicago Panthers' headquarters. After being thoroughly searched by two party members, the two men and about forty other potential members were escorted into a meeting room, where they listened to a Panther explain the Party's ideology, including the group's hatred of the capitalist power structure, antigovernment practices, and the importance of the art of self-defense. The unidentified Panther stated that the Chicago police had tried to infiltrate the group twice before and had been caught and dealt with accordingly. During the meeting, no pens or pencils were allowed, and no names were mentioned. Jackie, the taxi driver, appeared to be one of the high-ranking members. The potential members were given an application and told to return the following night for a meeting. The officer noted that there was one entrance/exit, that the recruits had to buzzed in, that their leader had to know the password ("Panther Power") and the appropriate response ("Right ON"), that the headquarters was never left unguarded at any time, and that Panthers were instructed never to give up their guns to police officers. Instead, the Party advocated that a member in this situation "shoot it out," and if a Panther gave up a weapon without a fight, that person would be in "hot water."[59] There was also a female self-defense karate class that night.[60]

The confidential investigator attended the next meeting, which was held at the Louis Theater, with Jordan and Panthers "Big Bear" Cleveland and another member. The undercover police officer drove the group to the meeting, and all were dressed in Panther regalia. About 200 people attended the event. When the group arrived, Julia Barnes was speaking. She advised all males to join the Party and to get a gun, because revolution was near. Fred Hampton and Cassandra Watson (secretary of education) also provided speeches. Watson spoke in place of Ruth Iris Shinn (secretary of communications). Both urged all Panthers to promote membership in the organization. The confidential investigator was told to bring a gun to the next meeting to increase the firepower of the group.[61]

On another occasion, a confidential investigator reported on a meeting held at Panther headquarters with the White Panther Party. The White Panthers donated $282 to the BPP's treasury, and a White Panther named Barry agreed to supply the Black Panthers with raw materials for making explosives. The investigator reported on the Panthers' plan to wire the telephone pole at the rear of their headquarters so that "if any pigs try to climb it to gain access to the headquarters, they'll be bar-b-qued pigs."[62] The investigator also submitted a floor plan of the Panthers' headquarters and a collection of formulas for making explosives.[63]

These accounts demonstrate just how easy it was for the Chicago Police Department to gather pertinent information and manufacture trumped-up charges and raids against the Panthers. There are numerous examples of Panthers arrested on bogus charges; to avoid repetition, only one incident will be discussed here. In January 1969, Bobby Rush and seven other Panthers, including two women, occupied the lobby of the Thirteenth District police station to make sure that members who were arrested earlier were released safely. The group declared that fellow members Robert Bruce, Clarence Clark, Peter Hammock, and James Stewart, along with SCLC brothers Robert and James Wilson, had been arrested on a false charge of robbery. Party members were released after being fingerprinted and processed, and as in most other intentional false arrests, the charges were dropped. The Wilson brothers were also cleared of the robbery allegation but were detained on charges of armed violence, aggravated battery, resisting arrest, and failure to register a firearm. Prior to leaving the police station, Rush was assured by attorney Dennis Cunningham that the Wilson brothers would get a defense counsel. Officers also discovered that Bruce had a film in the trunk of his car that the police wished they had known to take a look at. Officers described the film as being packaged to be shipped somewhere. Police followed all the cars and occupants back to the Panthers' headquarters and watched them for forty-five minutes.[64]

Such surveillance was a tactic exploited by officers that often resulted in police repression of Panthers. A two-hour observation of the meeting at Dog House Lounge on 7511 S. Cottage Grove between four Panthers, four Rangers, and four Black Elephants, for example, caused the Red Squad to intensify efforts to disrupt a possible union of the groups.[65]

The Media and the Panthers

The FBI utilized the media to plant fake and derogatory stories about the BPP in an attempt to discredit the organization and to obstruct recruitment and coalition building. More than 300 journalists, many of them nationally syndicated, served as propagandists for the FBI. Some of these members of the press simply signed their names to news stories and "opinion pieces written by FBI propaganda specialists."[66] The Chicago FBI field office alone listed 25 allied journalists, one of the more prominent being the *Chicago Tribune*'s Ronald Koziol. Chicago FBI special agent in charge Marlin Johnson routinely provided Koziol with false information about area Panthers. Koziol in turn published "a whole series of articles portraying the Panthers as 'highly violent.'" According to one history of the FBI, "The stories, replete with factual errors, 'were [intended] to support and lend credibility to [other] stepped up COINTELPRO operations' undertaken by Johnson's agents against the Chicago BPP chapter from January 1969 onward."[67]

Like the FBI, the Red Squad was able to effectively use the press to disseminate false and exaggerated information about those who opposed the Daley Democratic machine. Chicago Panthers were a special target, and a negative smear campaign was used to justify the police's violent attacks on the group. Red Squad–influenced media representations encouraged Chicagoans to be unsympathetic to the harassment, brutality, and deaths the police and other law enforcement agents inflicted on the members of the Party. Frank Donner documents that the *Chicago Tribune* "cooperated with the unit in a familiar trade-off by which reporters, in exchange for favorable press coverage, received information about targets or activities in disfavor with the red squad."[68]

Ronald Koziol, whom Donner calls "the undisputed dean of red squad collaborators," was supplied information from Red Squad reports to write negative articles in the *Tribune* about the reports' subjects. The information provided by the journalist via the newspaper was usually extremely exaggerated and severely contradicted police reports. For example, one article states that Panthers traveled to the South Side to meet with the BSR. Next, the police broke up the encounter, and eleven Panthers and five Rangers were arrested after a high-speed chase involving more than twenty-five police cars from the Grand Crossing district that also resulted in a few accidents.[69] An internal Red Squad document indicates a different version of the incident: there was a meeting between the Panthers and the Rangers, and after the assembly "one" of several Panther cars on its way back to the West Side was pulled over and searched, and the five occupants were arrested without any confrontation.[70]

In 1969, Koziol continued to use Red Squad reports to provide readers with sensationalized accounts about Chicago Panthers. In one article, the journalist stated that five Panthers (one of whom was Bobby Rush) had recently been arrested and a brown address book containing thirty-five names was confiscated; the report noted that the book might help authorities determine the number of new Panther recruits. The article failed to mention, however, that the members were arrested for informing a motorist of his rights as he was being issued a ticket by a policeman on Fifty-First Street and King Drive.

The journalist's piece cites a list of confiscated weapons and receipts for the Panthers' recent purchase of weapons. The purpose of Koziol's article was to produce a negative portrayal of the Party.[71]

These examples demonstrate the extent to which the mainstream press took on the function of implementing the Red Squad's "neutralization programs," playing an important part in discrediting certain targeted organizations.[72] Koziol's journalism substituted sensationalism for fact to portray the Panthers as a dangerous group that needed to be eliminated and to discourage the union of the Panthers and Rangers by identifying and presenting both groups to the public as violent gangs, thereby dissuading respectable community members and sympathetic individuals and groups from assisting the Party or its programs. Masquerading as objective journalism, these press reports misled readers and helped to fuel society's hostile misunderstanding of the BPP.[73] In addition to FBI and local Red Squad informants, police engaged paid journalists. The purpose of their articles was a classic counterrevolutionary three-step program that led to the destruction of the ILBPP: alienation, isolation, and elimination.

The Assassination of Fred Hampton

The efforts of city and federal law enforcement personnel to undermine the Panthers had borne obvious fruit by early 1969. In February of that year, a Red Squad informant reported, "Fred Hampton stated that he is scared that he will be killed. He believed that he was 'in it too deep to get out without being killed' because there has already been an attempt on his life. Hampton had all his pockets on his pants and jacket sewed shut so no one can say that he reached in his pocket for a weapon if he is killed."[74]

Hampton's concern for his life turned out to be prescient. On December 4, 1969, a little after 4:00 A.M., fourteen gang-intelligence-unit and subversive-unit police officers who had been organized into a special prosecution unit by Cook County state's attorney Edward Hanrahan raided Fred Hampton's apartment on 2337 West Monroe. The officers fired ninety-nine shots, killing both Fred Hampton and Mark Clark, the deputy defense minister from Peoria, Illinois.

The FBI's COINTELPRO has received warranted credit and criticism for its role in Hampton's death. With the help of confidential informant William O'Neal, the FBI was able to set up the political assassinations of Hampton and Clark. Yet, Chicago police officers controlled by state's attorney Hanrahan actually carried out the raid on the apartment and murdered the two Panthers.

Fred Hampton at Dirksen Federal Building in Chicago, October 1969
(Courtesy of Paul Sequeira)

This was the most egregious example of the Daley administration's efforts to silence Chicago's Black Panthers. Historians have not accorded enough accountability to the Chicago Police Department and the Daley Democratic machine for their part in the murders.

Chairman Fred Hampton and the Chicago Panthers made a priority of confronting police brutality, political corruption, and exploitation by Daley's Democratic machine.[75] Hampton helped to establish the Rainbow Coalition with civic, civil rights, religious, student, and community groups as well as gangs to form a collective front against their common oppressor, the Daley administration. As the face and voice of this movement, Hampton repeatedly challenged and threatened the Democratic machine in his speeches, press conferences, and television and radio appearances. As a consequence, the Daley administration made him a target and, ultimately, a candidate for political assassination.[76]

FBI agents were instructed by Director Hoover to neutralize the Panthers and thus had an equal incentive to eliminate the organization's charismatic leader, Fred Hampton. In 1969, Bobby Seale, Masai Hewitt, and Don Cox, members of the national BPP Central Committee, held a secret meeting with Fred Hampton and Bobby Rush in the office of attorney Kermit Coleman at the American Civil Liberties Union in Chicago to discuss the possibility of temporarily moving the BPP national headquarters to Chicago, as Bobby

Seale would soon be on trial in Chicago for his role in the protest demonstrations during the Democratic National Convention held in the city in 1968.[77] Hampton announced at a "meeting sponsored by Panthers held at the People's Church" in Chicago on September 25, 1969, that he had been chosen by national leadership to serve as "Assistant Chief of Staff" of the national BPP due to the success of the Illinois chapter and the incarceration and exile of the group's national leadership.[78] Panther founders Huey Newton and Bobby Seale were in jail facing murder charges. Newton's charges stemmed from an alleged shootout with police officers in California; Seale was accused of being involved in FBI provocateur George Sams's murder of Alex Rackley in Connecticut, as well as being a member of the Chicago Eight. Eldridge Cleaver was in exile in Algeria, and the Party's chief of staff, David Hilliard, was under indictment for threatening to kill President Richard Nixon.[79] Hampton would have assumed the highest position of national leadership in the Party, since he was not on trial, in jail, or under indictment. Furthermore, infiltrator William O'Neal informed the FBI that "Hampton kept the Party alive and growing through his leadership, and that the chapter [would falter] without him."[80] Consequently, Hampton became, in Ward Churchill's words, a "classic example of a COINTELPRO selective assassination" target in December 1969.[81]

Chicago has a long history of political assassinations of African Americans by the local power structure, for their opposition to its power, especially on the city's West Side. Fred Hampton was not the first African American West Side political icon to be murdered by the Chicago establishment, and he was not the first to be killed by Daley machine cronies. Politicians Octavious Granady (1928) and Ben Lewis (1963) are two others. Fred Hampton is, however, one of Chicago's most popular political martyrs. His death, as historians now understand, involved an unusual alliance between the city and the FBI. Moreover, his death led to a U.S. Senate hearing, a congressional investigation, and numerous trial proceedings, all of which jointly implicate the FBI and the Daley administration in both the assassination and the governmental cover-up of Hampton's murder.[82]

Before the raid that resulted in Hampton's murder in 1969, Chicago police had provoked violent confrontations with Panthers that resulted in deaths on both sides. On July 16, 1969, Panthers Larry Roberson and Grady Moore attempted to inform a resident of his rights as he was being interrogated by an officer. The officer was offended, and a dispute ensued that resulted in a shootout. Roberson was killed during the event, and Moore was arrested.[83] On November 13, 1969, another shootout occurred when two policemen reportedly responded to a call that men with guns were seen near an abandoned building on the South Side. Panther Spurgeon "Jake" Winters and two policemen, Frank Rappaport and John Gilhooly, were killed during the incident. Both sides claimed to have been attacked first, and eight officers and Panther Lance Bell suffered gunshot injuries. Bell was later indicted for the death of the two policemen.[84]

A month later, both law enforcement agencies used the deaths of officers Rappaport and Gilhooly as pretext to permanently silence Fred Hampton. Fully aware that Hampton was out of town during the incident, agents nonetheless blamed the chairman for causing the policemen's demise. Informant William O'Neal corroborated that the police sought revenge for the killings. However, not all policemen were willing to murder Panthers outright for retribution. Thomas Lyons, head of Chicago's GIU, canceled a shooting raid on the Panthers' office because he refused to allow the FBI to use him or his officers to attempt to destroy the Party by illegal means. Having conducted his own investigation into the incident, "Lyons discovered [what the FBI had known all along,] that Hampton had nothing to do with the officers' murders."[85]

The raid on Hampton's apartment was arranged by FBI Chicago special agent in charge Roy Mitchell and agent Robert Piper. O'Neal supplied his handlers with a hand-drawn floor plan of Hampton's apartment, which included the approximate height of the Panther's bed from the floor. Earlier that evening, the informant put a dose of secobarbital in Hampton's Kool-Aid, ensuring the target would be in a comatose sleep during the raid. Mitchell gave the floor plan to Hanrahan's office, and officers used it to carry out the raid.[86] Mitchell also falsely informed the Chicago Police Department that illegal weapons were stored in the apartment, despite O'Neal's reports that the weapons were purchased using "legal Illinois State Gun Registration Cards issued to female BPP members who [had] never been arrested."[87]

Armed with O'Neal's floor plan and informed of Hampton's sedation, fourteen police officers assigned to Hanrahan's Special Prosecutions Unit armed with a machine gun, semiautomatic rifles, shotguns, and handguns raided Hampton's apartment. The officers were led by Daniel Groth (who had suspected connections to the Central Intelligence Agency) and Edward Carmody (who was a childhood friend of an officer killed the previous month in a Panther/police shootout).[88]

The officers were transported to the apartment in a telephone company utility vehicle. The policemen used an illegally obtained search warrant for illegal weapons as a pretext for the raid. Immediately following two knocks on the door, Officer James "Gloves" Davis (an African American with a long list of police brutality complaints against him) kicked open the front door of the apartment and shot Mark Clark in the heart with a thirty-caliber M-1 carbine, killing him instantly. Having sustained the deadly wound, Clark reflexively fired the shotgun he held. This shot was the only one fired by a Panther during the raid. Harold Bell ran to Hampton's bedroom to attempt to warn and wake the chairman, to no avail. Officers Davis and Groth then shot eighteen-year-old Brenda Harris, who was asleep in a front-room bed. After securing the front of the apartment, Officers Davis and Joseph Gorman, armed with automatic submachine guns, blindly fired forty-two rounds into the wall of the front closet in the direction of Fred Hampton's bed.[89] The trajectory of the officers' rounds was low (at bed level), in a straight line, and toward the head of Hampton's bed as marked on O'Neal's floor plan.[90] Hampton's mattress was riddled with bullets. He was hit only a few times but was badly wounded. His pregnant girlfriend, Deborah Johnson, who was in bed with Hampton and lying adjacent to the wall, climbed over her boyfriend to avoid being shot.[91] She recalls the incident:

> Still half asleep, I looked up, and I saw bullets coming from what looked like the front of the apartment, from the kitchen area. They were, the pigs was just shooting, and about this time, I jumped on top of the chairman. He looked up, looked like all the pigs had converged at the entranceway to the bedroom area, the back bedroom area. The mattress is just going [starts shaking], you could just feel all the bullets going into it. I just knew we would be dead, everybody in there. When [Hampton] looked, he just looked up, he didn't say a word. He didn't move except for moving his head up. [Hampton] laid his head back down to the side like that. He never said a word; he never got up out of the bed.[92]

The police officers continued their indiscriminate shooting rampage. Three more Panthers sustained gunshot wounds. Verlina Brewer was shot twice, once in the left buttock and once in the left knee. Blair Anderson was hit three times, once in each thigh and once in the base of his penis. Doc Satchel, deputy minister of health, was shot five times with a machine gun and spent a month in the hospital.[93] Satchel recounted, "I was hit two times in the stomach, one time in the leg, and I was hit, grazed on each hand. . . . I had to have a section of my colon taken out because of an infection."[94]

After the police raiders had secured the apartment, one of the officers assassinated Fred Hampton. Policeman Edward Carmody and two unidentified officers entered Hampton's bedroom, as he was the only unaccounted-for

Panther at this point in the raid.[95] Scholar Curtis Austin contends that Panther Harold Bell's recollection of the incident offers proof of the officers' primary intent. Bell states that when the raiders discovered the wounded Hampton still lying in his bed, one officer shouted with excitement, "That's Fred Hampton, that's Fred Hampton!" indicating their intended target.[96] Panther survivors overheard the following exchange between Edward Carmody and the other two officers as they discussed what to do with Hampton as he lay wounded:[97]

(First Voice): "That's Fred Hampton."
(Second Voice): "Is he dead? Bring him out [of his bedroom]."
(First Voice): "He's barely alive; he'll make it."
(Two shots ring out and a third voice, believed to be Carmody's, states) "He's good and dead now."[98]

Fred Hampton was shot twice in the head at point-blank range as he lay immobile and unconscious. According to the second autopsy report, the wounds of the two fired shots "entered directly in front of the right ear and exited from the left side of the throat, and the other entered the right forehead and was probed to a point behind the left eye. They were consistent with two shots to the head at point blank range." The two bullets were never recovered.[99] The survivors' account suggests that Officer Carmody killed Fred Hampton. Carmody had a motive to murder Hampton, as his childhood friend had been killed the previous month by a Panther, and Carmody and other officers blamed Hampton for the policeman's death. The physical evidence and Carmody's later statements strongly suggest that he murdered Fred Hampton. Hampton's defense team argues that Carmody "was the only officer to enter from the rear [where Hampton's bedroom was located] and fire a gun of the [.38] caliber that could have caused bullet holes of the size found in Fred's head. We believe he was the officer who shot Fred inside the doorway to Fred's bedroom. The people in the back of the apartment testified that they heard a thump shortly after hearing shots and then saw Carmody dragging Fred's body out."[100] Scholars, activists, former Panthers, and government officials have also drawn this conclusion.[101]

The seven surviving Panthers in the apartment, including the wounded and female members, were beaten and arrested by the raiders. Wearing nothing but their pajamas and house shoes, the members were shuffled from one station to another in the Chicago winter snow. They were charged with attempted murder, aggravated assault, and assault with a deadly weapon, with bail set at at least $100,000 each.[102]

The Panthers were outraged by the assassination of Fred Hampton. Elbert "Big Man" Howard (minister of information for Oakland) stated, "Fred Hampton was murdered in his sleep by outlaws who masquerade as lawmen, who invade the man's home, his sanctuary, and attempted to massacre everyone in his home."[103] Eldridge Cleaver referred to Hampton being murdered in his sleep "by shock troopers of the power structure" as an example of a race war being conducted by the U.S. government.[104] The Panthers also advocated for a police control amendment to be implemented in American communities to end abuses that Panthers described as fascism and police brutality. The amendment called for control over the police to be given to neighborhood councils elected by their communities, the establishment of separate police departments for different ethnic and racial communities (black, white, Mexican, etc.), the creation of five community council divisions within each police department, and the residence of police officers in the communities where they worked.[105]

Other Panther messages, such as the one that follows, taunted and threatened police departments:

You are the agents of the power structure.
You are the flunkies of the fat ass businessman.
You are not here to "serve and protect" the masses of the people.
You are here to protect racism-capitalism-imperialism.
You are used by rich pigs to take the blame for the conditions in this
    country off of them.
The pig power structure will not and cannot protect you!!!
The wrath of the people will descend upon you.
Power to the people!
Panther power to the vanguard.[106]

State's attorney Hanrahan and special agent in charge Johnson played major roles in the disinformation campaign to cover up the political assassination of Fred Hampton. In addition, Ronald Koziol and reporters at the *Chicago Tribune* were called upon once again to utilize their positions to portray the party as a violence-prone group that was a threat to American society. Koziol printed at least seven articles during the three weeks following the police killings that documented supposedly violent actions by Panthers. The ulterior aim of the articles was to demonstrate to readers that the wounded and dead Panthers got exactly what they deserved.[107] The most egregious reports were a *Chicago Tribune* front-page exclusive and a CBS-affiliate WBBM reenactment of the raid. Both spectacles presented unchallenged police

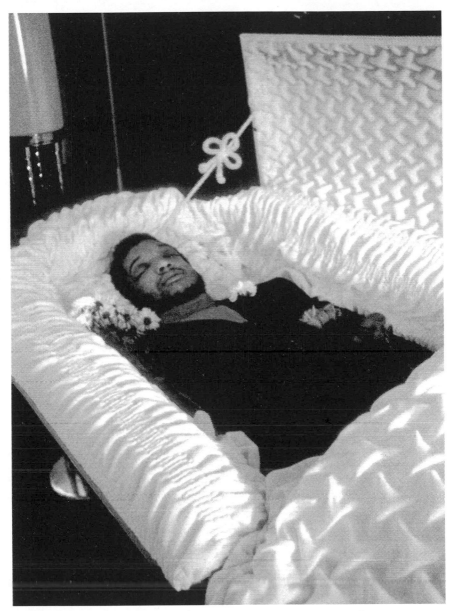

Fred Hampton lying in state, December 1969 (Courtesy of Paul Sequeira)

accounts. The *Tribune* even provided photos of supposed bullet holes in Hampton's apartment that state's attorney Hanrahan declared were proof that the Panthers fired first and that officers were forced to defend themselves. Several independent reporters revealed that what Hanrahan claimed to be bullet holes were actually nail heads, and more investigative journalism unraveled the cover-up of the raid.[108]

The discrepancies uncovered by independent investigative journalists led to a federal grand jury investigation. The grand jury highlighted the blatant contradictions in the officers' accounts:

This report contains the findings of the grand jury after hearing nearly one hundred witnesses and considering nearly one hundred thirty exhibits. Including police records and photographs, moving pictures, transcripts of testimonies before other bodies, voluminous investigative and scientific reports and reports of investigative interview with over one hundred potential witnesses who were not called. . . . Groth, Davis, Jones and Gorman, those are all officers, all insist that a shot was fired by Brenda Harris at them as they came in the door. None of them could explain what had become of this shot, and it is not possible to draw a line from the southeast corner of the living room where Harris was said by Davis and Groth to be on the bed holding a gun. Out through the living room door, the entrance hall door and the outside door, there are no holes in the west wall of the apartment. . . . By their own testimony, [the officers] admit that for twelve minutes . . . there was gun firing in that apartment. And yet the Federal Grand Jury concludes that only one possible shot could have come from a Panther weapon. And that shot could have come through the door from a man who had just been shot in the heart. [The officers] would have us believe, that even though there was only one Panther shot, they called for cease-fire on three different occasions and didn't get it and so they continued their firing. The great variance between the physical evidence and the testimony of the officers raises the question as to whether the officers are falsifying their accounts. Those officers fired ninety-nine shots through the walls of an apartment where they knew people were sleeping. . . . The Federal Grand Jury comes to its conclusions, unquestionably the raid was not professionally planned or properly executed and the result of the raid was two deaths, four injuries and seven improper criminal charges.

In spite of those conclusions, the report then goes on to say, "The physical evidence and the discrepancies in the officers' accounts are insufficient to establish probable cause to charge the officers with a willful violation of the occupants' civil rights."[109]

The raid on Hampton's apartment was declared illegal by the federal grand jury, but the police assassins did not suffer any repercussions. Notably, the officers failed to produce the Panthers' alleged illegal weapons, which were the pretext for the raid.[110] Moreover, the grand jury's decision that the officers' actions did not violate the Panthers' civil rights solidified that "indiscriminate targeting and autonomy were further assured by the power needs of the Daley administration and its political machine, which used the department's counter subversive resources as a weapon against critics."[111] In the immediate legal aftermath, a deal was brokered between the police and survivors of the raid: the grand jury would make no effort to indict the police raiders, and in exchange the police would drop the charges against the survivors. Koziol, the *Chicago Tribune*, and WBBM all failed to recant the bogus and doctored stories they reported about the raid to support the policemen. Nor did any of these news affiliates provide any criticism of the officers' flagrant abuse of force.[112] For the next thirteen years, the legal teams of the victims of the raid would battle Cook County, the city of Chicago, and the federal government in court before winning a settlement of $1.85 million in 1983. The FBI's chief infiltrator, William O'Neal committed suicide in the early 1980s. However, his work to dismantle to ILBPP was long done, as the chapter closed in 1974.

Conclusion

This chapter demonstrates that the Chicago Police Department's Red Squad resources and agenda were similar to those of the FBI's COINTELPRO. The unit, for example, was able to infiltrate the BPP not only in Chicago but also in California via undercover policemen and confidential informers—some of whom were officer's wives. The media, more specifically journalists and editors at the *Chicago Tribune*, collaborated with the Red Squad as a propaganda tool to sensationalize, tarnish the reputation and image of, and ultimately destroy the ILBPP.

The assassinations of Fred Hampton and Mark Clark were two of many political murders conducted by the Chicago Police Department. Their deaths illustrate the extremes of state repression to silence dissent and political opposition. To quote armed-self-defense advocate and African American liberation icon Robert Williams: "Due to the amount of legal protection given to police in controversial issues of violence and laws being passed that give those who kill police automatic death sentences, people are denied their right to defend one's own personal safety against brutal attacks by police. Fred Hampton and Mark Clark are . . . classical examples."[113] The subsequent civil trials by the Hampton family and the Panther survivors against the Chicago Police Department further indicated the state's role in the political assassination of Fred Hampton. This factor and others led to the demise of Daley Democratic machine politics in Chicago in the 1970s, which along with the Illinois chapter's legacy, is the subject of the next chapter.

The work of the Black Panther Party on the West Side
and South Side of Chicago built a strong movement
that clarified the issues.... Fred [Hampton] clarified the
issues—[that] these are our friends and these are our
enemies ... and that we need to unite with as many
people as possible.
—José "Cha Cha" Jiménez, September 14, 2009

SIX

The Legacy of the Illinois Chapter
of the Black Panther Party

The story of the ILBPP is a story of black politics and black radicalism in Chicago involving nontraditional political organizations and forces whose coalition politics have been neglected by conventional scholarship. It is a story,
too, of the battle of the city's poor and racially diverse populations for economic and political freedom from the stranglehold of Daley's Democratic
machine. And just as the story of the Illinois Panthers is a multifaceted one,
so too is the chapter's legacy, touching on poverty, race, and politics in Chicago and the nation. Fred Hampton's conviction that the Panthers had to
"unite with as many people as possible," as Jiménez puts it, lay behind the
three most significant elements of this legacy: the ILBPP's survival programs,
its influence on racial coalition politics (particularly through the Rainbow
Coalition), and its ongoing effect as a catalyst for twenty-first-century racial
and political conflict in Chicago.

Long after the Illinois chapter disbanded in 1974, its survival programs remained operative. Several former members and supportive community activists continued the free clinics and breakfast programs initiated by the chapter. The Rainbow Coalition continued to make strides in the political arena. The existence of the group in the early 1980s was a significant reason Chicago elected and later reelected its first African American mayor, Harold Washington, and both the coalition and its influence played major roles in the presidential campaigns of Jesse Jackson and Barack Obama. Though the Illinois Panthers solidified racial and class coalition-building politics in the city, few politicians have acknowledged the contribution that the Party's Rainbow Coalition made to their successful campaigns. Finally, Fred Hampton continues to be an icon and martyr of the city's class struggle. In recent years, several efforts to name a street on Chicago's West Side after Hampton ignited heated exchanges between the African American community and the power structure. The debate has exposed the continuation of the deep racial polarization that the Party's Rainbow Coalition attempted to address.

Survival Programs

The BPP's greatest legacy is its survival programs. These community service programs were initiated to circumvent the devastating effects of racism and capitalism on African Americans. Shortly after their implementation in Oakland, such programs were begun in cities such as Chicago, throughout the nation, and abroad to assist other impoverished and oppressed people. Former Chicago Panther Lynn French declared the survival programs to be a revolutionary aspect of the Party's legacy:

I believe the Black Panther Party left a permanent imprint in this country. You could talk about it on a lot of different levels. In practical terms of just day-to-day life, there was no such thing as having free breakfast in schools. I believe that there is not a city in this country that does not serve free breakfast to children in the mornings in public schools. Every medical institution or university in this country has now spawned health centers in communities that are a direct take off from what we had. Just in every aspect of every program that we had, it has become the accepted norm that that's what people should have. Now there may be people who say that's not a revolution, I say that's revolutionary. I think that we had a revolutionary impact, that's not to say that I think this is a perfect society, but I think that we had a revolutionary impact on how things were when we got together and started out.[1]

The most respected and utilized Panther community service project was its free breakfast for children initiative. There was no such successful government-run entity of its kind prior to the Panthers' program. The free breakfast for children program was instrumental in many poor American communities, as its success in poor black urban centers spilled over to other impoverished racial/ethnic communities. Its popularity spread as Panther field secretaries organized free breakfast programs in and outside black neighborhoods. The Party gained assistance from an array of supporters, including religious, civic, community, and student organizations, many of which were opposed to the Panthers' politics but respected, utilized, and relied upon their community service programs.

Kim Cloud, a former beneficiary of the Party's free breakfast program, recalls how the program's influence reached beyond simply feeding school-children: "Many times they fed my whole family. . . . The Panthers helped a lot of people."[2] Against the backdrop of Cold War politics, the free breakfast program highlighted the contradiction of the richest country in the world having one of the largest populations of hungry children in the world. "[J. Edgar] Hoover was quite aware," according to scholar Ward Churchill, "that it would be impossible to cast the party as merely 'a group of thugs' so long as it was meeting the daily nutritional requirements of an estimated 50,000 grade-schoolers in forty-five inner cities around the country."[3] As one high-ranking U.S. government official admitted, "The Panthers are feeding more kids [in the United States] than we are."[4] Not long after the Panther breakfast program demonstrated success, according to Bruce Dixon, "the city of Chicago began using federal funds to provide hot breakfasts to children in lower income neighborhoods across the city."[5] The Panthers' free breakfast for children program, Curtis Stephens points out, "ultimately served as the engine for an amendment to the federal Child Nutrition Act, which expanded access to free breakfast and lunch in schools to children from poor households."[6] In this way, American society as a whole still benefits today from the efforts of the Party.

The Party's free health clinic was another important survival project. Free community health centers were limited before the BPP commenced this program. Fred Hampton took the lead to open the clinic on the West Side, where local authorities claimed "there was no need for such services."[7] Panther clinics attempted to take the profit aspect out of the health care system and replace it with human rights. JoNina Abron points out that the Panther clinics provided a "variety of services, such as first aid care, physical examinations, prenatal care, and testing for lead poisoning, high blood pressure, and sickle cell anemia."[8] According to Hilliard's history of the Party, the clinics taught patrons that "as taxpayers" they ought not to put up with "the lackadaisical treatment given to them by county hospitals and other public health facilities."[9] Thus, entire communities were empowered as the clinics not only provided free health care but also specialized in preventative medicine and treatment that helped to foster collective agency and community interdependence. As the free breakfast program motivated government agencies to act, the success of the Panthers' health clinics persuaded the Chicago Board of Health to establish similar clinics in poor areas of the city.[10] The Panther clinics were also the first in the United States to offer free sickle-cell anemia testing. These examinations succeeded so well in highlighting that sickle cell was a persistent problem facing many Americans that President Richard Nixon mentioned the disease in a health message to Congress.[11] Also like the free breakfast program, the Party's free health clinics were adopted by other racial/ethnic poor communities.

Today, government programs offer free breakfast and lunches to schoolchildren, numerous nongovernmental organizations and charities provide free health clinics, and countless community centers are designed to supply an array of free services. Many such social services that target serving the poor, addressing hunger, combating police brutality, and working to strengthen education in underrepresented communities in the United States owe a debt to the BPP's survival programs.

The Rainbow Coalition

Probably the most underappreciated legacy of the Illinois Panthers is their creation of the Rainbow Coalition. This group and its popularization of the concept of class solidarity changed the political landscape of Chicago by helping to severely weaken the city's Democratic machine. The implicit role of the State's Attorney's Office and the FBI in the assassination of Fred Hampton galvanized the city.[12] Hampton became a martyr for the movement as Rainbow Coalition members stepped up efforts to organize against the Daley machine. State's attorney Edward Hanrahan, once heralded as Mayor Richard J. Daley's successor, was voted out of office in the early 1970s primarily as a result of the Daley administration's role in the cover-up of Hampton's murder.[13] Hanrahan's loss to his Republican opponent was, according

"Convict Hanrahan" billboard. A protester covered the word "reelect" with the word "convict" in reference to Hanrahan's role in the assassination of Fred Hampton and the subsequent cover-up, 1972. (Courtesy of Paul Sequeira)

to historian Gary Rivlin, the "Democratic organization's first citywide defeat under Daley's control and also a spur to black political empowerment."[14] For the first time in more than two decades, "a majority of black voters rejected the Democratic machine and voted for a Republican."[15] Hanrahan's defeat as a result of his involvement in Hampton's murder and the subsequent cover-up ended his political career.[16] In 1976, Mayor Daley died in office, and Republican, Democrat, and independent politicians who once lacked real political influence under the weight of the Daley Democratic machine intensified their challenges to Democrat-held seats in almost every political office.

On June 20, 1974, José Jiménez of the YLO held a press conference to announce to a coalition of blacks, whites, Latinos, Asians, and Native Americans that he would run for the North Side Forty-Sixth Ward alderman seat, openly advertising that he had once supported Fred Hampton and he still believed in the Rainbow Coalition.[17] His campaign kept the Rainbow Coalition movement alive as "fragments of the old SDS crowd, the old Black Panther crowd, and the old sympathetic media crowd" provided their services for his campaign; like Jiménez, they believed in the continuation of a "people's movement."[18] White allies in the Midwest who supported the Panthers under

Peace march against police repression, Michigan Avenue, Chicago, 1970
(Courtesy of Paul Sequeira)

the leadership of Walter "Slim" Coleman moved to Chicago to continue racial
coalition organizing under the rubric of the Intercommunal Survival Committee. Coleman later set up the Uptown Coalition, which included progressive whites who had supported the Rainbow Coalition before Hampton's
assassination and former members of the YPO, and he established chapters
throughout white communities in Chicago. Along with the Panthers, these
groups organized support for Jiménez's campaign for city alderman. Coleman explained that the coalition was "seeking support from what [he]
called the powerless masses." Coleman said, "If we can bury our differences
to elect an alderman, I'd say the revolution is not dead."[19] Jiménez was the
first Puerto Rican to run for office in Chicago against the Daley machine, and
his candidacy, though unsuccessful, opened up the Latino community as a
viable voting group. Others also had the audacity to challenge the machine
following Hampton's death. The Independent Voters of Illinois, a group of
progressive whites, ran William Singer for mayor against Daley; the group
also supported Jiménez's campaign.[20]

Fred Hampton's political assassination thus helped to unite African American, Latino, and progressive white groups and activists in a political movement against the Daley machine. Though the racial coalition's candidates
failed to gain a significant political office between 1970 and 1977, the groups
and activists continued to organize in their respective communities. Jiménez recalls that many activists burned out from the struggle against the

Democratic machine, but then Harold Washington announced his campaign for mayor of Chicago, reigniting the movement.[21]

Washington, an Illinois state senator, had become a Panther supporter following Hampton's death. After he "toured the bullet-ravaged apartment" where Fred Hampton and Mark Clark were assassinated, he found himself shaken and "outraged" by the Daley administration's wanton use of force, and he began to work politically with members of the original Rainbow Coalition.[22] The height of his political alliance with ILBPP-influenced grassroots organizers and organizations is best exhibited in his mayoral campaign. In 1983, Democratic candidate Washington, who had been elected to the U.S. House of Representatives in 1980, ran on a Rainbow Coalition platform—"a policy of racial justice and equality for working people and the poor"—and was elected Chicago's first African American mayor.[23] Congressman Bobby Rush, former deputy minister of defense of the Illinois Panthers, declared that Washington's election was "directly linked to the 'assassination' of Mr. [Fred] Hampton, and the outcry and change that it prompted."[24] According to Illinois Panther and Rainbow Coalition creator Bob Lee, "It was not until the election of Harold Washington that organizers realized the actual strength of the Rainbow Coalition, which also helped members to understand the local power structure's commitment to eliminating the group, as it was a real political threat to machine politics in Chicago."[25]

Robin D. G. Kelley points out that in order for Washington to win Chicago's mayoral election, "he would have to appeal to a significant proportion of white and Latino voters, and convince hundred of thousands of complacent, frustrated black adults to register and come out to the polls."[26] The Rainbow Coalition in Chicago had already paved the road of racial coalition and class solidarity in Chicago by 1983, and its members continued their work for Washington's mayoral campaign. Numerous individuals and organizations also participated in the African American voter registration drive on behalf of Washington.[27] The leaders of the organizations that made up the original Rainbow Coalition were key community organizers for Washington's campaign. They included Mike James of RUA, José "Cha Cha" Jiménez of the YLO, Bobby Rush of the ILBPP, and several other former Panthers, such as Yvonne King, who provided community-sensitive legal guidance for the Task Force for Black Political Empowerment, a group organized outside the formal campaign structure to "advance the struggle for political reform (symbolized by Washington's campaign) in a manner consistent with the broader goals of the movement."[28]

Original Rainbow Coalition members such as Jiménez supported Washington because his Rainbow Coalition platform addressed the nexus of the coalition's tenets, such as prioritizing neighborhoods over the needs of City Hall, opposing gentrification and urban renewal, and advocating for Puerto Rican liberation. Ironically, the strength of the Rainbow Coalition is in Chicago's staunch segregation. The city's various racial/ethnic neighborhoods were extremely territorial. Original Rainbow Coalition members understood that their coalition succeeded—despite failing to eradicate the deeply ingrained patterns of residential segregation—because of the organization's advocacy for neighborhoods to control the political, economic, and social dimensions of their own communities. Appalachian whites in Uptown, middle-class progressive whites in Logan Square, and Puerto Ricans in Lincoln Park and Humboldt Park accepted the guidance of the ILBPP in the late 1960s primarily because the Panthers made it clear that the group did not want to lead or control the aforementioned communities. The ILBPP's method was to train these communities how to be self-sufficient and develop empowerment; then the Panthers left the area for the residents to evolve on their own, understanding that the Panthers would return to assist the residents if and when the neighborhood needed their input and support. This factor was one of the primary tenets of Washington's platform: *neighborhoods first*. Washington's political grassroots organizers, many of whom were original members of the Rainbow Coalition, spread this message throughout the city.

These original Rainbow Coalition members organized and ran the Washington campaign's voter registration and turnout projects, and they used the strengths of their communities to extend to other areas of the city. Mike James of RUA, for instance, dealt with Chicago's North Side Logan Square and surrounding areas (a majority-white ethnic progressive community); José "Cha Cha" Jiménez served as Washington's North Side precinct coordinator and introduced the candidate to voters in Lincoln Park and bordering districts (mostly Puerto Rican and other Latino communities); and many former Panthers got involved in the campaign, predominately in African American communities. According to Robin D. G. Kelley, "The movement not only waged successful voter registration campaigns, increasing the number of black voters by 180,000 in 1982, but enjoyed substantial support from liberal whites."[29] In 1983, more than 100,000 people participated in a march from Lincoln Park to Humboldt Park to unite the community in favor of Washington's campaign. Thirty thousand of the marchers wore Young Lords buttons, as the group "was the first Latino organization to support Harold Washington for mayor."[30] Harold Washington did not necessarily have to state that his campaign was part of the original Rainbow Coalition (even though the title was a central advertisement of his campaign): his connection to the ILBPP-inspired group was understood by his supporters because of the activists and organizers who worked diligently for Washington.

In this way, the Illinois Panthers' Rainbow Coalition helped to lay the groundwork for the election of the city's first African American mayor. Coalition members rationalized that if a white woman, Jane Byrne, could be elected mayor, why not an African American man?[31] Byrne did not need a Rainbow Coalition because she was a Democratic machine politician, but Washington could not have defeated a machine candidate of any racial or ethnic background without the help of the Rainbow Coalition. Washington was elected, according to scholars Abdul Alkalimat and Doug Gills, because he rode the "crest of an unprecedented mobilization of the city's Black community, which included nearly 1.2 million people, or 40% of the total Chicago population." They explain: "Underpinning this campaign victory and augmenting the tremendous Black community mobilization was the significant coalition built among Latinos, white liberals from middle-class backgrounds, and poor whites from working-class origins"—again, the nexus of the original Rainbow Coalition. Washington's mayoral run was the most polarized election in Chicago's history along the lines of race and nationality to that time, and "more white people voted on the losing side than in any two successive elections in the city's history" due in part to racial coalition building.[32]

Once Washington was elected mayor of Chicago, the African American–led coalition remained focused on housing, affirmative action, and other progressive, cross-racial issues under his direction.[33] As mayor, Washington established what he called his "Rainbow Cabinet," which consisted of African American, Latino, and progressive white men and women—again, the core of the ILBPP's Rainbow Coalition. Scholar Manning Marable documented that Washington tried to reform Chicago's government "while addressing the basic grievances and problems of blacks and other constituents in the areas of housing, health care, employment, police brutality, and social services."[34] According to Gary Rivlin, Washington "hired people who were never before welcome on the premises, let alone offered positions at City Hall."[35] He appointed to the corporation council the civil rights attorney who had won the $1.85-million judgment against the city of Chicago, Cook County, and the U.S. government for the wrongful deaths of Illinois Panthers Fred Hampton and Mark Clark, as well as an attorney who filed suit against the Chicago Police Department's Red Squad. Washington also increased the number of women in positions of political power, bringing the proportion of women commissioners and deputy commissioners to just under 40 percent and appointing women as the city's two top financial officers before his death in office in 1987.[36] Robin D. G. Kelley documents that Washington's administration demonstrated its alliance to the ideology of the coalition that elected him by creating the Commission on Women's Affairs, in which Washington "successfully pushed for a state law giving public employees the right to form labor unions, and [he] implement[ed] affirmative action policies to increase the number of women and minorities in government."[37]

Washington's Rainbow Cabinet, appointments to office, and policies mirrored the position and politics of the ILBPP's Rainbow Coalition. Since Washington's coalition-based approach was a complete about-face from machine politics, old Democratic machine councilmen led by Aldermen Ed Vrdolyak and Ed Burke fought against almost every political initiative Washington attempted. The "Council Wars," as they were dubbed by the Chicago press, were so nasty and intense that a journalist from the *Wall Street Journal* once called the battles "Beirut by the Lake," comparing the racial animosity in Chicago's city council to the Lebanese civil war taking place during this period. According to Manning Marable, the primary factor motivating the political divide was not only racism but, more importantly, "patronage and power." By implementing "new cost controls, efficient management, and personnel cuts in the departments swollen by patronage," Washington's reformed government had taken away the privileges the Democratic machine had relied on for decades.[38] Original Rainbow Coalition member and ILBPP founder Bobby Rush participated in the battles, as he was also elected as an alderman "and served as one of Washington's lieutenants on the city council."[39] Rush, like other coalition members, supported Mayor Harold Washington because his politics and policies were in line with the essence of the Panther-inspired Rainbow Coalition, as the mayor supported an antiracist and anticlass coalition to fight political corruption and police brutality. Other Illinois politicians would later mimic Washington's organizing strategy for their campaigns, but unlike Washington, these politicians appropriated Rainbow Coalition politics for their own self-interest and were not married to the coalition's ideology.

Jesse Jackson, a Washington supporter who was director of Operation PUSH during the 1983 mayoral election, was inspired by Washington's campaign and witnessed the value of Rainbow Coalition politics firsthand.[40] Jackson and a group of black activists put an exploratory committee together with the goal of running a black candidate as a Democrat for the 1984

Chicago mayor Harold Washington and Jesse Jackson celebrating Washington's victory, 1983 (Courtesy of Paul Sequeira)

presidential election. "Because Jackson was so outspoken about the need to run a black candidate," declares Robin D. G. Kelley, "he quickly emerged as the movement's spokesman. In no time, the media dubbed him the next Presidential candidate, a label Jackson himself did little to dispel. By the spring of 1983, opinion polls revealed that Jackson ranked third among the potential slate of Democratic candidates."[41] Jackson may have figured that if racial coalition politics could get an African American elected in Chicago—a city with a long history of racial conflict, much of which played out during Washington's campaign—then the same strategy could assist in his bid for the White House. Scholar Peniel Joseph argues that "the successful political coalition that elected Harold Washington included veterans from the civil rights era and Black Power militants, along with progressives of all colors. Jackson's 'Rainbow Coalition' in effect attempted to duplicate at the national level the success of Chicago's local movement."[42] Gary Rivlin also documents that in Chicago, "Jackson learned the ways of the Rainbow, for it was on the heels of Washington's success at building his coalition that Jackson set out to recreate it on a national scale."[43] Thus, in 1984, Jackson co-opted the concept and name of the Rainbow Coalition and used them in his presidential campaigns of 1984 and 1988. In 1996, he merged the two organizations that he directed, Operation PUSH and the National Rainbow Coalition, into the

Rainbow Push Coalition. Today, this organization is commonly referred to simply as the "Rainbow Coalition," with no sense of its origin in the Illinois chapter of the Black Panther Party.

In Chicago, those who considered themselves participants in racial coalition politics looked upon Jackson's legal trademark of the Rainbow Coalition name and concept with skepticism. Rivlin describes Chicago activists' doubts about Jackson's qualifications as a coalition builder: "The problem was that in Chicago [people and activists] knew Jackson. He was never about rainbow politics or well-versed in coalition politics. . . . Jackson's realm had always been the black community. People did not offer this as a criticism so much as a statement of fact appropriate to judging someone seeking to lead a multiracial coalition."[44] "[Jesse Jackson] had to support the Rainbow Coalition concept because it was so well known," recalls José Jiménez, explaining, "He did not have a direct affiliation with us, but he had to support us because the concept was so alive."[45] Bob Lee, the chief organizer of the Illinois Panthers' Rainbow Coalition, says of Jackson's appropriation of the term, "Actually, Jesse Jackson pulled our little idea out of the trash bin, dusted it off, and gave it a new set of legs. It wasn't the same, but it was something. I do resent the idea that he could never admit where it all started, could never give credit [to the ILBPP]."[46]

Lee's disdain is warranted, considering that Jackson had fallen from the good graces of Fred Hampton and the ILBPP prior to Hampton's murder in 1969 because of his capitalist aspirations. At one point in 1969, Jackson was forcefully thrown out of the Panthers' headquarters on the West Side. However, after Hampton's assassination, Jackson threw his full support behind the Panthers and even provided a eulogy at Hampton's funeral. Nevertheless, Jackson was not an active member or supporter of the Rainbow Coalition until after the election of Harold Washington. According to Jiménez, in the late 1960s and early 1970s, Jackson was not interested in building a racial coalition united for class struggle. "Fred Hampton was sincere about uniting for class struggle. . . . Jesse Jackson was more cultural nationalist and capitalistic minded. He wasn't for the poor. I went to meetings with Jesse Jackson there, and you can tell that he had no choice but to support [Latinos] because he knew we were in coalition with Fred [Hampton]. He really didn't want to support [nonblacks]."[47]

Not all former Rainbow Coalition members are as understanding as Bob Lee on the issue of Jackson's adoption of the Rainbow Coalition tag. Denise Oliver-Velez, a community activist and former member of the New York Black Panther Party and the New York Young Lords Party, declares that not only did Jackson appropriate the term "Rainbow Coalition," but his rhetoric mirrors the slogan used by one of the organization's founders:

> I'm glad you brought up the Rainbow Coalition 'cause . . . it's a bugaboo of mine, which most of you, when you hear the words Rainbow Coalition, you think Jesse Jackson. [He] co-opted that. I remember Fred Hampton was one of the best speakers I ever heard in my life. And Fred used to say, "I am a revolutionary, and I love all my people," and he would go through all the colors, black people, brown, red people and yellow people, and people would respond. And Jesse changed it to "I am somebody." There's a very big difference between "I am a revolutionary" and "I am somebody." And so, he has never credited Fred Hampton for taking the name Rainbow Coalition, for the style, it's like he studied him and watered it down. Let's call spades a spade.[48]

Other original Rainbow Coalition members, mostly Panthers, have dubbed Jackson "Jesse James Jackson" for what they believe to be his theft of the title. Jiménez is one of the few original Rainbow Coalition members who support Jesse Jackson's use of the title. "Fred Hampton influenced everyone to use the Rainbow Coalition concept," explains Jiménez, continuing: "Even Jesse Jackson later used it. I don't attack Jesse Jackson for using it. I think it's great. He was keeping us alive. I respect him for that. . . . He came out and used it, and he was referring to us [Fred Hampton and the original members]."[49]

The title "Rainbow Coalition" has a symbolic purpose similar to the title of the Black Panther Party, however, and Jackson's appropriation and trademarking of the title violates its intention. In 1966, Huey Newton and Bobby Seale asked permission from Stokely Carmichael to use the title "Black Panther Party" and the Black Panther symbol. At the time, Carmichael was in Alabama politically organizing African American communities via a third political party called the Lowndes County Freedom Organization, and the party's symbol was the black panther. Carmichael informed Newton and Seale that the title belonged to the people and the movement, and that if the men intended to use the title to continue the struggle against oppression for African American liberation, then the title belonged to them as well.[50] The title "Rainbow Coalition" operated in the same manner. It was the code word for racial solidarity and class struggle against political and economic oppression in Chicago, and it belonged to the activists, the people, and the movement—a movement that in 1983 culminated in the election of Harold Washington as the city's first African American mayor. When Jesse Jackson appropriated the title, he was making a conscious effort to tap into a movement that he could possibly ride to the White House, but trademarking the term went too far.

The aforementioned resentment of Jackson by the originators and activists of the Rainbow Coalition is very much due to the fact that Jackson trademarked the term "Rainbow Coalition," thus taking legal ownership of the title that they believe belongs to the people and the movement. Jiménez argues that Jesse Jackson believes that he "inherited what Fred Hampton did. [Hampton] got killed so [he believes he] inherited [the movement] so [he took] it over [as his own]. He was trying to take over the movement of the Panthers; he was trying to steal the movement."[51] Jackson is popularly identified as representing a black agenda, which critically conflicts with the multiracial ideology of the original Rainbow Coalition. What Jackson attempted to do was use the proven methods of racial coalition politics as a campaign tool to get elected president. It was all about timing. Harold Washington's mayoral election provided Jackson with a model of how to inspire people of various racial and ethnic backgrounds to register to vote and to actually vote for a candidate with a Rainbow Coalition platform. By trademarking the title "Rainbow Coalition," Jackson displayed his selfish agenda by attempting to appropriate a movement and ideology he was not wedded to in order to get elected president. As an unintended consequence, Jackson's presidential campaigns helped to pave the way for future African American presidential candidates. According to scholar Peniel Joseph, "Jackson's 'Rainbow Coalition' emerged at a critical moment in American history and helped to decisively change a political playing field slanted against blacks." He continues: "During the 1980s, forces led by Jackson won a showdown within the Democratic Party that changed critical primary and caucus rules—a change that would lead to Barack Obama's 2008 presidential nomination."[52]

The legacy of the Party's Rainbow Coalition extends beyond Jesse Jackson to U.S. President Barack Obama. The chief concept of the organization's methodology, "racial and class solidarity," was present in Obama's U.S. presidential campaign in 2008. In 1969, Chicago Panthers were able to influence groups to form a powerful coalition despite their differences in race, class, age, gender, ethnicity, religion, and civic, community, or fraternal affiliations. Obama's successful presidential bid has essentially eclipsed what the Panthers were able to achieve in the late 1960s and early 1970s within the confines of Chicago by galvanizing individuals across the United States despite their varying and often conflicting backgrounds.

Like Jesse Jackson, Obama was also a witness to the success of Rainbow Coalition politics during Washington's mayoral campaign in 1983. He began working as a community organizer during Washington's first term in office and continued this work for three years.[53] Obama wanted to organize black folks at the grass roots for change, and he even tried to get a job working for Mayor Washington.[54] More importantly, he spent these years in Chicago working at the grassroots level and was exposed to the original Rainbow Coalition's legacy. Gerald Kellman, a white community organizer, recalls that when he hired Obama to organize in the South Side's black communities, he was looking for an African American because "it's tough to get doors opened."[55] Obama, however, was not immediately accepted by the black community. He had to earn their support. According to Lizy Mundy of the *Washington Post*, Obama "had to work with a lot of different church leaders, who weren't necessarily receptive to this young guy who came from the Ivy League and did not have Chicago roots."[56] Mike Krugliky, a community organizer in Chicago, reiterates: "You know, Chicago's a town that says, 'We don't want nobody that nobody sent.' Well, Barack was somebody that nobody sent."[57] Nevertheless, there was a model for Obama to follow in trying to determine how to put together a successful racial coalition in Chicago: that of recently elected mayor Harold Washington, whose coalition building linked to the original Rainbow Coalition. Obama's close friend Cassandra Butts explains how significant Washington's coalition was for Obama: "What Washington was able to do was to put together these coalitions, African-Americans, Latinos and progressive whites, and he was able to pull that together and beat the machine. And that kind of coalition building was incredibly influential for Barack."[58] Washington's success is one reason Obama aimed for political office.[59]

After leaving Chicago to earn a law degree from Harvard, Obama returned to the city in 1991, where he won an unopposed state senate seat in 1996 and was reelected in 1998. Then, in 2000, he attempted to dethrone former Illinois Black Panther and original Rainbow Coalition member Congressman Bobby Rush.[60] According to state senator Terry Link, Barack Obama ran against Bobby Rush because he "didn't feel Bobby was representing the area; he thought he could do a better job. . . . I think he misread it. He didn't analyze the strength of the Congressman in that area, the will of the people."[61] In this congressional race best described as the "Black Panther versus the professor" by Eric Adelstein, a media consultant in Chicago who worked on the Rush campaign, Obama was viewed as an outsider by the African American community, as opposed to Rush, who, like Harold Washington, owed his political career in part to the political assassination of Fred Hampton.[62] Edward McClelland documents that Bobby Rush "was a hero of the civil rights movement, the black power movement, and the Washington years."[63] Ron Lester, a pollster who worked for Barack Obama, stated that Congressman Rush's "support ran deep—to the extent that a lot of people who liked Barack [Obama] still wouldn't support him because they were committed to Bobby. He had built up this reserve of goodwill over 25 years in that community."[64]

Chicago's African American community rejected those who attempted to choose their leaders for them. Obama was supported by Richard M. Daley, the son of former mayor Richard J. Daley, whom the black community held responsible for the death of Fred Hampton. Rush was someone who struggled alongside the African American community in Chicago, while Obama was viewed as an outsider supported by white financial and political forces alien to and often at odds with the black community—a contemporary form of the Daley Democratic machine.[65] Jesse Jackson and President Bill Clinton endorsed Congressman Rush, as both understood that Chicago's black community was more nuanced than Obama's focus on the black working class.

Bobby Rush was a founding member of the original Rainbow Coalition, and his allies represented the elements that formed the nexus of the coalition: progressive African Americans, whites, and Latinos—folks Obama failed to account for prior to challenging the incumbent Rush. Obama had overstressed polling as a marker for success in the 2000 congressional race. Dan Shomon, Obama's campaign manager for the 2000 congressional race, stated that he and Obama conducted an "amateur poll to gauge his chances. They designed questions, recruited volunteers to telephone 300 people, and concluded that Mr. Rush was vulnerable." Shomon continues: "Obama will tell you that [the] poll was not the best poll in the world . . . because the results didn't turn out to be correct."[66] This points out a stark diversion from the Panthers' Rainbow Coalition ideology that Washington adopted. The Panthers, the original Rainbow Coalition, and Washington were not about polling but advocated *power to the people*. In the end, Rush defeated Obama by a two-to-one margin. President Barack Obama recalls, "I still burn, for example, with the thought of my one loss in politics, a drubbing in 2000 at the hands of incumbent Democratic Congressman Bobby Rush."[67] "The Bobby Rush defeat," Salim Muwakkil, editor of *In These Times*, argues, taught Obama "that his natural constituency were not these working class African-Americans with nationalist aspirations, but rather with progressive whites, progressive African-Americans, those who had a wider view of what politics was all about."[68]

Obama thus began to form racial coalitions in Chicago and throughout the state of Illinois. Marty Nesbitt, who served as finance chairman of Obama's congressional campaign, recalls that not long after Obama's loss to Bobby Rush in the 2000 congressional election, Obama announced to a small group of black professionals that he intended to run for U.S. Senate in 2004. "Obama said he believed he could bring together blacks and liberals into a coalition and come out on top in what was looking to be a crowded primary field."[69] Obama believes that "an emphasis on universal, as opposed to race-specific, programs isn't just good policy; it's also good politics."[70] Contrary to Peniel Joseph's position, it was not "Jesse Jackson's attempt to forge a 'rainbow coalition' . . . [that] provided a blueprint for the Obama campaign," but rather, it was Obama's political loss to original Rainbow Coalition founder Bobby Rush that galvanized him to adopt the strategy for his future elections.[71] This factor suggests that Barack Obama's own political ambitions, rather than a real desire to address the core issues that once defined the Panthers, drove his turn to ethnic coalition building. Like Jesse Jackson before him—whose slogan was "Keep Hope Alive" and who attempted to appropriate Washington's racial coalition strategy and message without being married to the political ideology—Obama would also lift this approach for his own self-interest. This appropriated platform and message would become the underlying meaning of Obama's campaign slogans, "hope" and "change." David Axelrod, who was well versed in original Rainbow Coalition ideology, would also influence Obama's decision to move in this direction.[72]

Barack Obama is a savvy politician. His defeat against Rush could have thwarted his political ambitions. Instead, Obama used his alliance with the current Daley Democratic machine to help him build his coalition and to support his campaign for U.S. Senate. Political scientist Dewey M. Clayton points out that Obama's first important step was to hire Mayor Daley's chief strategist, David Axelrod, to lead his campaign.[73] According to Marilyn Katz—a former member of SDS who was in charge of security for the organization during the 1968 Democratic National Convention antiwar demonstrations, and who later formed the media/press team for Harold Washington's mayoral campaign in 1983—David Axelrod is "a good maker of commercials" and "a good political consultant," and he has never been part "of the movement but he has been a friend to the movement."[74] As an associate of the movement, Axelrod made sure that his client tapped the right connections to forge his coalition.

In 2002, President George W. Bush gave the order to send American troops to invade Iraq in response to the 9/11 attacks. Many Americans opposed the invasion, and dozens of antiwar rallies took place around the country. In Chicago in October 2002, Marilyn Katz organized such a rally downtown at the Daley Center. Katz brought together the racial coalitions from the 1968 demonstrations and the Washington 1983 mayoral campaign to protest the Iraq war. Barack Obama, who was looking to forge such a racial coalition, delivered his now infamous antiwar speech at this rally. Three thousand people participated in the demonstration, including the racial coalition "that made up the core group of 1968 to 1982 to 2002." Katz explains: "Instead of putting out leaflets we turned to the rolodex and called [congressman] Danny Davis, [congresswoman] Jan Schakowsky, [alderwoman] Helen Shiller, and the pictures from that day [at the antiwar rally] are like 1968 grown up." Inspired by Obama's passionate speech, the organizers once again were "fired up" for the movement and decided to throw their support behind Obama. "And that gives Barack [Obama], who had a South Side base and whose been gathering a women's base in Chicago also, a newer side and a Latino base," continues Marilyn Katz; "that 2002 rally again coalesces the same people who fought against the war and organized against the war in summer of 1968, re-gathered with more gray hair . . . in October of 2002, which then becomes a very strong base for Barack [Obama's] candidacy for Senate, then President."[75]

David Axelrod wasted little time paralleling Obama's Senate bid in 2004 with Harold Washington's 1983 mayoral election to maintain the support of the racial coalition that was crucial to the election of Chicago's first African American mayor. David Mendell contends that Axelrod's television campaign was key to Obama's victory in his bid for the U.S. Senate in 2004: "[Obama] had a political story to tell, and Axelrod knew how to pick out the various aspects of that story and really sell them to voters. . . . His community organizing days went over extraordinarily well with blacks. His time at Harvard . . . Suddenly, whites are, like, 'Oh, OK.' They're very accepting of him. . . . That television campaign really sold voters on the story of Barack Obama."[76] Dewey M. Clayton documents that "the crafty advertising campaign orchestrated by David Axelrod aided Obama's candidacy by showing images of the late Mayor Harold Washington . . . [and thus] Obama emerged with 52 percent of the vote in the March primary."[77] More important, Obama's election to the U.S. Senate in 2004 was also a mirror image of Harold Washington's election in 1983. "At the victory party for his election," according to Salim Muwakkil, "it looked like a replay of Harold Washington's mayoral victory party. It really did. I mean, there were black people there who were ecstatic about the rise of this young brother and a range of white supporters, primarily these progressives who supported Harold Washington. It was extraordinary, really, the way that the crowds echoed each other."[78] Political scientist Baodong Liu posited that in 2008, Obama would utilize "an unprecedented multiracial coalition" that was empowering to voters because they "believed in the power of change and enjoyed the sense of unity that Obama brought together."[79] Much of this success was due to David Axelrod's leadership and guidance.

Axelrod himself brought to Obama's campaign a career built in part on long familiarity with Rainbow Coalition politics. During Harold Washington's campaign in 1983, Axelrod was a "star political reporter, columnist, and City Hall bureau chief" for the *Chicago Tribune*.[80] Axelrod studied the meteoric rise of Washington and Rainbow Coalition politics during his tenure as a *Tribune* political columnist. He also understood that the Rainbow Coalition ticket that elected Washington had ushered in a formidable political force in Chicago and offered an ideal model for defeating machine politicians. After all, Harold Washington's victory over Democratic machine incumbent Jane Byrne to become the city's first African American mayor was historic. As the *Chicago Tribune*'s City Hall bureau chief, Axelrod had a ringside seat, as he recalls: "Nineteen eighty-three, that was a phenomenal election. Harold Washington—extraordinary guy. I mean, he was the most kinetic campaigner and politician that I've ever met. It was inspiring the way the African-American community came alive around the prospect of electing Harold. There were those who mistook that for a negative [campaign], but it was one of the most positive campaigns I've ever seen, because people felt empowered."[81] Gary Rivlin points out that during Axelrod's tenure at the *Chicago Tribune*, he "was more sympathetic to Washington than most columnists" of the time.[82]

Marilyn Katz believes that it was her media team for Washington's mayoral election that inspired Axelrod to "quit the *Tribune*," because "we had more fun [running media for Washington's campaign] than he did [as a columnist for the local newspaper]."[83] In 1984, David Axelrod left the *Tribune* and became the press secretary for Democrat Paul Simon in his bid for a U.S. Senate seat from Illinois. Seven weeks later, he was named Simon's campaign manager. Having applied what he learned studying the methodology of political campaigns of both machine politicians and Washington's progressive and grassroots Rainbow Coalition, Axelrod helped Simon to win the Senate seat. Afterward, he established his own political consulting firm and was hired by Harold Washington to oversee the media strategy for his reelection campaign for Chicago mayor in 1987.[84] Axelrod's firm, now AKPD Message and Media, which includes partners John Kupper and David Plouffe, is best known for its reputation of successfully handling mayoral races, "with a particularly strong track record in electing black candidates."[85] Arguably, Axelrod acquired this skill by studying Washington's first election and by working with Rainbow Coalition activists on Washington's reelection campaign.

The original Rainbow Coalition members who worked on Washington's campaign also assumed the same positions during his reelection bid, but this time they were assisted by Axelrod, who used television commercials to broadcast Washington's Rainbow Coalition message. Axelrod's participation made Rainbow Coalition organizers' work of grassroots campaigning much easier, as the television commercials reached a much larger and a much more diverse audience. For example, in his first election under media consultant Marilyn Katz, Washington received only 8 percent of the white vote. David Axelrod's guidance in strategically delivering the campaign's message helped increase the white vote to 20 percent in Washington's reelection in 1987.[86]

Due in part to this success, Axelrod "has developed something of a novel niche for a political consultant: helping black politicians convince white voters to support them." He has assisted the successful campaigns of such candidates in city and state elections in Illinois, Michigan, Ohio, Texas, Pennsylvania, and Washington, D.C.[87] He has also managed media strategy and communications for more than 150 local, state, and national campaigns with a focus on progressive candidates and causes.[88] In addition to mayoral candidates, Axelrod's firm has represented candidates for governor, state supreme court justice, senator, and congressman. The firm attracted accolades for assisting the campaign of Deval Patrick, an African American who was elected governor of Massachusetts—a state that had not elected a Democratic governor in over twenty years.[89]

Barack Obama chose Axelrod as his chief strategist during his 2008 presidential campaign no doubt because Axelrod has a track record of winning elections for African American candidates. More importantly, he has effectively and repeatedly utilized Rainbow Coalition concepts and the methods he learned while studying and working with the group's organizers during Harold Washington's campaigns. While Jesse Jackson trademarked the title "Rainbow Coalition," Axelrod has transformed Rainbow Coalition ideology and methods into a commodity that he has sold to his clients, producing a remarkably high success rate.[90] The ways in which Axelrod has packaged and sold Rainbow Coalition ideology and messages to his clients have also evolved since the 1980s. Axelrod today is not simply a leader in message delivery but a "five-tool consultant" who uses his expertise as a planner of television and radio advertising, speechwriter, strategic planner, and crafter of campaign messages, as well as a spokesman.[91] He assumed all five roles during Obama's successful run for the White House as he crafted Obama's focused theme: "change that we can believe in." Communications scholars Quigwen Dong, Kenneth D. Day, and Raman Deol argue that according to self-efficacy theory, Obama's "campaign slogan resonated with the willingness and reasoned intention of many receivers of the message," which influenced receivers to become "involved in political action through working through grassroots networks."[92] Obama's election as the forty-fourth U.S. president is a direct result of David Axelrod's campaign skills, which he honed as a member of Harold Washington's team and which others have also documented was no doubt "a defining moment in the formation of his political consciousness."[93]

In contrast, David Axelrod's strategic genius demonstrates an evolution in racial coalition politics. The ILBPP's Rainbow Coalition (1968) and Washington's (1983) adoption of the group's methods and organizers relied on the same group of people: progressive African Americans, white ethnic progressive Chicagoans who were mostly working class, and Latinos who utilized grassroots organizing by way of door-to-door campaigning and rallies. "From the beginning, Jackson's primary base remained the African American community," declares Peniel Joseph, "despite the campaign's effort to appeal to disaffected working-class whites and Latinos. In contrast, Obama's primary base until his victory in the Iowa caucuses consisted of white voters who ranged from upscale professionals to college students."[94] In 2008, the Axelrod-induced racial coalition consisted of well-educated middle-class and some elite whites, "African Americans, Latinos, young people, and first-time voters, and the use of new technology—the Internet, databases, and social media—to organize and mobilize this new coalition, and to mount the most successful fundraising campaign of any presidential candidate in the history of this nation."[95] This point suggests that as with most political trends, there is change over time, and Axelrod has been able to broaden the base of racial coalitions and utilize the advancements in media such as the Internet, databases, and social networking to the benefit of his clients.

Harold Washington, Jesse Jackson, David Axelrod, and President Barack Obama all have a connection to the original Rainbow Coalition. However, with the exception of Washington, there is an egregious disconnect between what the Panthers and their allies hoped to accomplish and what their political strategy was ultimately used for by Jackson, Axelrod, and Obama. The ILBPP's Rainbow Coalition promoted a racial/ethnic coalition-building strategy as a means of challenging corruption and ensuring a voice for the voiceless. The coalition challenged members and allies to adopt democratic socialism as a model: "An ideal," scholar Lucius Outlaw points out, "as a concrete, real possibility that can be made actual through praxes, shared in by all of us 'different' folks, involving commitments to a possible future in which we maintain our own integrity without encroaching on the integrity and well-being of others."[96] Harold Washington was able to officially transfer and transform the group's ideology and methods from the fringes of Chicago politics into a revolutionary agent at the center of the city's political arena. As a result, the strategy was later appropriated by politicians, first by Jesse Jackson and, later, by David Axelrod and President Barack Obama. They saw it in many ways as a means to a political end rather than as the foundations for revolutionary reform that the Panthers and their allies sought. These later politicians mirrored Washington's election strategy as a method for their elections *only*, with no intention to adopt the ideology as their policy.[97] What does this mean and why is it important? Barack Obama's election to the U.S. Senate and as U.S. president is directly linked to the ILBPP's original Rainbow Coalition in Chicago by way of David Axelrod, who has used the methods and ideology of the group to achieve goals that neither the Panthers nor Harold Washington ever imagined were possible.

The Rainbow Coalition's goal when it was established was not to put an African American in the White House but, rather, to end the political corruption and stranglehold of the Daley Democratic machine. Although much has changed since the coalition was formed, the political movement that united many Chicagoans regardless of race, ethnicity, class, religion, or other affiliations in 1968 demonstrated its continuance and endurance on a national scale via Obama's presidential election in November 2008. "We were able to overcome a lot of the things that a lot of people thought were insuperable barriers in our politics," said Axelrod in a televised interview after the Democratic victory. "We put together a national coalition. . . . That is what we set out to do and that is what we did."[98] Axelrod and journalist Christopher Hayes reflect on the mirror images of Harold Washington's mayoral race and Obama's campaign for U.S. president:

> What Obama and Washington shared, Axelrod points out—a trait
> common to many of the successful black candidates he has worked
> for—is the direct, lived experience of the effects of injustice with a
> simultaneous faith that the injustice wasn't permanent, that it could

be overcome. "In many cases their personal stories are symbolic of the kinds of values that we as a society hold dear even if we haven't always honored them historically," Axelrod says. "The notion that you can overcome great obstacles—[they're] very hopeful figures, and I think that made them very potent politically. They've seen the obstacles and the barriers and they've also overcome them: It shows the work we have to do and the possibility that that work can get done, that you can work for a better future." . . . Axelrod and Obama call it "a new kind of politics," and in their imagining it is a rerun of the Washington race, but this time the empowerment can be shared across the racial divide.[99]

As Axelrod and many others know, what Obama accomplished in his election for U.S. president in 2008 is not a new phenomenon—at least not on the local level in Chicago.

Fred Hampton and the Chicago Panthers Today

In early March 2006, as I was waiting to take my doctoral oral exam, Jan Reiff gave me a recent *New York Times* article to read to calm my nerves and bolster my confidence in the importance of my research. The article was about a dispute in Chicago over the renaming of the 2300 block of West Monroe Street on the West Side. Fred Hampton Jr., with the help of Alderwoman Madeline L. Haithcock, proposed that the street be renamed in honor of his father, Fred Hampton. Most African American and many progressive residents regarded Hampton as a martyr assassinated by the establishment. In turn, the city's political establishment declared Hampton a dangerous and violent person who had consistently threatened the police and thus got what he deserved. The incident swiftly rekindled thirty-seven years of racial tension between Chicago's black community and the power structure—particularly the Chicago Police Department.[100]

The demand to post an honorary street sign in remembrance of Fred Hampton, the slain Panther, organizer, and revolutionary, reveals how Chicagoans, both black and white, remain divided over the legacy of Hampton and the meaning not only of the Black Panther Party but of the historical moment in which it flourished. The local government still refuses to admit that the political murder of Hampton was not only wrong but, in fact, an assassination. Also, black residents have not forgotten or forgiven the city for the murder of Hampton.

Almost 1,300 blocks in Chicago are named in honor of "all sorts of people," including the notorious mafia gangster Al Capone.[101] Some of the signs bear names in honor of disc jockeys (Herb Kent), the godfather of house music (Frankie Knuckles), and even household items (the flat iron). "When you talk about Chairman Fred Hampton," asserts Akua Njeri, Hampton's significant other, "you have to talk about a period of resistance. . . . It's something that happened back in the day, but its close enough in memory to be a shining example of resistance, of organization, of bringing people together to participate in their own fight for liberation and freedom. And this is a bad symbol, according to the state."[102] On March 29, 2006, Congressman Bobby Rush attended the City Hall council meeting to support the posting of the honorary street sign. Only two city officials supported the measure, Alderwomen Dorothy Tillman and Arenda Troutman. "[The Federal government] murdered Fred Hampton and Mark Clark," shouted Tillman during the meeting. She continued:

> What did they do [wrong]? They were feeding little children. They were standing up at a time when black folks were willing to die [for freedom]. I came up with Dr. Martin Luther King Jr. in the Southern Christian Leadership Conference who fought in the non-violent movement. But I know that during that struggle we had all kinds of resistance. We had SNCC, CORE, NAACP, and we had the Panthers—Mark Clark and Fred Hampton. Fred Hampton a very brilliant young man who said "We are going to feed our children; we are going to work with our children." They murdered him. . . . I think that it's a sin on this council floor that we are holding up just a simple sign.[103]

The Hampton sign never made it to a city council vote and is still undesignated due to pressure from the Fraternal Order of Police, former police superintendent Phil Cline, and then-mayor Richard M. Daley, who all opposed it because they believe that Hampton advocated violence. Thus, the collective essentially ignored the honorary sign of the violent mafia gangster Al Capone.[104]

The debate speaks to the problem of history versus public memory. Edward Morgan believes much of the problem is due to mass media culture.

> The lived history of the Black Panther Party has been reduced to a one-dimensionality that can safely be consigned to the black hole of public memory. . . . Stripped of their experimental context in violent inner-city America in the mid-to-late 1960s, and detached from their

political analysis of economic and racial exploitation, the Panthers are easy targets for the ongoing effort by the powerful to restore the hegemony threatened in the 1960s era. . . . No radical movement during or since the 1960s has been able to get its voice heard within the mainstream mass media. . . . Within the mass media culture, state repression pays off twice. It adds to the likely visibility of militancy and violence, widely viewed as alienating by mass audiences, while it runs these radical fringe elements into the ground.[105]

Much of the debate surrounding the honorary naming of one city block on the West Side of Chicago illustrates Morgan's point. The continued perpetuation of the official police report by those who have the power to define the terms, and which ignores the history and facts surrounding the controversy, sits at the center of the dispute of history versus public memory concerning Fred Hampton's legacy. The Chicago government's refusal to acknowledge the facts regarding Hampton's relationship to violence, for instance, demonstrates this point.

Mark Donahue, president of the Chicago chapter of the Fraternal Order of Police, opposed honoring Hampton and declared that it would be "a dark day when we honor someone who would advocate killing policemen and who took great advantage of the communities he claimed to have been serving."[106] Fred Hampton did not, in fact, advocate violence but, rather, promoted self-defense, which is a right of all Americans protected by the U.S. Constitution. Furthermore, Hampton and the Illinois Panthers served communities tirelessly, working long hours and earning no money for their services rendered. The Donahue accusations only heighten the divide between Chicago's progressive communities and the police and political establishment. The city officials who oppose the street sign ignore legal admission of guilt on the part of the state—guilt that is supported by the fact that the Hampton family was awarded a $1.85-million settlement by the federal government, Cook County, and the City of Chicago in 1983. This decision was made because of the abuse of force perpetrated by all the aforementioned levels of government in the wrongful death of Fred Hampton—a decision that highlighted police abuse and government misconduct.

According to Flint Taylor and Dennis Cunningham, in 1978 the U.S. Court of Appeals for the Seventh Circuit had concluded that

the FBI and their government lawyers "obstructed justice" by suppressing documents. Most significantly, the Court of Appeals also concluded that there was "serious evidence" to support the conclusion that the

FBI, Hanrahan, and his men, in planning and executing the raid, had participated in a "conspiracy designed to subvert and eliminate the Black Panther Party and its members," thereby suppressing a "vital radical Black political organization," as well as in a post-raid conspiracy to "cover up evidence" regarding the raid, "to conceal the true character of their pre-raid and raid activities," to "harass the survivors of the raid," and to "frustrate any legal redress the survivors might seek."[107]

In February 1983, "the U.S. Supreme Court refused to overturn this decision," and thus, "the federal government, Cook County and the City of Chicago, in a clear admission of guilt, finally agreed to settle the lawsuit."[108] This history of the controversy contradicts public memory of the incident put forth by the Chicago Fraternal Order of Police and Mayor Richard M. Daley. Moreover, the police and Daley are in positions of power to define the terms, legacy, and memory of the political assassination of Hampton and Clark.

An additional contradiction regarding the honorary street sign lay in the fact that two of the city's streets were "officially" not "honorarily" renamed in remembrance of violent white ethnics. In the 1930s, Crawford Avenue was renamed Pulaski Road in honor of Polish immigrant Casimir Pulaski. Pulaski, a Polish elite, received a death sentence for his role in a plot to murder the Polish king in the 1700s, which forced him to flee to America. Also in the 1930s, Seventh Street was renamed Balbo after Italian Italo Balbo. He was second in command under the fascist Italian leader Benito Mussolini. He was suspected of murdering a priest in Italy in 1923 and was known as the "model of the fascist generation."[109]

Nevertheless, Hampton's hometown, the village of Maywood, has honored him in two ways. In the early 1970s, town officials named the local swimming pool the Fred Hampton Aquatic Center in his honor. After all, Hampton exhausted years of protest to have the suburb of Maywood build a local swimming pool that would accommodate all who wanted to swim regardless of race—an issue that was violently contested by whites in the area even though segregation of public space violated federal law. The aquatic center now has a plaque dedicated to Hampton mounted on the entrance wall and a statue of Hampton greeting patrons as they enter the park. After Chicago refused to hang an honorary sign naming the 2300 block of W. Monroe "Fred Hampton Way," Maywood decided to officially change the name of the street on which the aquatic center is located from Oak Street to Fred Hampton Street.

Despite resistance to the historical remembrance of Fred Hampton by Chicago officials, students, activists, progressives, and organizations remain steadfast in passing on his legacy. Since the city council refused to honor Hampton in March 2006, a number of events have been held to memorialize the slain leader. Former members of the ILBPP established a not-for-profit group to archive oral histories and primary sources related to their work and later held an event at Northeastern Illinois University in Hampton's honor; Proviso East, Hampton's former high school, put on a play about the Panther chairman; Northwestern University held a panel discussion to remember him that aired on CSPAN; the University of Chicago held a two-day event in his honor; the DuSable Museum of African American History held an exhibit to remember Hampton and the entire BPP from April through August 2010 that included numerous panel discussions and events that brought in former members from all over the world; DePaul University held a two-day symposium on the original Rainbow Coalition that included members of all of the original organizations, who shared their memories of working with Fred Hampton; and movement lawyer Jeff Haas published his memoirs of Hampton's assassination and the subsequent trials. In the words of the slain revolutionary, "The beat goes on."

NOTES

INTRODUCTION

1. Miriam Ma'at-Ka-Re Monges, "'I Got a Right to the Tree of Life': Afrocentric Reflections of a Former Community Worker," in *The Black Panther Party Reconsidered*, ed. Charles E. Jones (Baltimore: Black Classic Press, 1998), 137.

2. My use of "murder" and "assassination" in this book reflects the consensus and popular understanding of Fred Hampton's death. See esp. *Murder of Fred Hampton* (The Film Group, 1971); Jeffrey Haas, *The Assassination of Fred Hampton: How the FBI and the Chicago Police Murdered a Black Panther* (Chicago: Lawrence Hill Books, 2009); and Flint Taylor and Dennis Cunningham, "The Assassination of Fred Hampton: 40 Years Later," *Police Misconduct and Civil Rights Law Report* 9, no. 12 (November/December 2009).

3. Peniel E. Joseph, "Black Liberation without Apology: Reconceptualizing the Black Power Movement," *Black Scholar* 31, no. 3/4, "Black Power Studies: A New Scholarship" (Fall/Winter 2001): 2–19; Peniel E. Joseph, "Dashikis and Democracy: Black Studies, Student Activism, and the Black Power Movement," *Journal of African American History* 88, no. 2, "The History of Black Student Activism" (Spring 2003): 182–203; Peniel E. Joseph, "The Black Power Movement, Democracy, and America in the King Years," *American Historical Review* 114, no. 4 (October 2009): 1001–16.

4. Clayborne Carson, ed., *The Autobiography of Martin Luther King, Jr.* (New York: Warner Books, 1998); Manning Marable, *Malcolm X: A Life of Reinvention* (New York: Viking, 2011); Komozi Woodard, *A Nation within a Nation: Amiri Baraka (LeRoi Jones) and Black Power Politics* (Chapel Hill: University of North Carolina Press, 1999).

5. Chana Kai Lee, *For Freedom's Sake: The Life of Fannie Lou Hamer* (Urbana: University of Illinois Press, 2000); Peter B. Levy, "Gloria Richardson and the Civil Rights Movement in Cambridge, Maryland," in *Groundwork: Local Black Freedom Movements in America*, ed. Jeanne Theoharis and Komozi Woodard (New York: New York University Press, 2005), 97–115; Barbara Ransby, *Ella Baker and the Black Freedom Movement: A Radical Democratic Vision* (Chapel Hill: University of North Carolina Press, 2003).

6. William Chafe, *Civilities and Civil Rights: Greensboro, North Carolina, and the Black Struggle for Freedom* (Oxford: Oxford University Press, 1981); John Dittmer, *Local People: The Struggle for Civil Rights in Mississippi* (Urbana: University of Illinois Press, 1995); Charles Payne, *I've Got the Light of Freedom: The Organizing Tradition and the Mississippi Freedom Struggle* (Berkeley: University of California Press, 2007).

7. Theoharis and Woodard, *Groundwork*; Jeanne Theoharis and Komozi Woodard, eds., *Freedom North: Black Freedom Struggles outside the South, 1940–1980* (New York: Palgrave Macmillan, 2003); Dayo Gore, Jeanne Theoharis, and Komozi Woodard, eds., *Want to Start*

a Revolution? Radical Women in the Black Freedom Struggle (New York: New York University Press, 2009).

8. Donna Jean Murch, *Living for the City: Migration, Education, and the Rise of the Black Panther Party in Oakland, California* (Chapel Hill: University of North Carolina Press, 2010); Matthew Countryman, *Up South: Civil Rights and Black Power in Philadelphia* (Philadelphia: University of Pennsylvania Press, 2005); Dittmer, *Local People*; Chafe, *Civilities and Civil Rights*; Payne, *I've Got the Light of Freedom*.

9. For a clear understanding of this debate, see Sundiata Keita Cha-Jua and Clarence Lang, "The 'Long Movement' as Vampire: Temporal and Spatial Fallacies in Recent Black Freedom Studies," *Journal of African American History* 92, no. 2 (Spring 2007): 265–88. The article won the Organization of American Historians' EBSCOhost America: History and Life Award for best scholarly article.

10. Gerald Horne, *The Fire This Time: The Watts Uprising and the 1960s* (Charlottesville: University Press of Virginia, 1995); Jeffrey O. G. Ogbar, *Black Power: Radical Politics and African American Identity* (Baltimore: Johns Hopkins University Press, 2004).

11. Hasan Jeffries, *Bloody Lowndes: Civil Rights and Black Power in Alabama's Black Belt* (New York: New York University Press, 2009); Murch, *Living for the City*; Peniel E. Joseph, ed., *Neighborhood Rebels: Black Power at the Local Level* (New York: Palgrave Macmillan, 2010); Judson L. Jeffries, ed., *On the Ground: The Black Panther Party in Communities across America* (Jackson: University Press of Mississippi, 2010); Yohuru Williams and Jama Lazerow, eds., *Liberated Territory: Untold Local Perspectives on the Black Panther Party* (Durham: Duke University Press, 2008).

12. Bridgette Baldwin, "In the Shadow of the Gun: The Black Panther Party, the Ninth Amendment, and Discourses of Self-Defense," in *In Search of the Black Panther Party: New Perspectives on a Revolutionary Movement*, ed. Jama Lazerow and Yohuru Williams (Durham: Duke University Press, 2006), 83; Devin Fergus, "The Black Panther Party in the Disunited States of America: Constitutionalism, Watergate, and the Closing of the Americanists' Mind," in Williams and Lazerow, *Liberated Territory*, 268.

13. Cha-Jua and Lang, "'Long Movement' as Vampire," 274, 278; Yohuru Williams, *Black Politics/White Power: Civil Rights, Black Power, and the Black Panthers in New Haven* (St. James, N.Y.: Brandywine Press, 2000).

14. Jeffries, *Bloody Lowndes*, 2, 153.

15. Murch, *Living for the City*, 4–7.

16. Charles E. Jones and Judson L. Jeffries, "'Don't Believe the Hype': Debunking the Panther Mythology," in Jones, *Black Panther Party Reconsidered*, 28.

17. Martin R. Delany, *The Condition, Elevation, Emigration and Destiny of the Colored People of the Unite States and Official Report of the Niger Valley Exploring Party* (1852; reprint, Humanity Books, 2004); Marilyn Richardson, ed., *Maria W. Stewart: America's First Black Woman Political Writer: Essays and Speeches* (Bloomington: Indiana University Press, 1987); David Walker, *Appeal* (Baltimore: Black Classic Press, 1993).

18. Robert Hill, "Racial and Radical: Cyril V. Briggs, *The Crusader* Magazine, and the African Blood Brotherhood, 1918–1922," in *The Crusader* (New York: Garland, 1987); Robert Hill, ed., *The Marcus Garvey and UNIA Papers*, vols. 1–5 (Los Angeles, University of California Press, 1983).

19. Timothy B. Tyson, *Radio Free Dixie: Robert F. Williams and the Roots of Black Power* (Chapel Hill: University of North Carolina Press, 1999).

20. Lance Hill, *The Deacons for Defense: Armed Resistance and the Civil Rights Movement* (Chapel Hill: University of North Carolina Press, 2004).

21. Martin Duberman, *Paul Robeson: A Biography* (New York: New Press, 1989).

22. Maxwell Stanford, "Revolutionary Action Movement (RAM): A Case Study of an Urban Revolutionary Movement in Western Capitalist Society" (master's thesis, Clark Atlanta University, 1986).

23. Clayborne Carson, *In Struggle: SNCC and the Black Awakening of the 1960s* (Cambridge, Mass.: Harvard University Press, 1981).

24. George Breitman, ed., *Malcolm X Speaks: Selected Speeches and Statements* (New York: Grove Weidenfeld, 1965).

25. Bobby Seale, "Chip Faces Death in Fascist Trial," *Black Panther Community Newsletter* (Southern California Chapter), March 11, 1970, 1.

26. Jones and Jeffries, "'Don't Believe the Hype,'" 28. For recent foundational books and essays that examine the African American tradition of self-defense, see Christopher B. Strain, *Pure Fire: Self Defense as Activism in the Civil Rights Era* (Athens: University of Georgia Press, 2005); Craig S. Pascoe, "The Monroe Rifle Club: Finding Justice in an 'Ungodly and Social Jungle Called Dixie,'" in *Lethal Imagination: Violence and Brutality in American History*, ed. Michael A. Bellesiles (New York: New York University Press, 1999), 393–424; Greta de Jong, *A Different Day: African American Struggles for Justice in Rural Louisiana, 1900–1970* (Chapel Hill: University of North Carolina Press, 2002); Akinyele Omowale Umoja, "1964: The Beginning of the End of Nonviolence in the Mississippi Freedom Movement," *Radical History Review* 85 (Winter 2003): 201–26; Akinyele Omowale Umoja, "'We Will Shoot Back': The Natchez Model and Paramilitary Organization in the Mississippi Freedom Movement," *Journal of Black Studies* 32, no. 3 (January 2002): 271–94; Emilye Crosby, "'This Nonviolent Stuff Ain't No Good. It'll Get Ya Killed': Teaching about Self-Defense in the African American Freedom Struggle," in *Teaching the American Civil Rights Movement: Freedom's Bittersweet Song*, ed. Julie Buckner Armstrong, Susan Hult Edwards, Houston Bryan Roberson, and Rhonda Y. Williams (New York: Routledge, 2002), 159–73; and Simon Wendt, "God, Gandhi, and Guns: The African American Freedom Struggle in Tuscaloosa, Alabama, 1964–1965," *Journal of African American History* 89, no. 1 (Winter 2004): 36–56.

27. Floyd W. Hayes III and Francis A. Kiene III, "'All Power to the People': The Political Thought of Huey P. Newton and the Black Panther Party," in Jones, *Black Panther Party Reconsidered*, 157–59.

28. Ibid.

29. Nikhil Pal Singh, "The Black Panthers and the 'Underdeveloped Country' of the Left," in Jones, *Black Panther Party Reconsidered*, 65–66.

30. Ibid.

31. Ibid., 66.

32. Chris Booker, "Lumpenization: A Critical Error of the Black Panther Party," in Jones, *Black Panther Party Reconsidered*, 341–43.

33. Ibid., 341.

34. Ibid., 341–42.

35. Ibid., 342; "SNCC, Panthers Announce Merger," *Guardian*, February 24, 1968, 1.

36. Booker, "Lumpenization," 343. Bay area legislator Don Mulford introduced a bill to repeal the law that permitted citizens to carry loaded weapons in public places so long as the weapons were openly displayed. The media dubbed the bill the "Panther Bill," the underlying purpose of which was to eliminate Black Panther Police Patrols and future Panther and police armed confrontations.

37. Ibid.

38. Ibid., 341–43.

39. Jane Rhodes, *Framing the Panthers: The Spectacular Rise of a Black Power Icon* (New York: New Press, 2007).

40. In 1969, Bobby Seale, Masai Hewitt, and Don Cox, members of the national BPP Central Committee, held a secret meeting with ILBPP leaders Fred Hampton and Bobby Rush in the office of attorney Kermit Coleman at the American Civil Liberties Union in Chicago to discuss the possibility of temporarily moving the BPP national headquarters to Chicago. Bobby Seale would soon be on trial for his participation in the protest during the Democratic National Convention in Chicago in 1968. The trial is infamously referred to as the Chicago Eight trial or conspiracy. A photo of this meeting is in the possession of the author, collected from the private archive of Howard Ann Kendrick (Campbell), former member of the ILBPP Central Staff (Communications Secretary).

41. Roy Wilkins and Ramsey Clark, *Search and Destroy: A Report* (New York: Metropolitan Applied Research Center, 1973); Michael J. Arlen, *An American Verdict* (Garden City, N.Y.: Doubleday, 1974), 196; E. Victor Wolfenstein, *The Victims of Democracy: Malcolm X and the Black Revolution* (Berkeley: University of California Press, 1981), xi, 422; Akua Njeri, *My Life with the Black Panther Party* (Oakland, Calif.: Burning Spear Publications, 1991), ii, 56; Huey P. Newton, *War against the Panthers: A Study of Repression in America* (New York: Harlem River Press, 1996); Akinyele Omowale Umoja, "Repression Breeds Resistance: The Black Liberation Army and the Radical Legacy of the Black Panther Party," in *Liberation, Imagination, and the Black Panther Party: A New Look at the Panthers and Their Legacy*, ed. Kathleen Cleaver and George N. Katsiaficas (New York: Routledge, 2001), 3–19.

42. Curtis Austin, *Up against the Wall: Violence in the Making and Unmaking of the Black Panther Party* (Fayetteville: University of Arkansas Press, 2006).

43. Haas, *Assassination of Fred Hampton*.

44. Arlen, *American Verdict*; Wilkins and Clark, *Search and Destroy*; Njeri, *My Life*; Melvin E. Lewis, "Once I Was a Panther," in Jones, *Black Panther Party Reconsidered*, 109–14; Mumia Abu-Jamal, "A Life in the Party: An Historical and Retrospective Examination of the Projections and Legacies of the Black Panther Party," in Cleaver and Katsiaficas, *Liberation, Imagination, and the Black Panther Party*, 40–50.

45. Jon Rice, "The World of the Illinois Panthers," in Theoharis and Woodard, *Freedom North*, 41–64.

46. Ibid., 41.

47. Ibid., 55–56.

48. Jesse Jackson's organization was originally titled Operation PUSH. Jackson would later rename the group the Rainbow Push Coalition. Today, it is simply called the Rainbow Coalition. Jackson has yet to properly acknowledge the origin of his group's title or give Fred Hampton and the ILBPP credit for Chicago's racial coalition atmosphere, from which Jackson and his organization now benefit.

49. Janny Scott, "In 2000, a Streetwise Veteran Schools a Bold Young Obama," *New York Times*, September 9, 2007, http://www.nytimes.com/2007/09/09/us/politics/09obama.html?pagewanted=all (accessed February 15, 2010).

50. The Red Squad was Chicago's equivalent of the FBI's COINTELPRO initiative. This segment of the police force was so sinister that even religious organizations and the Boy Scouts were victims of its assaults.

CHAPTER 1

1. James R. Grossman, "Great Migration," in *The Encyclopedia of Chicago*, ed. James R. Grossman, Ann Durkin Keating, and Janice L. Reiff (Chicago: University of Chicago Press, 2004), 363–64; Felecia G. Jones, "The Role of the Black Press during the 'Great Migration'" (paper presented at the Sixty-Ninth Annual Meeting of the Association for Education in Journalism and Mass Communication, Norman, Okla., August 3–6, 1986).

2. "Chicago Metropolitan Population," in Grossman, Keating, and Reiff, *Encyclopedia of Chicago*, 1005.

3. Grossman, "Great Migration," 363–64.

4. William J. Grimshaw, *Bitter Fruit: Black Politics and the Chicago Machine, 1931–1991* (Chicago: University of Chicago Press, 1992), 5.

5. Dempsey Travis, *An Autobiography of Black Politics* (Chicago: Urban Research Press, 1987), 70–71; "Riot Sweeps Chicago," *Chicago Defender*, August 2, 1919. For a detailed account of the event, see William M. Tuttle Jr., *Race Riot: Chicago in the Red Summer of 1919* (Chicago: Atheneum, 1970).

6. Travis, *Autobiography of Black Politics*, 70–71.

7. Ibid.; "List Of Slain in Four Days' Rioting," *Chicago Defender*, August 2, 1919; Steven Essig, "Race Riots," in Grossman, Keating, and Reiff, *Encyclopedia of Chicago*, 667.

8. Although it was common knowledge among Chicagoans that Daley was an active and popular member of the Hamburgs, he never admitted his participation in the riot—even though members of his gang were identified as stalwarts during the attacks on the South Side's black residents.

9. Mike Royko, *Boss: Richard J. Daley of Chicago* (New York: Dutton, 1971), 31.

10. Essig, "Race Riots," 667.

11. Travis, *Autobiography of Black Politics*, 66.

12. Ibid., 66–67.

13. Ibid., 67.

14. Jon Rice, "Black Radicalism on Chicago's West Side: A History of the Illinois Black Panther Party" (Ph.D. diss., Northern Illinois University, 1998), 11.

15. Harold Mayer and Richard Wade, *Chicago: Growth of a Metropolis* (Chicago: University of Chicago Press, 1969), 256.

16. Rice, "Black Radicalism," 11.

17. Travis, *Autobiography of Black Politics*, 110.

18. St. Clair Drake and Horace Cayton, *Black Metropolis* (New York: Harper and Row, 1970), 379–80.

19. Irish politicians John "Bathhouse" Coughlin and Michael "Hinky Dink" Kenna, for instance, both grabbed political power via ballot thievery and financial contributions to City Hall. See Travis, *Autobiography of Black Politics*, 35–36.

20. Ibid. Rev. Reverdy C. Ransom was an advocate of the Social Gospel and developed institutional church models for African Americans. Such models—along with his alliance with W. E. B. Du Bois—led to the eventual founding of the NAACP. See Calvin S. Morris, *Reverdy C. Ransom: Black Advocate of the Social Gospel* (Lanham, Md.: University Press of America, 1990), and Ralph E. Luker, "Reverdy C. Ransom: Black Advocate of the Social Gospel," book review, *Church History* 62, no. 4 (December 1993): 579–80.

21. Travis, *Autobiography of Black Politics*, 35–36.

22. Rice, "Black Radicalism," 18–19.

23. Travis, *Autobiography of Black Politics*, 40–44.

24. "Vote for De Priest," *Chicago Defender*, April 3, 1915; Travis, *Autobiography of Black Politics*, 55–56; "Exposition at Coliseum Aug. 23 to Sept. 22," *Chicago Defender*, April 3, 1915.

25. Travis, *Autobiography of Black Politics*, 55–56, 59–60.

26. Ibid., 60–61; "Oscar De Priest Set Free," *Chicago Defender*, June 16, 1917.

27. Travis, *Autobiography of Black Politics*, 89. During his terms, DePriest appointed African Americans to military positions in Annapolis and West Point. He stood defiant against the Ku Klux Klan and spoke in support of the Scottsboro boys. DePriest also attempted to revise the Fourteenth Amendment to guarantee all Americans equal protection under the law. See ibid., 89–90.

28. "Mayor Thompson Sweeps City Committeeman Fight," *Chicago Defender*, April 17, 1920; Travis, *Autobiography of Black Politics*, 73–76.

29. Travis, *Autobiography of Black Politics*, 76.

30. Ibid.

31. Harold Gosnell, *Machine Politics: Chicago Model* (Chicago: University of Chicago Press, 1937), 4; Grimshaw, *Bitter Fruit*, 5.

32. "Gangsters Murder Lawyer," *Chicago Defender*, April 14, 1928; "Arrest Granady Slayers," *Chicago Defender*, October 12, 1929; "Granady Murder Witness Slain," *Chicago Defender*, October 26, 1929; Rice, "Black Radicalism," 33–34.

33. Travis, *Autobiography of Black Politics*, 93–96; "So Is the Mayor," *Chicago Defender*, August 22, 1931; "Police Continue Drive on Policy, Handbooks and Slot Machines," *Chicago Defender*, December 24, 1932.

34. Travis, *Autobiography of Black Politics*, 96–98; "City Mourns at Bier of Mayor Anton Cermak," *Chicago Defender*, March 11, 1933; "Defender Flag at Half Mast for Mayor," *Chicago Defender*, March 11, 1933.

35. Kristi Anderson, *The Creation of a Democratic Majority, 1928–1936* (Chicago: University of Chicago Press, 1979), 106; Grimshaw, *Bitter Fruit*, 5.

36. Grimshaw, *Bitter Fruit*, 6–9.

37. Travis, *Autobiography of Black Politics*, 150–51.

38. "Dawson, Jackson Win 4-Year Terms," *Chicago Defender*, March 9, 1935; Travis, *Autobiography of Black Politics*, 150–51, 169; David K. Fremon, *Chicago Politics Ward by Ward* (Bloomington: Indiana University Press, 1988), 29–31.

39. Travis, *Autobiography of Black Politics*, 169, 174–76 (emphasis in original).

40. The American Communist Party was established in Chicago in 1919. The party's headquarters was in Chicago until 1927. In 1925, the group set up the American Negro Labor Congress to assist African American residents with their fight against racial discrimination in factories and other industries. During the 1930s, the Communist Party advocated against unemployment and evictions in Chicago's Black Belt. According to Randi Storch, "When police killed two black workers protesting an eviction in 1931, Communists led an interracial funeral procession estimated at 60,000 by the party and 15,000 by the *Chicago Daily News*" (Storch, "Communist Party," in Grossman, Keating, and Reiff, *Encyclopedia of Chicago*, 189–90).

41. Rice, "Black Radicalism," 12–16. Garveyites were members of Marcus Garvey's Universal Negro Improvement Association, which had hundreds of chapters worldwide. Garvey advocated a Black Nationalist agenda and is mostly identified for the institution of the Back

to Africa movement during the 1920s. For more information, see the Marcus Garvey Papers at UCLA, http://www.international.ucla.edu/africa/mgpp/.

42. See Stewart E. Tolnay, "The African American 'Great Migration' and Beyond," *Annual Review of Sociology* 29 (2003): 212–13.

> The most useful data source for studying the Great Migration has been a series of Public Use Microdata Samples (PUMS) derived from the decennial U.S. censuses. . . . The PUMS files have proven to be most useful for studying the educational selection of migrants from the South because the education level of an individual changes relatively little after a certain age. That evidence shows that early black southern migrants (in 1910 and 1920) were significantly more likely to be literate than blacks who remained in the South. In later years (from 1940 to 1970) the migrants had significantly higher levels of educational attainment (years of schooling) than the sedentary southern black population.

43. Rice, "Black Radicalism," 12–16.

44. Ibid., 19–20.

45. Grimshaw, *Bitter Fruit*, 48–49, 64.

46. Royko, *Boss*, 134; Rice, "Black Radicalism," 18–19.

47. Grimshaw, *Bitter Fruit*, 18–19.

48. Royko, *Boss*, 31; Grimshaw, *Bitter Fruit*, 19–20.

49. Royko, *Boss*, 134; Rice, "Black Radicalism," 34. See also "Democratic Voting—West Side Style," *Chicago Sun-Times*, November 11, 1968.

50. Wanda Ross, interview by author, May 25, 2007, Chicago, Ill. (audio file in possession of author). Ross was a member of the Chicago Panthers and was one of the main organizers for the group's free breakfast for children program.

51. Royko, *Boss*, 134.

52. Jon Rice, "The World of the Illinois Panthers," in *Freedom North: Black Freedom Struggles outside the South, 1940–1980*, ed. Jeanne Theoharis and Komozi Woodard (New York: Palgrave Macmillan, 2003), 43.

53. Ibid., 44.

54. Royko, *Boss*, 163–64.

55. Grimshaw, *Bitter Fruit*, 6.

56. Royko, *Boss*, 137.

57. Grimshaw, *Bitter Fruit*, 19, 11.

58. Royko, *Boss*, 32.

59. Grimshaw, *Bitter Fruit*, 12. For a detailed account of the power and duties of city aldermen under Daley, see Thomas M. Guterbock, *Machine Politics in Transition: Party and Community in Chicago* (Chicago: University of Chicago Press, 1980), 69–75.

60. Travis, *Autobiography of Black Politics*, 252–53.

61. Rice, "Black Radicalism," 35.

62. "In Defense of Self Defense: An Exclusive Interview with Minister of Defense, Huey P. Newton," *Black Panther*, March 16, 1968, 17.

63. "Campaigns, Politics, and Black People," *Black Liberator*, February 1969, 6. Gus Savage supported the Black Liberation Alliance. The group's national headquarters was located in Chicago on 75 East Thirty-Fifth Street. There were also other offices in Detroit, Cleveland, Columbus, Philadelphia, Gary, Indianapolis, Lexington, and New Orleans. See "Meet the Liberators," *Black Liberator*, February 1969, 5.

64. Grimshaw, *Bitter Fruit*, 20–21.

65. Ibid., 19–20.

66. Rice, "Black Radicalism," 34–35.

67. Rice, "World of the Illinois Panthers," 42–43.

68. Rice, "Black Radicalism," 36.

69. Ibid., 36–37; Thomas Millea, *Ghetto Fever* (Milwaukee, Wisc.: Bruce Publishing, 1968), 95–96.

70. Rice, "World of the Illinois Panthers," 44; Rice, "Black Radicalism," 37. See also *Chicago Sun-Times*, March 4, 1963.

71. Grimshaw, *Bitter Fruit*, 21.

72. Rice, "Black Radicalism," 27; "Community Areas, 1930–2000," in Grossman, Keating, and Reiff, *Encyclopedia of Chicago*, 1042. Also see Alphine Jefferson, "Housing Discrimination and Community Response in North Lawndale (Chicago), Illinois, 1948–1968" (Ph.D. diss., Duke University, 1979), 66–67.

73. Rice, "Black Radicalism," 27; "Community Areas, 1930–2000," 1038, 1042, 1044. Also see Evelyn Kitagawa and Karl Tauber, eds., *Local Community Fact Book for the Chicago Metropolitan Area, 1980* (Chicago: Chicago Community Inventory, University of Chicago, 1983), 79, 82.

74. Rice, "Black Radicalism," 29.

75. Darnell Wilson (pseud.), interview by Lawrence, in Louis Rosen, *The South Side: The Racial Transformation of an American Neighborhood* (Chicago: Ivan R. Dee, 1998), 60.

76. Linda Martin (pseud.), interview by Lawrence, in Rosen, *South Side*, 99.

77. Jeanine Galloway (pseud.), interview by Lawrence, in Rosen, *South Side*, 99–100 (emphasis in original).

78. Royko, *Boss*, 132–33.

79. "Billions for Urban Renewal but Not Enough to Go Around," *Sacramento Observer*, April 30, 1970.

80. Gerald Martin (pseud.), interview by Lawrence, in Rosen, *South Side*, 101.

81. Rice, "Black Radicalism," 28; Peter Lawrence, "Urban Renewal at Its Worst in Chicago's South Side," *Bay State Banner*, April 16, 1966; Peter Lawrence, "Feature Story of the Week: Robert Taylor Homes Poor Urban Renewal," *Bay State Banner*, May 28, 1966.

82. Royko, *Boss*, 133.

83. Ibid., 144.

84. Ibid., 203.

85. Ibid.

86. Ibid., 130.

87. "Labor Council Supports Open Occupancy Plan," *Tri-State Defender*, February 24, 1961.

88. Marilyn Kier (pseud.), interview by Lawrence, in Rosen, *South Side*, 80.

89. Royko, *Boss*, 130.

90. Ibid.

91. Ibid.

92. Ibid., 131–32.

93. "Fourth March to Daley Held by Demonstrators," *Chicago Daily Defender*, August 5, 1965; "Raby Hangs 'Lily White' Label on Bridgeport," *Chicago Daily Defender*, August 9, 1965; "Civil Rights Leaders Rip Alpha President," *New Pittsburgh Courier*, August 21, 1965.

94. Royko, *Boss*, 140; "Bridgeport Plays It Cool as the Marches Go On," *Chicago Daily Defender*, August 11, 1965.

95. Royko, *Boss*, 141.

96. Ibid., 135.

97. Jane Wysocker (pseud.), interview by Lawrence, in Rosen, *South Side*, 119 (emphasis in original).

98. Rice, "Black Radicalism," 28; "Two Societies," in *Eyes on the Prize* (PBS Home Video, 1987), 16:00–17:15.

99. Rice, "Black Radicalism," 28.

100. "Integration vs. Separation," *Bay State Banner*, October 1, 1966.

101. Rice, "Black Radicalism," 31.

102. Royko, *Boss*, 139–40.

103. "Rioting Hits in Chicago," *Chicago Defender*, August 14, 1965.

104. Royko, *Boss*, 143.

105. Keith Roberts (pseud.), interview by Lawrence, in Rosen, *South Side*, 86.

106. Royko, *Boss*, 142–43.

107. David J. Garrow, *Bearing the Cross: Martin Luther King, Jr., and the Southern Christian Leadership Conference* (New York: William Morrow, 1986), 427, 431.

108. Royko, *Boss*, 146; Garrow, *Bearing the Cross*, 444.

109. Garrow, *Bearing the Cross*, 448.

110. Royko, *Boss*, 146.

111. "Two Societies," 3:03–3:25.

112. Ibid.

113. Royko, *Boss*, 146–47.

114. "Two Societies," 5:32–6:00.

115. Rice, "World of the Illinois Panthers," 46.

116. Ibid.

117. Garrow, *Bearing the Cross*, 491.

118. Royko, *Boss*, 144–45.

119. Rice, "World of the Illinois Panthers," 45–46.

120. "Two Societies," 12:00–13:00.

121. Betty Washington and Donald Mosby, "300 Police Put Down Raging Westside Riot," *Chicago Daily Defender*, July 14, 1966; Royko, *Boss*, 149–51; Millea, *Ghetto Fever*, 38–39; "Two Societies," 13:00–14:25; *Report of the National Advisory Commission on Civil Disorders* (Washington, D.C.: U.S. Government Printing Office, 1968).

122. Royko, *Boss*, 149–51; "Two Societies," 14:27–14:60.

123. "Two Societies," 14:51–15:40.

124. Ibid.

125. Royko, *Boss*, 151.

126. Ibid., 147–48.

127. "Two Societies," 9:12–9:52.

128. Royko, *Boss*, 151–54; Donald Mosby, "Gage Park's Whites Stone Marchers," *Chicago Daily Defender*, August 1, 1966. For a detailed account of the Gage Park march, see Taylor Branch, *At Canaan's Edge: America in the King Years, 1965–1968* (New York: Simon and Schuster, 2006), 509–11.

129. "Two Societies," 18:18–18:30.

130. Rice, "World of the Illinois Panthers," 45, 48–49; Henry "Poison" Gaddis, telephone interview by author, May 17, 2008; "Wilson Admits Too Few Cops Sent to Gage Park," *Chicago Daily Defender*, August 3, 1966.

131. "Two Societies," 20:30–21:08; Branch, *At Canaan's Edge*, 520–22.

132. Royko, *Boss*, 151–54.

133. "Cicero Teens Bludgeon Youth with Baseball Bats: Attack Called 'Inhuman,'" *Chicago Defender*, May 28, 1966; "Four Cicero Teens Admit Ball Bat Killing," *Chicago Daily Defender*, May 31, 1966.

134. "Two Societies," 22:57–23:15.

135. "Cicero March Planned," *Chicago Daily Defender*, August 9, 1966; "Renewed Cicero Riot Forecast by Al Raby," *Chicago Daily Defender*, August 18, 1966; "Kerner Ponders Calling Guard into Cicero," *Chicago Daily Defender*, August 24, 1966; "Violence No Stranger in Riot Torn Cicero," *Chicago Daily Defender*, August 29, 1966.

136. "Two Societies," 25:30–26:55.

137. Branch, *At Canaan's Edge*, 507.

138. "Two Societies," 27:00–27:39.

139. Royko, *Boss*, 154.

140. "Two Societies," 27:50–28:15.

141. "WSO Plans to 'Mobilize' March into Cicero Sunday," *Chicago Daily Defender*, August 29, 1966.

142. "Two Societies," 28:29–29:04.

143. Ibid., 30:00–31:53; "The Big March," *Chicago Daily Defender*, September 6, 1966; Branch, *At Canaan's Edge*, 524.

144. J. F. Rice, *Up on Madison, Down on 75th Street: A History of the Illinois Black Panther Party*, pt. 1 (Evanston: The Committee, 1983), 10.

145. Royko, *Boss*, 154; "Leaders Concerned: Does Keane Speak for Daley?" *Chicago Daily Defender*, November 28, 1966.

146. Branch, *At Canaan's Edge*, 558.

147. "Across the Nation—When the Storm Was Over," *Bay State Banner*, April 18, 1968.

148. Royko, *Boss*, 163; John L. Taylor, "Seven Minutes of Hell in Westside Riot," *Chicago Daily Defender*, April 8, 1968.

149. Royko, *Boss*, 164–65; "'Kill Rioters' Daley Ordered," *Chicago Daily Defender*, April 16, 1968.

150. *American Revolution II* (Chicago: The Film Group, 1969), 18:20–20:50.

151. Donald Mosby, "Black Cops, Lawyers 'Shocked' by 'Shoot to Kill' Statement," *Chicago Daily Defender*, April 16, 1968; Betty Washington, "Rights Leaders, Clergy Call Mayor to Task on 'Shoot to Kill' Stand," *Chicago Daily Defender*, April 16, 1968; Betty Washington, "CORE Adds Voice to Furor over Mayor's Shooting Statement," *Chicago Daily Defender*, April 17, 1968; Dave Potter, "Daley Gets Bad Review from Sammy Davis," *Chicago Daily Defender*, April 17, 1968.

152. "Hotline," *Black Panther*, May 18, 1968, 3.

153. "Arm Ourselves or Harm Ourselves," *Black Panther*, May 4, 1968, 2.

154. The Democratic machine would regain political power in the late 1980s under the leadership of Richard J. Daley's son, Richard M. Daley, after the death of Harold Washington.

155. Grimshaw, *Bitter Fruit*, xii.

156. Royko, *Boss*, 161–62.

CHAPTER 2

1. William Gardner Smith, *Return to Black America* (Englewood Cliffs, N.J.: Prentice-Hall, 1970), 173; Nikhil Pal Singh, "The Black Panthers and the 'Underdeveloped Country' of the Left," in *The Black Panther Party Reconsidered*, ed. Charles E. Jones (Baltimore: Black Classic Press, 1998), 63.

2. Jeffrey Haas, *The Assassination of Fred Hampton: How the* FBI *and the Chicago Police Murdered a Black Panther* (Chicago: Lawrence Hill Books, 2009), 15.

3. The Hamptons bought a new home in Maywood in 1958, and Iberia Hampton still resides there today. Francis Hampton, born on May 12, 1922, in Haynesville, Louisiana, died on March 7, 2008, in Maywood.

4. Iberia Hampton interview and William Hampton interview, in *The Essence of Fred Hampton: An Attempt to Capture the Spirit of a Young Man Who Influenced So Many and to Pass It on to Those Who Didn't Have the Opportunity to Meet Him* (Chicago: Salsedo Press, [1989]), 2, 4. This document is a collection of interviews of people who had close relationships with Fred Hampton. It is unclear who conducted the interviews, and the date the document was printed is not present in the pamphlet. The document was given to the author by William Hampton, the brother of Fred Hampton.

When direct attribution is not made in the text, the accompanying citation contains the name of the person whose opinions are being relayed in the sentence.

5. Francis Hampton interview, in *Essence Of Fred Hampton*, 4.

6. Harland Walton interview, in *Essence Of Fred Hampton*, 7; Edward Penny Hatchett interview, in *Essence Of Fred Hampton*, 46. Walton is Fred Hampton's cousin and a community activist. Hatchett grew up in Maywood and attended both Irving Elementary School and Proviso East High School with Fred Hampton.

7. Haas, *Assassination of Fred Hampton*, 18.

8. Iberia Hampton interview, 4.

9. Paul Wade interview, in *Essence Of Fred Hampton*, 10; Eugene Moore interview, in *Essence Of Fred Hampton*, 51. Wade was a schoolmate of Fred Hampton and a community activist in Maywood. Moore was elected as an Illinois state representative.

10. William Hampton interview, 2.

11. J. F. Rice, *Up on Madison, Down on 75th Street: A History of the Illinois Black Panther Party*, pt. 1 (Evanston: The Committee, 1983), 12.

12. Hatchett interview, 46.

13. Judge Shelvin Hall interview, in *Essence Of Fred Hampton*, 53. Hall was a classmate of Fred Hampton.

14. Darren Arnson interview, in *Essence Of Fred Hampton*, 47. Arnson, an accountant, was a schoolmate of Fred Hampton.

15. Jim Ivory interview, in *Essence Of Fred Hampton*, 20. Ivory, an educator and community activist, had numerous conversations with Hampton regarding activism at Proviso East High School.

16. Charles Anderson interview, in *Essence Of Fred Hampton*, 19. Anderson, a teacher, was a staff member during Hampton's time at Proviso East High School.

17. Donald Williams interview, in *Essence Of Fred Hampton*, 13.

18. Dr. Jeremy Spooner interview, in *Essence Of Fred Hampton*, 6. Spooner, an educator at Southern University in Louisiana, met Hampton in college.

19. William Taylor interview, in *Essence Of Fred Hampton*, 53. Taylor, a local labor leader, worked with Hampton at the Corn Products Company in Argo, Illinois, in the summer of 1967.

20. Rev. Claude Porter interview, in *Essence Of Fred Hampton*, 44. Porter worked with Hampton on various community activist projects.

21. Don Johnson, Francis Ward, Ralph Whitehead, and Brian Boyer, "Chairman Fred Died a Natural Death," *Chicago Journalism Review* 2, no. 12, "The Death of Fred Hampton: A Special Report" (December 1969): 10.

22. Williams interview, 12.

23. Ibid.

24. Ivory interview, 21; Rev. Ron Graham interview, in *Essence of Fred Hampton*, 38.

25. Williams interview, 12; Johnson, Ward, Whitehead, and Boyer, "Chairman Fred Died a Natural Death," 10.

26. William Hampton interview, 2; Hatchett interview, 46; Kevin Johnson interview, in *Essence Of Fred Hampton*, 54; Dr. Conrad Worrill interview, in *Essence of Fred Hampton*, 58; Jon Rice, "The World of the Illinois Panthers," in *Freedom North: Black Freedom Struggles outside the South, 1940–1980*, ed. Jeanne Theoharis and Komozi Woodard (New York: Palgrave Macmillan, 2003), 50. Johnson grew up with Hampton and declares that Hampton's activism led him to transcend a life of negativity to pursue a more positive direction. Worrill was a member of Black United Front, and he and Hampton worked as a team on numerous civil rights campaigns when Hampton was a member of the NAACP.

27. Williams interview, 13; Marvin Carter interview, in *Essence of Fred Hampton*, 50. Carter grew up with Hampton and used to help him collect food and clothes to send to civil rights workers in the South.

28. Iberia Hampton interview, 5; Rev. Gregory Perkins interview, in *Essence Of Fred Hampton*, 54–55. Perkins was Hampton's assistant when they were members of the NAACP.

29. Williams interview, 13; William Hampton interview, 2.

30. Graham interview, 38; Rice, *Up on Madison*, 12. Graham is the minister of First Methodist Church, which was used by the NAACP and black and white Maywood residents as a meeting place after the riot at Proviso East High School.

31. Ron Burke interview, in *Essence of Fred Hampton*, 9. Burke, a community activist, was an advisor to Hampton when he was in both the NAACP and the BPP.

32. Rev. Joseph Richardson interview, in *Essence Of Fred Hampton*, 52. Richardson was the pastor of St. James Baptist Church in Broadview, Illinois, and he worked and marched with Hampton on numerous occasions.

33. Rev. Jesse Jackson interview, in *Essence Of Fred Hampton*, 48; Dick Gregory interview, in *Essence Of Fred Hampton*, 56. Jackson was a member of the SCLC at this time. Gregory, a comedian and activist, was heavily involved in organizing against the Daley machine for open housing and at the Democratic National Convention in Chicago in 1968.

34. Stokely Carmichael interview, in *Essence Of Fred Hampton*, 49.

35. Dr. Russ Meeks interview, in *Essence Of Fred Hampton*, 44; Warner Saunders interview, in *Essence Of Fred Hampton*, 49. Meeks is an activist who was involved in the arts. Saunders is a Chicago television personality.

36. Hall interview, 53; Michael McCarty, "Presentation on Illinois Black Panther Party and Fred Hampton" (40th Reunion of the Black Panther Party, Oakland, Calif., October 13, 2006) (audio file in possession of author).

37. Wade interview, 11.

38. Bob Wiggins interview, in *Essence Of Fred Hampton*, 51. Wiggins was a West Side activist who worked with Hampton on various operations.

39. Danny Davis interview, in *Essence Of Fred Hampton*, 50. Davis was an activist and politician who challenged the Daley machine during this time.

40. Tyrone Davis interview, in *Essence Of Fred Hampton*, 52.

41. Richard G. Hatcher interview, in *Essence Of Fred Hampton*, 48.

42. James Montgomery interview, in *Essence Of Fred Hampton*, 23. Montgomery was one of the lead attorneys who successfully sued the federal government, Cook County, and the City of Chicago after Hampton was assassinated.

43. Iberia Hampton interview, 4.

44. Rice, "World of the Illinois Panthers," 50.

45. Robert Wells interview, in *Essence of Fred Hampton*, 15. Wells was a Maywood resident who was also concerned about his children having a place to swim.

46. "Remarks by Ted Elbert at the Village Board Meeting Concerning the Naming of the Pool, 1970," in *Essence of Fred Hampton*, 29.

47. Wade interview, 10; Carter interview, 50.

48. Jim Brewer interview, in *Essence of Fred Hampton*, 51; Tyrone Gladney interview, in *Essence Of Fred Hampton*, 52. Brewer is a former basketball player for the Cleveland Cavaliers who went to high school with Hampton and marched with him in numerous swimming pool campaigns. Gladney also was a schoolmate of Hampton and participated in numerous swimming pool campaigns.

49. McCarty, "Presentation."

50. Rev. Harry McNelty interview, in *Essence of Fred Hampton*, 46. McNelty was pastor of First Baptist Church in Melrose Park, where the Chicago area memorial service for Fred Hampton was held.

51. Jackson interview, 49.

52. Yvonne King, "Presentation on the Illinois Black Panther Party" (40th Reunion of the Black Panther Party, Oakland, Calif., October 13, 2006) (audio and video files in possession of author).

53. Singh, "Black Panthers and the 'Underdeveloped Country' of the Left," 78.

54. "In Defense of Self Defense: An Exclusive Interview with Minister of Defense, Huey P. Newton," *Black Panther*, March 16, 1968, 16.

55. Ibid.

56. *Black Panther Community Newsletter*, June 16, 1969.

57. Joan Elbert interview, in *Essence of Fred Hampton*, 30; Rice, *Up on Madison*, 13.

58. Rice, "World of the Illinois Panthers," 50–51; Rice, *Up on Madison*, 13.

59. Jon Rice, "Black Radicalism on Chicago's West Side: A History of the Illinois Black Panther Party" (Ph.D. diss., Northern Illinois University, 1998), 70.

60. Ibid., 71. This location would later be known as "the Fort" and would serve as headquarters for the black street gang the Black Stone Rangers.

61. Bobby Rush, "A Gathering of Friends: Honoring Reverend Congressman Bobby Lee Rush" (reflection, private ceremony, Chicago, Ill., October 10, 2009) (audio file in possession of author); Rice, "World of the Illinois Panthers," 51; Rice, "Black Radicalism," 71; King, "Presentation."

62. Joann Lombard interview, in *Essence Of Fred Hampton*, 47. Lombard grew up in Maywood with Hampton, and the two attended the same high school. He recruited her into the Youth Branch of the NAACP, and she later joined him as a member of the ILBPP.

63. Rice, "World of the Illinois Panthers," 51; Rice, "Black Radicalism," 72.

64. Rush, "Gathering of Friends."

65. Ibid.; King, "Presentation"; "Interview Report: Black Panthers Issue Charter for Chicago Chapter," November 7, 1968, box 228, folder 9, items 119, 119-1, 119-2, Surveillance Unit, Intelligence Section, Bureau of Investigative Services, Chicago Police Department–Red Squad, Chicago History Museum (hereafter Red Squad papers); "Report Regarding Black Panther Party," December 18, 1968, box 229, folder 1, item 22, Red Squad papers.

66. Henry English interview, in *Essence of Fred Hampton*, 50. English is the director of Black United Fund and a former ILBPP member.

67. Fred Hampton, "You Can Murder a Liberator, but You Can't Murder Liberation," in *The Black Panthers Speak*, ed. Philip S. Foner (Philadelphia: Lippincott, 1970), 138–44.

68. Lu Palmer interview, in *Essence of Fred Hampton*, 35. Palmer was a close friend of Hampton and other Panthers.

69. "Panthers in Chicago," *Militant*, October 25, 1968.

70. Ronald Koziol, "Find Black Panthers Are Recruiting Here," *Chicago Tribune*, October 10, 1968.

71. Ibid.; "Information Report: Wilson Jr. College," October 10, 1968, box 228, Red Squad papers.

72. Ronald Koziol, "Panther Chief Pushes Drive among Gangs," *Chicago Tribune*, January 24, 1969.

73. Michael McCarty, interview by author, September 15, 2006, Chicago, Ill. (audio file in possession of author); "Report to District 11: Black Panther Party," January 13, 1969, box 229, folder 1, items 46, 46-1, Red Squad papers; Rice, "Black Radicalism," 75; Rice, *Up on Madison*, 23.

74. McCarty interview; Rice, "Black Radicalism," 75–76.

75. "Interview Report: Black Panther Party," February 8, 1969, box 229, folder 3, item 49, Red Squad papers.

76. "Report Regarding Black Panther Party," December 18, 1968, box 229, folder 1, item 22, Red Squad papers.

77. King, "Presentation."

78. On September 18, 1968, San Francisco State became the first university to institute a black studies program as a result of student protests. UCLA capitulated to similar student dissent in January 1969. There, Los Angeles Panthers Alprentice "Bunchy" Carter and John Huggins were killed in Campbell Hall during a dispute among students over who would head up the newly established program. The incident took place between the US Organization (cultural nationalists) and the Black Panthers (at this time revolutionary nationalists) on January 17, 1969. Both groups that represented students at UCLA clashed, resulting in the shooting death of the two Panthers. The episode was instigated by the FBI COINTELPRO, which exacerbated the rivalry between the groups. The FBI's goal was to have the groups engage in a war that would ultimately lead to their destruction. Such a war did not take place. See *Black Panther Community Newsletter* (Southern California Chapter), September 1, 1969; "Pigs Sacrifice Pigs," *Black Panther Community Newsletter* (Southern California Chapter), September 15, 1969, 1; *Black Community News Service* (Southern California Chapter), January 19, 1970; Scot Brown, *Fighting for Us: Maulana Karenga, the US Organization, and Black Cultural Nationalism* (New York: New York University Press, 2003); Curtis Austin, *Up against the Wall: Violence in the Making and Unmaking of the Black Panther Party* (Fayetteville: University of Arkansas Press, 2006).

79. For decades, the black student movement in Chicago received only scant scholarly attention. In 2003, however, works by Joy Ann Williamson and Dionne Danns were published that examine the role of Chicago African American high school and college students in the fight for quality education and a curriculum that encompassed the African and African American experiences. This chapter parallels Donna Murch's, *Living for the City* by displaying how the students attending the high schools and community colleges have a very different class composition than the traditional student movements examined by scholars in the past. See Joy Ann Williamson, *Black Power on Campus: The University of Illinois, 1965–75* (Urbana: University of Illinois Press, 2003); Dionne Danns, *Something Better for Our Children: Black Organizing in Chicago Public Schools, 1963–1971* (New York: Routledge, 2003); Dionne Danns, "Chicago High School Students' Movement for Quality Public Education, 1966–1971," *Journal of African American History* 88, no. 2, "The History of Black Student Activism" (Spring 2003): 138–50; Donna Jean Murch, *Living for the City: Migration, Education, and the Rise of the Black Panther Party in Oakland, California* (Chapel Hill: University of North Carolina Press, 2010).

80. Rice, *Up on Madison*, 6–7; Henry "Poison" Gaddis, telephone interview by author, May 17, 2008. The Coordinating Council of Community Organizations was based on the South Side. It was a civil rights group whose goals mirrored those of the SCLC and the NAACP.

81. Rice, *Up on Madison*, 7–8.

82. "Daley Charges Red Plot: Prove It! Leaders Demand," *Chicago Daily Defender*, July 1, 1965, 1, 3, 14.

83. Rice, *Up on Madison*, 8.

84. Black Students Association, *R.A.P.*, vol. 2, no. 2 (Chicago: Roosevelt University, 1968), 5.

85. Ibid.

86. Black Students Association, "Merit Is What?," in ibid., 4–5.

87. Ibid. National statistics for dropout rates in 1968 indicate that black students were more likely to drop out of high school than their white counterparts. For instance, the dropout rate in 1968 for cohorts ages 16–17 overall was 15.7 percent (black males, 23.8 percent; black females, 24.7 percent; white males, 14.3 percent; white females, 14.6 percent) and ages 18–19 overall was 7.8 percent (black males, 10.1 percent; black females, 14.2 percent; white males, 6.9 percent; white females, 7.6 percent). See Russell W. Rumberger, "High School Dropouts: A Review of Issues and Evidence," *Review of Educational Research* 57, no. 2 (Summer 1987): 101–21.

88. "Interview Report: Black Student Association, Roosevelt University," January 13, 1969, box 229, folder 3, item 11, Red Squad papers. I assume that the undercover officer was African American because he was able to gather information about James Turner's workshop after Turner insisted that all white people "leave the room" before he spoke.

89. "Interview Report: For Blacks Only (TV Program) ABC-Channel 7," January 14, 1969, box 229, folder 2, items 15, 17, Red Squad papers. In March 1968, Chicano students from six East Los Angeles area high schools staged a five-day walkout to protest what they believed to be deplorable conditions and a lack of quality education in their schools. Sal Castro, a teacher at Lincoln High School, along with the Brown Berets and student leaders of the schools involved, led the walkouts. See Jack McCurdy, "But Won't Remove Police: School Board Yields to Some Student Points in Boycotts," *Los Angeles Times*, March 12, 1968.

90. "Information Report: Harper High School," February 6, 1969, box 229, folder 3, item 60, Red Squad papers.

91. William Galloway (pseud.), interview by Lawrence, in Louis Rosen, *The South Side: The Racial Transformation of an American Neighborhood* (Chicago: Ivan R. Dee, 1998), 81, 84.

92. Darnell Wilson (pseud.), interview by Lawrence, in Rosen, *South Side*, 84, 85.

93. Rosen, *South Side*, 104–11.

94. Keith Roberts (pseud.), interview by Lawrence, in Rosen, *South Side*, 109.

95. Bill Van Alstine, "Race Riot Flares at Gage Park School," *Chicago Defender*, February 5, 1966, 1.

96. Betty Washington, "Black Students Boycott Gage Park High," *Chicago Daily Defender*, May 25, 1968, 1.

97. "Arrest Three in Gage Park Student Row: Black White Pupils Clash," *Chicago Daily Defender*, May 13, 1969, 1, 3, 20.

98. "Police Arrest Nineteen at Gage Park School Fracas," *Chicago Daily Defender*, October 16, 1969, 2.

99. Tony Anthony, "Gage Park Race Tensions Mount," *Chicago Daily Defender*, March 14, 1970, 1, 4; Tony Anthony, "Students March at Gage Park High," *Chicago Daily Defender*, March 25, 1970, 1, 3; Rosemary Terry, "Gage Park Boundary Changes Cause Rift," *Chicago Daily Defender*, December 4, 1971, 3; "Asks Court to Close High School," *Chicago Daily Defender*, September 21, 1972, 3; Michael L. Culbert, "Racists Use Tapes in Gage Park Row," *Chicago Daily Defender*, September 23, 1972, 1, 36; James M. Stephens, "PUSH Men Guard School," *Chicago Daily Defender*, October 24, 1972, 1, 3, 20; Tony Griggs, "Twenty-Six Arrested in Gage Park Riot," *Chicago Daily Defender*, November 16, 1972, 1, 3, 35; Tony Griggs, "Tells Gage Park Horror," *Chicago Daily Defender*, November 18, 1972, 1, 22.

100. Griggs, "Twenty-Six Arrested"; Griggs, "Tells Gage Park Horror."

101. Tony Griggs, "Four Hundred in Harper Walkout," *Chicago Daily Defender*, November 22, 1972, 1, 3.

102. Robert McClory, "Protest Nazi Rally Here," *Chicago Defender*, April 30, 1975, 1, 3.

103. Warner Saunders, "Racism Consumes Gage Park," *Chicago Daily Defender*, October 3, 1972, 8; Earl Nelson, "Gage Park Like Selma," *Chicago Daily Defender*, October 9, 1972, 3, 22; James W. Compton, "More Than Meets the Eye," *Chicago Daily Defender*, November 20, 21, 25, 1972; "Daley Enters Gage Furor," *Chicago Daily Defender*, November 21, 1972, 1, 2; "Gage Park Racists," *Chicago Daily Defender*, December 19, 1972, 13; Robert McClory, "Blacks Sold Out by School Deal," *Chicago Defender*, August 25, 1973, 1; "Sorry School Decision," *Chicago Defender*, August 27, 1973, 13; Robert McClory, "To Halt Racial Strife," *Chicago Defender*, August 29, 1973, 1, 3.

104. Clarence Thomas, "College Students Come Home," *Black Panther*, May 18, 1968, 20.

105. Don McAllister, presenter, "United Front against Fascism Conference," Oakland, Calif., July 18–20, 1969, sponsored by the Black Panther Party, in *Transcription: United Front against Fascism Conference*, 1969, box 229, folder 4, item 1, Red Squad papers.

106. Chaka, "How to Relate to Black Community," *Black Liberator*, February 1969, 3.

107. "Interview Report: Interview with Mr. Charles Monroe, Dean at Wilson Jr. College, Regarding Participation of Black Panthers in Current School Problems at Wilson Jr. College," November 12, 1968, box 229, folder 1, items 19, 19-1, Red Squad papers.

108. "Interview Report: 'The Hole,'" October 17, 1968, box 228, folder 9, items 100, 100-1, Red Squad papers.

109. "Interview Report: Activities at Wilson Jr. College," February 12, 1969, box 229, folder 3, item 71, Red Squad papers.

110. Bobby Rush and Bob Brown would later team up with Fred Hampton (NAACP) and members of other organizations in 1968 to form the ILBPP.

111. King, "Presentation."

112. "Interview Report: Information Concerning Black Panthers Recruiting in Woodlawn Area," December 20, 1968, box 229, folder 3, item 6, Red Squad papers.

113. "Information Report: Hyde Park High School," January 22, 1969, box 229, folder 3, item 22, Red Squad papers.

114. "Information Report: Recruitment Notice," 1969, box 228, Red Squad papers.

115. "Panther Visitors," *Champaign–Urbana Courier*, January 12, 1969.

116. Carolann Rodriguez, "Panthers Eject Whites from Meeting . . . Blacks Urge Guns," *Daily Illini*, January 11, 1969.

117. "Black Panthers," *Champaign–Urbana Courier*, January 11, 1969.

118. Mike Hilfrink, "Black Panther Party Recruits," *Champaign–Urbana Courier*, January 11, 1969.

119. Ibid.

120. Rodriguez, "Panthers Eject Whites."

121. Hilfrink, "Black Panther Party Recruits."

122. Ibid.

123. Ibid.; Rodriguez, "Panthers Eject Whites."

124. "Two Black Panthers Arrested in Disturbance at Illini Union," *Daily Illini*, February 8, 1969.

125. Ibid.

126. "Black Student Association, University of Illinois–Urbana, Illinois Black Panther Party," February 7–9, 1969, box 229, folder 3, items 21-4 through 21-6, Red Squad papers; "Nine Black Panthers Plead Guilty in Arraignment Court," *Daily Illini*, February 11, 1969.

127. Brenda Harris, interview by author, September 21, 2009, Chicago, Ill. (audio file in possession of author).

128. Bernard Farber, "Purpose of Black Panthers Outlined by Panther Speaker Here," *Roosevelt Torch*, December 9, 1968.

129. Ibid.

130. Ibid.

131. Ibid. John Brown was an abolitionist who in 1859 led a raid on the federal arsenal at Harpers Ferry, Virginia, with the intention of igniting a slave revolt that he believed could end slavery in the United States.

132. Ibid.

133. Ibid.

134. "Panthers Featured in Black Revival Week," *Roosevelt Torch*, January 13, 1969.

135. "Information Report: Wilson Jr. College," October 10, 1968, box 228, Red Squad papers.

136. "Information Report: Dr. Bruckman, Head of Social Science Department at Wilson Junior College," December 16, 1968, box 229, folder 1, items 56, 56-1, Red Squad papers.

137. Ibid.

138. "Human Relations Report," January 29, 1969, box 229, folder 3, item 48, Red Squad papers.

139. Ibid.

140. "Information Report: Black Panthers Activity at Crane Jr. College," November, December 1968, box 228, folder 1, item 37, Red Squad papers.

141. "Interview Report: 'Free Huey Newton Rally,' Held at University of Illinois, Circle Campus," November 26, 1968, box 229, folder 1, item 2, Red Squad papers.

142. "Interview Report: Robert L. Carter," January 27, 1969, box 229, folder 3, item 32, Red Squad papers.

143. "Interview Report: Memorial for Dr. Martin Luther King at the U of I Circle Campus," January 15, 1969, box 229, folder 2, item 25, Red Squad papers.

144. "Information Report: Black Student Organization of IIT," January 8, 1969, box 229, folder 2, item 5, Red Squad papers; "Surveillance Report: The Black Panther Party at the Herman Hall, IIT," January 9, 1969, box 229, folder 2, item 18, Red Squad papers.

145. "Information Report: Known Members of Black Panthers Have Been Frequenting Pool Hall," October 28, 1968, box 228, Red Squad papers.

146. "Information Report: Militant Group," August 23, 1968, box 228, Red Squad papers.

147. "Information Report: Members of Black Panther Party and Deacons for Defense and Justice," August 19, 1968, box 228, Red Squad papers.

148. "Information Report: Meeting of Black Panthers at Louis Theater," January 16, 1969, box 229, folder 2, item 27, Red Squad papers.

149. Rice, "Black Radicalism," 33, 38–39; Lance Hill, *The Deacons for Defense: Armed Resistance and the Civil Rights Movement* (Chapel Hill: University of North Carolina Press, 2004), 227–30. The Deacons for Defense and Justice was organized in Jonesboro, Louisiana, in July 1964 by African American World War II and Korean War veterans to protect civil rights workers from the Ku Klux Klan and white vigilante residents and police. The group provided protection for CORE voter registration workers, SNCC organizers, and other civil rights activists who visited Louisiana. More importantly, it demonstrates that, contrary to popular belief that the civil rights movement was singularly nonviolent, armed resistance was a significant tool of the civil rights movement. For a critique of Hill's book, see Emilye Crosby, "It Wasn't the Wild West: Keeping Local Studies in Self-Defense Historiography," in *Civil Rights History from the Ground Up: Local Struggles, a National Movement*, ed. Emilye Crosby (Athens: University of Georgia Press, 2011), 194–255.

150. Hill, *Deacons for Defense*, 232.

151. Rice, "Black Radicalism," 33, 38–39; Hill, *Deacons for Defense*, 230, 232.

152. Rice, "Black Radicalism," 39–40. There is no consistent official record of exactly how many Panthers were in the Chicago chapter. Most of the Panthers' records were destroyed by police during raids, and officers set the Panthers' headquarters on fire during one raid. Unofficially, according to former ILBPP members and various police reports, there were more than 500 members at its height, and the number dwindled to about 50 after Hampton's murder.

153. Rice, "World of the Illinois Panthers," 46; Lamar Billy "Che" Brooks, telephone interview by author, January 13, 2007 (digital audio file in possession of author).

154. Rice, "World of the Illinois Panthers," 43

155. Ibid., 43; Rice, *Up on Madison*, 3.

156. "Information Report: Visit by Senator McCarthy, Presidential Candidate, to SCLC's Operation Breadbasket," August 17, 1968, box 228, folder 9, item 26, Red Squad papers.

157. "Surveillance Report: West Englewood Citizens Committee for Better Police Protection," November 23, 1968, box 229, folder 1, item 30, Red Squad papers.

158. "Information Report: Benefit Show for Huey Newton," October 5, 1968, box 228, folder 9, items 90, 90-1, Red Squad papers.

159. Ibid.

160. Ibid. A recognizance bond is a promise to appear in court with no monetary binder between the court and the person out on bond. This type of bond is usually used when there is absolutely no risk of the person skipping out on bond. Crawford makes the case that racism in the Cook County court system prevented African Americans from taking advantage of recognizance bonds.

161. Ibid.

162. William Stewart, "How to Organize Co-Ops," *Black Liberator*, February 1969, 4.

163. There was a shootout in Oakland, California, between Panthers and police on April 6, 1968, two days after Martin Luther King's assassination, that resulted in the arrest of the Party's minister of information, Eldridge Cleaver, and the death of the Party's first recruit, Bobby Hutton. Forced to surrender, seventeen-year-old Hutton was unarmed when he was shot and killed by police. Betty Shabazz, now deceased, was the wife of human rights leader Malcolm X, who was slain in February 1965.

164. Betty Shabazz, "Western Union Telegram: Bobby James Hutton Family and Kathleen Cleaver," *Black Panther*, May 4, 1968, 17.

165. McCarty interview.

166. Ibid.

167. Henry "Poison" Gaddis, interview by author, October 14, 2006, at the Black Panther Party 40th Reunion in Oakland, Calif. (audio file in possession of author).

168. Gaddis interview, October 14, 2006.

169. Wanda Ross, interview by author, May 25, 2007, Chicago, Ill. (audio file in possession of author).

CHAPTER 3

1. Mumia Abu-Jamal, "A Life in the Party: An Historical and Retrospective Examination of the Projections and Legacies of the Black Panther Party," in *Liberation, Imagination, and the Black Panther Party: A New Look at the Panthers and Their Legacy*, ed. Kathleen Cleaver and George N. Katsiaficas (New York: Routledge, 2001), 46–47.

2. *American Revolution II* (Chicago: The Film Group, 1969), 21:55–26:00.

3. L. F. Palmer Jr., "Black Panthers Carve a Foothold in Chicago," *Daily News*, January 25, 1969.

4. Ibid.

5. Ibid.

6. Ward Churchill, "'To Disrupt, Discredit and Destroy': The FBI's Secret War against the Black Panther Party," in Cleaver and Katsiaficas, *Liberation, Imagination, and the Black Panther Party*, 108–9. In 1971, tensions between Eldridge Cleaver and Huey Newton over the direction of the Party were exacerbated by the FBI's counterintelligence agents. Tensions between the New York chapter and Oakland were also a result of COINTELPRO operations.

7. Robert Justin Goldstein, *Political Repression in Modern America from 1870 to the Present* (Boston: G. K. Hall, 1978).

8. Susan Cantor, "Fred Hampton: A Case of Political Assassination," *First Principles: National Security and Civil Liberties* 2, no. 3 (November 1976), in series 2, subseries 6: Legal Papers, box 37, folder 1, Dr. Huey P. Newton Foundation, Incorporated Papers, Green Library, Department of Special Collections, Stanford University, Palo Alto, Calif.

9. Ibid.

10. Angela D. LeBlanc-Ernest, "'The Most Qualified Person to Handle the Job': Black Panther Party Women, 1966–1982," in *The Black Panther Party Reconsidered*, ed. Charles E. Jones (Baltimore: Black Classic Press, 1998), 311.

11. Yvonne King, "Presentation on the Illinois Black Panther Party" (40th Reunion of the Black Panther Party, Oakland, Calif., October 13, 2007) (audio and video files in possession of author); Brenda Harris, interview by author, September 21, 2009, Chicago, Ill. (audio file in possession of author). Harris worked for several of the chapter's survival programs. The Better Boys Foundation was founded in 1961 by Joseph Kellman, chairman and CEO of Globe Glass and Mirror. It is a nonprofit organization that serves Chicago's West Side community of North Lawndale. Its purpose is to help North Lawndale youth break the cycle of poverty via academic achievement. The foundation remains a thriving force in the community today. For more information, see Better Boys Foundation, http://www.bbfchicago.org (accessed May 2, 2007).

12. J. F. Rice, *Up on Madison, Down on 75th Street: A History of the Illinois Black Panther Party*, pt. 1 (Evanston: The Committee, 1983), 38. There was a free breakfast site at the Marcy Center on Sixteenth Street and Hamon, the People's Church at 201 South Ashland, Precious Blood Church on Congress and Western, the Madden Center near Twenty-Second and State Streets, on Thirty-Fifth Street near Indiana, on Forty-Fifth Street near State Street, and at the Panther office on 2350 West Madison.

13. Donna Jean Murch, *Living for the City: Migration, Education, and the Rise of the Black Panther Party in Oakland, California* (Chapel Hill: University of North Carolina Press, 2010), 172.

14. *Black Panther Community Newsletter*, June 16, 1969.

15. Wanda Ross, interview by author, May 25, 2007, Chicago, Ill. (audio file in possession of author). Philanthropist Lucille Montgomery was a benefactor of several politically radical activists and groups in the 1960s and 1970s. Her Chicago home was often used as a fundraising site for the party and other groups, where activists would meet celebrities and other wealthy individuals who donated to their causes. A&P, originally called the Great Atlantic and Pacific Tea Company, was at this time the world's largest grocer. The company had stores in more than 3,100 U.S. cities and grossed $2.9 billion per year. See "Red Circle & Gold Leaf," *Time*, November 13, 1950.

16. Lynn French, interview by Phyllis J. Jackson, in *Comrade Sisters* (documentary produced by Phyllis J. Jackson and Christine L. Minor, 2005), 19:07–19:21. The documentary is a collection of interviews of former female Panthers conducted by former Panther Phyllis J. Jackson. The quotations and accounts provided by the documentary *Comrade Sisters* utilized in this book cannot be quoted, copied, or duplicated without the express written consent of Phyllis J. Jackson.

17. Yvonne King, interview by Phyllis J. Jackson, in *Comrade Sisters*, 14:35–15:41.

18. *Murder of Fred Hampton* (The Film Group, 1971), 11:23–12:02.

19. Rice, *Up on Madison*, 38.

20. Harris interview.

21. Cantor, "Fred Hampton."

22. JoNina M. Abron, "'Serving the People': The Survival Programs of the Black Panther Party," in Jones, *Black Panther Party Reconsidered*, 184.

23. *Murder of Fred Hampton*, 17:33–17:41.

24. Abron, "'Serving the People,'" 184.

25. *Murder of Fred Hampton*, 18:46–19:30.

26. Abron, "'Serving the People,'" 184.

27. Cantor, "Fred Hampton."

28. Richard Romo, "Mexican-Americans Fight Racism," *Black Panther*, May 4, 1968, 2. The Peace and Freedom Party is based in California. It is an open, multitendency, socialist, and feminist political party. It opposes capitalism, racism, imperialism, sexism, and elitism. The Brown Caucus is a Latino/Latina constituency of the organization. For more information, see Peace and Freedom Party, http://www.peaceandfreedom.org (accessed March 5, 2006).

29. Bernard Farber, "Purpose of Black Panthers Outlined by Panther Speaker Here," *Roosevelt Torch*, December 9, 1968, 3.

30. The Rainbow Coalition is discussed in detail in Chapter 4.

31. Operation Breadbasket was the economic arm of the SCLC. There were offices in numerous American cities.

32. "Information Report: Visit by Senator McCarthy, Presidential Candidate, to SCLC's Operation Breadbasket," August 17, 1968, box 228, Surveillance Unit, Intelligence Section, Bureau of Investigative Services, Chicago Police Department–Red Squad, Chicago History Museum (hereafter Red Squad papers).

33. Sheryl Fitzgerald, "Chicago Panthers Staging Liquor Boycott," *Daily Defender*, October 30, 1968. The East Garfield Organization was a community-based group located on Chicago's West Side in the East Garfield district. The community was about 70 percent African American by the late 1960s and housed three large Chicago Housing Authority projects.

34. Ibid.

35. Ibid.

36. Ibid. The Vice Lords were a gang located in the East Garfield area.

37. Ronald Koziol, "Find Black Panthers Are Recruiting Here," *Chicago Tribune*, October 10, 1968. Located on Chicago's South Side, the BSR was America's largest street gang, with well over 5,000 members.

38. "Cleaver Will Teach History of Racism at UCLA," *Chicago Defender*, September 13, 1968. The class's objective traced racism from slavery to its contemporary effects in the United States. Various state politicians threatened to sanction the University of California college system if UCLA allowed the Panther to teach the course. University of California professors and students banded together to oppose what they perceived to be outside pressure—which allowed students to enroll in Cleaver's class.

39. Palmer, "Panthers Carve a Foothold"; King, "Presentation."

40. *Stronghold: Panther Film*, series 2, subseries 4: Stronghold, box 27, folder 8, item 1, Newton Foundation, Stanford University.

41. "Interview Report: Black Panther Party," February 8, 1969, box 229, folder 3, item 49, Red Squad papers.

42. Ibid. John Henry Altofer was a wealthy businessman and civic leader from Peoria, Illinois, who had political ambitions but was mostly known as a philanthropist. Before being elected Illinois governor in 1969, Richard Buell Ogilvie was known for his battles against Chicago's mafia as Cook County sheriff. Ogilvie's lieutenant governor was future Democratic U.S. senator Paul Simon. Their single term was the first and only time that opposite parties occupied the Illinois governor and lieutenant governor positions.

43. Mike Hilfrink, "Black Panther Party Recruits," *Champaign–Urbana Courier*, January 11, 1969.

44. "Surveillance Report: Revolutionary Contingent," December 30, 1968, box 229, folder 1, item 80, Red Squad papers.

45. Ibid.

46. Yvonne King, panelist, "Women and the Black Panther Party," DuSable Museum of African American History, Chicago, Ill., May 13, 2010 (audio file in possession of author).

47. Koziol, "Find Panthers Are Recruiting Here."

48. Rufus Walls, Minister of Information, "Black Panther Weekend Newsletter," Chicago, February 1, 1969, in box 229, folder 3, item 56-1, Red Squad papers. Eldridge Cleaver was the Party's minister of information. At this time, he was in exile in Algeria after jumping bail after a shootout with police that left seventeen-year-old Bobby Hutton dead. H. Rap Brown was national chairman of SNCC before he joined the BPP in 1968. Stokely Carmichael also left SNCC to join the Black Panthers and was named the organization's prime minister. The Progressive Labor Party was founded in 1962 by Milt Rosen and Mort Sheer as a result of a split in the Communist Party of the United States. The group advocated against unemployment, racism, and war. For more information on the Progressive Labor Party, see Robert J. Alexander, *Maoism in the Developed World* (London: Praeger, 2001), 11–24.

49. Walls, "Black Panther Weekend Newsletter." The Party often referred to the African American population as the "black colony" to equate its plight with other colonized peoples abroad. The Mau Mau was a Kenyan rebel group that led a failed military uprising against British colonizers. Their movement hastened Kenya's independence, which came to fruition in 1963. *The Dirty Dozen* was a 1967 movie about a group of convicted murderers who were involved in a mass assassination mission of German officers in World War II. The National Liberation Front was the force engaged in battle against the United States in the Vietnam War. It was made up of more than a dozen different political and religious groups. They used small cells of three to ten men per unit to wage guerrilla warfare against the U.S. military presence in Vietnam.

50. "Interview Report: For Blacks Only (TV Program) ABC-Channel 7," January 14, 1969, box 229, folder 2, items 15, 17, Red Squad papers. *For Blacks Only* usually aired on Sunday afternoons at 3:00 P.M. Fred Hampton also stated that the Panthers had been underground in Chicago for six months before the organization decided to open its office on 2350 West Madison. He explained that the current economic system had to be overturned because it contained two main evils: capitalism and racism. Hampton declared that the U.S. political system was in need of an absolute and drastic change because blacks had not been involved in the establishment of the American government when the founding fathers drew up the political process. He compared the Panthers to the Dirty Dozen, Garrison's Gorillas, and the Green Berets, whom he deemed as ready for spot jobs in urban settings, and the army could not come into a city and cope with such methods. *Garrison's Gorillas* was a 1967 television series about a group of prisoners turned commandos who used their special skills against the Germans in World War II. *The Green Berets* was a 1968 movie starring John Wayne. It was the first American movie about the Vietnam War depicting gung-ho soldiers waging battle against the "Viet Cong."

51. Ibid.

52. Ibid.

53. Linda Williams, "Black Political Progress in the 1980s: The Electoral Arena," in *The New Black Politics: The Search for Political Power*, ed. Michael B. Preston, Lenneal J. Henderson, and Paul Lionel Puryear (New York: Longman, 1987), 111; Clarence Lusane, "To Fight for the People: The Black Panther Party and Black Politics in the 1990s," in Jones, *Black Panther Party Reconsidered*, 451.

54. Lusane, "To Fight for the People," 451.

55. Ibid.

56. Ollie A. Johnson III, "Explaining the Demise of the Black Panther Party: The Role of Internal Factors," in Jones, *Black Panther Party Reconsidered*, 405.

57. "Chicago Model Cities Election—December 19th People's Candidates Campaign for Public Offices," *Black Panther*, December 7, 1972, 6; LeBlanc-Ernest, "'Most Qualified Person to Handle the Job,'" 319. Model Cities was an initiative of President Lyndon Johnson's War on Poverty federal urban aid program. It was established in 1966 in an attempt to improve coordination of existing urban programs and provide additional funds for local plans.

58. "In Defense of Self Defense: An Exclusive Interview with Minister of Defense, Huey P. Newton," *Black Panther*, March 16, 1968, 16.

59. "Interview Report: Civil Disturbance Regarding Democratic National Convention," August 6, 1968, box 228, folder 9, Red Squad papers.

60. Ibid.

61. Ibid.; "Interview Report: Democratic National Convention," August 6, 1968, box 228, folder 9, item 18, Red Squad papers.

62. "Interview Report: Democratic National Convention."

63. Ibid. Yippies were members of the Youth International Party, a group founded in 1967 by Abbie Hoffman and Jerry Rubin. The group was originally part of SDS.

64. "Interview Report: Mike Noonan," October 20, 1968, box 228, folder 9, items 106 through 106-2, Red Squad papers. Mike James cofounded the political group Rising Up Angry, located on Chicago's North Side. The group was one of the initial representatives of the original Rainbow Coalition, which is discussed in detail in Chapter 4. Eldridge Cleaver was the Peace and Freedom Party's U.S. presidential candidate in 1968. He was scheduled to visit the campuses of UIC, Northwestern, and the University of Chicago during the aforementioned speaking tour.

65. "Interview Report: Black Militants Arming Themselves on the South Side of Chicago," August 21, 1968, box 228, folder 9, Red Squad papers. The police interview report identified the interviewee as an employee of Marzano's Clearing Bowl.

66. "Interview Report: Mr. Ciralski," August 5, 7, 1968, box 228, folder 9, Red Squad Papers. The interview took place in Skyway Liquors on 7018 South Stony Island. The African American civil unrest dubbed the Glenville Shootout took place July 23–28, 1968. There was a confrontation between a number of armed black men and Cleveland police that erupted into the shootout. Four of the men and three policeman were killed, which ignited two days of conflict. A race riot also took place on July 27, 1968, in Gary, Indiana.

67. *American Revolution II*, 7:00–10:34.

68. Ibid., 10:05–10:10.

69. Ibid., 10:35–10:44.

70. "Democratic National Convention," Chicago History Museum, http://www.chicagohs.org/history/politics/1968.html (accessed February 23, 2008). For a detailed account of the riots at the 1968 Democratic National Convention, see David Farber, *Chicago '68* (Chicago: University of Chicago Press, 1988). For information on the riots during the convention from the perspective of Chicago police officers, see Frank Kusch, *Battleground Chicago: The Police and the 1968 Democratic National Convention* (Chicago: University of Chicago Press, 2008).

71. *American Revolution II*, 12:15–17:44.

72. "Chicago, 1968," CNN, http://www.cnn.com/ALLPOLITICS/1996/conventions/chicago/facts/chicago68/index.shtml (accessed February 21, 2008). The trial opened on September 24, 1969. Two main groups were targeted by the grand jury: the National Mobilization

to End the War in Vietnam and the Yippies, along with the Panthers. The Chicago Eight were members of these groups. Those on trial included Abbie Hoffman, Jerry Rubin, David Dellinger, Tom Hayden, Rennie Davis, John Froines, Lee Weiner, and Bobby Seale.

73. CNN, http://www.cnn.com/ALLPOLITICS/1996/conventions/chicago/facts/chicago68/index.shtml. For more information on the Chicago Eight trial, see John Schultz, *The Chicago Conspiracy Trial* (New York: Da Capo, 1993), and Jon Wiener, *Conspiracy in the Streets: The Extraordinary Trial of the Chicago Eight* (New York: New Press, 2006).

74. "In Defense of Self Defense," 18.

75. Nikhil Pal Singh, "The Black Panthers and the 'Underdeveloped Country' of the Left," in Jones, *Black Panther Party Reconsidered*, 65–66. The civil rights movement is traditionally identified as a middle-class movement. However, in Chicago, civil rights was very much a working-class agenda, as the majority of black residents were working poor.

76. Ibid.

77. Ibid., 65.

78. "Interview Report: Black Panthers Issue Charter for Chicago Chapter," November 7, 1968, box 228, folder 9, items 119, 119-1, 119-2, Red Squad papers.

79. "Information Report: Recruiting and Organizing of the Black Panthers," November 21, 1968, box 228, folder 9, item 131, Red Squad papers.

80. "Baldwin, Seale, Eckels Talk Revolution," *Black Panther*, May 18, 1968, 2, 25. In 1831, Nat Turner led the most successful slave revolt in the history of American slavery.

81. Jon Rice, "Black Radicalism on Chicago's West Side: A History of the Illinois Black Panther Party" (Ph.D. diss., Northern Illinois University, 1998), 86.

82. Farber, "Purpose of Black Panthers Outlined by Panther Speaker Here," 3.

83. Ibid.

84. "Surveillance Report: Revolutionary Contingent," December 30, 1968, box 229, folder 1, item 80, Red Squad papers.

85. "Surveillance Report: West Englewood Citizens Committee for Better Police Protection," November 23, 1968, box 229, folder 1, item 30, Red Squad papers. CORE, established in 1942, had pioneered the use of sit-ins and other civil disobedience. In Chicago, the group worked to desegregate public schools and housing.

86. Palmer, "Panthers Carve a Foothold."

87. "Information Report: 'Pray In,'" January 5, 1969, box 229, folder 2, items 3, 3-1, Red Squad papers. Archbishop Cody was allegedly an obstacle to the promotion of black priests in the Catholic Church.

88. Ibid.

89. Elaine Brown, *A Taste of Power: A Black Woman's Story* (New York: Pantheon, 1992); Assata Shakur, *Assata: An Autobiography* (Chicago: Lawrence Hill Books, 1987).

90. Robyn Ceanne Spencer, "Engendering the Black Freedom Struggle: Revolutionary Black Womanhood and the Black Panther Party in the Bay Area, California," *Journal of Women's History* 20, no. 1 (Spring 2008): 91.

91. Jeffrey O. G. Ogbar, "Brown Power to Brown People: Radical Ethnic Nationalism, the Black Panthers, and Latino Radicalism, 1967–1973," in *In Search of the Black Panther Party: New Perspectives on a Revolutionary Movement*, ed. Jama Lazerow and Yohuru Williams (Durham: Duke University Press, 2006), 276–77.

92. Charles E. Jones, "Arm Yourself or Harm Yourself: People's Party II and the Black Panther Party in Houston, Texas," in *On the Ground: The Black Panther Party in Communities across America*, ed. Judson L. Jeffries (Jackson: University Press of Mississippi, 2010), 23–24.

93. Jeffries, *On the Ground*; Judson L. Jeffries, ed., *Comrades: A Local History of the Black Panther Party* (Bloomington: Indiana University Press, 2007); Judson L. Jeffries, ed., *Black Power in the Belly of the Beast* (Urbana: University of Illinois Press, 2006); Peniel E. Joseph, ed., *Neighborhood Rebels: Black Power at the Local Level* (New York: Palgrave Macmillan, 2010); Lazerow and Williams, *In Search of the Black Panther Party*; Yohuru Williams and Jama Lazerow, eds., *Liberated Territory: Untold Local Perspectives on the Black Panther Party* (Durham: Duke University Press, 2008).

94. Paul Alkebulan, *Survival Pending Revolution: The History of the Black Panther Party* (Tuscaloosa: University of Alabama Press, 2007), 98–116. Alkebulan's chapter on women and the BPP exhibits experiences from women from local chapters as well as the national headquarters in Oakland. The book chapter fulfills its goal of providing informative and rich details of the various roles of female BPP members across chapters. However, Tracye Matthews's piece is a critical analysis of the gender politics of the BPP.

95. Tracye Matthews, "'No One Ever Asks What a Man's Role in the Revolution Is': Gender and the Politics of the Black Panther Party, 1966–1971," in Jones, *Black Panther Party Reconsidered*, 268.

96. Ibid., 280–81.

97. Ibid., 293.

98. Ibid., 280–81.

99. Tracye Matthews, panelist, "Women and the Black Panther Party."

100. Murch, *Living for the City*, 211.

101. Robyn Ceanne Spencer, "Inside the Panther Revolution: The Black Freedom Movement and the Black Panther Party in Oakland, California," in *Groundwork: Local Black Freedom Movements in America*, ed. Jeanne Theoharis and Komozi Woodard (New York: New York University Press, 2005), 306–7.

102. Reynaldo Anderson, "Practical Internationalists: The Story of the Des Moines, Iowa, Black Panther Party," in Theoharis and Woodard, *Groundwork*, 283–84, 290; Ericka Huggins, interview by author, March 24, 2011, Lexington, Ky. The Des Moines chapter allied with the National Welfare Rights Organization to oppose the treatment of poor women and the forced breakup of black families in the city. See Anderson, "Practical Internationalists," 290.

103. C. Clark Kissinger, "Serve the People," *Guardian*, May 17, 1969, 7.

104. King, "Presentation"; Joan McCarty, interview by author, October 19, 2009, Atlanta, Ga.

105. Joan Gray, panelist, "Women and the Black Panther Party."

106. Kissinger, "Serve the People," 7; LeBlanc-Ernest, "'Most Qualified Person to Handle the Job,'" 311.

107. King, "Presentation." Joan Gray was respected as an intellectual and community organizer.

108. Ibid.; Joan McCarty interview.

109. Rice, "Black Radicalism," 101.

110. *Comrade Sisters*, 4:39–5:45.

111. Murch, *Living for the City*, 190.

112. French interview, in *Comrade Sisters*, 5:54–6:13.

113. Murch, *Living for the City*, 266 (n. 33). The survey consisted of 119 members from across the country. The study revealed that 81 percent of female members held high school diplomas, as opposed to 68 percent of male members. Sixty-three percent of female members had at least one semester of college, as opposed to 43 percent of male members. For

more information about the surveys, see Alkebulan, *Survival Pending Revolution*, 98–99, 151 (n. 1).

114. Joan McCarty interview.

115. Joan Kelley-Williams, interview by Phyllis J. Jackson, in *Comrade Sisters*, 7:45–8:44.

116. Yvonne King, panelist, "Women and the Black Panther Party."

117. Harris interview; Joan McCarty interview; Ann Kendrick and Donna Calvin, interview by author, January 5, 2011, Chicago, Ill.

118. Rice, "Black Radicalism," 100–101. For anecdotal examples of female members who would not accept gender inequality in Detroit, see Ahmad Rahman, "Marching Blind: The Rise and Fall of the Black Panther Party in Detroit," in Williams and Lazerow, *Liberated Territory*, 187–88, 204–5.

119. "Note," *Black Panther* (1968), 24.

120. Harris interview.

121. Farber, "Purpose of Black Panthers Outlined by Panther Speaker Here," 3.

122. King interview, in *Comrade Sisters*, 32:51–33:20.

123. Henry "Poison" Gaddis, supplement during question and answer session to King, "Presentation." Gaddis was a field secretary of the Illinois chapter and helped to organize the Rainbow Coalition.

124. King interview, in *Comrade Sisters*, 30:36–31:40.

125. Joan Gray, interview, *The HistoryMakers African American Video Oral History Collection*, tape 3, reel 6, August 22, 2003, 00:28:43.

126. Joan Gray, panelist, "Women and the Black Panther Party."

127. Henry "Poison" Gaddis, interview by author, October 14, 2006, Oakland, Calif.

128. Harris interview; Ross interview; Gray interview, *HistoryMakers African American Video Oral History Collection*; Kendrick and Calvin interview.

129. Spencer, "Inside the Panther Revolution," 310.

130. Joan McCarty interview.

131. Akua Njeri, *My Life with the Black Panther Party* (Oakland, Calif.: Burning Spear Publications, 1991), 45–46.

132. French interview, in *Comrade Sisters*, 39:33–39:58.

133. Kathleen Neal Cleaver, "Back to Africa: The Evolution of the International Section of the Black Panther Party (1969–1972)," in Jones, *Black Panther Party Reconsidered*, 239.

134. Ibid.

135. Murch, *Living for the City*, 192.

136. French interview, in *Comrade Sisters*, 37:21–38:27.

137. Ibid., 45:26–47:15.

138. Johnson, "Explaining the Demise of the Black Panther Party," 401.

CHAPTER 4

1. Michael Coakley, "A Year Later—Same Old Tune," *Chicago Today*, August 29, 1969.

2. Ibid.

3. Jon Rice, "The World of the Illinois Panthers," in *Freedom North: Black Freedom Struggles outside the South, 1940–1980*, ed. Jeanne Theoharis and Komozi Woodard (New York: Palgrave Macmillan, 2003), 55–56.

4. *American Revolution II* (Chicago: The Film Group, 1969), 28:05–29:17.

5. José "Cha Cha" Jiménez, remarks delivered at "Young Lords and Black Panther Party Symposium" (Sonja Haynes Stone Center for Black Culture and History, University of North Carolina, Chapel Hill, 2007), disc 2, 24:00–26:11.

6. Rice, "World of the Illinois Panthers," 43, 50.

7. Henry "Poison" Gaddis, telephone interview by author, May 17, 2008. Gaddis served as security/organizer under Bob Lee during his tenure as a member of the ILBPP.

8. Yvonne King, "Presentation on the Illinois Black Panther Party" (40th Reunion of the Black Panther Party, Oakland, Calif., October 13, 2007) (audio and video files in possession of author); Robert "Bobby" E. Lee, interview by author, October 22, 2008, Houston, Tex. King served as a field secretary and organized for the Rainbow Coalition and later was appointed deputy minister of labor for the ILBPP. Lee was a member of the ILBPP from the fall of 1968 to May 1970.

9. Lee interview.

10. Ibid.

11. Ibid.

12. James Tracy, "The (Original) Rainbow Coalition," *Solidarities*, September 30, 2006.

13. Gaddis interview, May 17, 2008; Tracy, "(Original) Rainbow Coalition"; Lee interview.

14. Gaddis interview, May 17, 2008; Tracy, "(Original) Rainbow Coalition."

15. Lee interview.

16. Rice, "World of the Illinois Panthers," 54; "Young Lords Running Log, 1968–1970: Misc. File Rainbow Coalition, Item 37, Pages 1–2," box 386, folder 15, item 1, p. 22, and "Young Lords Running Log, 1968–1970: Black Panther Party Vol. 11, Item 448, Page 1," box 386, folder 15, item 1, p. 23, Surveillance Unit, Intelligence Section, Bureau of Investigative Services, Chicago Police Department–Red Squad, Chicago History Museum (hereafter Red Squad papers). A greaser was a young white male, usually of working-class background, who identified with the countercultural trend of using grease to slick back his hair.

17. Gaddis interview, May 17, 2008.

18. King, "Presentation."

19. Henry "Poison" Gaddis, remarks delivered at "Young Lords and Black Panther Party Symposium" (Sonja Haynes Stone Center for Black Culture and History, University of North Carolina, Chapel Hill, 2007), disc 2, 00:00–00:53.

20. Jon Rice, "Black Radicalism on Chicago's West Side: A History of the Illinois Black Panther Party" (Ph.D. diss., Northern Illinois University, 1998), 98–99.

21. Kathleen Neal Cleaver, "Back to Africa: The Evolution of the International Section of the Black Panther Party (1969–1972)," in *The Black Panther Party Reconsidered*, ed. Charles E. Jones (Baltimore: Black Classic Press, 1998), 230–31.

22. Mike James, "Live from the Heartland: Young Lords Radio Interview," interview of José "Cha Cha" Jiménez, WLUW Chicago, November 2005, Michael James Archive (Rising Up Angry), Chicago, Ill.

23. Gaddis interview, May 17, 2008; King, "Presentation."

24. Gaddis interview, May 17, 2008; Wanda Ross, interview by author, May 25, 2007, Chicago, Ill. (audio file in possession of author); Michael McCarty, interview by author, September 15, 2006, Chicago, Ill. (audio file in possession of author); Tracy, "(Original) Rainbow Coalition"; Lee interview.

25. James, "Live from the Heartland"; *Bulletin, Ministry of Information, People News Service*, July 5, 1969; King, "Presentation"; Tracy, "(Original) Rainbow Coalition."

26. Roger Flaherty, "Uptown's Village Plan—to Oblivion and Back Again," *Ravenswood-Lincolnite, Lerner Newspapers*, September 16, 1969, box 304, folder 4, item 1-1, Red Squad papers; Gaddis remarks, disc 2, 29:18–32:02; *American Revolution II*, 38:28–55:05. JOIN Community Union was initiated by SDS in Uptown in 1968.

27. Lee interview.

28. James, "Live from the Heartland."

29. *Rising Up Angry* 1, no. 1 (July 1969): 7. The photo, taken by Linn Ehrlich, is at the bottom of the page.

30. Amanda Seligman, "Uptown," in *The Encyclopedia of Chicago*, ed. James R. Grossman, Ann Durkin Keating, and Janice L. Reiff (Chicago: University of Chicago Press, 2004), 1293.

31. Mike James, *Rising Up Angry and Chicago's Early Rainbow Coalition, 1968–1975: Remembering the Black Panther Party, Young Lords Organization, Young Patriots, and Rising Up Angry* (Center for Latino Research, DePaul University, September 19, 2008), pamphlet, p. 4.

32. Ibid.

33. "Information Report: Possible Meeting of the Black Panthers (Young Patriots)," February 11, 1969, box 229, folder 3, item 65, Red Squad papers; Lee interview.

34. *American Revolution II*, 38:28–45:45.

35. Ibid.

36. Tracy, "(Original) Rainbow Coalition."

37. Todd Gitlin and Nanci Hollander, *Uptown: Poor Whites in Chicago* (New York: Harper and Row, 1970).

38. Lee interview. Charlotte Engelmann later would provide legal defense for members of the Rainbow Coalition—members of the BPP, the YPO, and the Young Lords.

39. Ibid.

40. Gaddis remarks, disc 2, 29:18–32:02; Tracy, "(Original) Rainbow Coalition."

41. Lee interview.

42. Henry "Poison" Gaddis, interview by author, October 14, 2006, Oakland, Calif.

43. *American Revolution II*, 38:28–45:45.

44. Lee interview.

45. Gaddis interview, October 14, 2006.

46. *American Revolution II*, 45:46–55:05.

47. Ibid., 29:18–30:52, 34:36–35:07.

48. Ibid., 35:08–36:28.

49. Ibid., 1:00:23–1:11:28.

50. Ibid.

51. Lee interview.

52. *American Revolution II*, 29:18–30:52.

53. "Human Relations," February 17, 1969, box 229, folder 3, item 76, Red Squad papers.

54. *American Revolution II*, 59:06–1:00:22.

55. Ibid., 38:28–45:45.

56. "Surveillance Report: Young Patriots and Black Panthers," February 12, 1969, box 229, folder 3, item 72, Red Squad papers.

57. Flaherty, "Uptown's Village Plan," Red Squad papers.

58. *American Revolution II*, 45:46–55:05; Lee interview. For more information on Uptown residents' struggle with the Model Cities Board, see Stephen S. Young, *Indicators of the Failure of the Chicago Model Cities Program to Effectively and Substantially Involve Uptown Model Area Residents* (Chicago, 1969).

59. Lee interview.

60. *American Revolution II*, 45:46–55:05.

61. "Stone Grease Grapevine: The Young Patriots, Uptown," *Rising Up Angry* 1, no. 1 (July 1969): 7; Lee interview.

62. Lee interview.

63. "The Young Patriots, Lincoln Park," *Rising Up Angry* 1, no. 1 (July 1969): 8.

64. "United Front against Fascism Conference," July 19, 1969, folder 4, item 1, pp. 13–14, Red Squad papers.

65. National Young Lords timeline, http://nationalyounglords.com/YoungLords Timeline.html; José "Cha Cha" Jiménez, interview by author, September 14–15, 2009, Chicago, Ill.

66. Amanda Seligman, "Lincoln Park," in Grossman, Keating, and Reiff, *Encyclopedia of Chicago*, 746.

67. Mike Royko, *Boss: Richard J. Daley of Chicago* (New York: Dutton, 1971), 148–49.

68. José (Cha Cha) Jiménez biography, National Young Lords website, http://national younglords.com/Jose%20bio.html (accessed January 25, 2009); Jiménez interview by author.

69. "Young Lords," *Rising Up Angry* 1, no. 1 (July 1969): 14; James, "Live from the Heartland"; Jiménez interview by author.

70. James, "Live from the Heartland"; Jiménez interview by author.

71. James, "Live from the Heartland."

72. "Young Lords," *Rising Up Angry*.

73. James, "Live from the Heartland"; Jiménez interview by author.

74. "Information Report: Attention—Third World Unity Conference, Blacks and Latins Unite," February 12, 1969, box 304, folder 10, item 5-6, and "Interview Report: Young Lords," February 7, 1969, box 304, folder 10, item 2, Red Squad papers; "Young Lords," *Rising Up Angry*.

75. "Police Harrassment of Young Lords Reported," Young Lords Organization newsletter, no date, box 304, folder 10, item 10, Red Squad papers.

76. Jiménez interview by author.

77. Ibid.; Jiménez biography; "Information Report: Police Harrassment—Political Repression," Young Lords Organization newsletter, February 12, 1969, box 304, folder 10, items 5-4, 5-5, Red Squad papers.

78. James, "Live from the Heartland"; National Young Lords timeline; Jiménez interview by author.

79. "Young Lords," *Rising Up Angry*.

80. James, "Live from the Heartland"; Jiménez interview by author.

81. James, "Live from the Heartland"; Jiménez biography; Jiménez interview by author.

82. "Young Lords," *Rising Up Angry*; Jiménez interview by author. McCormick Theological Seminary was located at Halsted and Belden Streets. It was a Presbyterian Divinity School that had about 250 students. Later, it was bought by DePaul University.

83. Felix M. Padilla, *Puerto Rican Chicago* (Notre Dame: University of Notre Dame Press, 1987), 121; *Chicago Sun-Times*, May 19, 1969.

84. James, "Live from the Heartland"; Jiménez biography; Jiménez interview by author.

85. "Young Lords," *Rising Up Angry*; Jiménez interview by author.

86. "Young Lords," *Rising Up Angry*; Jiménez interview by author.

87. James, "Live from the Heartland"; Jiménez interview by author.

88. "Young Lords," *Rising Up Angry*; National Young Lords timeline; Jiménez interview by author.

89. James, "Live from the Heartland"; National Young Lords timeline; Jiménez interview by author. Dr. Pedro Albizu Campos was a Puerto Rican nationalist who advocated for the independence of Puerto Rico beginning in the 1930s. See Frederic Ribes Tovar, *Albizu Campos: Puerto Rican Revolutionary* (New York: Plus Ultra Educational Publishers, 1971).

90. James, "Live from the Heartland"; Jiménez interview by author.

91. Jiménez interview by author.

92. "Pigs Break Up YLO March," *Rising Up Angry* 1, no. 2 (August 1969): 16; Jiménez interview by author. The Comancheros was a group of young Chicanos who had developed a political consciousness.

93. Padilla, *Puerto Rican Chicago*, 121.

94. "Young Lords," *Rising Up Angry*; William C. Harsh Jr., "Young Lords Charge City Using Laws to Block Day-Care Center," *Chicago Sun-Times*, September 6, 1969; Jiménez interview by author.

95. Padilla, *Puerto Rican Chicago*, 121; Pat Krochmal, "Form 'People's' Church: Young Lords Seek $10,000," *Chicago Today*, September 7, 1969.

96. "YLO," *Rising Up Angry* 1, no. 3 (October 1969): 8; Jiménez interview by author.

97. "Surveillance Report: Young Lords," February 5, 1969, box 304, folder 10, items 1-3, 1-4, Red Squad papers. Johnson was not an official member of the YLO, but he served as a de facto member and advisor.

98. Padilla, *Puerto Rican Chicago*, 121; "Lincoln Park," *Rising Up Angry* 1, no. 3 (October 1969): 8; Jiménez interview by author.

99. "Lincoln Park," *Rising Up Angry*; Jiménez interview by author.

100. James, "Live from the Heartland"; Jiménez interview by author.

101. "Memorial Rally," September 10, 1969, box 301, folder 12, item 8-1, Red Squad papers; *Rising Up Angry* 1, no. 3 (October 1969): 8; Jiménez interview by author.

102. Denise Oliver-Velez, remarks delivered at "Young Lords and Black Panther Party Symposium" (Sonja Haynes Stone Center for Black Culture and History, University of North Carolina, Chapel Hill, 2007), disc 1, 45:06–51:02.

103. Ibid.

104. James, "Rising Up Angry," 4.

105. Mike James, presentation on Rising Up Angry at "Rising Up Angry and Chicago Early Rainbow Coalition, 1968–1975" (opening reception, photo exhibit, Center for Latino Research, DePaul University, Chicago, Ill., September 19, 2008); "Transmittal Report: Mike G. James," box 304, folder 4, item 22-1, March 25, 1970, Red Squad papers.

106. James, "Rising Up Angry," 4.

107. Ibid., 6.

108. Mike James, "Getting Ready for the Firing Line: Organizing in Uptown in the 60s; Remembering JOIN Community Union," *Heartland Journal* 51 (Summer 2005): 26.

109. Elizabeth A. Patterson, "Logan Square," in Grossman, Keating, and Reiff, *Encyclopedia of Chicago*, 761.

110. James, "Rising Up Angry," 6.

111. Ibid.

112. "Rising Up Angry," *Rising Up Angry* 1, no. 2 (August 1969): 16.

113. "Stone Grease Grapevine: Corp," *Rising Up Angry* 1, no. 1 (July 1969): 7.

114. James, "Live from the Heartland."

115. "The Black Panthers," *Rising Up Angry* 1, no. 1 (July 1969): 3.

116. James, "Rising Up Angry," 5.

117. Ibid., 6.

118. *Rising Up Angry* 1, no. 3 (October 1969): 2.

119. "Drivin' the Snakes out Again," "Delvin," "Connolly," and "An American Letter," *Rising Up Angry* 1, no. 3 (October 1969): 10–11.

120. "Boil the Pigs in the Melting Pot! Revolution in Ireland, Italy and America," *Rising Up Angry* 2, no. 1 (Summer 1970): 14.

121. "Senn" and "Gaylords at Foreman High School," *Rising Up Angry* 1, no. 2 (August 1969): 8–9; "A Message from RISING UP ANGRY to the Brothers and Sisters on the Fights in the Schools," *Rising Up Angry* 1, no. 6 (Midwinter 1970): 2.

122. "CORP," "Southwest Side," and "Wells High School," *Rising Up Angry* 1, no. 3 (October 1969): 7.

123. "Austin High School" and "Tilden Tech," *Rising Up Angry* 1, no. 3 (October 1969): 7.

124. "Black Panthers," *Rising Up Angry*.

125. "Latin Kings Organization," *Rising Up Angry* 1, no. 6 (Midwinter 1970): 8.

126. "West Side," *Rising Up Angry* 1, no. 2 (August 1969): 8.

127. "Example of Changes in the Gangs: From a Leaflet Put Out by the Latin Eagles," *Rising Up Angry* 1, no. 1 (July 1969): 8.

128. James, "Rising Up Angry," 6.

129. Ibid.

130. Ibid.

131. Ibid.

132. Ibid.

133. Ibid.

134. Ibid.

135. Ibid.

136. Ibid.

137. Ibid.

138. Ibid., 7.

139. "Doc Gandalf's," *Rising Up Angry* 1, no. 3 (October 1969): 8.

140. "Logan Square," *Rising Up Angry* 1, no. 2 (August 1969): 9.

141. "Lowering the Construction Boom," *Rising Up Angry* 1, no. 3 (October 1969): 6.

142. Ibid.

143. James, "Rising Up Angry," 7.

144. Ibid., 6.

145. *Chicago Police Department, Red Squad and Selected Records Catalogue: Historical Sketch of the Gang Unit*, Red Squad papers, 72.

146. "Gang Busters," *Rising Up Angry* 1, no. 1 (July 1969): 11.

147. *Chicago Police Department*, Red Squad papers, 73.

148. "Things to Watch for as the Gang Intelligence Unit Comes Messing in Our Affairs," *Rising Up Angry* 1, no. 1 (July 1969): 9; James, "Rising Up Angry," 7.

149. For additional analysis of various Chicago black gangs and their relationships with the ILBPP and the YLO, see Jeffrey O. G. Ogbar, "Brown Power to Brown People: Radical Ethnic Nationalism, the Black Panthers, and Latino Radicalism, 1967–1973," in *In Search of the Black Panther Party: New Perspectives on a Revolutionary Movement*, ed. Jama Lazerow and Yohuru Williams (Durham: Duke University Press, 2006), 252–88.

150. Gaddis interview, October 14, 2006.

151. Gaddis interview, May 17, 2008.

152. For a nuanced history of street gangs in Chicago during the twentieth century, see Andrew J. Diamond, *Mean Streets: Chicago Youth and the Everyday Struggle for Empowerment in the Multiracial City, 1908–1969* (Berkeley: University of California Press, 2009).

153. "Information Report: Black Panthers and Their Recruiting Drive in Englewood," October 30, 1968, box 229, folder 1, item 16; "Interview Report: Democratic National Convention," August 6, 1968, box 228; and "Interview Report: Black Panther Party," February 8, 1969, box 229, folder 3, item 49, all in Red Squad papers; Ronald Koziol, "Find Black Panthers Are Recruiting Here," *Chicago Tribune*, October 10, 1968; "Panther Chief Pushes Drive among Gangs," *Chicago Tribune*, January 24, 1969.

154. Phil Hamlin, "Groups Vow End to Police Brutality," *Black Liberator*, May 1969, 1, 9.

155. *Rising Up Angry* 1, no. 1 (July 1969): 9.

156. Gaddis interview, May 17, 2008.

157. *Hampton v. Hanrahan*, 600 F. 2d 600 (7th Cir. 1979), brief. This brief summarizes the *Hampton v. Hanrahan* case, which was won by the plaintiffs. In 1983, the Hampton family was awarded a $1.85-million settlement by the federal government, Cook County, and the City of Chicago when the U.S. Supreme Court refused to overturn the 1979 decision of the U.S. Court of Appeals for the Seventh Circuit.

U.S. Senate, Select Committee to Study Governmental Operations with Respect to Intelligence Activities, "The FBI's Covert Action Program to Destroy the Black Panther Party," in *Supplementary Detailed Staff Reports on Intelligence Activities and the Rights of Americans*, book 3, *Final Report* (Washington, D.C.: U.S. Government Printing Office, 1976), 197.

158. J. F. Rice, *Up on Madison, Down on 75th Street: A History of the Illinois Black Panther Party*, pt. 1 (Evanston: The Committee, 1983), 30.

159. "Interview Report: Activity of the Chicago Chapter of the Black Panther Party," December 19, 1968, box 229, folder 1, item 59, p. 66, Red Squad papers.

160. *Hampton v. Hanrahan*; U.S. Senate, "FBI's Covert Action Program," 197.

161. "The Young Comancheros," *Rising Up Angry* 1, no. 1 (July 1969): 9. It was later revealed by reports of public hearings that the Young Comancheros were given start-up money for their organization in exchange for supplying information to the police department to discredit the YLO. See National Young Lords timeline.

162. Gaddis interview, May 17, 2008.

163. "United Front against Fascism Conference," July 19, 1969, box 229, folder 4, item 1, p. 9, Red Squad papers. Bill Kunstler was the preeminent movement lawyer from New York. He participated in the Chicago Eight conspiracy trial. Ron Dellums later served as a U.S. congressman and was mayor of Oakland, California, from 2007 until 2011.

164. Ibid.

165. Gaddis remarks, disc 2, 29:18–32:02.

166. Gaddis interview, May 17, 2008.

167. Lee interview.

168. Jiménez remarks, disc 2, 24:00–26:11; Lee interview; Jiménez interview by author.

169. Gaddis interview, October 14, 2006.

170. Lee interview.

171. Roger Ebert's words and four-star rating are printed on the cover of the documentary *American Revolution II*.

172. Lee interview.

173. King, "Presentation."

174. Oliver-Velez remarks, disc 2, 26:13–28:44.

175. Richard Romo, "Mexican-Americans Fight Racism," *Black Panther*, May 4, 1968, 2.

176. "Editorial: Black Panther Party and Peace and Freedom Party," *Black Panther*, March 15, 1968, 3; Gaddis interview, May 17, 2008.

177. James, "Getting Ready for the Firing Line," 26; Ollie A. Johnson III, "Explaining the Demise of the Black Panther Party: The Role of Internal Factors," in Jones, *Black Panther Party Reconsidered*, 405–6.

178. Lee interview. For in-depth analysis of the People's Party II, see Charles E. Jones, "Arm Yourself or Harm Yourself: People's Party II and the Black Panther Party in Houston, Texas," in *On the Ground: The Black Panther Party in Communities across America*, ed. Judson L. Jeffries (Jackson: University Press of Mississippi, 2010), 3–40.

179. Gaddis interview, May 17, 2008.

180. "'Country Dialectics': Poor, Texas Whites Organize to Survive Racist America," *Black Panther*, August 19, 1972, 7, 11, 14.

181. Gaddis interview, May 17, 2008; Oliver-Velez remarks, disc 2, 26:13—28:44.

182. Gaddis interview, May 17, 2008.

183. Cleaver, "Back to Africa," 225–26.

184. "Interview Report: Susan Rosenblum," June 19, 1973, box 229, folder 5, items 16-1, 16-2, Red Squad papers.

CHAPTER 5

1. Jon Rice, "Black Radicalism on Chicago's West Side: A History of the Illinois Black Panther Party" (Ph.D. diss., Northern Illinois University, 1998), 126.

2. Ibid., 132.

3. Donald Mosby, "Murder Suspected in Jail Cell Death: Youth's Remains Examined," *Chicago Daily Defender*, May 6, 1969.

4. Donald Mosby, "IID Probes Another Death," May 8, 1969; "'Policeman Beat Me,' Bus Driver Charges," May 15, 1969; Donald Mosby, "Police Get Another Brutality Complaint," May 17, 1969; George Montgomery, "Crime 'n' Police," May 24, 1969; "Says Cops Wrecked Home," May 29, 1969, all in *Chicago Daily Defender*.

5. J. F. Rice, *Up on Madison, Down on 75th Street: A History of the Illinois Black Panther Party*, pt. 1 (Evanston: The Committee, 1983), 47.

6. "Dismiss and Jail Two Policemen in Panther Case," *Chicago Sun-Times*, September 11, 1968.

7. Donald Mosby, "Two Black Cops on Trial," *Chicago Daily Defender*, May 28, 1969; Donald Mosby, "One Cop Guilty, Another Released in Arrest Case," *Chicago Daily Defender*, May 29, 1969.

8. Rice, "Black Radicalism," 132.

9. "Policeman Admits He's a Klansman," *Black Panther*, March 15, 1968, 3.

10. Rice, "Black Radicalism," 128. Also see *Chicago Sun-Times*, December 28, 1967, front page.

11. "Klan Headquarters Claim Fifty Police Officers in Chicago Police Department Belong to Klan," *Chicago Sun-Times*, December 28, 1967.

12. *American Revolution II* (Chicago: The Film Group, 1969), 1:00:23–1:11:28.

13. Mike Royko, *Boss: Richard J. Daley of Chicago* (New York: Dutton, 1971), 203.

14. Rice, "Black Radicalism," 134.

15. Rice, *Up on Madison*, 49.

16. Ibid.

17. Royko, *Boss*, 203.

18. Frank Donner, *Protectors of Privilege: Red Squads and Police Repression in Urban America* (Berkeley: University of California Press, 1990), 97. The Chicago History Museum houses the records of the Chicago Police Department's Red Squad files. In these files is a large section dedicated to the surveillance and infiltration of the Afro-American Patrolman's League.

19. Rice, "Black Radicalism," 136. Also see *Chicago Tribune*, March 13, 1975.

20. Donner, *Protectors of Privilege*, 1.

21. Ibid.

22. *Chicago Police Department, Red Squad and Selected Records Catalogue Introduction*, Surveillance Unit, Intelligence Section, Bureau of Investigative Services, Chicago Police Department–Red Squad, Chicago History Museum (hereafter Red Squad papers), p. 2. HUAC was set up by the House of Representatives beginning in 1934 to investigate persons suspected of subversion or disloyalty to the United States. At its height, HUAC's blacklisting practice was used by Wisconsin senator Joseph McCarthy to root out Communists in America. HUAC and Senator McCarthy used such tactics primarily against members of the Communist Party but also against most leftists, as right-wing conservative groups and individuals were often not questioned or prosecuted.

23. Ibid. The Alien Registration Act is better known as the Smith Act. The measure was passed by Congress in 1940 and made it illegal for any person or group in the United States to advocate the overthrow of the U.S. government. The law's main target was the Communist Party. The McCarran Acts are also known as the Internal Security Act of 1950. The legislation was passed by both the Senate and the House, and it required Communist and leftist organizations to register with the U.S. attorney general. The purpose of the law was to protect the United States from subversive activities.

24. Donner, *Protectors of Privilege*, 90. The moniker is the title of chapter 4 of the text.

25. Ibid.

26. Ibid.

27. "Interview Report: Civil Disturbance Regarding Democratic National Convention," August 6, 1968, box 228, folder 9, Red Squad papers; "United Front against Fascism Conference," July 19, 1969, box 229, folder 4, item 1, Red Squad papers.

28. Donner, *Protectors of Privilege*, 126.

29. Ibid., 146.

30. Ibid., 90.

31. Alliance to End Repression, *Chicago's Secret Police* (pamphlet published after December 30, 1985) (in possession of author—given to author by Richard Gutman, P.C., attorney for the Alliance to End Repression). Also see sec. 11b of the September 22, 1987, Order Concerning Disposition of Documents, in *Alliance to End Repression v. City of Chicago*, Nos. 74 C 3268/75 C 3295 (N.D. Ill. 1974).

32. Ward Churchill, "'To Disrupt, Discredit and Destroy': The FBI's Secret War against the Black Panther Party," in *Liberation, Imagination, and the Black Panther Party: A New Look at the Panthers and Their Legacy*, ed. Kathleen Cleaver and George N. Katsiaficas (New York: Routledge, 2001), 79.

33. Richard Gid Powers, *Secrecy and Power: The Life of J. Edgar Hoover* (New York: Free Press, 1987), 5–35.

34. Churchill, "'To Disrupt, Discredit and Destroy,'" 83.

35. U.S. Senate, Select Committee to Study Governmental Operations with Respect to Intelligence Activities, "The FBI's Covert Action Program to Destroy the Black Panther Party," in *Supplementary Detailed Staff Reports on Intelligence Activities and the Rights of Americans*, book 3, *Final Report* (Washington, D.C.: U.S. Government Printing Office: 1976), 187.

36. Ibid., 188.

37. Ibid., 1.

38. Churchill, "'To Disrupt, Discredit and Destroy,'" 78–117.

39. Donner, *Protectors of Privilege*, 143.

40. Winston A. Grady-Willis, "The Black Panther Party: State Repression and Political Prisoners," in *The Black Panther Party Reconsidered*, ed. Charles E. Jones (Baltimore: Black Classic Press, 1998), 368.

41. *Hampton v. Hanrahan*, 600 F. 2d 600 (7th Cir. 1979), brief; U.S. Senate, "FBI's Covert Action Program," 222–23.

42. Grady-Willis, "Black Panther Party," 372–73.

43. *Hampton v. Hanrahan*; Churchill, "'To Disrupt, Discredit and Destroy,'" 98.

44. Ward Churchill and Jim Vander Wall, *The* COINTELPRO *Papers: Documents from the FBI's Secret Wars against Domestic Dissent* (Cambridge: South End Press, 2002), 146, 360 (n. 114). For a detailed account of the Rackley murder and trial, see Paul Bass and Douglas W. Rae, *Murder in the Model City: The Black Panthers, Yale, and the Redemption of a Killer* (New York: Basic Books, 2006).

45. Churchill, "'To Disrupt, Discredit and Destroy,'" 98.

46. Churchill and Vander Wall, COINTELPRO *Papers,* 360 (n. 114).

47. *Hampton v. Hanrahan*; "The Black Panthers," *Rising Up Angry* 1, no. 1 (July 1969): 3; Churchill, "'To Disrupt, Discredit and Destroy,'" 98.

48. *Hampton v. Hanrahan*; "Black Panthers," *Rising Up Angry* 1, no. 2 (August 1969): 9; Churchill, "'To Disrupt, Discredit and Destroy,'" 98. The three Panthers were Pete, Alvin, and Larry—surnames unknown.

49. Grady-Willis, "Black Panther Party," 372–73.

50. Churchill, "'To Disrupt, Discredit and Destroy,'" 95.

51. Ibid.

52. *Hampton v. Hanrahan*; Jon Rice, "The World of the Illinois Panthers," in *Freedom North: Black Freedom Struggles outside the South, 1940–1980*, ed. Jeanne Theoharis and Komozi Woodard (New York: Palgrave Macmillan, 2003), 58; U.S. Senate, "FBI's Covert Action Program," 222–23.

53. *Hampton v. Hanrahan*; Churchill, "'To Disrupt, Discredit and Destroy,'" 96.

54. *Hampton v. Hanrahan*; Churchill, "'To Disrupt, Discredit and Destroy,'" 101.

55. Churchill, "'To Disrupt, Discredit and Destroy,'" 96.

56. Ollie A. Johnson III, "Explaining the Demise of the Black Panther Party: The Role of Internal Factors," in Jones, *Black Panther Party Reconsidered*, 402.

57. Henry "Poison" Gaddis, interview by author, October 14, 2006, at the Black Panther Party 40th Reunion in Oakland, Calif. (audio file in possession of author); Michael McCarty, interview by author, September 15, 2006, Chicago, Ill. (audio file in possession of author).

58. "Interview Report: Black Panther Party," January 22, 1969, box 228, folder 3, item 17, Red Squad papers.

59. Ibid.

60. Ibid.

61. Ibid.

62. "Interview Report: Chicago Chapter of the Black Panther Party," December 22, 1968, box 229, folder 1, item 74, Red Squad papers.

63. Ibid. The White Panther Party's headquarters were at the Church of the Covenant, 945 W. Diversey.

64. "Interview Report: Black Panthers," January 14, 1969, box 229, folder 3, items 12, 12-1, Red Squad papers.

65. "Interview Report: Members of Black Panther Party, Black Elephants, Black Peace Stones at Dog House Lounge," August 31, 1968, box 228, Red Squad papers. According to the report, the Black Elephants were a militant black power organization, prone to violence, and very close to the Panther movement.

66. Churchill, "'To Disrupt, Discredit and Destroy,'" 84. For more information on such reporters, see U.S. Senate, "FBI's Covert Action Program," 35–36, 218–20.

67. Churchill, "'To Disrupt, Discredit and Destroy,'" 84.

68. Donner, *Protectors of Privilege*, 139.

69. Ronald Koziol, "16 Panthers, Rangers Seized after a Chase," *Chicago Tribune*, December 19, 1968.

70. "Interview Report: Activity of the Chicago Chapter of The Black Panthers," December 19, 1968, box 229, folder 1, item 59, Red Squad papers.

71. Ronald Koziol, "Panther Chief Pushes Drive among Gangs," *Chicago Tribune*, January 24, 1969. Panthers arrested were Nathaniel Junior (21), William O'Neal (19), Bobby Rush (20), Weldon Young (22), and a seventeen-year-old youth.

72. Donner, *Protectors of Privilege*, 140.

73. Koziol, "16 Panthers, Rangers Seized"; "Interview Report: Activity of the Chicago Chapter of the Black Panthers," December 19, 1968, box 229, folder 1, item 59, Red Squad papers.

74. "Interview Report: Black Panther Party," February 8, 1969, box 229, folder 3, item 49, Red Squad papers.

75. Johnson, "Explaining the Demise of the Black Panther Party," 401.

76. The Chicago Police Department Red Squad files contain an extensive collection on Fred Hampton and a smaller collection on the ILBPP. The large amount of material demonstrates that Hampton was highly targeted by the police department, which has been proven by successful class-action lawsuits brought by the Alliance to End Repression and the American Civil Liberties Union against the city of Chicago to have been a tool against dissent utilized by the Daley administration.

77. See the illustration in the Introduction of this volume. Photo of meeting in possession of author. Collected from the private archive of Howard Ann Kendrick (Campbell), former member of ILBPP Central Staff (Communications Secretary).

78. "Young Lords Running Log, 1968–1970: Gang File Black Panther Party, Item 389, Pages 1/4," box 386, folder 15, item 1, p. 17, Red Squad papers. The report indicates that Bernardine Dohrn and members of SDS, the YLO, the YPO, and other groups were invited to the meeting to be informed of the Panthers' upcoming demonstration at the Federal Building during the Chicago Eight conspiracy trial.

79. *Hampton v. Hanrahan*; Curtis Austin, *Up against the Wall: Violence in the Making and Unmaking of the Black Panther Party* (Fayetteville: University of Arkansas Press, 2006), 189.

80. *Hampton v. Hanrahan*.

81. Churchill, "'To Disrupt, Discredit and Destroy,'" 106.

82. U.S. Senate, "FBI's Covert Action Program"; Roy Wilkins and Ramsey Clark, *Search and Destroy: A Report* (New York: Metropolitan Applied Research Center, 1973); Iberia Hampton, Plaintiff-Appellant, The United States Court of Appeals for the Seventh Circuit: Appeals from the United States District Court for the Northern District of Illinois, Eastern Division, No. 70-C-1384, Joseph Sam Perry, Judge: Argued August 14, 1978—Decided April 23, 1979.

83. *Rising Up Angry* 1, no. 3 (October 1969): 8.

84. "Chicago Youth, Policeman Die in Gun Battle," *Los Angles Times*, November 14, 1969; John D. Vasilopulos and Julius J. Blakeny, "Ask U.S. Probe of Shootout," *Chicago Daily Defender*, November 15, 1969; Donald Mosby, "Black Panther Indicted," *Chicago Daily Defender*, December 23, 1969; "Shoot-out Deaths Are Ruled Murder," *New York Times*, December 25, 1969.

85. Austin, *Up against the Wall*, 212–13.

86. *Hampton v. Hanrahan*; Churchill, "'To Disrupt, Discredit and Destroy,'" 106.

87. Austin, *Up against the Wall*, 213.

88. *Hampton v. Hanrahan*; Donner, *Protectors of Privilege*, 90; Flint Taylor and Dennis Cunningham, "The Assassination of Fred Hampton: 40 Years Later," *Police Misconduct and Civil Rights Law Report* 9, no. 12 (November/December 2009): 4. The other officers were Joseph Gorman, William Corbett, Raymond Broderick, Lynwood Harris, John Ciszewski, George Jones, James "Gloves" Davis, John Marisuch, Fred Howard, Philip Joseph, and William Kelly. Davis, Joseph, Jones, and Howard were black.

89. *Hampton v. Hanrahan*; Austin, *Up against the Wall*, 190–91, 217; Churchill, "'To Disrupt, Discredit and Destroy,'" 106.

90. *Hampton v. Hanrahan*; Donner, *Protectors of Privilege*, 90; *Murder of Fred Hampton* (The Film Group, 1971), 1:03:46–1:17:29.

91. *Hampton v. Hanrahan*; Austin, *Up against the Wall*, 217; Churchill, "'To Disrupt, Discredit and Destroy,'" 106.

92. *Murder of Fred Hampton*, 1:03:46–1:17:29.

93. *Hampton v. Hanrahan*; Austin, *Up against the Wall*, 191.

94. *Murder of Fred Hampton*, 1:03:46–1:17:29.

95. The physical evidence strongly suggests that "Gloves" Davis shot and killed Mark Clark and that Edward Carmody murdered Fred Hampton.

96. Austin, *Up against the Wall*, 218.

97. Akua Njeri, *My Life with the Black Panther Party* (Oakland, Calif.: Burning Spear Publications, 1991), 30; *Murder of Fred Hampton*, 1:03:46–1:17:29.

98. Churchill and Vander Wall, *COINTELPRO Papers*, 358 (n. 93); Njeri, *My Life*, 38; *Murder of Fred Hampton*, 1:03:46–1:17:29.

99. Jeffrey Haas, *The Assassination of Fred Hampton: How the FBI and the Chicago Police Murdered a Black Panther* (Chicago: Lawrence Hill Books, 2010), 91–92; *Hampton v. Hanrahan*; Austin, *Up against the Wall*, 191.

100. Haas, *Assassination of Fred Hampton*, 274.

101. *Hampton v. Hanrahan*; Donner, *Protectors of Privilege*, 90; Taylor and Cunningham, "Assassination of Fred Hampton," 4; Churchill and Vander Wall, COINTELPRO *Papers*, 358 (n. 93); Churchill, "'To Disrupt, Discredit and Destroy,'" 106; Njeri, *My Life*, 38; *Murder of Fred Hampton*, 1:03:46–1:17:29; Wilkins and Clark, *Search and Destroy*, 140–42; Haas, *Assassination of Fred Hampton*, 301, 346.

102. *Hampton v. Hanrahan*; Njeri, *My Life*, 39; Austin, *Up against the Wall*, 191. The seven survivors were Louis Trulock, Harold Bell, Deborah Johnson (now Akua Njeri), Doc Satchel, Blair Anderson, Brenda Harris, and Verlina Brewer.

103. Bigman, "The Role of the Black Panther Party—Reviewed," *Black Panther Community News Service* (Southern California Chapter), March 11, 1970, 8–9.

104. Eldridge Cleaver, "The Fascists Have Already Decided in Advance to Murder Chairman Bobby Seale in the Electric Chair," *Black Panther Community News Service*, March 11, 1970, 6–7.

105. "Petition Statement for Community Control of Police," *Black Panther Community News Service*, March 20, 1970, 7.

106. "Note to the Pig," *Black Panther Community News Service*, March 20, 1970, 14.

107. *Hampton v. Hanrahan*; Churchill, "'To Disrupt, Discredit and Destroy,'" 84–85.

108. *Murder of Fred Hampton*, 1:03:46–1:20:32.

109. Ibid., 1:20:33–1:26:27. I only have the documentary, *Murder of Fred Hampton*, and not the actual federal grand jury report as a source. In the documentary, Skip Andrews, the Hampton family's attorney, reads several sections of the report during a press conference. He then goes on to read the definition of murder under Illinois law. The report and the definition are almost identical, but the report does not use the word "murder." Andrews highlights the parallels between the federal grand jury report and the definition of murder under Illinois law to make the case that Hampton was actually murdered by the raiding police officers according to Illinois law. I essentially transcribed this section of the documentary as quoted in the manuscript.

110. *Hampton v. Hanrahan*; Austin, *Up against the Wall*, 191.

111. Donner, *Protectors of Privilege*, 90.

112. *Hampton v. Hanrahan*; Austin, *Up against the Wall*, 191; Churchill, "'To Disrupt, Discredit and Destroy,'" 84–85.

113. Robert Williams, "Message from Robert Williams—POW," *Black Panther Community News Service*, March 11, 1970, 5.

CHAPTER 6

1. Lynn French, interview by Phyllis J. Jackson, in *Comrade Sisters* (documentary produced by Phyllis J. Jackson and Christine L. Minor, 2005), 18:00–19:06. The documentary is a collection of interviews of former female Panthers conducted by former Panther Phyllis J. Jackson. The quotations and accounts provided by the documentary *Comrade Sisters* utilized in this book cannot be quoted, copied, or duplicated without the express written consent of Phyllis J. Jackson.

2. Don Terry, "Souls on Wheels: A Bus Tour of Black Panther Turf," *New York Times*, November 10, 1997.

3. Ward Churchill, "'To Disrupt, Discredit and Destroy': The FBI's Secret War against the Black Panther Party," in *Liberation, Imagination, and the Black Panther Party: A New Look at the Panthers and Their Legacy*, ed. Kathleen Cleaver and George Katsiaficas (New York: Routledge, 2001), 87.

4. David Hilliard, ed., *The Black Panther Party: Service to the People Programs* (Albuquerque: University of New Mexico Press, 2008), 31.

5. Bruce A. Dixon, "In Honor of Fred Hampton and Mark Clark: Executed by Chicago Cops—Dec. 4, 1969," *Black Commentator*, December 7, 2004, http://www.hartford-hwp.com/archives/45a/716.html (accessed December 9, 2004).

6. Curtis Stephens, "Life of a Party," *Crisis*, September/October 2006, 34.

7. Ibid.

8. JoNina M. Abron, "'Serving the People': The Survival Programs of the Black Panther Party," in *The Black Panther Party Reconsidered*, ed. Charles E. Jones (Baltimore: Black Classic Press, 1998), 183.

9. Hilliard, *Black Panther Party*, 23.

10. Dixon, "In Honor of Fred Hampton and Mark Clark."

11. Abron, "'Serving the People,'" 33.

12. Edward McClelland, *Young Mr. Obama: Chicago and the Making of a Black President* (New York: Bloomsbury Press, 2010), 36–37.

13. Gary Rivlin, *Fire on the Prairie: Chicago's Harold Washington and the Politics of Race* (Henry Holt: New York, 1992), 26–27; McClelland, *Young Mr. Obama*, 37.

14. Rivlin, *Fire on the Prairie*, 26; McClelland, *Young Mr. Obama*, 37.

15. Rivlin, *Fire on the Prairie*, 26.

16. Trevor Jensen, "Edward V. Hanrahan, 1921–2009: Political Career Ended by Black Panther Raid," *Chicago Tribune*, June 10, 2009; Jo Napolitano, "Edward Hanrahan, Prosecutor Tied to '69 Panthers Raid, Dies at 88," *New York Times*, June 12, 2009; Abdon M. Pallasch, "Former State's Attorney Edward Hanrahan," *Chicago Sun-Times*, June 9, 2009; Patricia Sullivan, "Prosecutor Oversaw Fatal 1969 Raid of Black Panthers in Chicago," *Washington Post*, June 12, 2009.

17. "Background Report: José Jiménez," September 9, 1974, box 304, folder 11, Surveillance Unit, Intelligence Section, Bureau of Investigative Services, Chicago Police Department–Red Squad, Chicago History Museum (hereafter Red Squad papers); "José Jiménez Statement of Candidacy," June 20, 1974, box 304, folder 11, items 33-1, 33-2, Red Squad papers; "Leader of Young Lords Is Candidate for Alderman," *Chicago Today*, June 21, 1974. A Red Squad observation report indicates that there were approximately 100 people at the press conference consisting of "40% Caucasians, 40% Puerto Ricans, and 20% Negroes, of mixed gender, ranging in ages from 5 to 50 years of age" ("Surveillance Report: José 'Cha-Cha' Jiménez," June 20, 1974, box 304, folder 11, items 30-1, 30-2, Red Squad papers).

18. Ellis Cose, "Why Latino Ex-Gang Leader Will Run for Alderman," *Chicago Sun-Times*, June 24, 1974.

19. José "Cha Cha" Jiménez, interview by author, September 14–15, 2009, Chicago, Ill.; "Leader of Young Lords is Candidate for Alderman," *Chicago Today*, June 21, 1974.

20. Jiménez interview by author.

21. Ibid.

22. Ibid.; Rivlin, *Fire on the Prairie*, 55.

23. Robin D. G. Kelley, "Into the Fire: 1970 to the Present," in *To Make Our World Anew: A History of African Americans*, ed. Robin D. G. Kelley and Earl Lewis (Oxford: Oxford University Press, 2000), 580.

24. Monica Davey, "Chicago Divided over Proposal to Honor a Slain Black Panther," *New York Times*, March 5, 2006.

25. Robert "Bobby" E. Lee, interview by author, October 22, 2008, Houston, Tex.

26. Kelley, "Into the Fire," 580.

27. While traditional organizations such as the NAACP, the Chicago Urban League, and Jesse Jackson's Operation PUSH had for years tried to mobilize the city's black vote, the most significant participants represented grassroots community efforts within and outside the black community. These groups and advocates were the Chicago Black United Community

(headed by Lu Palmer), Citizens for Self-Determination (led by Mercedes Maulette), activist Al Sampson, Concerned Young Adults, Independent Grassroots Youth Organization, Vote Community (founded by Ed Gardner of Soft Sheen hair products and Tim Black), African Community of Chicago, People's Movement for Voter Registration and Education, and Political Action Committee of Illinois (headed by Sam Patch). See Abdul Alkalimat and Doug Gills, *Harold Washington and the Crisis of Black Power in Chicago* (Chicago: Twenty First Century Books, 1989), 40–41.

28. Ibid., 40–41, 64–65.

29. Kelley, "Into the Fire," 581.

30. Jiménez interview by author.

31. McClelland, *Young Mr. Obama*, 37.

32. Alkalimat and Gills, *Harold Washington and the Crisis of Black Power*, 52–53.

33. Rivlin, *Fire on the Prairie*, xii.

34. Manning Marable, *Black Leadership: Four Great American Leaders and the Struggle for Civil Rights* (New York: Penguin, 1998), 127.

35. Rivlin, *Fire on the Prairie*, 246.

36. Ibid.

37. Kelley, "Into the Fire," 581.

38. Marable, *Black Leadership*, 128, 129.

39. David Mendell, *Obama: From Promise to Power* (New York: Harper Collins, 2007), 129.

40. Peniel E. Joseph, *Dark Days, Bright Nights: From Black Power to Barack Obama* (New York: Basic Civitas Books, 2010), 170, 174.

41. Kelley, "Into the Fire," 582.

42. Joseph, *Dark Days, Bright Nights*, 176.

43. Rivlin, *Fire on the Prairie*, xiii.

44. Ibid., 298.

45. Jiménez interview by author.

46. James Tracy, "The (Original) Rainbow Coalition," *Solidarities*, September 30, 2006.

47. Jiménez interview by author.

48. Denise Oliver-Velez, remarks delivered at "Young Lords and Black Panther Party Symposium" (Sonja Haynes Stone Center for Black Culture and History, University of North Carolina, Chapel Hill, 2007), disc 2, 26:13–28:44 (in possession of author).

49. Jiménez interview by author.

50. Hasan Jeffries, *Bloody Lowndes: Civil Rights and Black Power in Alabama's Black Belt* (New York: New York University Press, 2009), 2, 153.

51. Jiménez interview by author.

52. Joseph, *Dark Days, Bright Nights*, 177–78.

53. For an in-depth look at Barak Obama in his early years in Chicago, see McClelland, *Young Mr. Obama*.

54. Barack Obama, *Dreams from my Father: A Story of Race and Inheritance* (New York: Random House, 1995), 123, 131.

55. Gerald Kellman, interview, *Frontline: The Choice 2008*, PBS, July 24, 2008, http://www.pbs.org/wgbh/pages/frontline/choice2008/interviews/kellman.html (accessed September 18, 2008).

56. *Frontline: Dreams of Obama* (PBS Home Video, 2009), 17:03–17:17.

57. Ibid., 17:18–17:28.

58. Ibid., 18:05–18:18.

59. McClelland, *Young Mr. Obama*, 26.

60. Mendell, *Obama*, 128.

61. Janny Scott, "In 2000, a Streetwise Veteran Schooled a Bold Young Obama," *New York Times*, September 9, 2007, http://www.nytimes.com/2007/09/09/us/politics/09obama. html?pagewanted=all (accessed February 15, 2010).

62. Ibid.

63. McClelland, *Young Mr. Obama*, 146.

64. Scott, "In 2000, a Streetwise Veteran Schooled a Bold Young Obama."

65. Mendell, *Obama*, 129–30.

66. Scott, "In 2000, a Streetwise Veteran Schooled a Bold Young Obama."

67. Barack Obama, *The Audacity of Hope: Thoughts on Reclaiming the American Dream* (New York: Crown, 2006), 105.

68. *Frontline: Dreams of Obama*, 34:44–35:03.

69. Mendell, *Obama*, 153.

70. Obama, *Audacity of Hope*, 247.

71. Joseph, *Dark Days, Bright Nights*, 188.

72. Mendell, *Obama*, 230.

73. Dewey M. Clayton, *The Presidential Campaign of Barack Obama: A Critical Analysis of a Racially Transcendent Strategy* (New York: Routledge, 2010), 19–20.

74. Marilyn Katz, interview by author, August 17, 2011, Chicago, Ill. (audio and video files in possession of author). Katz is president of MK Communications: Public Strategies in the Public Interest. She cut her teeth as a political strategist/consultant in the Richard M. Daley mayoral administration in Chicago.

75. Ibid.

76. *Frontline: Dreams of Obama*, 35:55–36:33.

77. Clayton, *Presidential Campaign of Barack Obama*, 19.

78. *Frontline: Dreams of Obama*, 36:47–37:13.

79. Baodong Liu, *The Election of Barack Obama: How He Won* (New York: Palgrave Macmillan, 2010), 124.

80. Patrick T. Reardon, "The Agony and the Agony," *Chicago Tribune*, June 24, 2007.

81. Christopher Hayes, "Obama's Media Maven," *Nation*, February 19, 2007.

82. Rivlin, *Fire on the Prairie*, 130.

83. Katz interview.

84. Reardon, "Agony and the Agony"; Debra Bell, "Ten Things You Didn't Know about David Axelrod," *U.S. News and World Report*, December 2, 2008, http://www.usnews.com/articles/news/politics/2008/12/02/10-things-you-didnt-know-about-david-axelrod.html (accessed December 5, 2008).

85. Hayes, "Obama's Media Maven." AKPD Message and Media is a Chicago-based consulting firm. Axelrod was the chief strategist for Barack Obama's 2004 U.S. Senate election and his 2008 U.S. presidential election. Axelrod next served as President Obama's top political advisor and also served as the chief strategist for President's Obama reelection campaign.

86. Ibid.

87. Ibid. David Axelrod was responsible for the victories in the mayoral races of African Americans Dennis Archer in Detroit, Michael White in Cleveland, Anthony Williams in D.C., Lee Brown in Houston, and John Street in Philadelphia.

88. AKPD Message and Media, http://akpdmedia.com/clients/ (accessed January 28, 2009).

89. Hayes, "Obama's Media Maven"; Bell, "Ten Things."

90. AKPD Message and Media.

91. Reardon, "Agony and the Agony."

92. Quigwen Dong, Kenneth D. Day, and Raman Deol, "The Resonant Message and the Powerful New Media: An Analysis of the Obama Presidential Campaign," in *The Obama Effect: Multidisciplinary Renderings of the 2008 Campaign*, ed. Heather E. Harris, Kimberly R. Moffitt, and Catherine R. Squires (Albany: State University of New York Press, 2010), 75–76. For a comprehensive analysis of the use of media and message during President Obama's 2008 election, see Kate Kenski, Bruce W. Hardy, and Kathleen Hall Jamieson, eds., *The Obama Victory: How Media, Money, and Message Shaped the 2008 Election* (Oxford: Oxford University Press, 2010).

93. Hayes, "Obama's Media Maven."

94. Joseph, *Dark Days, Bright Nights*, 189.

95. Clayton, *Presidential Campaign of Barack Obama*, 4.

96. Lucius Outlaw, "On Race and Class, or, On the Prospects of 'Rainbow Socialism,'" in *The Year Left 2: An American Socialist Yearbook*, ed. Mike Davis, Manning Marable, Fred Pfeil, and Michael Sprinker (London: Verso, 1987), 121.

97. For a recent evaluation of President Obama's first term, see James A. Thurber, ed., *Obama in Office* (Boulder: Paradigm Publishers, 2011). The breakdown of President Obama's policy highlights his disconnect from the original Rainbow Coalition ideology. However, the extreme partisanship that President Obama has experienced during his first term unfortunately parallels Washington's first term in office as mayor of Chicago (Beirut on the Lake).

98. "Profile: David Axelrod," *BBC NEWS*, November 7, 2008, http://news.bbc.co.uk/go/pr/fr/-/2/hi/americas/us_elections_2008/7716677.stm (accessed December 5, 2008).

99. Hayes, "Obama's Media Maven."

100. Davey, "Chicago Divided."

101. Ibid.

102. Ray Baker Jr., dir., *Chairman Fred Hampton Way* (2009). This documentary has yet to be released to the public.

103. Ibid.

104. Euan Hague, "Street Lessons," *Area Chicago: How We Learn*, October 11, 2007, http://www.areachicago.org/p/issues/how-we-learn/street-lessons/ (accessed November 5, 2007).

105. Edward P. Morgan, "Media Culture and the Public Memory of the Black Panther Party," in *In Search of the Black Panther Party: New Perspectives on a Revolutionary Movement*, ed. Jama Lazerow and Yohuru Williams (Durham: Duke University Press, 2006), 356–57.

106. Fran Spielman, "Chicago Cops Fight Black Panther Street Naming," *Chicago Sun Times*, February 28, 2006.

107. Flint Taylor and Dennis Cunningham, "The Assassination of Fred Hampton: 40 Years Later," *Police Misconduct and Civil Rights Law Report* 9, no. 12 (November/December 2009): 6.

108. Ibid.

109. Hague, "Street Lessons"; Eric Zorn, "Fred Hampton Way? No Way!" *Chicago Tribune*, February 28, 2006.

BIBLIOGRAPHY

Primary Sources

ARCHIVES

California
Department of Special Collections, Green Library, Stanford University, Palo Alto
    Dr. Huey P. Newton Foundation, Incorporated Papers
Special Collections, Young Research Library, University of California, Los Angeles
    Black Community News Service (Southern California Chapter), 1969–71
    Bluck Panther, 1968–80
    Black Panther Community Newsletter (Southern California Chapter), 1969–71

Illinois
Chicago Films Archive
    American Revolution II. Chicago: The Film Group, 1969.
Chicago History Museum
    Afro-American Patrolman's League Papers
    Chicago Police Department–Red Squad, Bureau of Investigative Services, Intelligence
        Section, Surveillance Unit (Red Squad papers, U.S. Circuit Court Sealed Records)
William Hampton Archive, Maywood
    *The Essence of Fred Hampton: An Attempt to Capture the Spirit of a Young Man Who
        Influenced So Many and to Pass It On to Those Who Didn't Have the Opportunity to
        Meet Him*. Chicago: Salsedo Press, [1989].
Michael James Archive (Rising Up Angry), Chicago
    Heartland Journal, 2005
    "Live from the Heartland: Young Lords Radio Interview"
        Interview of José "Cha Cha" Jiménez, WLUW Chicago, November 2005
    Rising Up Angry, 1968–70
Special Collections, Carter G. Woodson Library, Chicago
    The Black Liberator, 1969
    The Militant, 1968

Online
Federal Bureau of Investigation
    Fred Hampton
    Black Panther Party

PERIODICALS

Bay State Banner, 1966–70
Bulletin, Ministry of Information, People News Service, 1969–70
Champaign–Urbana Courier, 1969–70
Chicago Daily Defender, 1965–72
Chicago Defender, 1915–73
Chicago Sun-Times, 1967–69, 2006, 2009
Chicago Today, 1969–70
Chicago Tribune, 1968–70, 2006, 2007, 2009
Daily Illini, 1969–70
Daily News, 1969–70
Guardian, 1968–70
Los Angeles Times, 1968–70
Nation, 1978–79, 2007
New Pittsburgh Courier, 1965–70
New Yorker, 1971–72
New York Times, 1965–78, 1997, 2006, 2009
Roosevelt Torch, 1968–69
Sacramento Observer, 1968–70
Time, 1950–51
Tri-State Defender, 1961–62
Washington Post, 2009

INTERVIEWS

Conducted by the Author
Brooks, Lamar Billy "Che." January 13, 2007, telephone interview.
Calvin, Donna. January 5, 2011, Chicago, Ill.
Gaddis, Henry "Poison." October 14, 2006, Oakland, Calif.
————. May 17, 2008, telephone interview.
Harris, Brenda. September 21, 2009, Chicago, Ill.
Huggins, Ericka. March 24, 2011, Lexington, Ky.
Jiménez, José "Cha Cha." September 14–15, 2009, Chicago, Ill.
Katz, Marilyn. August 17, 2011, Chicago, Ill.
Kendrick, Ann. January 5, 2011, Chicago, Ill.
Lee, Robert "Bobby" E. October 22, 2008, Houston, Tex.
McCarty, Joan. October 19, 2009, Atlanta, Ga.
McCarty, Michael. September 15, 2006, Chicago, Ill.
Ross, Wanda. May 25, 2007, Chicago, Ill.

From Other Sources
Comrade Sisters. Documentary produced by Phyllis J. Jackson and Christine L. Minor, 2005.
    French, Lynn
    Kelley-Williams, Joan
    King, Yvonne

The Essence of Fred Hampton: An Attempt to Capture the Spirit of a Young Man Who Influenced So Many and to Pass It On to Those Who Didn't Have the Opportunity to Meet Him. Chicago: Salsedo Press, [1989].

Anderson, Charles
Arnson, Darren
Brewer, Jim
Burke, Ron
Carmichael, Stokely
Carter, Marvin
Davis, Danny
Davis, Tyrone
Elbert, Joan
English, Henry
Gladney, Tyrone
Graham, Ron
Gregory, Dick
Hall, Shelvin
Hampton, Francis
Hampton, Iberia
Hampton, William
Hatcher, Richard G.
Hatchett, Edward Penny
Ivory, Jim
Jackson, Jesse
Johnson, Kevin
Lombard, Joann
McNelty, Harry
Meeks, Russ
Montgomery, James
Moore, Eugene
Palmer, Lu
Perkins, Gregory
Porter, Claude
Richardson, Joseph
Saunders, Warner
Spooner, Jeremy
Taylor, William
Wade, Paul
Walton, Harland
Wells, Robert
Wiggins, Bob
Williams, Donald
Worrill, Conrad

The HistoryMakers African American Video Oral History Collection. Tape 3, reel 6. August 22, 2003.

Gray, Joan

James, Michael. "Live from the Heartland: Young Lords Radio Interview." WLUW Chicago, November 2005.
José "Cha Cha" Jiménez
Jones, Charles E. "'Talkin' the Talk and Walkin' the Walk': An Interview with Panther Jimmy Slater." In *The Black Panther Party Reconsidered*, edited by Charles E. Jones, 147–53. Baltimore: Black Classic Press, 1998.
Slater, Jimmy
Rosen, Louis. *The South Side: The Racial Transformation of an American Neighborhood*. Chicago: Ivan R. Dee, 1998.
Dreyer, Arthur
Galloway, Jeanine
Galloway, William
Kier, Marilyn
Martin, Gerald
Martin, Linda
Roberts, Keith
Wilson, Darnell
Wysocker, Jane

REPORTS

Report of the National Advisory Commission on Civil Disorders. Washington, D.C.: U.S. Government Printing Office, 1968.
U.S. Senate. Select Committee to Study Governmental Operations with Respect to Intelligence Activities. "The FBI's Covert Action Program to Destroy the Black Panther Party." In *Supplementary Detailed Staff Reports on Intelligence Activities and the Rights of Americans*. Book 3, *Final Report*. Washington, D.C.: U.S. Government Printing Office, 1976.
Wilkins, Roy, and Ramsey Clark. *Search and Destroy: A Report*. New York: Metropolitan Applied Research Center, 1973.

LEGAL PROCEEDINGS

Alliance to End Repression v. City of Chicago, Nos. 74 C 3268/75 C 3295 (N.D. Ill. 1974).
Hampton, Iberia, Plaintiff-Appellant. The United States Court of Appeals for the Seventh Circuit: Appeals from the United States District Court for the Northern District of Illinois, Eastern Division. No. 70-C-1384—Joseph Sam Perry, Judge: Argued August 14, 1978—Decided April 23, 1979.
Hampton v. Hanrahan, 600 F. 2d 600 (7th Cir. 1979). Brief.
"Hearings on Intelligence Activities." Vol. 6, "The Federal Bureau of Investigation." In *U.S. Senate Select Committee to Study Government Operations with Respect to Intelligence Activities*. Washington D.C.: U.S. Government Printing Office, 1975.

REFLECTIONS

Abu-Jamal, Mumia. "A Life in the Party: An Historical and Retrospective Examination of the Projections and Legacies of the Black Panther Party." In *Liberation, Imagination, and the Black Panther Party: A New Look at the Panthers and Their Legacy*, edited by Kathleen Cleaver and George N. Katsiaficas, 40–50. New York: Routledge, 2001.

————. *We Want Freedom: A Life in the Black Panther Party*. Cambridge: South End Press, 2004.

Foner, Philip S., ed. *The Black Panthers Speak*. Philadelphia: Lippincott, 1970.

Hayden, Tom. *Reunion: A Memoir*. New York: Random House, 1988.

Jennings, Regina. "Why I Joined the Party: An Africana Womanist Reflection." In *The Black Panther Party Reconsidered*, edited by Charles E. Jones, 257–65. Baltimore: Black Classic Press, 1998.

Lewis, Melvin E. "Once I Was a Panther." In *The Black Panther Party Reconsidered*, edited by Charles E. Jones, 109–14. Baltimore: Black Classic Press, 1998.

Monges, Miriam Ma'at-Ka-Re. "'I Got a Right to the Tree of Life': Afrocentric Reflections of a Former Community Worker." In *The Black Panther Party Reconsidered*, edited by Charles E. Jones, 135–46. Baltimore: Black Classic Press, 1998.

Njeri, Akua. *My Life with the Black Panther Party*. Oakland, Calif.: Burning Spear Publications, 1991.

"Remarks by Ted Elbert at the Village Board Meeting Concerning the Naming of the Pool, 1970." In *The Essence of Fred Hampton: An Attempt to Capture the Spirit of a Young Man Who Influenced So Many and to Pass It On to Those Who Didn't Have the Opportunity to Meet Him*, 29. Chicago: Salsedo Press, [1989].

Rush, Bobby. "A Gathering of Friends: Honoring Reverend Congressman Bobby Lee Rush." Reflection, private ceremony, Chicago, Ill., October 10, 2009.

AUTOBIOGRAPHIES

Anthony, Earl. *Spitting in the Wind: The True Story behind the Violent Legacy of the Black Panther Party*. Santa Monica: Roundtable Publishers, 1990.

Brent, William Lee. *Long Time Gone: A Black Panther's True-Life Story of His Skyjacking and Twenty-Five Years in Cuba*. New York: Times Books, 1996.

Brown, Elaine. *A Taste of Power: A Black Woman's Story*. New York: Pantheon, 1992.

Fletcher, Jim, Tanaquil Jones, Sylvère Lotringer, Dhoruba Bin Wahad, Mumia Abu-Jamal, and Assata Shakur, eds. *Still Black, Still Strong: Survivors of the U.S. War against Black Revolutionaries*. Active Agents Series. New York, 1993.

Hilliard, David, and Lewis Cole. *This Side of Glory: The Autobiography of David Hilliard and the Story of the Black Panther Party*. Boston: Little, Brown, 1993.

Shakur, Assata. *Assata: An Autobiography*. Chicago: Lawrence Hill Books, 1987.

SYMPOSIUMS, PRESENTATIONS, AND SPEECHES

Breitman, George, ed. *Malcolm X Speaks: Selected Speeches and Statements*. New York: Grove Weidenfeld, 1965.

Gaddis, Henry "Poison." Supplement during question and answer session to Yvonne King, "Presentation on Illinois Black Panther Party." 40th Reunion of the Black Panther Party, Oakland, Calif., October 13, 2006.

————. Remarks delivered at "Young Lords and Black Panther Party Symposium." Sonja Haynes Stone Center for Black Culture and History, University of North Carolina, Chapel Hill, 2007.

Gray, Joan, panelist. "Women and the Black Panther Party." DuSable Museum of African American History, Chicago, Ill., May 13, 2010.

Hampton, Fred. "You Can Murder a Liberator, but You Can't Murder Liberation." In *The Black Panthers Speak*, edited by Philip S. Foner, 138–44. Philadelphia: Lippincott, 1970.

James, Michael. "Rising Up Angry and Chicago's Early Rainbow Coalition, 1968–1975." Presentation on Rising Up Angry, opening reception, photo exhibit, Center for Latino Research, DePaul University, Chicago, Ill., September 19, 2008.

Jiménez, José "Cha Cha." Remarks delivered at "Young Lords and Black Panther Party Symposium." Sonja Haynes Stone Center for Black Culture and History, University of North Carolina, Chapel Hill, 2007.

King, Yvonne. "Presentation on the Illinois Black Panther Party." 40th Reunion of the Black Panther Party, Oakland, Calif., October 13, 2006.

———, panelist. "Women and the Black Panther Party." DuSable Museum of African American History, Chicago, Ill., May 13, 2010.

McCarty, Michael. "Presentation on Illinois Black Panther Party and Fred Hampton." 40th Reunion of the Black Panther Party, Oakland, Calif., October 13, 2006.

Oliver-Velez, Denise. Remarks delivered at "Young Lords and Black Panther Party Symposium." Sonja Haynes Stone Center for Black Culture and History, University of North Carolina, Chapel Hill, 2007.

"Young Lords and Black Panther Party Symposium." Sonja Haynes Stone Center for Black Culture and History, University of North Carolina, Chapel Hill, 2007.

PAMPHLETS, TELEGRAMS, AND NEWSLETTERS

Alliance to End Repression. *Chicago's Secret Police*. December 30, 1985. Pamphlet.

Amos, Rex. *Black Panther in Fat City, 1965*. Pamphlet.

Black Panther Party. *Fallen Comrades of the Black Panther Party*. N.d. Pamphlet.

Black Students Association. *R.A.P.* Vol. 2, no. 2. Chicago: Roosevelt University, 1968.

James, Mike. *Rising Up Angry and Chicago's Early Rainbow Coalition, 1968–1975: Remembering the Black Panther Party, Young Lords Organization, Young Patriots, and Rising Up Angry*. Center for Latino Research, DePaul University, Chicago, Ill., September 19, 2008. Pamphlet.

Shabazz, Betty. "Cleaver, Bobby James Hutton Family, and Kathleen." Western Union telegram in *Black Panther* 2, no. 17 (1968).

Walls, Rufus. *Black Panther Weekend Newsletter*. Chicago, Ill., February 1, 1969.

MISCELLANEOUS PUBLISHED SOURCES

The Crusader. New York: Garland, 1987.

Hill, Robert, ed. *The Marcus Garvey and UNIA Papers*. Vols. 1–5. Los Angeles: University of California Press, 1983.

Jackson, George. *Blood in My Eye*. New York: Random House, 1972.

———. *Soledad Brother: The Prison Letters of George Jackson*. New York: Coward-McCann, 1970.

DOCUMENTARIES

Chairman Fred Hampton Way. Produced and directed by Ray Baker Jr., 2009. Documentary has yet to be released to the public.

Comrade Sisters. Produced by Phyllis J. Jackson and Christine L. Minor, 2005.

Frontline: Dreams of Obama. PBS Home Video, 2009.

Murder of Fred Hampton. The Film Group, 1971.

"Two Societies." In *Eyes on the Prize*. PBS Home Video, 1987.

Secondary Sources

BOOKS

Alexander, Robert J. *Maoism in the Developed World*. London: Praeger, 2001.

Alkalimat, Abdul, and Doug Gills. *Harold Washington and the Crisis of Black Power in Chicago*. Chicago: Twenty First Century Books, 1989.

Alkebulan, Paul. *Survival Pending Revolution: The History of the Black Panther Party*. Tuscaloosa: University of Alabama Press, 2007.

Anderson, Benedict R. *Imagined Communities: Reflections on the Origin and Spread of Nationalism*. Rev. and extended ed. London: New York, 1991.

Anderson, Kristi. *The Creation of a Democratic Majority, 1928–1936*. Chicago: University of Chicago Press, 1979.

Arlen, Michael J. *An American Verdict*. Garden City, N.Y.: Doubleday, 1974.

Armstrong, Julie Buckner, Susan Hult Edwards, Houston Bryan Roberson, and Rhonda Y. Williams, eds. *Teaching the American Civil Rights Movement: Freedom's Bittersweet Song*. New York: Routledge, 2002.

Ashmore, Harry S. *Civil Rights and Wrongs: A Memoir of Race and Politics, 1944–1994*. New York: Pantheon, 1994.

Austin, Curtis. *Up against the Wall: Violence in the Making and Unmaking of the Black Panther Party*. Fayetteville: University of Arkansas Press, 2006.

Balbus, Isaac D. *The Dialectics of Legal Repression: Black Rebels before the American Criminal Courts*. New York: Russell Sage Foundation, 1973.

Bass, Paul, and Douglas W. Rae. *Murder in the Model City: The Black Panthers, Yale, and the Redemption of a Killer*. New York: Basic Books, 2006.

Bellesiles, Michael A., ed. *Lethal Imagination: Violence and Brutality in American History*. New York: New York University Press, 1999.

Branch, Taylor. *At Canaan's Edge: America in the King Years, 1965–1968*. New York: Simon and Schuster, 2006.

Brown, Scot. *Fighting for Us: Maulana Karenga, the Us Organization, and Black Cultural Nationalism*. New York: New York University Press, 2003.

Carson, Clayborne. *In Struggle: SNCC and the Black Awakening of the 1960s*. Cambridge, Mass.: Harvard University Press, 1981.

———, ed. *The Autobiography of Martin Luther King, Jr*. New York: Warner Books, 1998.

Chafe, William. *Civilities and Civil Rights: Greensboro, North Carolina, and the Black Struggle for Freedom*. Oxford: Oxford University Press, 1981.

Churchill, Ward, and Jim Vander Wall, eds. *Agents of Repression: The FBI's Secret Wars against the Black Panther Party and the American Indian Movement*. Boston: South End Press, 1988.

———. *The* COINTELPRO *Papers: Documents from the* FBI's *Secret Wars against Domestic Dissent*. Boston: South End Press, 1990.

Clayton, Dewey M. *The Presidential Campaign of Barack Obama: A Critical Analysis of a Racially Transcendent Strategy*. New York: Routledge, 2010.

Cleaver, Kathleen, and George N. Katsiaficas, eds. *Liberation, Imagination, and the Black Panther Party: A New Look at the Panthers and Their Legacy*. New York: Routledge, 2001.

Collier, Peter, and David Horowitz. *Destructive Generation: Second Thoughts about the Sixties*. New York: Summit Books, 1989.

Collins, Sheila D. *The Rainbow Challenge: The Jackson Campaign and the Future of U.S. Politics*. New York: Monthly Review Press, 1986.

Countryman, Matthew. *Up South: Civil Rights and Black Power in Philadelphia*. Philadelphia: University of Pennsylvania Press, 2005.

Crosby, Emilye, ed. *Civil Rights History from the Ground Up: Local Struggles, a National Movement*. Athens: University of Georgia Press, 2011.

Cunningham, David. *There's Something Happening Here: The New Left, the Klan, and FBI Counterintelligence*. Berkeley: University of California Press, 2004.

Danns, Dionne. *Something Better for Our Children: Black Organizing in Chicago Public Schools, 1963–1971*. New York: Routledge, 2003.

Davis, Mike, Manning Marable, Fred Pfeil, and Michael Sprinker, eds. *The Year Left 2: An American Socialist Yearbook*. London: Verso, 1987.

de Jong, Greta. *A Different Day: African American Struggles for Justice in Rural Louisiana, 1900–1970*. Chapel Hill: University of North Carolina Press, 2002.

Delany, Martin R. *The Condition, Elevation, Emigration and Destiny of the Colored People of the United States and Official Report of the Niger Valley Exploring Party*. 1852. Reprint, Humanity Books, 2004.

Diamond, Andrew J. *Mean Streets: Chicago Youth and the Everyday Struggle for Empowerment in the Multiracial City, 1908–1969*. Berkeley: University of California Press, 2009.

Dittmer, John. *Local People: The Struggle for Civil Rights in Mississippi*. Urbana: University of Illinois Press, 1995.

Donner, Frank. *Protectors of Privilege: Red Squads and Police Repression in Urban America*. Berkeley: University of California Press, 1990.

Drake, St. Clair, and Horace Cayton. *Black Metropolis*. New York: Harper and Row, 1970.

Duberman, Martin. *Paul Robeson: A Biography*. New York: New Press, 1989.

Farber, David. *Chicago '68*. Chicago: University of Chicago Press, 1988.

Fraser, Ronald. *1968: A Student Generation in Revolt*. 1st American ed. New York: Pantheon, 1988.

Fraser, Steve, and Gary Gerstle. *The Rise and Fall of the New Deal Order, 1930–1980*. Princeton, N.J.: Princeton University Press, 1989.

Fremon, David K. *Chicago Politics Ward by Ward*. Bloomington: Indiana University Press, 1988.

Garrow, David J. *Bearing the Cross: Martin Luther King, Jr., and the Southern Christian Leadership Conference*. New York: William Morrow, 1986.

Gitlin, Todd. *The Sixties: Years of Hope, Days of Rage*. New York: Bantam, 1987.

Gitlin, Todd, and Nanci Hollander. *Uptown: Poor Whites in Chicago*. New York: Harper and Row, 1970.

Goldstein, Robert Justin. *Political Repression in Modern America from 1870 to the Present*. Boston: G. K. Hall, 1978.

Gore, Dayo F., Jeanne Theoharis, and Komozi Woodard, eds. *Want to Start a Revolution? Radical Women in the Black Freedom Struggle*. New York: New York University Press, 2009.

Gosnell, Harold. *Machine Politics: Chicago Model*. Chicago: University of Chicago Press, 1937.

Grimshaw, William J. *Bitter Fruit: Black Politics and the Chicago Machine, 1931–1991*. Chicago: University of Chicago Press, 1992.

Grossman, James R., Ann Durkin Keating, and Janice L. Reiff, eds. *The Encyclopedia of Chicago*. Chicago: University of Chicago Press, 2004.

Guterbock, Thomas M. *Machine Politics in Transition: Party and Community in Chicago*. Chicago: University of Chicago Press, 1980.

Haas, Jeffrey. *The Assassination of Fred Hampton: How the FBI and the Chicago Police Murdered a Black Panther*. Chicago: Lawrence Hill Books, 2009.

Harris, Heather E., Kimberly R. Moffitt, and Catherine R. Squires, eds. *The Obama Effect: Multidisciplinary Renderings of the 2008 Campaign*. Albany: State University of New York Press, 2010.

Hill, Lance. *The Deacons for Defense: Armed Resistance and the Civil Rights Movement*. Chapel Hill: University of North Carolina Press, 2004.

Hilliard, David, ed. *The Black Panther Party: Service to the People Programs*. Albuquerque: University of New Mexico Press, 2008.

Horne, Gerald. *The Fire This Time: The Watts Uprising and the 1960s*. Charlottesville: University Press of Virginia, 1995.

Jeffries, Hasan. *Bloody Lowndes: Civil Rights and Black Power in Alabama's Black Belt*. New York: New York University Press, 2009.

Jeffries, Judson L., ed. *Black Power in the Belly of the Beast*. Urbana: University of Illinois Press, 2006.

———. *Comrades: A Local History of the Black Panther Party*. Bloomington: Indiana University Press, 2007.

———. *On the Ground: The Black Panther Party in Communities across America*. Jackson: University Press of Mississippi, 2010.

Jones, Charles E., ed. *The Black Panther Party Reconsidered*. Baltimore: Black Classic Press, 1998.

Joseph, Peniel E. *Dark Days, Bright Nights: From Black Power to Barack Obama*. New York: Basic Civitas Books, 2010.

———, ed. *Neighborhood Rebels: Black Power at the Local Level*. New York: Palgrave Macmillan, 2010.

Katsiaficas, George N. *The Imagination of the New Left: A Global Analysis of 1968*. Boston: South End Press, 1987.

Kelley, Robin D. G., and Earl Lewis, eds. *To Make Our World Anew: A History of African Americans*. Oxford: Oxford University Press, 2000.

Kenski, Kate, Bruce W. Hardy, and Kathleen Hall Jamieson, eds. *The Obama Victory: How Media, Money, and Message Shaped the 2008 Election*. Oxford: Oxford University Press, 2010.

Kitagawa, Evelyn, and Karl Tauber, eds. *Local Community Fact Book for the Chicago Metropolitan Area, 1980*. Chicago: Chicago Community Inventory, University of Chicago, 1983.

Kusch, Frank. *Battleground Chicago: The Police and the 1968 Democratic National Convention*. Chicago: University of Chicago Press, 2008.

Lazerow, Jama, and Yohuru Williams, eds. *In Search of the Black Panther Party: New Perspectives on a Revolutionary Movement*. Durham: Duke University Press, 2006.

Lee, Chana Kai. *For Freedom's Sake: The Life of Fannie Lou Hamer*. Urbana: University of Illinois Press, 2000.

Liu, Baodong. *The Election of Barack Obama: How He Won*. New York: Palgrave Macmillan, 2010.

Marable, Manning. *Black Leadership: Four Great American Leaders and the Struggle for Civil Rights*. New York: Penguin, 1998.

———. *Malcolm X: A Life of Reinvention*. New York: Viking, 2011.

Mayer, Harold, and Richard Wade. *Chicago: Growth of a Metropolis*. Chicago: University of Chicago Press, 1969.

McClelland, Edward. *Young Mr. Obama: Chicago and the Making of a Black President*. New York: Bloomsbury Press, 2010.

Mendell, David. *Obama: From Promise to Power*. New York: Harper Collins, 2007.

Millea, Thomas. *Ghetto Fever*. Milwaukee, Wisc.: Bruce Publishing, 1968.

Morris, Calvin S. *Reverdy C. Ransom: Black Advocate of the Social Gospel*. Lanham, Md.: University Press of America, 1990.

Murch, Donna Jean. *Living for the City: Migration, Education, and the Rise of the Black Panther Party in Oakland, California*. Chapel Hill: University of North Carolina Press, 2010.

Newton, Huey P. *War against the Panthers: A Study of Repression in America*. New York: Harlem River Press, 1996.

Obama, Barack. *The Audacity of Hope: Thoughts on Reclaiming the American Dream*. New York: Crown, 2006.

———. *Dreams from My Father: A Story of Race and Inheritance*. New York: Random House, 1995.

Ogbar, Jeffrey O. G. *Black Power: Radical Politics and African American Identity*. Baltimore: Johns Hopkins University Press, 2004.

Olsen, Jack. *Last Man Standing: The Tragedy and Triumph of Geronimo Pratt*. New York: Anchor Books, 2001.

Omi, Michael, and Howard Winant. *Racial Formation in the United States: From the 1960s to the 1980s*. Critical Social Thought. New York: Routledge and Kegan Paul, 1986.

Padilla, Felix M. *Puerto Rican Chicago*. Notre Dame: University of Notre Dame Press, 1987.

Payne, Charles. *I've Got the Light of Freedom: The Organizing Tradition and the Mississippi Freedom Struggle*. Berkeley: University of California Press, 2007.

Pearson, Hugh. *The Shadow of the Panther: Huey Newton and the Price of Black Power in America*. Reading: Addison-Wesley, 1994.

Phillips, Kevin P. *The Emerging Republican Majority*. New Rochelle, N.Y.: Arlington House, 1969.

Powers, Richard Gid. *Secrecy and Power: The Life of J. Edgar Hoover*. New York: Free Press, 1987.

Preston, Michael B., Lenneal J. Henderson, and Paul Lionel Puryear, eds. *The New Black Politics: The Search for Political Power*. New York: Longman, 1987.

Ransby, Barbara. *Ella Baker and the Black Freedom Movement: A Radical Democratic Vision*. Chapel Hill: University of North Carolina Press, 2003.

Rice, J. F. *Up on Madison, Down on 75th Street: A History of the Illinois Black Panther Party*. Pt. 1. Evanston: The Committee, 1983.

Richardson, Marilyn, ed. *Maria W. Stewart: America's First Black Woman Political Writer: Essays and Speeches*. Bloomington: Indiana University Press, 1987.

Rivlin, Gary. *Fire on the Prairie: Chicago's Harold Washington and the Politics of Race.* New York: Henry Holt, 1992.

Royko, Mike. *Boss: Richard J. Daley of Chicago.* New York: Dutton, 1971.

Sayres, Sohnya, Anders Stephanson, Stanley Aronowitz, and Fredric Jameson, eds. *The 60s without Apology.* Minneapolis: University of Minnesota Press in cooperation with Social Text, 1984.

Smith, William Gardner. *Return to Black America.* Englewood Cliffs, N.J.: Prentice-Hall, 1970.

Strain, Christopher B. *Pure Fire: Self-Defense as Activism in the Civil Rights Era.* Athens: University of Georgia Press, 2005.

Theoharis, Jeanne, and Komozi Woodard, eds. *Freedom North: Black Freedom Struggles outside the South, 1940–1980.* New York: Palgrave Macmillan, 2003.

———. *Groundwork: Local Black Freedom Movements in America.* New York: New York University Press, 2005.

Thurber, James A., ed. *Obama in Office.* Boulder: Paradigm Publishers, 2011.

Tovar, Frederic Ribes. *Albizu Campos: Puerto Rican Revolutionary.* New York: Plus Ultra Educational Publishers, 1971.

Travis, Dempsey. *An Autobiography of Black Politics.* Chicago: Urban Research Press, 1987.

Tuttle, William M., Jr. *Race Riot: Chicago in the Red Summer of 1919.* Chicago: Atheneum, 1970.

Tyson, Timothy B. *Blood Done Sign My Name: A True Story.* New York: Crown, 2004.

———. *Radio Free Dixie: Robert F. Williams and the Roots of Black Power.* Chapel Hill: University of North Carolina Press, 1999.

Van Peebles, Mario, Ula Y. Taylor, and J. Tarika Lewis. *Panther: A Pictorial History of the Black Panthers and the Story Behind the Film.* A Newmarket Pictorial Moviebook. New York: Newmarket Press, 1995.

Walker, David. *Appeal.* Baltimore: Black Classic Press, 1993.

Williams, Yohuru. *Black Politics/White Power: Civil Rights, Black Power, and the Black Panthers in New Haven.* St. James, N.Y.: Brandywine Press, 2000.

Williams, Yohuru, and Jama Lazerow, eds. *Liberated Territory: Untold Local Perspectives on the Black Panther Party.* Durham: Duke University Press, 2008.

Williamson, Joy Ann. *Black Power on Campus: The University of Illinois, 1965–75.* Urbana: University of Illinois Press, 2003.

Wolfe, Tom. *Radical Chic and Mau-Mauing the Flak Catchers.* New York: Farrar Straus and Giroux, 1970.

Wolfenstein, E. Victor. *The Victims of Democracy: Malcolm X and the Black Revolution.* Berkeley: University of California Press, 1981.

Woodard, Komozi. *A Nation within a Nation: Amiri Baraka (LeRoi Jones) and Black Power Politics.* Chapel Hill: University of North Carolina Press, 1999.

Young, Stephen S. *Indicators of the Failure of the Chicago Model Cities Program to Effectively and Substantially Involve Uptown Model Area Residents.* Chicago, 1969.

ARTICLES AND ESSAYS

Abron, JoNina M. "'Serving the People': The Survival Programs of the Black Panther Party." In *The Black Panther Party Reconsidered*, edited by Charles E. Jones, 177–92. Baltimore: Black Classic Press, 1998.

Anderson, Reynaldo. "Practical Internationalist: The Story of the Des Moines, Iowa, Black Panther Party." In *Groundwork: Local Black Freedom Movements in America*, edited by Jeanne Theoharis and Komozi Woodard, 282–99. New York: New York University Press, 2005.

Baldwin, Bridgette. "In the Shadow of the Gun: The Black Panther Party, the Ninth Amendment, and Discourses of Self-Defense." In *In Search of the Black Panther Party: New Perspectives on a Revolutionary Movement*, edited by Jama Lazerow and Yohuru Williams, 67–93. Durham: Duke University Press, 2006.

Black Students Association. "Merit Is What?" In *R.A.P.*, vol. 2, no. 2, pp. 4–5. Chicago: Roosevelt University, 1968.

Booker, Chris. "Lumpenization: A Critical Error of the Black Panther Party." In *The Black Panther Party Reconsidered*, edited by Charles E. Jones, 337–62. Baltimore: Black Classic Press, 1998.

Cantor, Susan. "Fred Hampton: A Case of Political Assassination." *First Principles: National Security and Civil Liberties* 2, no. 3 (November 1976). In series 2, subseries 6: Legal Papers, box 37, folder 1, Dr. Huey P. Newton Foundation, Incorporated Papers, Green Library, Department of Special Collections, Stanford University, Palo Alto, Calif.

Cha-Jua, Sundiata Keita, and Clarence Lang. "The 'Long Movement' as Vampire: Temporal and Spatial Fallacies in Recent Black Freedom Studies." *Journal of African American History* 92, no. 2 (Spring 2007): 265–88.

"Chicago Metropolitan Population." In *The Encyclopedia of Chicago*, edited by James R. Grossman, Ann Durkin Keating, and Janice L. Reiff, 1005. Chicago: University of Chicago Press, 2004.

Churchill, Ward. "'To Disrupt, Discredit and Destroy': The FBI's Secret War against the Black Panther Party." In *Liberation, Imagination, and the Black Panther Party: A New Look at the Panthers and Their Legacy*, edited by Kathleen Cleaver and George N. Katsiaficas, 78–117. New York: Routledge, 2001.

Cleaver, Kathleen Neal. "Back to Africa: The Evolution of the International Section of the Black Panther Party (1969–1972)." In *The Black Panther Party Reconsidered*, edited by Charles E. Jones, 211–54. Baltimore: Black Classic Press, 1998.

"Community Areas, 1930–2000." In *The Encyclopedia of Chicago*, edited by James R. Grossman, Ann Durkin Keating, and Janice L. Reiff, 1042. Chicago: University of Chicago Press, 2004.

Crosby, Emilye. "It Wasn't the Wild West: Keeping Local Studies in Self-Defense Historiography." In *Civil Rights History from the Ground Up: Local Struggles, a National Movement*, edited by Emilye Crosby, 194–255. Athens: University of Georgia Press, 2011.

———. "'This Nonviolent Stuff Ain't No Good. It'll Get Ya Killed': Teaching about Self-Defense in the African American Freedom Struggle." In *Teaching the American Civil Rights Movement: Freedom's Bittersweet Song*, edited by Julie Buckner Armstrong, Susan Hult Edwards, Houston Bryan Roberson, and Rhonda Y. Williams, 159–73. New York: Routledge, 2002.

Danns, Dionne. "Chicago High School Students' Movement for Quality Public Education, 1966–1971." *Journal of African American History* 88, no. 2, "The History of Black Student Activism" (Spring 2003): 138–50.

Davenport, Christian A. "Reading the 'Voice of the Vanguard': A Content Analysis of the Black Panther Intercommunal News Service, 1969–1973." In *The Black Panther Party*

Reconsidered, edited by Charles E. Jones, 193–209. Baltimore: Black Classic Press, 1998.

Dong, Quigwen, Kenneth D. Day, and Raman Deol. "The Resonant Message and the Powerful New Media: An Analysis of the Obama Presidential Campaign." In *The Obama Effect: Multidisciplinary Renderings of the 2008 Campaign*, edited by Heather E. Harris, Kimberly R. Moffitt, and Catherine R. Squires, 75–88. Albany: State University of New York Press, 2010.

Doss, Erika. "Revolutionary Art Is a Tool for Liberation." In *Liberation, Imagination, and the Black Panther Party: A New Look at the Panthers and Their Legacy*, edited by Kathleen Cleaver and George N. Katsiaficas, 175–87. New York: Routledge, 2001.

Essig, Steven. "Race Riots." In *The Encyclopedia of Chicago*, edited by James R. Grossman, Ann Durkin Keating, and Janice L. Reiff, 667. Chicago: University of Chicago Press, 2004.

Fergus, Devin. "The Black Panther Party in the Disunited States of America: Constitutionalism, Watergate, and the Closing of the Americanists' Mind." In *Liberated Territory: Untold Local Perspectives on the Black Panther Party*, edited by Yohuru Williams and Jama Lazerow, 265–94. Durham: Duke University Press, 2008.

Grady-Willis, Winston A. "The Black Panther Party: State Repression and Political Prisoners." In *The Black Panther Party Reconsidered*, edited by Charles E. Jones, 363–89. Baltimore: Black Classic Press, 1998.

Grossman, James R. "Great Migration." In *The Encyclopedia of Chicago*, edited by James R. Grossman, Ann Durkin Keating, and Janice L. Reiff, 363–64. Chicago: University of Chicago Press, 2004.

Hague, Euan. "Street Lessons." *How We Learn*, October 11, 2007.

Hayes, Floyd W., III, and Francis A. Kiene III. "'All Power to the People': The Political Thought of Huey P. Newton and the Black Panther Party." In *The Black Panther Party Reconsidered*, edited by Charles F. Jones, 157–76. Baltimore: Black Classic Press, 1998.

Hill, Robert. "Racial and Radical: Cyril V. Briggs, *The Crusader* Magazine, and the African Blood Brotherhood, 1918–1922." In *The Crusader*. New York: Garland, 1987.

James, Mike. "Getting Ready for the Firing Line: Organizing in Uptown in the 60s; Remembering JOIN Community Union." *Heartland Journal* 51 (Summer 2005): 26.

Jameson, Fredric. "Periodizing the Sixties." *The 60s without Apology*, edited by Sohnya Sayres, Anders Stephanson, Stanley Aronowitz, and Fredric Jameson. Minneapolis: University of Minnesota Press in cooperation with Social Text, 1984.

Jeffries, Judson L. "An Unexamined Chapter of Black Panther History." In *Black Power in the Belly of the Beast*, edited by Judson L. Jeffries, 185–223. Urbana: University of Illinois Press, 2006.

Johnson, Don, Francis Ward, Ralph Whitehead, and Brian Boyer. "Chairman Fred Died a Natural Death." *Chicago Journalism Review* 2, no. 12, "The Death of Fred Hampton: A Special Report" (December 1969): 10.

Johnson, Ollie A., III. "Explaining the Demise of the Black Panther Party: The Role of Internal Factors." In *The Black Panther Party Reconsidered*, edited by Charles E. Jones, 391–414. Baltimore: Black Classic Press, 1998.

Jones, Charles E. "Arm Yourself or Harm Yourself: People's Party II and the Black Panther Party in Houston, Texas." In *On the Ground: The Black Panther Party in Communities across America*, edited by Judson L. Jeffries, 3–40. Jackson: University Press of Mississippi, 2010.

————. "Reconsidering Panther History: The Untold Story." In *The Black Panther Party Reconsidered*, edited by Charles E. Jones, 1–21. Baltimore: Black Classic Press, 1998.

Jones, Charles E., and Michael L. Clemons. "Global Solidarity: The Black Panther Party in the International Arena." In *Liberation, Imagination, and the Black Panther Party: A New Look at the Panthers and Their Legacy*, edited by Kathleen Cleaver and George N. Katsiaficas, 20–39. New York: Routledge, 2001.

Jones, Charles E., and Judson L. Jeffries. "'Don't Believe the Hype': Debunking the Panther Mythology." In *The Black Panther Party Reconsidered*, edited by Charles E. Jones, 25–56. Baltimore: Black Classic Press, 1998.

Joseph, Peniel E. "Black Liberation without Apology: Reconceptualizing the Black Power Movement." *Black Scholar* 31, no. 3/4, "Black Power Studies: A New Scholarship" (Fall/ Winter 2001): 2–19.

————. "The Black Power Movement, Democracy, and America in the King Years." *American Historical Review* 114, no. 4 (October 2009): 1001–16.

————. "Dashikis and Democracy: Black Studies, Student Activism, and the Black Power Movement." *Journal of African American History* 88, no. 2, "The History of Black Student Activism" (Spring 2003): 182–203.

Kelley, Charles R. "The Black Panthers and the University of California." In *American Security Council: Washington Report*, edited by Charles R. Kelley, 1–4. Washington, D.C.: American Security Council Press, 1968.

Kelley, Robin D. G. "Into the Fire: 1970 to the Present." In *To Make Our World Anew: A History of African Americans*, edited by Robin D. G. Kelley and Earl Lewis, 543–613. Oxford: Oxford University Press, 2000.

LeBlanc-Ernest, Angela D. "'The Most Qualified Person to Handle the Job': Black Panther Party Women, 1966–1982." In *The Black Panther Party Reconsidered*, edited by Charles E. Jones, 305–34. Baltimore: Black Classic Press, 1998.

Levy, Peter B. "Gloria Richardson and the Civil Rights Movement in Cambridge, Maryland." In *Groundwork: Local Black Freedom Movements in America*, edited by Jeanne Theoharis and Komozi Woodard, 97–115. New York: New York University Press, 2005.

Luker, Ralph E. "Reverdy C. Ransom: Black Advocate of the Social Gospel." Book review. *Church History* 62, no. 4 (December 1993): 579–80.

Lusane, Clarence. "To Fight for the People: The Black Panther Party and Black Politics in the 1990s." In *The Black Panther Party Reconsidered*, edited by Charles E. Jones, 443–67. Baltimore: Black Classic Press, 1998.

Matthews, Tracye. "'No One Ever Asks, What a Man's Role in the Revolution Is': Gender and the Politics of the Black Panther Party, 1966–1971." In *The Black Panther Party Reconsidered*, edited by Charles E. Jones, 267–304. Baltimore: Black Classic Press, 1998.

Morgan, Edward P. "Media Culture and the Public Memory of the Black Panther Party." In *In Search of the Black Panther Party: New Perspectives on a Revolutionary Movement*, edited by Jama Lazerow and Yohuru Williams, 356–57. Durham: Duke University Press, 2006.

Ogbar, Jeffrey O. G. "Brown Power to Brown People: Radical Ethnic Nationalism, the Black Panthers, and Latino Radicalism, 1967–1973." In *In Search of the Black Panther Party: New Perspectives on a Revolutionary Movement*, edited by Jama Lazerow and Yohuru Williams, 252–88. Durham: Duke University Press, 2006.

Outlaw, Lucius. "On Race and Class, or, On the Prospects of 'Rainbow Socialism.'" In *The*

Year Left 2: An American Socialist Yearbook, edited by Mike Davis, Manning Marable, Fred Pfeil, and Michael Sprinker, 106–21. London: Verso, 1987.

Pascoe, Craig S. "The Monroe Rifle Club: Finding Justice in an 'Ungodly and Social Jungle Called Dixie.'" In Lethal Imagination: Violence and Brutality in American History, edited by Michael A. Bellesiles, 393–424. New York: New York University Press, 1999.

Patterson, Elizabeth A. "Logan Square." In The Encyclopedia of Chicago, edited by James R. Grossman, Ann Durkin Keating, and Janice L. Reiff, 761. Chicago: University of Chicago Press, 2004.

Preston, Michael B. "Black Politics and Public Policy in Chicago: Self-Interest Versus Constituent Representation." In The New Black Politics: The Search for Political Power, edited by Michael B. Preston, Lenneal J. Henderson, and Paul Lionel Puryear. New York: Longman, 1982.

Rahman, Ahmad. "Marching Blind: The Rise and Fall of the Black Panther Party in Detroit." In Liberated Territory: Untold Local Perspectives on the Black Panther Party, edited by Yohuru Williams and Jama Lazerow, 181–231. Durham: Duke University Press, 2008.

"Red Circle & Gold Leaf." Time, November 13, 1950.

Reitan, Ruth. "Cuba, the Black Panther Party, and the U.S. Black Movement in the 1960s." In Liberation, Imagination, and the Black Panther Party: A New Look at the Panthers and Their Legacy, edited by Kathleen Cleaver and George N. Katsiaficas, 164–74. New York: Routledge, 2001.

Rice, Jon. "The World of the Illinois Panthers." In Freedom North: Black Freedom Struggles outside the South, 1940–1980, edited by Jeanne Theoharis and Komozi Woodard, 41–64. New York: Palgrave Macmillan, 2003.

Rumberger, Russell W. "High School Dropouts: A Review of Issues and Evidence." Review of Educational Research 57, no. 2 (Summer 1987): 101–21.

Schultz, John. The Chicago Conspiracy Trial. New York: Da Capo, 1993.

Seligman, Amanda. "Lincoln Park." In The Encyclopedia of Chicago, edited by James R. Grossman, Ann Durkin Keating, and Janice L. Reiff, 746. Chicago: University of Chicago Press, 2004.

———. "Uptown." In The Encyclopedia of Chicago, edited by James R. Grossman, Ann Durkin Keating, and Janice L. Reiff, 1293. Chicago: University of Chicago Press, 2004.

Singh, Nikhil Pal. "The Black Panthers and the 'Underdeveloped Country' of the Left." In The Black Panther Party Reconsidered, edited by Charles E. Jones, 57–105. Baltimore: Black Classic Press, 1998.

Spencer, Robyn Ceanne. "Engendering the Black Freedom Struggle: Revolutionary Black Womanhood and the Black Panther Party in the Bay Area, California." Journal of Women's History 20, no. 1 (Spring 2008): 90–113.

———. "Inside the Panther Revolution: The Black Freedom Movement and the Black Panther Party in Oakland, California." In Groundwork: Local Black Freedom Movements in America, edited by Jeanne Theoharis and Komozi Woodard, 300–318. New York: New York University Press, 2005.

Stephens, Curtis. "Life of a Party." Crisis, September/October 2006.

Storch, Randi. "Communist Party." In The Encyclopedia of Chicago, edited by James R. Grossman, Ann Durkin Keating, and Janice L. Reiff, 189–90. Chicago: University of Chicago Press, 2004.

Taylor, Flint, and Dennis Cunningham. "The Assassination of Fred Hampton: 40 Years Later." *Police Misconduct and Civil Rights Law Report* 9, no. 12 (November/December 2009).

Tolnay, Stewart E. "The African American 'Great Migration' and Beyond." *Annual Review of Sociology* 29 (2003): 209–32.

Tracy, James. "The (Original) Rainbow Coalition." *Solidarities*, September 30, 2006.

Umoja, Akinyele Omowale. "1964: The Beginning of the End of Nonviolence in the Mississippi Freedom Movement." *Radical History Review* 85 (Winter 2003): 201–26.

———. "Repression Breeds Resistance: The Black Liberation Army and the Radical Legacy of the Black Panther Party." In *Liberation, Imagination, and the Black Panther Party: A New Look at the Panthers and Their Legacy*, edited by Kathleen Cleaver and George N. Katsiaficas, 3–19. New York: Routledge, 2001.

———. "Set Our Warriors Free: The Legacy of the Black Panther Party and Political Prisoners." In *The Black Panther Party Reconsidered*, edited by Charles E. Jones, 417–41. Baltimore: Black Classic Press, 1998.

———. "'We Will Shoot Back': The Natchez Model and Paramilitary Organization in the Mississippi Freedom Movement." *Journal of Black Studies* 32, no. 3 (January 2002): 271–94.

Wendt, Simon. "God, Gandhi, and Guns: The African American Freedom Struggle in Tuscaloosa, Alabama, 1964–1965." *Journal of African American History* 89, no. 1 (Winter 2004): 36–56.

Wiener, Jon. *Conspiracy in the Streets: The Extraordinary Trial of the Chicago Eight*. New York: New Press, 2006.

Williams, Linda. "Black Political Progress in the 1980s: The Electoral Arena." In *The New Black Politics: The Search for Political Power*, edited by Michael B. Preston, Lenneal J. Henderson, and Paul Lionel Puryear. New York: Longman, 1987.

THESES AND DISSERTATIONS

Hopkins, Charles. "The Deradicalization of the Black Panther Party, 1967–1973." Ph.D. diss., University of North Carolina, Chapel Hill, 1978.

Jefferson, Alphine. "Housing Discrimination and Community Response in North Lawndale (Chicago), Illinois, 1948–1968." Ph.D. diss., Duke University, 1979.

Rice, Jon. "Black Radicalism on Chicago's West Side: A History of the Illinois Black Panther Party." Ph.D. diss., Northern Illinois University, 1998.

Stanford, Maxwell. "Revolutionary Action Movement (RAM): A Case Study of an Urban Revolutionary Movement in Western Capitalist Society." Master's thesis, Clark Atlanta University, 1986.

Umoja, Akinyele. "Eye for an Eye: The Role of Armed Resistance in the Mississippi Freedom Movement." Ph.D. diss., Emory University, 1996.

PAPERS AND PRESENTATIONS

Jones, Felecia G. "The Role of the Black Press during the 'Great Migration.'" Paper presented at the Sixty-Ninth Annual Meeting of the Association for Education in Journalism and Mass Communication, Norman, Okla., August 3–6, 1986.

McAllister, Don, presenter. "United Front against Fascism Conference," Oakland, Calif., July 18–20, 1969. Sponsored by the Black Panther Party.

INTERNET

AKPD Message and Media. http://akpdmedia.com/clients/ (accessed January 28, 2009).

Bell, Debra. "Ten Things You Didn't Know about David Axelrod." *U.S. News and World Report*, December 2, 2008. http://www.usnews.com/articles/news/politics/2008/12/02/10-things-you-didnt-know-about-david-axelrod.html (accessed December 5, 2008).

The Better Boys Foundation. http://www.bbfchicago.org (accessed May 2, 2007).

"Chicago, 1968." *CNN*. http://www.cnn.com/ALLPOLITICS/1996/conventions/chicago/facts/chicago68/index.shtml (accessed February 21, 2008).

"Democratic National Convention." *The Chicago History Museum*. http://www.chicagohs.org/history/politics/1968.html (accessed February 23, 2008).

Dixon, Bruce A. "In Honor of Fred Hampton and Mark Clark: Executed by Chicago Cops— Dec. 4, 1969." *Black Commentator*, December 7, 2004. http://www.hartford-hwp.com/archives/45a/716.html (accessed December 9, 2004).

Hague, Euan. "Street Lessons." *Area Chicago: How We Learn*, October 11, 2007. http://www.areachicago.org/p/issues/how-we-learn/street-lessons/ (accessed November 5, 2007).

Jiménez, José "Cha Cha." Biography. National Young Lords website. http://nationalyounglords.com/Jose%20bio.html (accessed January 25, 2009).

Kellman, Gerald. Interview. *Frontline: The Choice 2008*. PBS, July 24, 2008. http://www.pbs.org/wgbh/pages/frontline/choice2008/interviews/kellman.html (accessed September 18, 2008).

The Marcus Garvey Papers at UCLA. http://www.international.ucla.edu/africa/mgpp/ (accessed March 6, 2006).

National Young Lords timeline. http://nationalyounglords.com/YoungLordsTimeline.html (accessed January 25, 2009).

Peace and Freedom Party. http://www.peaceandfreedom.org (accessed March 5, 2006).

"Profile: David Axelrod." *BBC NEWS*, November 7, 2008. http://news.bbc.co.uk/go/pr/fr/-/2/hi/americas/us_elections_2008/7716677.stm (accessed December 5, 2008).

Scott, Janny. "In 2000, a Streetwise Veteran Schools a Bold Young Obama." *New York Times*, September 9, 2007. http://www.nytimes.com/2007/09/09/us/politics/09obama.html?pagewanted=all (accessed February 15, 2010).

INDEX

Hoover, J. Edgar, 172–73, 181, 193
House Un-American Activities Committee
(HUAC), 171
Housing discrimination, 5, 15–16, 19, 27–29,
35, 37–38, 40–41, 42–49, 57–58, 60, 67, 105,
112, 115, 126, 135–36, 142, 150, 156, 168,
171, 199. See also Covenants; Segregation:
residential; Slums
Howard, Elbert "Big Man," 186
Huggins, Ericka, 112, 121
Humboldt Park, 144, 147–48, 198
Hutton, Bobby, 8, 85, 240 (n. 48)
Hyde Park High School, 68, 74

Illinois Chapter of the Black Panther Party
(ILBPP): founding of, 8, 53, 61–64; and
gender, 13, 92, 110–23; and colleges
and universities, 53, 66, 74–79, 89, 97,
99–100, 123, 163; and the media, 58,
68, 99–101, 102, 178–80, 181; structure
and early goals of, 64–66; and the
Lumpenproletariat, 65, 89; rank and file
of, 65–66, 85–89, 115–16, 122–23; and
recruitment, 74–80; membership demographics of, 85–89, 115, 123, 129; relationship of with national BPP headquarters, 91–103; and the 1968 Democratic
National Convention, 92, 103–7, 123, 125;
and civil rights programs, 107–10; and
the founding of the Rainbow Coalition,
125–31; and gangs, 128–29, 160–63;
and the Young Patriots Organization,
129, 130, 132–35, 136–37, 141–42; and the
Young Lords, 142, 145–46, 149–50;
and Rising Up Angry, 149, 152–53, 155,
156, 159; and law enforcement repression, 167–78, 180–90; positive legacy
of, 191–200; political appropriation of
ideals of, 201–12. See also Black Panther
Party for Self Defense; Hampton, Fred;
Rainbow Coalition
Independent Voters of Illinois, 196
Informants, 104–5, 161, 168, 171, 174–75,
180, 183
Intelligence Section and Surveillance Unit,
Chicago Police Department. See Red Squad
Intercommunal Survival Committee, 196
Irish community, 18, 20, 28–32, 69, 153–54,
170

Ivory, Jim, 56–57, 59
I Wor Kuen, 166

Jackson, Jesse: presidential campaigns
of, 4, 10–11, 13–14, 192, 200–204, 207,
210–21; and Chicago in the 1960s, 43,
45–46, 48, 58, 60, 78; and Operation
Breadbasket, 83, 98
James, Mike, 105, 128, 131, 151–53, 156, 159,
197–98
Jiménez, José "Cha Cha," 128–29, 143–49,
191, 195–98, 202–4
Jobs Or Income Now (JOIN), 129, 131–32,
150–51, 153
John Brown Revolutionary League, 165
Johnson, Bruce, 149
Johnson, Deborah, 111, 184. See also Njeri,
Akua
Johnson, Marlin, 178–79, 186
Jones, Henry "Teenan," 21–22
Jones, Jeff, 163
Junior, Nathaniel, 76, 131, 254 (n. 71)

Katz, Marilyn, 207–10
Kelley, Robin D. G., 197–98, 200–201
Kendrick, Howard Ann (Ann Campbell), 65,
113–14
King, Martin Luther, Jr.: and the Chicago
Freedom Movement, 2, 15, 26, 42–48, 67,
82, 87, 126, 171, 214; assassination of, 8, 49,
70, 84, 127; and Fred Hampton, 58–59, 87,
109; and the BPP, 78, 79, 108–10
King, Yvonne, 60, 65, 95, 103, 113–14, 116–18,
121, 165, 197
Koziol, Ronald, 178–80, 186, 189
Ku Klux Klan, 5, 78, 108, 133, 169–70, 224
(n. 27), 236 (n. 149)

Labor relations, 16, 18, 127, 158–59, 171, 200
Latin Eagles, 146, 155
Latin Kings, 148, 154
Law enforcement. See COINTELPRO; Daley
Democratic machine: and the Chicago
Police Department; Federal Bureau of
Investigation; Illinois Chapter of the Black
Panther Party: and law enforcement
repression; Police brutality; Red Squad;
Subversive Unit, Chicago Police
Department